# Democracy, Bonapartism and Fascism: Class Struggle in the 1930s

# *Democracy, Bonapartism and Fascism*

*Class Struggle in the 1930s*

Leon Trotsky & Ted Grant

Wellred Books
London

*Democracy, Bonapartism and Fascism: Class Struggle in the 1930s*
Leon Trotsky and Ted Grant

First edition
Wellred Books, April 2025


wellred-books.com

Publisher information:
Wellred Books Ltd, 4th Floor, 18 St. Cross Street,
London, EC1N 8UN, books@wellred-books.com



UK distribution: Wellred Books Britain, wellredbooks.co.uk
contact@wellredbooks.co.uk

EU distribution: 1917 Verlag e. U.
Lustkandlgasse 10/1, 1090 Vienna/Wien, Austria
william.haemmerle@gmail.com

USA distribution: Marxist Books, marxistbooks.com
sales@marxistbooks.com

DK distribution: Forlaget Marx, forlagetmarx.dk
Vermlandsgade 2, st., 2400 København NV
forlag@forlagetmarx.dk

Cover image: *Rechtsradikale Gefahr! Rechtzeitig zupacken!*
SPD Poster, 1945

Cover design by Deep Sohelia

Layout by Wellred Books

ISBN: 978 1 916936 15 7

# *Contents*

Introduction .......... vii

*Part 1: Germany – Writings by Leon Trotsky*

Problems of the International Left Opposition .......... 3
What is Fascism? .......... 31
Germany: The Only Road .......... 35
The Tragedy of the German Proletariat .......... 109
What is National Socialism? .......... 123
German Bonapartism .......... 135

*Part 2: France – Writings by Leon Trotsky*

Bonapartism and Fascism .......... 145
Whither France? .......... 155
France at the Turning Point .......... 195
The French Revolution Has Begun! .......... 215
Revolutionary Interlude in France .......... 223

*Part 3: Europe After the War – Writings by Trotsky and Ted Grant*

Bonapartism, Fascism and War....233
By Leon Trotsky

Democracy or Bonapartism in Europe....245
By Ted Grant

The Menace of Fascism....275
By Ted Grant

*Timeline*....339

*Index*....345

*Titles by Wellred Books*....349

# *Introduction*

The 1930s was one of the most tumultuous decades in human history. The world was shaken in a series of convulsions, starting with the Wall Street Crash and ending in the horrors of the Second World War.

Parallels are frequently drawn between the crisis of that time and this third decade of the twenty-first century. The most obvious is the economic crisis, which has plagued the world since 2007-08. There's a crisis in international relations, with a major conflict taking place between the main imperialist powers. Finally, of course, there's the sharpness of the class antagonisms, which, in the case of the 1930s, led to the regimes of Adolf Hitler in Germany, Benito Mussolini in Italy, Francisco Franco in Spain and Philippe Pétain in France etc.

Historical parallels are useful, but insufficient, to understand the new elements in the situation today. This can then frequently lead to exaggerations and mistaken tactics. It has led to the policy of 'lesser-evilism', giving the workers' leaders – whether trade unions or political parties – an excuse to capitulate before the ruling class.

Not only do they frequently exaggerate the strength of the enemy, but they also fail to look at the other side of the coin. The massive revolutionary potential that existed in the past, and that is even greater today, is to them a closed book.

The leaders of the labour movement are cynically exploiting the natural revulsion of many youth and working class people against divisive reactionary parties, in order to drag them into supporting the so-called 'lesser evil'. With the excuse of fighting the 'danger of fascism', an utterly false perspective, they have supported draconian attacks on the working class as well as the 'middle class', which they so often claim to want to win.

In the mistaken policy of the workers' leaders and the petty-bourgeois left, we find perhaps the clearest possible parallels with the past. The popular fronts of the 1930s have had many modern echoes, and just like in the past, their only achievements is to tie the working class organisations to the stinking corpse of liberalism.

What the workers' movement needs is a clear-sighted strategy, which is based on a sober analysis of phenomena and what they represent. The texts contained in this volume are therefore, not just of historical interest, but are of vital importance in training a new generation of communists, if they are to succeed where their predecessors failed.

For Marxists, there are valuable lessons to be learnt from this period, but in drawing historical parallels we must always be careful. History never repeats itself exactly in the same way, and we will therefore not find in it exact analogies which we can use as a blueprint for our tactics today. In fact, one of the important threads running through the present volume is precisely the need, not to attempt to find in the texts of the past a formula, but to understand the method that the authors applied.

Leon Trotsky was the most acute observer of this period, and his writings are second to none. After Lenin's death, it was left to Trotsky to carry on the legacy of Marxism. This was, on the one hand, the theoretical legacy left by Marx, Engels and Lenin, and on the other hand, the struggles of the revolutionary movement in Russia, including the successful seizing of power in October 1917.

In these texts, Trotsky carefully analyses the events as they are taking place and points the way forward. For us to learn from them, it is insufficient just to learn by rote the conclusions that he drew. It is necessary to understand how he draws out the analysis from events, how he analyses the consciousness of different layers in society and how he arrives from that to a conclusion about the correct tactics and slogans for the communists.

The whole period was one of revolution and counter-revolution and Trotsky never failed to see the connection between the two: how, under the right circumstances, counter-revolutionary coups would push the working class in a revolutionary direction; and how correct tactics on behalf of the leadership of the working class could lead from defensive action to offensive.

It was clear to him that only the seizure of power by the proletariat, led by a party, could defeat reaction. Therefore, the struggle against fascism and reaction was always intimately linked to the struggle to win the confidence of the working class and the petty bourgeoisie.

But to do that one needed to start from a concrete and careful analysis of things as they were. Trotsky make this point repeatedly when criticising the policy of the Communist International[1] in the article 'Bonapartism and Fascism':

> The vast practical importance of a correct theoretical orientation is most strikingly manifested in a period of acute social conflict of rapid political shifts, of abrupt changes in the situation… It is in just such periods that all sorts of transitional, intermediate situations and combinations arise, as a matter of necessity, which upset the customary patterns and doubly require a sustained theoretical attention. In a word, if in the pacific and 'organic' period (before the war) one could still live on the revenue from a few ready-made abstractions, in our time each new event forcefully brings home the most important law of the dialectic: The truth is always concrete.[2]

Trotsky's method of analysing things concretely stood in stark contrast to the Communist International, which, under the leadership of

1 The Third, or Communist, International (Comintern), formed of communist parties across the world, was the successor to the Second International, which collapsed with the outbreak of the First World War.

2 Trotsky, 'Bonapartism and Fascism', 15 July 1934, in this volume, p. 145.

Nikolai Bukharin and Joseph Stalin, adopted a completely schematic approach. In 1926, Bukharin drew up a schema for a defensive struggle of the then 'second period' which would then turn into the offensive in a 'third period'.

This completely absurd characterisation of 'periods' freed the national sections of any need to concretely analyse the real conditions on the ground and the consciousness of different layers, because the answers were already provided by the general characterisation of the period.

The zig-zagging of the Comintern, between the opportunism of the 'second period' and the ultra-leftism of the 'third period' found a theoretical justification in this schema. But one can not derive slogans and tactics simply from the general characterisation of the period.

If one were to use a military analogy, it would be like insisting that the army is now in an offensive posture, which is going to last for some years, and this would mean that there can be no digging of trenches, no retreats, but only advance, and it has to be on the entire front. This on the basis that the conditions in general are suitable for an advance, while at the same time not considering the state of your troops, not considering the terrain, not considering the strength and weaknesses of different units, etc.

Such an approach would be a sure way of guaranteeing defeat. Indeed, the Comintern managed to do precisely that. The history of the 1930s and its ending in the horrors of the Second World War is the history of the failures of the Communist International – the organisation that was meant to lead the proletariat internationally to victory.

## *Germany and the collapse of the Weimar Republic*

If one looks at each stage of this process, this becomes clear. In a sense, the perspectives of the Communist International of the 'third period' seemed to be confirmed by events. The policy was launched at the February 1928 plenum of the ECCI (the Executive Committee of the Communist International). This was confirmed at the Sixth Congress of the Communist International six months later.

One year after that, October 1929, the Wall Street Crash happened. It turned everything upside down. The temporary boom (from 1921-29) had stabilised the political situation, but now that all went out the window. The US was dragged into the crisis, and in a big way. This had important consequences for Germany.

Industries were idle, mass employment emerged. Crucially, heavily indebted farmers were facing ruin with banks forcing sales of farms. Hitler found fertile soil in the countryside in this period for his demagogy against the banks and finance capital.

The crisis led in March 1930 to the fall of the Social Democratic government of Herman Müller. Heinrich Brüning, of the Catholic Centre Party, became Chancellor.

The new government proceeded to attempt to resolve the crisis by a savage assault on wages, but this was rejected by the Reichstag. An attempt to pass it using President Paul von Hindenburg's decree powers also failed. This left no option but to dissolve the Reichstag and call new elections.

Behind the scenes, Major General Kurt von Schleicher[3] was operating to undermine parliamentary rule – and particularly the SPD – using Hindenburg's powers. Around him was a military clique who saw parliament, and 'Marxism', as an obstacle to German recovery.

The outcome of the elections did little to solve the problems of the German bourgeoisie. Compared to 1928, the Nazi Party went from 12 seats to 107 and became the second-largest party, the Communist Party went from 54 to 77 seats, becoming the third largest.

The new political situation was even more unstable than the previous one. This is the point at which the articles in this volume begin, with Trotsky's 'The Turn in the Communist International and the Situation in Germany'.

In the article, Trotsky lays out the danger posed by fascism in Germany. He criticises the Communist Party for its ultra-left stance

3 Kurt von Schleicher was a German military officer and the penultimate Chancellor of Germany. He was assassinated during the Night of the Long Knives, 30 June 1934.

towards the SPD. He did this not to support the Social Democrats who were playing a treacherous role, but because the Communist Party was closing the door to the millions of workers who still supported Social Democracy.

He criticises the leaders of the party for underestimating the danger of fascism, and because they were underestimating the difficulties that lay on the road to the revolution:

> Under the impact of the crisis, the petty bourgeoisie swung, not in the direction of the proletarian revolution, but in the direction of the most extreme imperialist reaction, pulling behind it considerable sections of the proletariat.[4]

This posed a mortal threat to the workers' movement and required the skilful use of the tactic of the united front. What was needed was to offer fighting agreements to the Social-Democratic workers, not shrill denunciations.

But shrillness was precisely what issued forth from the Communist leadership, who justified their position pointing to the role that the Social-Democratic leaders were playing. Particular bitterness was caused by the massacre of Communists on 1 May 1929, which became known as 'Blutmai'. This was carried out by the police under the leadership of SPD police chiefs Karl Zörgiebel and Albert Grzesinski.

Yet, even such treacherous actions should not have determined the policy of the Communist Party. What was needed was a level-headed policy to win the confidence of the social-democratic workers, and thereby pull them away from their treacherous leaders. And this, the Communist Party completely failed to put forward.

The economic situation turned from bad to worse. In May 1931, the Creditanstalt bank collapsed in Vienna, which had a ripple effect across the continent. Then in July, Germany's biggest bank, Danat, collapsed. By February 1932, there were six million unemployed. The situation was dire.

---

4 Trotsky, 'The Turn in the Communist International', 26 September 1930, in this volume, p. 8.

The Social-Democratic policy in these circumstances was to prop up the liberals in order, as they argued it, to keep the fascists out. They had supported the new ministry of Brüning which was governing with the use of Hindenburg's presidential decrees, and in the election of April 1932, they supported Hindenburg as the only means of defeating Hitler. The same Hindenburg who less than a year later would hand the Chancellorship to Hitler.

## *Von Papen's coup*

After winning the elections, Hindenburg and the military clique around him moved against Brüning. They replaced him with Franz von Papen.[5]

Von Papen began by lifting the ban on the Nazi street gangs, the SA and the SS, understanding that they would unleash a wave of violence. Schleicher was preparing a move against the Social-Democratic government of the Free State of Prussia, which at the time consisted of over 62 per cent of German territory and 61 per cent of the population. He got a commitment from the Social-Democratic unions not to participate in a general strike in its defence, in return for some promises.

On 17 July, seven thousand SA men staged a provocation with a march through Altona, a Jewish working class suburb of Hamburg. The Communist Youth, supported by local workers, attempted to block the march. In the clashes that followed the police shot and killed eighteen people, two of whom were SA men.

Papen used the event as a pretext to remove the Prussian government three days later. According to Papen, they had failed to maintain 'order'. In one swoop, the military clique around Hindenburg had thus removed the main bastion of the SPD, and the SPD barely whimpered in response.

At the end of July came new parliamentary elections, where Hitler's Nazi Party (NSDAP) got 37 per cent of the vote, well ahead of the SPD.

5 Franz von Papen was Chancellor of Germany for the latter half of 1932. He became Vice-Chancellor after Hitler took power in 1933. He fled the country after the Night of the Long Knives in 1934.

Again, the Communists made small steps forward. The combined vote of the workers' parties was now 35 per cent, a small decrease on the previous election, but only five points lower than 1928.

Numerically, the workers' parties had retained the bulk of their support, and they both had paramilitary organisations numbering hundreds of thousands. To that should be added the trade unions who remained a massive force. The drop in the overall support for the working class parties was a sign of demoralisation as neither party could offer a way forward.

## *The 'third period' madness*

The programme of the SPD was nothing short of a capitulation to the bourgeoisie. Yet the communists, who ought to have provided an alternative, failed to do so. The KPD was pursuing an ultra-left policy, declaring that society was already fascist, and that the SPD was 'social fascist'. Because of this policy they were unable to win over the rank-and-file social-democratic workers to communism. Trotsky pointed this out:

> The workers cannot simply leave the Social Democracy, in spite of all the crimes of that party; they must be able to replace it by another party. Meanwhile the German Communist Party, in the person of its leaders, has for the past nine years done everything in its power to repel the masses or at least prevent them from rallying around the Communist Party.[6]

In 1931, six months before Papen's coup, at the height of their ultra-left madness, the KPD joined forces with the reactionary Stahlhelm – an armed veterans organisation tied to the monarchist German National People's Party (DNVP) – and the Nazis, attempting to oust the Prussian SPD government in a referendum. They also made local agreements with the SA and other reactionary outfits to break up Social-Democratic meetings.

As Trotsky points out, this tactic was doing the Social-Democratic leaders a huge favour. It was very easy for them to portray the Communists and the Nazis as being the same.

---

6 Trotsky, *Germany: The Only Road*, 14 September 1932, in this volume, p. 38.

It is in this frenzied atmosphere that Trotsky writes his pamphlet *Germany: The Only Road.* It was one of a series of articles directed at the German Communist movement, warning them of the impending disaster. Here he again takes up the problems with the schematic approach that the Communist Party, and its leader, Ernst Thälmann, had taken in analysing the situation, and the political mistakes that flowed from it:

> By disregarding the social and political distinctions between Bonapartism, that is, the regime of 'civil peace' resting upon military-police dictatorship, and fascism, that is, the regime of open civil war against the proletariat, Thälmann deprives himself in advance of the possibility of understanding what is taking place before his very eyes. If Papen's cabinet is a fascist cabinet then what fascist 'danger' is he talking about?[7]

In other words, by insisting on calling Brüning, Papen and the SPD all fascist, and declaring that Germany was already in a fascist regime, they helped disarm the proletariat before the genuine fascist threat coming from Hitler.

Instead, Trotsky carefully analyses the then-regime of Papen and what it reflected. He points out that the crisis was bringing about the need for the ruling class to do away with the concessions granted in the wake of the German Revolution of 1918. The Reichstag and the labour organisations were an obstacle to that.

This was another reason why the labelling of the Social Democrats as 'social fascist' was mistaken. Not because they did not prepare the way for fascism, but because on that road, they, and particularly the millions of workers behind them, would inevitably enter into conflict with the fascists.

The policy of the Communists should therefore have been to seek a united front with the Social Democrats against the fascists. That is, they should have proposed to the Social Democratic Party and trade union leaders a united struggle against the Nazis on a programme of specific demands. If the proposal were

7 Ibid, p. 61.

accepted, it would have enabled a united struggle, strengthening the proletariat by raising its self-confidence, and if the leaders refused, the communists would have gained influence over the social democratic workers who would have seen them as willing to take up the necessary struggle. However, this is not what the Communist Party leaders did:

> The Stalinist bureaucracy acts in the opposite manner: it not only rejects fighting agreements, but still worse, it maliciously destroys those agreements which arise from below. At the same time, it proposes to the Social Democratic deputies a parliamentary accord. This means that at the moment of danger it declares its own ultraleftist theory and praxis to be worthless; yet it is replaced not with the policy of revolutionary Marxism but with an unprincipled parliamentary combination in the spirit of the 'lesser evil'.[8]

After the coup of 20 July, when it became increasingly obvious in which direction things were moving, the Communist Party shifted their position, but the way they did it, as Trotsky says, was with "an unprincipled parliamentary combination". Foreshadowing the popular front policy of 1934, they were supporting parliamentary coalitions including the SPD and the Centre Party.

In other words, whilst refusing an agreement for a united struggle of the whole working class on the streets, in the factories, etc., the Communist Party joined with the Social Democrats and one of the liberal bourgeois parties in a bloc in parliament. Thus what you got was not a united workers' front, but a cross-class parliamentary bloc.

On the eve of 20 July, the Communist Party of Germany issued an appeal to the German trade union movement for joint action in defence of proletarian interests. Although technically correct, coming after four years of ultra-left madness, and with no explanation, it could only have the effect of exposing the leadership's previous policy and inconsistency, rather than achieving the stated aim.

8 Ibid, p. 74.

To top it off, they maintained their opposition to negotiations with the social democratic leaders for united action. They weren't honest and open with the working class. They felt it too important to protect the prestige of the party and its leaders. So, they resorted to behind-the-scenes negotiations and combinations, including with pacifists and other petty-bourgeois elements. For example, they organised the World Congress Against War which was held in August 1932 and led to the formation of the World Committee Against War and Fascism, which was led by people like Albert Einstein, Upton Sinclair and Bertrand Russell.

Once again, the Communist International was jumping from one mistake to the opposite mistake. Yet this latest turn was not to have any impact before it was overtaken by events, as Trotsky had suggested.

## *Hindenburg hands power to Hitler*

In September 1932, the Reichstag was once again dissolved after Papen had been defeated in a confidence vote. New elections were held on 6 November, which changed little in the parliamentary equation. Worryingly, from the point of view of the Bonapartist clique around Schleicher, the NSDAP was entering into crisis, as money had run out and the party had just lost two million votes in the elections, whilst the Communist Party was continuing to gain ground.

Schleicher had lost confidence in Papen and manoeuvred to get him out, taking over as Chancellor on 3 December. Schleicher insisted that it was necessary to prevent the collapse of the NSDAP. He wanted to bring them into government, but not with the position of Chancellor, which Hitler was demanding. Instead, Schleicher negotiated with a leading Nazi deputy and SA commander, Gregor Strasser, to overcome Hitler's opposition. However, Hitler managed to prevent the manoeuvre.

This sealed Schleicher's fate. Von Papen manoeuvred with Hindenburg (the 'lesser evil') to install Hitler as chancellor. The army, seeing Hitler as the only guarantee for stability, supported this move. On 30 January, Hitler was installed as Chancellor and the Reichstag was dissolved.

The terror campaign intensified on the streets. A few days before the new elections, Hitler and his new allies found the excuse they were looking for. The Reichstag was set on fire on the night of 27 February. The deed was blamed on the Communist Party, which was banned, and democratic rights were suspended. The election was a farce, the Communist Party vote was reduced by one million and Hitler managed to pick up 44 per cent of the vote.

Trotsky wrote his article 'The Tragedy of the German Proletariat' after this 'election'. He drew the balance sheet of the past decade of the Communist International in a damning verdict:

> Since 1923, that is, since the beginning of the struggle against the Left Opposition, the Stalinist leadership, although indirectly, assisted the Social Democracy with all its strength to derail, to befuddle, to enfeeble the German proletariat: it restrained and hindered the workers when the conditions dictated a courageous revolutionary offensive; it proclaimed the approach of the revolutionary situation when it had already passed; it worked up agreements with petty-bourgeois phrasemongers and windbags; it limped impotently at the tail of the Social Democracy under cover of the policy of the united front; it proclaimed the "third period" and the struggle for the conquest of the streets under conditions of political ebb and the weakness of the Communist Party; it replaced the serious struggle by leaps, adventures or parades; it isolated the Communists from the mass trade unions; it identified the Social Democracy with fascism and rejected the united front with the mass workers' organisations in face of the aggressive bands of the National Socialists; it sabotaged the slightest initiative for the united front for local defence, at the same time it systematically deceived the workers as to the real relationship of forces, distorted the facts, passed off friends as enemies and enemies as friends – and drew the noose tighter and tighter around the neck of the party, not permitting it to breathe freely any longer, nor to speak, nor to think.[9]

9 Trotsky, 'The Tragedy of the German Proletariat', 14 March 1933, in this volume, p. 110.

He continued:

> Not a single national congress, no international congress, nor even a plenum of the ECCI; no preparation in the press of the party, no analysis of the policy of the past.[10]

Indeed, the Communist International had proved itself incapable of learning, of absorbing the lessons of past struggles and had transformed itself into an obedient tool of the Moscow bureaucracy In so doing, it had bound the hands behind the back of the international proletariat. It had now led to an absolute disaster.

After the election, the Communist deputies were rounded up and sent to concentration camps. The SPD deputies were not far behind. On 23 March, the enabling act was passed, giving the government the right to pass laws without Parliament. In other words, it effectively abolished Parliament.

The Social-Democratic unions declared their 'neutrality' and promised to work with the Nazis. Such weakness, which these leaders had shown time and time again, only invited aggression. On 2 May, after a massive May Day rally organised by the NSDAP, all trade union offices were attacked and taken over. In the following months, hundreds of thousands of communists, social-democrats and trade unionists were sent to the concentration camps. The proud German labour movement had been annihilated without a fight.

'The Tragedy of the German Proletariat' was Trotsky's balance sheet of the tactics and strategy of the Communist Party and Social Democracy, and the article 'What is National Socialism?' drew theoretical conclusions about the nature of the new regime.

Trotsky puts particular focus on the role that the petty bourgeoisie played in the rise of Hitler, but, he pointed out, this layer handed power to the very same people they had rebelled against:

> German fascism, like Italian fascism, raised itself to power on the backs of the petty bourgeoisie, which it turned into a battering ram

10 Ibid, p.117.

> against the organisations of the working class and the institutions of democracy. But fascism in power is least of all the rule of the petty bourgeoisie. On the contrary, it is the most ruthless dictatorship of monopoly capital. Mussolini is right: the middle classes are incapable of independent policies.[11]

Since the petty bourgeoisie was incapable of playing an independent role, they wound up handing power back to the big bourgeoisie. Using the Gestapo secret police, in The Night of the Long Knives, between 30 June and 2 July 1934, Hitler arrested and executed the leaders of the SA. This eliminated a threat to his alliance with the army and German finance capital. Thus the small farmers, shopkeepers etc., having helped to butcher the working class, now brought to power a regime of monopoly capital.

## *The collapse of the French Third Republic*

In 1934, after the disastrous defeat of the German working class, the focus of the advanced workers of Europe shifted away from Germany and towards France, where on 6 February, gangs of fascists and monarchists had organised a provocation, leading to riots and clashes with the police in which 2,000 people were injured and seventeen killed.

These riots were followed by a response from the working class organisations: a massive demonstration on 9 February followed by a general strike three days later. The divide between the Socialist and the Communist Party was pushed to the side, as both their trade union confederations and their parties were united in action on the day.

The actions of the working class pushed back the fascists, but it resolved nothing. Instead the Gaston Doumergue regime rose to power, balanced, as Trotsky points out, between the two. The bourgeoisie attempted to find a new stability in an outsider, the retired previous president Doumergue, backed by two generals. The new government attempted to restore order, but it did not last long.

11 Trotsky, 'What is National Socialism?', 2 November 1933, in this volume, p. 131.

The article 'Bonapartism and Fascism', written in July 1934, tackles the theoretical questions raised by the period. Trotsky explains what the nature of the new regime in France was:

> A government which raises itself above the nation is not, however, suspended in air. The true axis of the present government passes through the police, the bureaucracy, the military clique. It is a military-police dictatorship with which we are confronted, barely concealed with the decorations of parliamentarism. But a government of the sabre as the judge arbiter of the nation – that's just what Bonapartism is.[12]

Trotsky pointed out precisely how the new government, in spite of nominally being based in parliament, in reality had raised itself above it. He makes this important theoretical point about the nature of both Bonapartism and democracy:

> The strength of finance capital does not reside in its ability to establish a government of any kind and at any time, according to its wish; it does not possess this faculty. Its strength resides in the fact that every non-proletarian government is forced to serve finance capital; or better yet, that finance capital possesses the possibility of substituting for each one of its systems of domination that decays, another system corresponding better to the changed conditions. However, the passage from one system to another signifies the political crisis which, with the concourse of the activity of the revolutionary proletariat may be transformed into a social danger to the bourgeoisie. The passage of parliamentary democracy to Bonapartism itself was accompanied in France by an effervescence of civil war. The perspective of the passage from Bonapartism to fascism is pregnant with infinitely more formidable disturbances and consequently also revolutionary possibilities.[13]

The new regime, being based on the unsteady equilibrium between fascists and the workers, was very weak, and it was to end in a revolutionary movement two years later.

12 Trotsky, 'Bonapartism and Fascism', 15 July 1934, in this volume, p. 148.
13 Ibid, p. 150.

As Trotsky was writing his article 'Whither France?' in November 1934, Doumergue resigned and was replaced by Flandin, who was not long after replaced by Bouisson, then Laval, then Sarraut – five governments in two years.

The reason for the instability of the governments was the collapse of the Radicals, the political centre. Their political base, the petty bourgeoisie, was being crushed by the crisis and became politically restless.

Society was in a crisis and it needed to be resolved either one way or another:

> The social crisis in its political expression is the crisis of power. The old master of society is bankrupt. A new master is needed.[14]

Who was that master to be? Was it to be the fascists or the working class? That was the real question. The petty bourgeoisie needed to be won over to the proletariat, or they would be won over by the fascists:

> The petty bourgeoisie will reject the demagogy of fascism only if it puts its faith in the reality of another road. That other road is the road of proletarian revolution.[15]

Now, however, the policy of the Communist International had shifted from the ultra-left period to opportunism. It now aligned its policy with the failed policy of social democracy; in other words, an alliance with the collapsing liberal Radicals, to try to shore them up.

This was preparing a very similar disaster to that of Germany, and the very opposite of what was needed:

> The working-class party must occupy itself not with a hopeless effort to save the party of the bankrupts. It must, on the contrary, with all its strength, accelerate the process of liberation of the masses from Radical influence.[16]

---

14 Trotsky, 'Whither France?', 9 November 1934, in this volume, p. 192.

15 Ibid, p. 167.

16 Ibid, p. 169.

## *The Popular Front*

Of course, the small forces of the Left Opposition[17] in France, the Trotskyists, were unable to affect events. The Communist Party and the Socialist Party joined with the Radicals in a Popular Front in 1935, in time for the elections the next year.

The elections of May 1936 produced a wave of enthusiasm. Already in March, Trotsky was writing 'France at the Turning Point'. He took up again the question of the Popular Front. He again pointed out that the crisis of capitalism could not be resolved by attempting to prop up the status quo. The leaders of the workers in France were preparing another disaster:

> The People's Front [Popular Front], the conspiracy between the labour bureaucracy and the worst political exploiters of the middle classes [the Radicals] is capable only of killing the faith of the masses in the revolutionary road and of driving them into the arms of the fascist counter-revolution.[18]

Precisely because it was a cross-class alliance, it was bound to break down at the first impact of events:

> The People's Front will fall to pieces at the first serious test, and deep fissures will open up in all of its component sections. The policy of the People's Front is the policy of betrayal.[19]

Indeed, these words were to prove prophetic. The victory of the Popular Front led to a massive strike wave, starting on 26 May. It became a general strike involving more than a million workers and factory occupations.

But this was not suited to the new alignment on the French left. The line was that one mustn't upset the coalition, and naturally the bourgeois Radicals were not at all happy about this turn of events:

---

17 The Left Opposition was founded by Trotsky in 1923 to combat the bureaucratic degeneration of the Soviet Union. The Left Oppositionists referred to themselves as the 'Bolshevik-Leninists'.

18 Trotsky, 'France at the Turning Point', 26 March 1936, in this volume, p. 209.

19 Ibid, p. 210.

> The leading centres of the working-class organisations, including those of the Communist Party, have been caught unawares. They are afraid, above all, lest the strike spoil all their blueprints.[20]

In order to preserve the Popular Front, the movement needed to be betrayed. Much like what was to happen thirty years later in May 1968, a massive revolutionary movement that could have taken power and abolished capitalism, was betrayed for lofty promises from the bourgeoisie.

An agreement was signed, which included major concessions to the workers. After all, when their back is against the wall, the bourgeoisie is willing to make all kinds of concessions, in order to save the system as a whole. However, far from creating a lasting basis on which to get further concessions, once the movement has died down, the bourgeoisie will exact their revenge.

Trotsky warned of the consequences:

> The very essence of the matter lies in the fact that the reforms, very meagre as they are in substance, upon which the capitalists and the leaders of the labour organisations agreed in June, are not viable, because they are already beyond the powers of declining capitalism, taken as a whole.[21]

The big bourgeois of course could weather the crisis, with their massive financial reserves and monopoly power, and the cost would be borne by the small and medium producers. The consequences of the political support for the Popular Front were not hard to work out.

> 'Do not expect miracles from us!', the pedants in power keep repeating. But the gist of the matter lies precisely in the fact that without 'miracles', without heroic decisions, without a complete overturn in property relations – without the concentration of the banking system, of the basic branches of industry and of foreign trade in the hands of the state – there is no salvation for the petty bourgeoisie of the city and country.[22]

20 Trotsky, 'The French Revolution Has Begun!', 9 June 1936, in this volume, p. 217.
21 Trotsky, 'Revolutionary Interlude in France', 9 July 1936, in this volume, p. 224.
22 Ibid, p. 226.

The betrayal of the strikes and the capitulation to the Radicals spelled the end of the movement. The Popular Front was wound up in 1938, after having moved to the right. From then on, each new government represented a further move to the right, until the French bourgeoisie could take their revenge with the capitulation to Hitler in 1940.

## *The Second World War and its aftermath*

In his last article, 'Bonapartism, Fascism and War', Trotsky summarises how this disaster took place. The betrayal that was the Popular Front, and the campaign for a block with 'democracy' against Hitler, was followed by another zig-zag. Stalin entered into an alliance with Hitler through the Molotov-Ribbentrop Pact of August 1939. The treaty promised Soviet non-aggression, and carved Eastern Europe up into spheres of influence. This disoriented the ranks of the party, but also had further, more devastating, consequences:

> The French working class proved caught unaware. The war provoked a terrible disorientation and the mood of passive defeatism, or to put it more correctly, the indifferentism of an impasse. From this web of circumstances arose first the unprecedented military catastrophe and then the despicable Pétain regime.[23]

Trotsky referred to the new regime of reactionary French general Philippe Pétain as 'senile Bonapartism', as this eighty-year-old symbolically represented the best that French capitalism could offer.

In the article, he summarised the experiences of the previous decade. He describes how under pressure of the crisis: "the 'fuses' of democracy 'blow out'. Hence the short-circuits of dictatorship."[24]

The important question to understand is that parliamentary democracy is based on the ability of the ruling class to buy off at least a layer of the working class to keep the class struggle in check. When it loses that ability, the class struggle eventually reaches a

23 Trotsky, 'Bonapartism, Fascism and War', 20 August 1940, in this volume, p. 243.
24 Ibid, p. 239.

point at which the fuses 'blow out'. Should the workers in such a situation fail to take power, should the revolution be defeated, then Bonapartism and dictatorship follows.

He emphasised that the decisive point in the struggle against fascism and Bonapartism was the question of the working class taking power. Fascism wasn't simply a policy of the ruling class that they picked up and imposed at will, nor was it a new economic system that had replaced capitalism. On the contrary, it was a consequence of the ruling class' inability to govern society in the way it used to.

Trotsky was assassinated in August 1940, and the Trotskyists who attempted to take up the leadership of the Fourth International after his death, unfortunately, made mistake after mistake.

One of these mistakes was resurrecting the old schematism of Bukharin and Stalin, of course with some differences. As the Second World War was coming to an end, one of the leaders, Pierre Frank, declared that Bonapartism was now in place everywhere. So, whereas the Stalinists had declared that all regimes had become fascist as a result of the crisis in 1928-31, now Frank declared that since 1934 all regimes in France had been Bonapartist. This included the Popular Front government, and Frank claimed the same was true for the rest of Europe, except Britain where the regime was on the cusp of becoming Bonapartist.

Starting from the general statement on the period, that bourgeois democracy had exhausted its role, Frank declared in March 1946 that "we do not generally have in Europe at the present time democratic regimes, because there is literally no place for them".

Almost alone in the Fourth International, Ted Grant and the leadership of the Revolutionary Communist Party (RCP) argued against the leadership of the International, that a new world situation was unfolding. One that could not have been envisaged in 1938-40. Ted Grant was to become the founder of the forces that have developed into the Revolutionary Communist International (RCI) today.

In 1946, he wrote in reply to the first part of Frank's article that:

> Each stage must be examined concretely by the vanguard who could thus understand and interpret events and draw the correct practical conclusions for activity therefrom.[25]

He quoted Trotsky's 'Bonapartism and Fascism' about ready-made abstractions (see above) and said that some of the cadres of the International, like Frank, were precisely trying to live off of ready-made abstractions. They were drawing slogans and categories from the general position of capitalism, rather than proceeding from the concrete.

There was another wave of intense class struggle at the end of the Second World War, combined with strong partisan movements in Italy, Greece and Yugoslavia and a big movement in France. All these movements, with the exception of Yugoslavia, were diverted down the path of the bourgeois-democratic revolution by the Stalinists. In the same period, the Labour Party came to power in Britain with a landslide electoral victory, and it not only got into power, but was actually able to implement many of the reforms on which it had been elected.

Starting from reality as it was developing, Ted Grant and the British RCP drew the conclusion that what Europe was facing was not Bonapartism in general, but counter-revolution in a democratic form. That is, the movement had been betrayed and diverted towards stabilising a bourgeois-democratic regime by the Communist Parties and Social Democracy. Time was to prove beyond a shadow of a doubt that Ted Grant was correct.

The final text in this collection is Ted Grant's pamphlet 'The Menace of Fascism'. In this pamphlet, Grant summarises the position of the Trotskyists on Bonapartism and fascism, with a particular emphasis on Italy, but he also draws out how the fascists were being used in bourgeois-democratic Britain after the war. He clarifies the methods and the tactics that should be employed, and

25 Grant, 'Democracy and Bonapartism in Europe', August 1946, in this volume, p. 246.

once again warns against the dangers of Popular Frontism and of appeals to the state:

> Historical experience has shown that it is not possible to legislate fascism out of existence. The very nature of the capitalist state precludes that, for fascism in the nature of things is the naked weapon of capitalist class rule.

This warning now not only had to be directed to the Social-Democratic, but also the Communist workers. The remnants of the Communist International were now working hand-in-hand with the Social-Democratic leaders to disarm the working class ideologically and preach the virtues of class collaboration and reformism.

## *Lessons for today*

The aim of this collection is not to provide a prescription of measures for the movement – a kind of cookbook of fixed categories and slogans. Rather, the point is to learn the real lessons of the 1930s and the failure of the working class to take power.

Hitler, Mussolini, Franco and Pétain did not come to power because of any supposed oratorical skills, or even because of the crisis of capitalism. They came to power because, when the question of power was posed, when the workers had the opportunity to take power, because of the fatal role of their leaders, the workers were unable to seize the opportunity.

As the conditions in the 1930s ripened, and even became over-ripe, Bonapartism, and eventually fascism, stepped in to resolve the question of power in favour of the capitalists.

The key point there, however, is that fascism came to power at the end of a revolutionary process, in which the workers, particularly in Germany, had the opportunity to take power many times. It was the failure to do so that paved the wave for Bonapartism and fascism. In other words: it was the disastrous mistakes of the Social Democratic and Communist leaders that led to Hitler.

The decades that have passed since Trotsky and Ted Grant wrote these texts have produced some important new developments. We once again face a crisis, but the balance of forces has changed. The post-war upswing massively strengthened the working class, leaving the petty-bourgeoisie as a rump and turning the bulk of them into proletarians. The farmers, who played such a key role in the rise of Hitler, are a tiny group in society, as are the small shop keepers. The bulk of teachers, lecturers and civil servants, who formed a privileged layer in the past, have been reduced to the status of workers.

Therefore, the working class today is far stronger than it was in the 1930s. The potential strength of the revolution is thus much greater, and the counter-revolution much weaker. Further, we find ourselves today at an early stage of this process, not at the end, which means the working class will have many opportunities to take power before counter-revolution has a chance to take control of the situation.

However, the leadership of the workers' organisations, which was already degenerate in the 1930s, has now degenerated to an unprecedented level. The social democrats are in crisis everywhere. The Communist Parties have disappeared or merged with Social Democracy. The trade union leaders have become the worst strike breakers. All of them fight to defend the status quo at a time when it has once again become repugnant to the vast majority of workers and the petty bourgeoisie, in its weakened form. This is the biggest obstacle facing the working class at the present moment.

It will be the task of the coming period to rediscover the militant traditions of the workers' movement, and in this the ideas of Leon Trotsky and Ted Grant will play a key role.

Niklas Albin Svensson,
London,
21 March 2025

# *Part 1: Germany*

## *Writings by Leon Trotsky*

*September 1930 – October 1932*

# *Problems of the International Left Opposition*

## *The Turn in the Communist International and the Situation in Germany*

Written 26 September 1930

### *The sources of the latest turn*

Tactical turns, even wide ones, are absolutely unavoidable in our epoch. They are necessitated by the abrupt turns of the objective situation (a lack of stable international relations; sharp and irregular fluctuations of conjuncture; sharp reflections of the economic fluctuations in politics; the impulsiveness of the masses under the influence of a feeling of helplessness, etc., etc.). Careful observation of the changes in the objective situation is now a far more important and at the same time immeasurably more difficult task than it was before the war, in the epoch of the 'organic' development of capitalism. The leadership of the party now finds itself in the position of someone who drives his automobile on a mountain, over the sharp zig-zags of the road. An untimely turn, incorrectly applied speed, threaten the passengers and the car with the greatest danger, if not with destruction.

The leadership of the Communist International[1] in recent years has given us examples of very abrupt turns. The latest of them we have observed in the last months. What has called forth the turns of the Communist International since the death of Lenin? The changes in the objective situation? No. It can be said with confidence: beginning with 1923, not a single tactical turn was made in time, under the influence of correctly estimated changes in the objective conditions, by the Comintern. On the contrary: every turn was the result of the unbearable sharpening of the contradictions between the line of the Comintern and the objective situation. We are witnessing the very same thing this time, too.

The Ninth Plenum of the ECCI, the Sixth Congress, and particularly the Tenth Plenum,[2] adopted a course towards an abrupt and direct revolutionary rise (the 'third period'), which was absolutely excluded at the time by the objective situation existing after the great defeats in Britain and China,[3] the weakening of the Communist parties throughout the world, and particularly under the conditions of a commercial and industrial boom, which embraced a series of the most important capitalist countries. The tactical turn in the Communist International begun in February 1928 was therefore directly contrary to the actual turn of the historic road. From these contradictions arose the tendencies of adventurism, the further isolation of the parties from the masses, the weakening of the organisations, etc.

1 The leading body of the Third, or Communist, International (Comintern) was the Executive Committee of the Communist International (ECCI). By the 1930s, the bureaucracy of the Soviet Union dominated the ECCI and the Comintern, transforming it into a tool for its foreign policy.

2 The Ninth and Tenth Plenums of the ECCI occurred in February 1928 and July 1929 respectively. The Sixth Congress met July-September 1928. At these meetings, the ultra-left theory of the 'third period' was put forward, which argued that a deep, worldwide revolutionary crisis was imminent.

3 The defeats of the 1926 General Strike in Britain and the Chinese Revolution of 1925-27.

Only after all these phenomena had clearly assumed a menacing character did the leadership of the Comintern make a new turn in February 1930, backward from, and to the right of, the tactics of the 'third period'.

It is the irony of fate, unmerciful to all *chvostism*,[4] that the new tactical turn in the Comintern coincided chronologically with the new turn in the objective conditions.[5] An international crisis of unprecedented acuteness undoubtedly opened the prospect of mass radicalisation and social convulsions. Precisely under such circumstances, a turn to the left could and should have been made, that is, boldly speeding up on the curve of the revolutionary upsurge. This would have been absolutely correct and necessary if, in the last three years, the leadership of the Comintern had utilised, as it should have, the period of economic revival and revolutionary ebb to strengthen the positions of the party in the mass organisations, above all in the trade unions. Under such circumstances, the driver could and should have shifted his gears in 1930 from second into third, or at least prepared for such a change in the near future. In reality, the directly opposite process took place. So as not to go over the cliff, the driver had to change from a prematurely adopted speed down to second and slow down the pace. When? Under circumstances in which a correct strategic line would have demanded acceleration.

Such is the crying contradiction between tactical necessity and strategic perspective, a contradiction in which, by the logic of the mistakes of their leadership, the communist parties find themselves in a number of countries.

We see this contradiction most strikingly and dangerously now in Germany, where the last elections revealed an exceptionary peculiar relation of forces, resulting not only from the two periods of Germany's postwar stabilisation, but also from the three periods of the Comintern's mistakes.

---

4 *Chvostism* (tail-ism) refers to the practice of following behind and reacting after events.

5 Referring to the Wall Street crash of 1929.

## *The parliamentary victory of the Communist Party in the light of the revolutionary tasks*

The official press of the Comintern is now depicting the results of the German elections as a prodigious victory of communism, which places the slogan of a Soviet Germany on the order of the day. The bureaucratic optimists do not want to reflect upon the meaning of the relationship of forces which is disclosed by the election statistics. They examine the figure of communist votes gained independently of the revolutionary tasks created by the situation and the obstacles it sets up.

The Communist Party[6] received around 4,600,000 votes as against 3,300,000 in 1928. From the viewpoint of 'normal' parliamentary mechanics, the gain of 1,300,000 votes is considerable even if we take into consideration the rise in the total number of voters. But the gain of the party pales completely beside the leap of fascism from 800,000 to 6,400,000 votes. Of no less significance for evaluating the elections is the fact that the Social Democracy, in spite of substantial losses, retained its basic cadres and still received a considerably greater number of workers' votes than the Communist Party.[7]

Meanwhile, if we should ask ourselves what combination of international and domestic circumstances could be capable of turning the working class towards communism with greater velocity, we could not find an example of more favourable circumstances for such a turn than the situation in present-day Germany: Young's

6 Referring to the Communist Party of Germany (KPD), which was founded at the beginning of the November Revolution, 9 November 1918, led by Rosa Luxemburg and Karl Liebknecht.

7 The votes for the 1930 German federal election are as follows:

| *Party* | *Votes* | *Share (per cent)* |
|---|---|---|
| SPD | 8,575,244 | 24.5 (down from 29.8 in 1928) |
| NSDAP | 6,379,672 | 18.3 (up from 2.6 in 1928) |
| KPD | 4,590,160 | 13.1 (up from 10.6 in 1928) |
| Centre Party | 4,127,000 | 11.8 (down from 12.1 in 1928) |

noose,[8] the economic crisis, the disintegration of the rulers, the crisis of parliamentarism, the terrific self-exposure of the Social Democracy in power.[9] From the viewpoint of these concrete historical circumstances, the specific gravity of the German Communist Party in the social life of the country, in spite of the gain of 1,300,000 votes, remains proportionately small.

The weakness of the positions of communism, inextricably bound up with the policy and regime of the Comintern, is revealed more clearly if we compare the present social weight of the Communist Party with those concrete and unpostponable tasks which the present historical circumstances put before it.

It is true that the Communist Party itself did not expect such a gain. But this proves that under the blows of mistakes and defeats, the leadership of the Communist parties has become unaccustomed to big aims and perspectives. If yesterday it underestimated its own possibilities, then today it once more underestimates the difficulties. In this way, one danger is multiplied by another.

In the meantime, the first characteristic of a real revolutionary party is to be able to look reality in the face.

## *The vacillations of the big bourgeoisie*

With every turn of the historic road, with every social crisis, we must over and over again examine the question of the mutual relations of the three classes in modern society: the big bourgeoisie, led by finance capital; the petty bourgeoisie, vacillating between the basic camps; and finally, the proletariat. The big bourgeoisie, making up a negligible part of the nation, cannot hold power without the support

8 Referring to the Young Plan of 1929, which followed a number of similar plans attempting to get Germany to pay the reparations of the Treaty of Versailles. The plan only lasted three years before it became clear that Germany could not meet the terms of this plan. Payments were reduced by 90 per cent in 1932.

9 The Social-Democratic Party (SPD) was a mass reformist party, founded in 1875. The SPD had power handed to them through the November Revolution in 1918, but due to their reformist outlook and fear of the masses, they betrayed the masses and led the crushing of the January 1919 Spartacist rising, culminating in the murder of the leaders of the KPD, Rosa Luxemburg and Karl Liebknecht.

of the petty bourgeoisie of the city and the village, that is, of the remnants of the old, and the masses of the new, middle classes. In the present epoch, this support acquires two basic forms, politically antagonistic to each other but historically supplementary: Social Democracy and fascism. In the person of the Social Democracy, the petty bourgeoisie, which follows finance capital, leads behind it millions of workers.

The *big German bourgeoisie* is vacillating at present; it is split up. Its disagreements are confined to the question: Which of the two methods of cure for the social crisis shall be applied at present? The social-democratic therapy repels one part of the big bourgeoisie by the uncertainty of its results, and by the danger of too large levies (taxes, social legislation, wages). The surgical intervention of fascism seems to the other part to be uncalled for by the situation and too risky. In other words, the finance bourgeoisie as a whole vacillates in the evaluation of the situation, not seeing sufficient basis as yet to proclaim an offensive of its own 'third period', when the Social Democracy is unconditionally replaced by fascism, when, generally speaking, it undergoes a general annihilation for its services rendered. The vacillations of the big bourgeoisie – with the weakening of its basic parties – between the Social Democracy and fascism are an extraordinarily clear symptom of a pre-revolutionary situation. With the approach of a real revolutionary situation, these vacillations will of course immediately come to an end.

## *The petty bourgeoisie and fascism*

For the social crisis to bring about the proletarian revolution, it is necessary that, besides other conditions, a decisive shift of the petty-bourgeois classes occur in the direction of the proletariat. This will give the proletariat a chance to put itself at the head of the nation as its leader.

The last election revealed – and this is its principal symptomatic significances – a shift in the opposite direction. Under the impact of the crisis, the petty bourgeoisie swung, not in the direction of the proletarian revolution, but in the direction of the most extreme imperialist reaction, pulling behind it considerable sections of the proletariat.

The gigantic growth of National Socialism[10] is an expression of two factors: a deep social crisis, throwing the petty-bourgeois masses off balance, and the lack of a revolutionary party that would today be regarded by the popular masses as the acknowledged revolutionary leader. If the Communist Party is the *party of revolutionary hope*, then fascism, as a mass movement, is the *party of counter-revolutionary despair*. When revolutionary hope embraces the whole proletarian mass, it inevitably pulls behind it on the road of revolution considerable and growing sections of the petty bourgeoisie. Precisely in this sphere, the election revealed the opposite picture: counter-revolutionary despair embraced the petty-bourgeois mass with such force that it drew behind it many sections of the proletariat.

How is this to be explained? In the past, we have observed (Italy, Germany) a sharp strengthening of fascism, victorious, or at least threatening, as the result of a spent or missed revolutionary situation, at the conclusion of a revolutionary crisis in which the proletarian vanguard revealed its inability to put itself at the head of the nation and change the fate of all its classes, the petty bourgeoisie included. This is precisely what gave fascism its peculiar strength in Italy. But at present the problem in Germany does not arise at the conclusion of a revolutionary crisis, but just at its approach. From this, the leading Communist Party officials, optimists *ex officio*, draw the conclusion that fascism, having come 'too late', is doomed to inevitable and speedy defeat (*Die Rote Fahne*).[11] These people do not want to learn anything. Fascism comes 'too late' in relation to old revolutionary crises. But it appears sufficiently early – at the dawn – in relation to the new revolutionary crisis. The fact that it gained the possibility of taking up such a powerful starting position on the

10 The National Socialist German Workers' Party (abbreviated as NSDAP) was the official name of the Nazis. The Nazi's had appropriated the word 'Socialist' in order to tap into the popular mood of support for the SPD.

11 *Die Rote Fahne* (*The Red Flag*) was the daily newspaper of the KPD.

eve of a revolutionary period and not at its conclusion, is not the weak side of fascism but the weak side of communism. The petty bourgeoisie does not wait, consequently, for new disappointments in the ability of the party to improve its fate; it bases itself upon the experiences of the past, remembering the lesson of 1923, the capricious leaps of the ultra-left course of Maslow-Thälmann,[12] the opportunist impotence of the same Thälmann, the clatter of the 'third period', etc. Finally – and this is the most important – its lack of faith in the proletarian revolution is nourished by the lack of faith in the Communist Party on the part of millions of social-democratic workers. The petty bourgeoisie, even when completely thrown off the conservative road by circumstances, can turn to social revolution only when the sympathies of the majority of the working class are for a social revolution. Precisely this most important condition is still lacking in Germany, and not by accident.

The programmatic declaration of the German Communist Party before the elections was completely and exclusively devoted to fascism as the main enemy. Nevertheless, fascism came out the victor, gathering not only millions of semi-proletarian elements, but also many hundreds of thousands of industrial workers. This is an expression of the fact that in spite of the parliamentary victory of the Communist Party, the proletarian revolution as a whole suffered a serious defeat in this election – to be sure, of a preliminary, warning and not decisive character. It can become decisive and will inevitably become decisive, if the Communist Party is unable to evaluate its partial parliamentary victory in connection with this 'preliminary' character of the defeat of the revolution as a whole, and draw from this all the necessary conclusions.

---

12 Arkadi Maslow and Ernst Thälmann were figures in the KPD. Maslow, alongside his partner and Chair of the KPD, Ruth Fischer, led the party in an ultra-left direction, following Zinoviev on the question of the united front.
However, only a year later, Zinoviev considered the pair as "unreliable" and removed them from the party leadership, replacing them with Thälmann, who had collaborated closely with Maslow and Fischer in the preceding period. Thälmann would go on to completely subordinate himself and the party to the leadership in Moscow.

*Fascism in Germany has become a real danger*, as an acute expression of the helpless position of the bourgeois regime, the conservative role of the Social Democracy in this regime and the accumulated powerlessness of the Communist Party to abolish it. Whoever denies this is either blind or a braggart.

In 1923, Brandler,[13] in spite of all our warnings, monstrously exaggerated the forces of fascism. From the wrong evaluation of the relationship of forces grew a hesitating, evasive, defensive, cowardly policy. This destroyed the revolution. Such events do not pass without leaving traces in the consciousness of all the classes of the nation. The overestimation of fascism by the communist leadership created one of the conditions for its further strengthening. The contrary mistake, this very underestimation of fascism by the present leadership of the Communist Party, may lead the revolution to a more severe crash for many years to come.

The danger becomes especially acute in connection with the question of the *tempo* of development, which does not depend upon us alone. The malarial character of the political curve revealed by the election speaks for the fact that the tempo of development of the national crisis may turn out to be very speedy. In other words, the course of events in the very near future may resurrect in Germany, on a new historical plane, the old tragic contradiction between the maturity of a revolutionary situation on the one hand and the weakness and strategical impotence of the revolutionary party on the other. This must be said clearly, openly, and above all, in time.

## *The Communist Party and the working class*

It would be a monstrous mistake to console oneself with the fact, for instance, that the Bolshevik Party in April 1917, after the arrival of Lenin, when the party first began to prepare for the seizure of power, had fewer than 80,000 members and led behind itself,

13 Heinrich Brandler was Chairman of the KPD from 1921-24, where he was on the right wing of the party. He was expelled from the KPD in 1928 and went on to form the KPO (Communist Party of Germany, Opposition). The Brandlerites, as they came to be known, aligned themselves with Nikolai Bukharin and the Right Opposition.

even in Petrograd, not more than a third of the workers and a far smaller part of the soldiers. The situation in Russia was altogether different. The revolutionary parties came out of the underground only in March, after an almost three-year interruption of even that strangled political life which existed prior to the war. The working class during the war renewed itself approximately 40 per cent. The overwhelming mass of the proletariat did not know the Bolsheviks, had not even heard of them. The voting for the Mensheviks[14] and SRs[15] in March-June was simply an expression of the first hesitant steps after the awakening. In this voting there was not even a shadow of disappointment with the Bolsheviks or accumulated lack of faith in them, which can arise only as the result of a party's mistakes, verified by the masses through experience. On the contrary. Every day of revolutionary experience in 1917 pushed the masses away from the conciliators and to the side of the Bolsheviks. From this followed the stormy, inexorable growth of the ranks of the party and particularly of its influence.

The situation in Germany has at its root a different character, in this respect as well as in others. The German Communist Party did not come upon the scene yesterday, nor the day before. In 1923, it had behind it, openly or in a semi-concealed form, the majority of the working class. In 1924, on the ebbing wave, it received 3,600,000 votes, a greater percentage of the working class than at present. This means that those workers who remained with the Social Democracy, as well as those who voted this time for the National Socialists, did so not out of simple ignorance, not because they awakened only yesterday, not because they have as yet had no chance to know what the Communist Party is, but because they have *no faith*, on the basis of their own experience in the recent years.

14 The Mensheviks were the reformist wing of the Russian Social-Democratic Labour Party (RSDLP), of which the Bolsheviks were also a part until 1912, when both parties formally split.

15 The Party of Socialist-Revolutionaries (SRs) were a petty-bourgeois party of agrarian socialists who based themselves on the peasantry. In 1917, they split between the Left and Right SRs. Like the Mensheviks, they were divided on the question of the First World War, with the majority supporting the war.

Let us not forget that in February 1928, the ninth plenum of the Executive Committee of the Comintern gave the signal for an intensified, extraordinary, irreconcilable struggle against 'social fascism'.[16] The German Social Democracy was in power almost all this time, revealing to the masses at every step its criminal and shameful role. And all this was supplemented by an enormous economic crisis. It would be difficult to invent circumstances more favourable for the weakening of the Social Democracy. Nevertheless, it retained its basic positions. How is this striking fact to be explained? Only by the fact that the leadership of the Communist Party, by its whole policy, assisted the Social Democracy, supporting it from the left.

This does not at all mean that by voting for the Social Democracy, 5 to 6 million working men and women expressed their full and unlimited confidence in it. The Social Democratic workers should not be considered blind. They are not at all so naive about their own leaders, but they do not see a different way out for themselves in the given situation. Of course, we are not speaking of the labour aristocracy and bureaucracy, but of the rank-and-file workers. The policy of the Communist Party does not inspire them with confidence, not because the Communist Party is not a revolutionary party, but because they do not believe in its ability to gain a revolutionary victory, and do not wish to risk their heads in vain. Voting reluctantly for the Social Democracy, these workers do not express confidence in it but rather they express their lack of confidence in the Communist Party. This is where the great difference lies between the present position of the German Communists and the position of the Russian Bolsheviks in 1917.

But by this alone, the difficulties are not exhausted: inside the Communist Party itself, and particularly in the circle of its supporters and the workers voting for it, is a great reserve of vague

16 The so-called theory of 'social fascism' argued that in the 'third period' of capitalism, a world revolution was imminent, society was already 'fascist' and the reformists and social-democrats constituted "the moderate wing of fascism". (Stalin, 'Concerning the International Situation', *Works*, Vol. 6, Foreign Languages Publishing House, 1924, p. 294.) The latter idea was originally raised in 1924, but was resurrected in 1928 to serve the purpose of the new ultra-left turn.

lack of faith in the leadership of the party. From this grows what is called the 'disparity' between the general influence of the party and its numerical strength, and particularly its role in the trade unions – in Germany such a disparity undoubtedly exists. The official explanation of the disparity is that the party has not been able to 'strengthen' its influence organisationally. Here the mass is looked upon as purely passive material, which enters or does not enter the party, depending exclusively upon whether the secretary can grab every worker by the throat. The bureaucrat does not understand that workers have their own mind, their experience, their will and their active or passive policy toward the party. The worker votes for the party – for its banner, for the October Revolution, for his own future revolution. But by refusing to join the Communist Party or to follow it in the trade-union struggle, he says that he has no faith in its daily policy. The 'disparity' is consequently, in the final analysis, an expression of the lack of confidence of the masses in the present leadership of the Communist International. And this lack of confidence, created and strengthened by mistakes, defeats, fictions and direct deception of the masses from 1923 to 1930, is one of the greatest hindrances on the road to the victory of the proletarian revolution.

Without an internal confidence in itself, the party will not conquer the class. Not to conquer the proletariat means not to break the petty-bourgeois masses away from fascism. One is inextricably bound up with the other.

## *Back to the 'second' period or once more towards the 'third'?*

If we were to use the official terminology of centrism,[17] we would formulate the problem in the following way: the leadership of the Comintern foisted the tactic of the 'third period', that is, the tactic of an immediate revolutionary upsurge, upon the national sections at a time (1928) when the features of the 'second period' were most clearly visible, that is, the stabilisation of the bourgeoisie and the

17 Centrism describes those tendencies in the workers' movement that vacillate between reformism and revolutionary Marxism.

ebb and decline of the revolution. The turn from this, which came in 1930, meant a rejection of the tactic of the 'third period' in favour of the tactic of the 'second period'. In the meantime, this turn made its way through the bureaucratic apparatus at a moment when the most important symptoms began, at any rate in Germany, to signal plainly the real approach of a 'third period'. Does the need for a new tactical turn flow from all this – in the direction of the recently abandoned tactic of the 'third period'?

We use these designations so as to make the posing of this problem more accessible to those circles whose minds are clogged up by the methodology and terminology of the centrist bureaucracy. But we have no intention whatever to adopt this terminology, which conceals a combination of Stalinist bureaucratism and Bukharinist metaphysics.[18] We reject the apocalyptic presentation of the 'third' period as the final one: how many periods there will be before the victory of the proletariat is a question of the relation of forces and the changes in the situation; all this can be tested only through action. We reject the very essence of this strategic schematism with its numbered periods; there is no abstract tactic established in advance for the 'second' and the 'third' periods. It is understood that we cannot achieve victory and the seizure of power without an armed uprising. But how shall we reach this uprising? By what methods? And at what tempo shall we mobilise the masses? This depends not only upon the objective situation in general, but in the first place upon the state in which the arrival of the social crisis in the country finds the proletariat, upon the relation between the party and the class, the proletariat and the petty bourgeoisie, etc. The state of the proletariat at the threshold of the 'third period' depends in its turn upon the tactic the party applied in the period preceding it.

18 Nikolai Bukharin was an 'old Bolshevik' and was Stalin's closest ally from 1923-28. He was the chief architect of the theory of 'socialism in one country'. From 1928, Bukharin led the Right Opposition. He was executed in Stalin's purges in 1938. Trotsky here describes his philosophy as 'metaphysics', that is, formalistic thinking, with concepts and principles that are divorced from the material world.

The normal, natural change of tactics, with the present turn of the situation in Germany, should have been the *acceleration of tempo, the sharpening of slogans and methods of struggle*. This tactical turn would have been normal and natural only if the tempo and slogans of struggle of yesterday had corresponded to the conditions of the preceding period. But this never occurred. The sharp discordance of the ultra-left policy and the stabilised situation is precisely the reason for the tactical turn. What has resulted is that at the moment when the new turn of the objective situation, along with the unfavourable general regrouping of the political forces, brought communism a big gain in votes, the party turned out to be strategically and tactically more disoriented, entangled and off the track than ever before.

To make clearer the contradiction fallen into by the German Communist Party – like most of the other sections of the Comintern, only far deeper than the rest of them – let us take the simplest comparison. In order to jump over a barrier, a preliminary running start is necessary. The higher the barrier, the more important it is to start the run on time, not too late and not too early, in order to approach the obstruction with the necessary reserve of strength. Beginning with February 1928, and especially since July 1929, however, the German Communist Party did nothing but take the running start. It is no wonder that the party began to lose its wind and drag its feet. The Comintern finally gave the command: "Single quick time!" But no sooner had the winded party started to change to a more normal step than before it began to appear not an imaginary but an actual barrier, which might require a revolutionary jump. Will there be enough distance for taking the run? Shall the turn be rejected and changed to a counter-turn? These are the tactical and strategic questions which appear before the German party in all their acuteness.

In order that the leading cadres of the party should be able to find a correct reply to these questions, they must have the chance to judge the next section of the road in connection with the strategy of the past years and its consequences, as revealed in this election.

If, in opposition to this, the bureaucracy should succeed, by cries of victory, in drowning the voice of political self-criticism, this would inevitably lead the proletariat to a catastrophe more terrible than that of 1923.

## *The possible variations of the further development*

A revolutionary situation, confronting the proletariat with the immediate problem of seizing power, is made up of objective and subjective elements, each bound with the other and to a large extent conditioning each other. But this mutual dependence is relative. The law of uneven development applies fully also to the factors of a revolutionary situation. An insufficient development of one of them may produce a condition in which the revolutionary situation either does not come to an explosion and spends itself, or, coming to an explosion, ends in defeat for the revolutionary working class. What is the situation in Germany in this respect?

1. A deep national crisis (economy, international situation) is unquestionably at hand. There appears to be no way out along the normal road of the bourgeois parliamentary regime.

2. The political crisis of the ruling class and its system of government is absolutely indubitable. This is not a parliamentary crisis, but a crisis of class rule.

3. The revolutionary class, however, is still deeply split by internal contradictions. The strengthening of the revolutionary party at the expense of the reformists is as yet at its inception, and has been proceeding thus far at a tempo which is far from corresponding with the depth of the crisis.

4. The petty bourgeoisie, at the very beginning of the crisis, has already assumed a position antagonistic to the *present system* of capitalist rule, but at the same time mortally hostile to the proletarian revolution.

In other words, there are at hand the basic objective conditions for a proletarian revolution. There is one of its political conditions (the state of the ruling class); the other political condition (the state of the proletariat) has only begun to change in the direction of revolution, and because of the heritage of the past, cannot change rapidly; finally, the third political condition (the state of the petty bourgeoisie) is not directed towards the proletarian revolution but towards a bourgeois counter-revolution. The change of this last condition into a favourable one cannot be accomplished without radical changes in the proletariat itself, that is, without the political liquidation of the Social Democracy.

We have, thus, a deeply contradictory situation. Some of its factors put the proletarian revolution on the order of the day: others, however, exclude the possibility of its victory in the next period, that is, without a previous deep change in the political relation of forces.

Theoretically, several variations of the further development of the present situation in Germany can be considered, depending upon objective factors, the policy of the class enemies included, as well as the conduct of the Communist Party itself. Let us note schematically four possible variations of development.

1. The Communist Party, frightened by its own strategy of the 'third period', moves ahead gropingly, with extreme caution, avoiding risky steps and – without giving battle – misses a revolutionary situation. This would mean a repetition of the policy of Brandler in 1921-23, only changed in form. Reflecting the pressure of the Social Democracy, the Brandlerites and semi-Brandlerites, outside the party as well as inside of it, will drive in this direction.

2. Under the influence of the election success, the party, on the contrary, makes a new sharp turn to the left, in the direction of a direct struggle for power, and being a party of the active minority, suffers a catastrophic defeat. Driving in this direction are: fascism; the clamorous, senseless agitation of the apparatus which does not weigh anything, which does not enlighten, but stupefies; the despair and impatience of a part of the working class, particularly the unemployed youth.

3. It is possible, furthermore, that the leadership, rejecting nothing, will attempt empirically to find a middle course between the dangers of the first two variations, and in this connection, will commit a series of new mistakes and, in general, will so slowly eliminate the lack of confidence of the proletarian and semi-proletarian masses, that by that time the objective conditions will have changed in a direction unfavourable for a revolution, giving way to a new period of stabilisation. It is chiefly in this eclectic direction, combining *chvostism* in general with adventurism in particular, that the Moscow Stalinist top is pushing the German party, fearing to take a clear position and preparing an alibi for itself beforehand, that is, a possibility of putting the blame on the 'performers' – at the right or at the left, depending upon the results. This policy, with which we are familiar enough, sacrifices the international historical interests of the proletariat to the interests of the 'prestige' of the bureaucratic top. Intimations of such a course have already been given in *Pravda* on 16 September.

4. Finally, the most propitious, or more correctly, the only propitious variation: the German party, through the efforts of its best and most conscious elements, takes a careful survey of the whole present contradictory situation. By a correct, audacious and flexible policy, the party, on the basis of the present situation, succeeds in uniting the majority of the proletariat and thus secures a reversal in the direction of the semi-proletarian and most oppressed petty-bourgeois masses. The proletarian vanguard, as leader of the nation of the toiling and oppressed, comes to victory. To help the party change its policy towards this course is the task of the Bolshevik-Leninists (Left Opposition).

It would be fruitless to guess which of these variations has better chances of happening in the next period. Such questions are not decided by guesses but by struggle.

One necessary element is an irreconcilable ideological struggle against the centrist leadership of the Comintern. From Moscow, the signal has already been given for a policy of bureaucratic prestige which covers up yesterday's mistakes and prepares tomorrow's through false cries about the new triumph of the line. Monstrously exaggerating the victory of the party, monstrously underestimating the difficulties, interpreting even the success of fascism as a positive factor for the proletarian revolution, *Pravda*[19] necessarily makes one small stipulation. "The successes of the party should not make us dizzy." The treacherous policy of the Stalinist leadership is true to itself even here. An analysis of the situation is given in the spirit of uncritical ultra-leftism. The party is thus deliberately pushed onto the road of adventurism. At the same time, Stalin prepares his alibi in advance with the aid of the ritualistic phrase about "dizziness". It is precisely this policy, short-sighted, unscrupulous, that may ruin the German revolution.

## *Where is the way out?*

We have given above, without any glossing over or embellishment an analysis of difficulties and dangers related as a whole to the political and subjective sphere, which grew primarily out of the mistakes and crimes of the epigone leadership, and which now definitely threaten to demolish a new revolutionary situation developing before our very eyes. The officials will either close their eyes to our analysis or else they will replenish their stock of slander. But it is not a matter of hopeless officials; it concerns the fate of the German proletariat. In the party, as well as in the apparatus, there are not a few people who observe and think and who will be compelled tomorrow by sharp circumstances to think with doubled intensity. It is to them that we direct our analysis and our conclusions.

Every critical situation has great sources of uncertainty. Moods, views and forces, hostile and friendly, are formed in the very process

19 *Pravda* was a Bolshevik daily newspaper published in St. Petersburg, founded on the initiative of the St. Petersburg workers in April 1912. By the late 1920s it had become the mouthpiece of the Stalinist bureaucracy.

of the crisis. They cannot be foreseen mathematically. They must be measured in the process of the struggle, through struggle; and on the basis of these living measurements, necessary corrections must be made in the policy.

Can the strength of the conservative resistance of the social-democratic workers be calculated beforehand? It cannot. In the light of the events of the past years, this strength seems to be gigantic. But the truth is that what helped most of all to weld together Social Democracy was the wrong policy of the Communist Party, which found its highest expression in the absurd theory of social fascism. To measure the real resistance of the Social-Democratic ranks, a different measuring instrument is required, that is, a correct Communist tactic. Given this condition – and it is not a small condition – the degree of internal corrosion of the Social Democracy can be revealed in a comparatively brief period.

In a different form, what has been said above also applies to fascism: it arose, among the other conditions present from the tremblings of the Zinoviev-Stalin strategy.[20] What is its offensive power? What is its stability? Has it reached its culminating point as the optimists *ex officio* assure us, or is it only on the first step of the ladder? This cannot be foretold mechanically. It can be determined only through action. Precisely in regard to fascism, which is a razor in the hands of the class enemy, the wrong policy of the Comintern may produce fatal results in a brief period. On the other hand, a correct policy – not in such a short period, it is true – can undermine the positions of fascism.

A revolutionary party, at the time of a crisis in the regime, is much stronger in the extra-parliamentary mass struggles than within the framework of parliamentarism. But again, on one condition: if it understands the situation correctly and can connect in practice the vital needs of the masses with the task of seizing power. Everything is now reduced to this. It would therefore be the greatest mistake to see in the present situation in Germany only difficulties and dangers. No, the situation also reveals tremendous possibilities, provided it is clearly and thoroughly understood and correctly utilised.

20 Referring to the theory of 'social fascism'.

What is needed for this?

1. A forced turn to the right at the time when the situation is swinging to the left calls for particularly attentive, honest and skilful observation for further changes in all the factors of the situation. The abstract contrasting of the methods of the 'second' and 'third' periods must be rejected at once. The situation must be taken as it is, with all its contradictions and the living dynamics of its development. We must carefully watch the real changes in the situation and influence it in the direction of its real development – not to suit the schemes of Molotov[21] or Kuusinen.[22] To be oriented in the situation – that is the most important and most difficult part of the problem. It cannot be solved at all by bureaucratic methods. Statistics, important though they are by themselves, are insufficient for this purpose. It is necessary to sound the very deepest mass of the proletariat and the toilers generally. We must not only advance the vital and gripping slogans; we must trace the hold they get on the masses. This can be achieved only by an active party which puts out tens of thousands of feelers everywhere, which gathers the testimony, considers all the questions and actively works out its collective viewpoint.

2. The question of the party regime is inextricably bound up with this. People appointed by Moscow, independent of the confidence or lack of confidence of the party, will not be able to lead the masses in an assault upon capitalist society. The more artificial the present regime, the deeper will be its crisis in the days and hours of decision. Of all the 'turns', the most important and urgent one concerns the party regime. It is a question of life or death.

---

21 Vyacheslav Molotov was an 'old Bolshevik' and an ally of Stalin. He became Chairman of the Council of People's Commissars from 1930-41 and remained a leading bureaucrat in the USSR until 1957.

22 Otto Kuusinen was the leader of the Finnish Social-Democratic Party and played a leading role in the Finnish Socialist Worker's Republic, where he was People's Commissar for Education. After the defeat of the republic in 1918 he fled to the USSR and became the Secretary of the ECCI.

3. A change in the regime is the precondition for a change in the course and its consequence at the same time. One is inconceivable without the other. The party must break away from the false atmosphere of conventionality, of hushing up real trouble, of glorifying spurious values – in a word, from the disastrous atmosphere of Stalinism, which is not created by ideological and political influence but by the crude, material dependence of the apparatus and the methods of command based on that.

   One of the necessary conditions for the liberation of the party from bureaucratic bondage is a general examination of the 'general line' of the German leadership, beginning with 1923, and even with the March Days of 1921.[23] The Left Opposition, in a number of documents and theoretical works, has given its evaluation of all the stages of the unfortunate official policy of the Comintern. This criticism must become the property of the party. To avoid it or to be silent about it will not be possible. The party will not rise to the height of its great tasks if it does not freely evaluate its present in the light of its past.

4. If the Communist Party, in spite of the exceptionally favourable circumstances, has proved powerless seriously to shake the structure of the Social Democracy with the aid of the formula of 'social fascism', then real fascism now threatens this structure, no longer with wordy formulas of so-called radicalism, but with the chemical formulas of explosives. No matter how true it is that the Social Democracy prepared the blossoming of fascism by its whole policy, it is no less true that fascism comes forward as a deadly threat primarily to that same Social Democracy, all of

---

23 Referring to the infamous 'March Action', where the KPD called for an ill-prepared general strike, attempting to 'spark' a revolution with a premature insurrection. Despite the heroism shown by sections of workers, the whole episode was a fiasco, without any plan or direction. Workers were expected to heed the general strike call at the drop of a hat. As expected, the movement collapsed. The communists took to derailing trains, organising sham kidnapping of communists and even blowing up a munitions depot, blaming it on the local police. The March Action was a bitter failure, leading to the arrest of 6,000 workers and communists, and significantly harming the reputation of the party.

whose magnificence is inextricably bound up with parliamentary-democratic-pacifist forms and methods of government.

There can be no doubt that at the crucial moment the leaders of the Social Democracy will prefer the triumph of fascism to the revolutionary dictatorship of the proletariat. But precisely the approach of such a choice creates exceptional difficulties for the Social-Democratic leaders among their own workers. The policy of a united front of the workers against fascism flows from this whole situation. It opens up tremendous possibilities for the Communist Party. A condition for success, however, is the rejection of the theory and practice of 'social fascism', the harm of which becomes a positive menace under the present circumstances.

The social crisis will inevitably produce deep cleavages within the Social Democracy. The radicalisation of the masses will affect the social-democratic workers long before they cease to be social-democrats. We will inevitably have to make agreements against fascism with the various social-democratic organisations and factions, putting definite conditions to the leaders in full view of the masses. Only the frightened opportunists, yesterday's allies of Purcell and Cook,[24] of Chiang Kai-shek and Wang Jingwei,[25] can bind themselves by formal commitments beforehand against such agreements. We must return from the official's empty phrase about the united

24 Albert Purcell and Arthur Cook were British trade unionists. Purcell was the president of the Trade Union Congress and member of the Communist Party, Cook was the chairman of the Miners' Federation from 1924. During the 1926 General Strike, the Communist Party, under directives from the Comintern, had a policy of uncritical support for the trade union leaders, who led the strike to defeat.

25 Chiang Kai-Shek and Wang Jingwei were leading figures in the Kuomintang (KMT), the bourgeois-nationalist party in China. During the Chinese Revolution of 1925-27, the Comintern's directives to the Chinese Communist Party were to subordinate themselves to the KMT, which they characterised as the party of the 'progressive' bourgeoisie. Chiang was even elected an honorary member of the Executive Committee of the Comintern in 1926 – Trotsky's was the solitary vote against this decision. The KMT, led by Chiang, brutally crushed the revolution, and then headed the Chinese government until 1948.

front to the policy of the united front as it was formulated by Lenin and always applied by the Bolsheviks in 1917.

5. The problem of unemployment is one of the most important elements of the political crisis. The struggle against capitalist rationalisation and for the seven-hour working day remains entirely on the order of the day. But only the slogan of an extensive, planned collaboration with the Soviet Union can raise this struggle to the height of the revolutionary tasks. In the programmatic declaration for the election, the Central Committee of the German party states that *after achieving power* the Communists will establish economic collaboration with the Soviet Union. There is no doubt of this. But a historical perspective cannot be counterposed to the political tasks of the day. The workers, and the unemployed in the first place, must be mobilised right now under the slogan of extensive economic collaboration with the Soviet Republic. The State Planning Commission of the Union of Soviet Socialist Republics should work out a plan of economic collaboration with the help of the German Communists and trade unionists, which, using the present unemployment as its point of departure, would spread out into a comprehensive collaboration embracing all the basic branches of the economy. The problem does not lie in promising to reconstruct the economy after the seizure of power; it lies in seizing power. The problem is not to promise the collaboration of Soviet Germany with the USSR, but to win the working masses for this collaboration today, linking it closely with the crisis and unemployment and spreading it further into a gigantic plan for the socialist reconstruction of both countries.

6. The political crisis in Germany calls into question the Versailles regime in Europe[26] The Central Committee of the German

26 The Treaty of Versailles of June 1919 returned Alsace-Lorraine to France from Germany and deprived Germany of other territory in Europe and overseas colonies and also established punitive war reparations. The Treaty had a disastrous effect on the German economy and led to a revolutionary crisis when France occupied the Ruhr in 1923.

> Communist Party says that once in power, the German proletariat will abolish the Versailles documents. Is that all? The overthrow of the Versailles Treaty as the supreme achievement of the proletarian revolution! What will be put in its place? Not a word about it. This negative formulation of the question brings the Party closer to the National Socialists. The *Soviet United States of Europe* is the only correct slogan, pointing the way out of European fragmentation, which threatens not only Germany but the whole of Europe with complete economic and cultural decline.
>
> The slogan of the proletarian unification of Europe is at the same time a very important tool in the struggle against the abominations of fascist chauvinism, bullying of France and so on. The most wrong, the most dangerous policy is that which consists in passively adapting to the enemy, in painting yourself to match him. The slogans of national despair and national frenzy must be counteracted by slogans of international withdrawal. And for this purpose it is necessary to purge one's own party of the poison of National Socialism, the main element of which is the theory of socialism in a separate country.

To boil all the above down to one simple formula, let us put the question this way: Should the tactics of the German Communist Party in the immediate period be conducted under the banner of *defence* or *offensive*? We answer: defence.

If the clash were to take place today, as a result of the offensive of the Communist Party, the proletarian vanguard would smash its head on the bloc of the state with fascism, with the frightened and bewildered neutrality of the majority of the working class and with the direct support of the majority of the petty bourgeoisie for fascism.

A position of defence means a policy of rapprochement with the majority of the German working class and a united front with the Social Democratic and non-party workers against the fascist danger.

To deny this danger, to minimise it, to treat it lightly is the greatest crime that can be committed today against the proletarian revolution in Germany.

What will the Communist Party 'defend'? The Weimar Constitution?[27] No, we will leave this task to Brandler. The Communist Party must call for the defence of those material and spiritual positions which the working class has managed to win for itself in the German state. It is a matter of, most directly, the fate of its political organisations, its trade unions, its newspapers and printing houses, its clubs and libraries and so on. The working communist should say to the working social-democrat: "The policy of our parties is irreconcilable; but if the fascists come tonight to smash the premises of your organisation, I will come to your aid with weapons in my hands. Do you promise, in case danger threatens my organisation, to rush to my aid?" Here is the quintessence of the policy of the present period. All agitation must be tuned to this key.

The more persistently, more seriously, more thoughtfully – without the squealing and boasting which so quickly bore the workers – shall we conduct this agitation, the more sound organisational measures of defence shall we propose in every factory, in every workers' quarter and district, the less is the danger that the fascist offensive will take us by surprise, the greater is the certainty that this offensive will unite rather than splinter the workers' ranks.

It is the fascists, owing to their dizzying success thanks to the petty-bourgeois, impatient and undisciplined composition of their army, who will be inclined in the immediate period to bury themselves in the offensive. To compete with them on this path at present would be not only hopeless but also mortally dangerous. On the contrary, the more the fascists will have in the eyes of the social-democratic workers and the working masses in general the appearance of the offensive side and we of the defensive side, the better will be our

27 The November Revolution of 1918 abolished the monarchy and declared a new republic. Fearing the revolutionary workers in Berlin, the national assembly, which adopted the new constitution, decided to meet in Weimar until August 1919. This regime became the Weimar Republic, and lasted until Hitler took power in 1933.

chances not only of defeating the fascist offensive, but also of moving into a successful offensive ourselves. Defence must be vigilant, active and courageous. The headquarters must review the entire field of struggle, taking into account all changes, so as not to miss a new turning point in the situation, when it will be necessary to give the signal for a general assault.

There are strategists who are always and under all conditions in favour of defence. The Brandlerites, for example, belong to this group. It would be sheer childishness to be embarrassed if they were to talk about defence *today* too: they always do. The Brandlerites are one of the mouthpieces of Social Democracy. Our task is to get closer to the Social-Democratic workers on the basis of defence and then lead them into a decisive offensive. The Brandlerites are absolutely incapable of this. At the moment when the balance of forces radically changes in favour of the proletarian revolution, the Brandlerites will again be a ballast and a brake on it. That is why a policy of defence calculated to move closer to the Social-Democratic masses does not in any case mean a softening of contradictions with the Brandlerite headquarters, behind which there are not and never will be any masses.

* * *

In connection with the characterised above grouping of forces and the tasks of the proletarian vanguard, the methods of physical violence used by the Stalinist bureaucracy in Germany and in other countries against the Bolshevik-Leninists take on a very special significance. This is a direct favour to the Social-Democratic police and the strike gangs of fascism. In fundamental contradiction to the traditions of the revolutionary proletarian movement, these methods, more than anything else, correspond to the spirit of the petty-bourgeois officials who are sitting on a salary secured from above and are afraid of losing it at the onset of party democracy. A widespread explanatory work, as concrete as possible, is necessary against the Stalinist abominations, exposing the role of the most unworthy officials of the party apparatus. The experience of the USSR, as well as that of other countries, shows that it is those gentlemen who need to cover up their sins and crimes before their high superiors: embezzlement of public funds, abuse of office, or simply their complete unfitness, that fight against the leftist opposition with the greatest fury. It is quite clear that the exposure of the fist fighting of the Stalinist apparatus against the Bolshevik-Leninists will be all the more successful the more widely will we develop our general agitation on the basis of the tasks outlined above.

* * *

We have considered the question of the tactical turn of the Comintern solely in the light of the German situation, because, first, the German crisis now places the German Communist Party once again at the centre of the attention of the world proletarian vanguard, and because in the light of this crisis all problems appear with the greatest prominence. It would not be difficult, however, to show that what has been said here applies, in one way or another, to other countries as well.

In France, all forms of class struggle after the war have an immeasurably less acute and decisive character than in Germany. But the general tendencies of development are the same, not to mention the direct dependence of the fate of France on that of Germany. The turns of the Comintern have, at any rate, a universal character. The French Communist Party, announced by Molotov as the first candidate for power as early as 1928, has pursued an absolutely suicidal policy during the last two years. It has overlooked, in particular, the economic upturn. The tactical turn was announced in France at a moment when industrial revival was clearly beginning to be replaced by crisis. Thus the same contradictions, difficulties and challenges that we are talking about with regard to Germany are also the order of the day in France.

The turn of the Comintern, combined with the turn of the situation, poses new and extremely important tasks for the left communist opposition. Its forces are few in number. But each current grows with the growth of its tasks. To understand them clearly means to seize one of the most important prerequisites of victory.

# *What is Fascism?*

## *Extracts From a Letter to a Comrade*

Written 15 November 1931

I am writing you today regarding the question of fascism. It would be well if you were to discuss three questions with the English comrades, since in this manner we can arrive at conclusions and definite views.

What is fascism? The name originated in Italy. Were all the forms of counter-revolutionary dictatorship fascist or not? That is, prior to the advent of fascism in Italy.

The former dictatorship in Spain, of Primo de Rivera,[1] is called a fascist dictatorship by the Comintern. Is this correct or not? We believe that it is incorrect.

The fascist movement in Italy was a spontaneous movement of large masses, with new leaders from the rank and file. It is a plebeian movement in origin, directed and financed by big capitalist powers. It issued forth from the petty bourgeoisie, the slum proletariat and

1 Miguel Primo de Rivera was a military officer and Prime Minister of Spain from 1923 until his fall in 1930.

even to a certain extent, from the proletarian masses, Mussolini, a former socialist, is a 'self-made' man arising from this movement.[2]

Primo de Rivera was an aristocrat. He occupied a high military and bureaucratic post, and was chief governor of Catalonia. He accomplished his overthrowal with the state and military forces. The dictatorships of Spain and Italy are two totally different forms of dictatorship. It is necessary to distinguish between them. Mussolini had great difficulty in reconciling many old military institutions with the fascist militia. This problem did not exist for Primo de Rivera.

The movement in Germany is analogous mostly to the Italian movement. It is a mass movement, with its leaders employing a great deal of socialist demagogy. This is necessary for the creation of the mass movement.

The genuine basis is the petty bourgeoisie. In Italy it is a very large base – the petty bourgeoisie of the towns and cities, and the peasantry. In Germany likewise, there is a large base for fascism. In England there is less of that base because the proletariat is the overwhelming majority of the population: the peasant or farming stratum only an insignificant section.

It may be said, and this is true to a certain extent, that the new middle class, the functionaries of the state, the private administrators, etc., etc., can constitute such a base. But this is a new question that must be analysed. This is a supposition. It is necessary to analyse just what it will be. It is necessary to foresee the fascist movement growing from this or that element. But this is only a perspective which is controlled by events. I am not affirming that it is impossible for a fascist movement to develop in England or for a Mosley[3] or someone else to become a dictator. This is a question for the future. It is a far-fetched possibility.

---

2 Benito Mussolini was the fascist Prime Minister of Italy from 1922 to 1943. He was the son of an Italian revolutionary and edited the Italian Socialist Party paper *Avanti!* from 1912-14 but was expelled from the Socialist Party when he came out in favour of Italy intervening in the war.

3 Oswald Mosley was a British aristocrat and fascist. He was a Labour MP from 1924-31 before founding and leading the British Union of Fascists in 1932 until it was banned in 1940.

To speak of it now as an imminent danger is not a prognosis but a mere prophecy. In order to be capable of foreseeing anything in the direction of fascism, it is necessary to have a definition of that idea. What is fascism? What is its base, its form and its characteristics? How will its development take place?

The aim of this is to show the English comrades that the question is not a simple one. It is necessary to proceed in a scientific and Marxist manner.

Now another question. Naturally, it is important that you occupy yourself with the isolated elements of the Left Opposition, but it is no less important to pay close attention to what is taking place in the Communist Party, the Independent Labour Party[4] and the Labour Party. The first tremors of the earthquake must have produced very great cracks in the wall of the house, and the Bolshevik-Leninists can gain an influence among a large section of the labour movement. It is necessary to direct your attention not only to our little section but to everything that is happening in this great organism.

This letter is in very rough form. I have not even checked its contents but I trust that you will get the general sense of the ideas expressed…

L Trotsky
15 November 1931
Kadıköy, Istanbul

4 The Independent Labour Party (ILP) was formed in 1893 and became a component party of the Labour Party. Although it had a reformist leadership, the ILP represented the most left-wing members of the Labour Party. By the time of this letter, in late 1931, it was on the verge of breaking from the Labour Party.

# *Germany: The Only Road*

Written 14 September 1932

Editor's note: This pamphlet analysing the tumultuous political situation in Germany and the tasks of the communists was written by Trotsky in exile in Turkey, September 1932. Hitler had run for the presidency earlier in April, losing narrowly to Paul von Hindenburg, and in the July elections the Nazis had become the largest party in the Reichstag.

* * *

## *Foreword*

The decline of capitalism promises to be still more stormy, dramatic and bloody than its rise. German capitalism will surely prove no exception. If its agony is being stretched out too long, the fault lies – we must speak the truth – with the parties of the proletariat.

German capitalism appeared late on the scene, and was deprived of the privileges of the first-born. Russia's development placed it somewhere between England and India; Germany, in such a scheme, would have to occupy the place between England and Russia, but without the enormous overseas colonies of Great Britain and without the 'internal colonies' of tsarist Russia. Germany, squeezed into the heart of Europe, was faced – at a time when the whole world had already been divided up – with the necessity of conquering foreign markets and redividing colonies which had already been divided.

German capitalism was not destined to swim with the stream, to give itself up to the free play of forces. Only Great Britain could afford this luxury, and then only for a limited historical period, which has recently ended before our eyes. German capitalism could not even afford the 'sense of moderation' of French capitalism, which is entrenched within its limitations and in addition, is equipped with rich colonial possessions as a reserve.

The German bourgeoisie, opportunist through and through in the domain of internal politics, had to rise to heights of audacity and rapidity in that of economy and of world politics; it had to expand its production immeasurably, to catch up with the older nations, to rattle the sword and hurl itself into the war. The extreme rationalisation of German industry after the war likewise resulted from the necessity of overcoming the unfavourable conditions of historical delay, the geographical situation and military defeat.

If the economic evils of our epoch, in the last analysis, result from the fact that the productive forces of humanity are incompatible with private ownership of the means of production as well as the national boundaries, German capitalism is going through the severest convulsions just because it is the most modern, most advanced and most dynamic capitalism on the continent of Europe.

The physicians of German capitalism are divided into three schools: liberalism, planned economy and autarky.

Liberalism would like to restore the *'natural' laws of the market*. But the wretched political fate of liberalism only reflects the fact that German capitalism could never base itself on Manchesterism,[1] but went through protectionism to trust and monopolies. The German economy cannot be brought back to a 'healthy' past which never existed.

1 Referring to the nineteenth century liberal movement that advocated for the free market and free trade, originating amongst the textile manufacturers of Manchester, England.

'National Socialism' promises to revise the work of Versailles in its own manner, i.e. to carry further the offensive of Hohenzollern[2] imperialism. At the same time, it wants to bring Germany to *autarky*, i.e. onto the road of provincialism and voluntary restriction. The lion's roar in this case hides the psychology of the whipped dog. To adapt German capitalism to its national boundaries is about the same as to cure a sick man by cutting off his right hand, his left foot and part of his skull.

To cure capitalism by means of *planned economy* would mean to eliminate competition. In such a case we must begin with the abolition of private ownership of the means of production. The bureaucratic-professorial reformers do not even dare to think of it. German economy is, least of all, purely German: it is an integral constituent of world economy. A German plan is conceivable only in the perspective of an international economic plan. A planned system within closed national boundaries would mean the abnegation of world economy, i.e. the attempt to retreat to the system of autarky.

These three systems, with their mutual feuds, in reality resemble each other in the respect that they are all shut in within the magic circle of reactionary utopianism. What must be saved is not German capitalism, but Germany – from its capitalism.

In the years of the crisis, the German bourgeoisie, or its theoreticians at least, have uttered speeches of repentance – yes, they had carried out much too risky policies, they had too lightly resorted to the help of foreign credits, had pushed forward too fast the modernisation of factory equipment etc. In the future one must be more careful! In reality, however, as the Papen programme[3] and the attitude of finance capital toward it have shown, the leaders of the German bourgeoisie incline today more than ever to economic adventurism.

---

2 The House of Hohenzollern was the ruling imperial dynasty of Germany in the early 1900s, until they were deposed by the November Revolution of 1918.

3 Referring to the programme pursued by the short-lived government of Franz von Papen, Chancellor of Germany for the latter half of 1932.

At the first signs of an industrial revival, German capitalism will show itself to be what its historical past has made it, and not what the liberal moralists would like to make it. The entrepreneurs, hungry for profits, will again raise the steam pressure without looking at the pressure gauge. The chase after foreign credits will again take on a feverish character. Are the possibilities of expansion slight? All the more necessary to monopolise them for oneself. The terrified world will again see the picture of the preceding period, but in the form of still more violent convulsions. At the same time, the restoration of German militarism will proceed as if the years 1914-18 had never existed. The German bourgeoisie is again placing East Elbe barons[4] at the head of the nation. Under Bonapartist auspices they are even more inclined to risk the head of the nation than under those of the legitimate monarchy.

In their lucid moments, the leaders of German Social Democracy must ask themselves by what miracle their party, after all the damage that it has done, still leads millions of workers. Certainly, great importance must be given to the conservatism innate in every mass organisation. Several generations of the proletariat have gone through Social Democracy as a political school; this has created a great tradition. Yet that is not the main reason for the vitality of reformism. The workers cannot simply leave the Social Democracy, in spite of all the crimes of that party; they must be able to replace it by another party. Meanwhile the German Communist Party, in the person of its leaders, has for the past nine years done everything in its power to repel the masses or at least prevent them from rallying around the Communist Party.

The policy of capitulation of Stalin-Brandler in the year 1923; the ultra-left zigzag of Maslow-Ruth Fischer-Thälmann in 1924-25; the opportunistic crawling before the Social Democracy in 1926-28; the adventurism of the 'third period' in 1928-30; the theory and practice of 'social fascism' and of 'national liberation'

4 The region east of the River Elbe was renowned for its reactionary, monarchist, aristocrats (Junkers), who ruled their large landholdings with an iron fist.

in 1930-32 – those are the items of the bill. The total reads: Hindenburg-Papen-Schleicher and co.[5]

On the capitalist road, there is no future for the German people. Therein lies the most important source of strength for the Communist Party. The example of the Soviet Union shows through experience that there is a way out on the socialist road. Therein lies the second source of strength for the Communist Party.

But, thanks to the conditions of development of the isolated proletarian state, there has come to leadership of the Soviet Union a national opportunistic bureaucracy, which does not believe in the world revolution, which defends its independence of the world revolution and at the same time maintains an unlimited domination over the Communist International. And that is at the present time the greatest misfortune for the German and the international proletariat.

The situation in Germany is as if purposely created to make it possible for the Communist Party to win the majority of the workers in a short time. Only, the Communist Party must understand that as yet, today, it represents the minority of the proletariat, and must firmly tread the road of united front tactics. Instead of this, the Communist Party has made its own a tactic which can be expressed in the following words: not to give the German workers the possibility of carrying on economic struggles, or offering resistance to fascism, or seizing the weapon of the general strike, or creating soviets – before the entire proletariat recognises in advance the leadership of the Communist Party. The political task is converted into an ultimatum.

From where could this destructive method have come? The answer to this is the policy of the Stalinist faction in the Soviet

---

5 Paul von Hindenburg was a prominent General who spent nearly fifty years in the Imperial German Army. He came out of retirement to lead the army during the First World War, becoming the Chief of the General Staff in 1916. Together with the arch-reactionary General Ludendorff he ran Germany as a military dictatorship in the final years of the war. He appointed Hitler Chancellor in 1933 and remained as President until his death in 1934, when the office of the President was abolished.

Union. There the apparatus has converted political leadership into administrative command. In refusing to permit the workers to discuss, or criticise, or vote, the Stalinist bureaucracy speaks to them in no other language than that of the ultimatum. The policy of Thälmann is an attempt to translate Stalinism into bad German. But the difference consists in the fact that the bureaucracy of the USSR has at the disposal of its policy of command the state power, which it received at the hands of the October Revolution. Thälmann, on the other hand, has, for the reinforcement of his ultimatum, only the formal authority of the Soviet Union. This is a great source of moral assistance, but under the given conditions it only suffices to close the mouths of the communist workers, but not to win over the social-democratic workers. But the problem of the German revolution is now reduced to this latter task.

Continuing the previous works of the author devoted to the policy of the German proletariat, the present pamphlet attempts to investigate the questions of German revolutionary policy in a new stage.

## *Bonapartism and fascism*

Let us endeavour to analyse briefly what has occurred and where we stand.

Thanks to the Social Democracy, the Brüning government[6] had at its disposal the support of parliament for ruling with the aid of emergency decrees. The Social-Democratic leaders said: "In this manner we shall block the road of fascism to power." The Stalinist bureaucracy said: "No, fascism has already triumphed; it is the Brüning regime which is fascism." Both were false. The social-democrats palmed off a passive retreat before fascism as the struggle against fascism. The Stalinists presented the matter as if the victory of fascism was already behind them. The fighting power of the

6 Heinrich Brüning was a Centre Party politician and Chancellor of Germany 1930-32, before being ousted and replaced by Franz von Papen.
The Centre Party was a Catholic bourgeois party. It was the third-largest party in the Reichstag during the years of the Weimar Republic and played a role in the formation of several coalition governments.

proletariat was sapped by both sides and the triumph of the enemy facilitated and brought closer.

In its time, we designated the Brüning government as *Bonapartism* ('a caricature of Bonapartism'), that is, as a regime of military police dictatorship. As soon as the struggle of two social strata – the haves and the have-nots, the exploiters and the exploited – reaches its highest tension, the conditions are established for the domination of bureaucracy, police, soldiery. The government becomes 'independent' of society. Let us once more recall: if two forks are stuck symmetrically into a cork, the latter can stand even on the head of a pin. That is precisely the schema of Bonapartism. To be sure, such a government does not cease being the clerk of the property owners. Yet the clerk sits on the back of the boss, rubs his neck raw and does not hesitate at times to dig his boots into his face.

It might have been assumed that Brüning would hold on until the final solution. Yet, in the course of events, another link inserted itself: the Papen government. Were we to be exact we should have to make a rectification of our old designation: the Brüning government was a pre-Bonapartist government. Brüning was only a precursor. In a perfected form, Bonapartism came upon the scene in the Papen-Schleicher government.

Wherein lies the difference? Brüning asserted that he knew no greater happiness than to "serve" Hindenburg and Article 48.[7] Hitler 'supported' Brüning's right flank with his fist. But with the left elbow Brüning rested on Wels'[8] shoulder. In the Reichstag, Brüning found a majority which relieved him of the necessity of reckoning with the Reichstag.

The more Brüning's independence from the parliament grew, the more independent did the summits of the bureaucracy feel themselves from Brüning and the political groupings standing

7 Article 48 of the Weimar Constitution gave the President emergency powers. President Hindenburg used this decree 109 times between 1930 and 1932 to bypass the Reichstag.

8 Otto Wels was Chairman of the SPD from 1919 until his death in 1939.

behind him. There only remained finally to break the bonds with the Reichstag. The Papen government emerged from an immaculate bureaucratic conception. With the right elbow it rests upon Hitler's shoulder. With the police fist it wards off the proletariat on the left. Therein lies the secret of its 'stability', that is of the fact that it did not collapse at the moment of its birth.

The Brüning government bore a clerical-bureaucratic-police character. The Reichswehr[9] still remained in reserve. The 'Iron Front'[10] served as a direct prop of order. The essence of the Hindenburg-Papen coup d'état[11] lay precisely in eliminating dependence on the Iron Front. The generals moved up automatically to first place.

The Social-Democratic leaders turned out to be completely duped. And this is no more than is proper for them in periods of social crisis. These petty-bourgeois intriguers appear to be clever only under those conditions where cleverness is not necessary. Now they pull the covers over their heads at night, sweat and hope for a miracle: perhaps in the end we may yet be able to save not only our necks, but also the overstuffed furniture and the little, innocent savings. But there will be no more miracles...

Unfortunately, however, the Communist Party has also been completely taken by surprise by the events. The Stalinist bureaucracy was unable to foresee a thing. Today Thälmann, Remmele,[12] and others speak on every occasion of "the coup d'état

9 The Reichswehr was the official name of the German armed forces after the November Revolution.

10 The Eiserne Front (Iron Front) was a German paramilitary organisation set up to defend the Weimar Constitution. While officially independent, it was de facto tied to the SPD. Its members fought both communists and fascists in the streets.

11 In May 1932, after campaigning against the government, Papen was appointed Chancellor after a deal between himself, President Hindenburg and Hitler, who agreed to allow a new government to form. He replaced Brüning, whose government had governed with the support or tolerance of the SPD.

12 Hermann Remmele was a member of the KPD and on its Central Committee from 1920-33. He was also a member of the Reichstag for these years. From 1923-26, he was editor of *Die Rote Fahne*, and from 1926 a member of the ECCI.

of 20 July".[13] How is that? At first they contended that fascism had already arrived and that only "counter-revolutionary Trotskyists" could speak of it as something in the future. Now it turns out that to pass over from Brüning to Papen – for the present not to Hitler but only to Papen – a whole 'coup d'état' was necessary. Yet the class content of Severing,[14] Brüning and Hitler, these sages taught us, is "one and the same thing." Then whence and wherefore the *coup d'état?*

But the confusion doesn't come to an end with this. Even though the difference between Bonapartism and fascism has now been revealed plainly enough, Thälmann, Remmele and others speak of the *fascist* coup d'état of 20 July. At the same time, they warn the workers against the approaching danger of the Hitlerite, that is, the equally fascist, overturn. Finally, the Social Democracy is designated just as before as social fascist. The unfolding events are in this way reduced to this, that species of fascism take the power from each other with the aid of 'fascist' coups d'état. Isn't it clear that the whole Stalinist theory was created only for the purpose of gumming up the human brain?

The less prepared the workers were, the more the advent of the Papen government was bound to produce the impression of strength: complete ignoring of the parties, new emergency decrees, dissolution of the Reichstag, reprisals, state of siege in the capital, abolition of the Prussian 'democracy'. And with what ease! A lion you kill with a shot; the flea you squash between the fingernails; Social-Democratic ministers are finished off with a flick.

However, in spite of the visibility of concentrated forces, the Papen government as such is weaker yet than its predecessor. The Bonapartist regime can attain a comparatively stable and durable

13 On 20 July 1932, Hindenburg disbanded the SPD government of the Free State of Prussia, which covered half of Germany, and installed German Chancellor von Papen instead, effectively abolishing the Prussian government and centralising power in the federal government.

14 Carl Severing was a member of the SPD, Minister of the Interior for Prussia from 1920 until the 20 July coup and for Germany from 1928-30.

character only in the event that it brings a revolutionary epoch to a close; when the relationship of forces has already been tested in battles; when the revolutionary classes are already spent, but the possessing classes have not yet freed themselves from the fear: will not tomorrow bring new convulsions? Without this basic condition that is, without a preceding exhaustion of the mass energies in battles, the Bonapartist regime is in no position to develop.

Through the Papen government, the barons, the magnates of capital and the bankers have made an attempt to safeguard their interests by means of the police and the regular army. The idea of giving up all power to Hitler, who supports himself upon the greedy and unbridled bands of the petty bourgeoisie, is a far from pleasant one to them. They do not, of course, doubt that in the long run Hitler will be a submissive instrument of their domination. Yet this is bound up with convulsions, with the risk of a long and weary civil war and great expense. To be sure, fascism, as the Italian example shows, leads in the end to a military bureaucratic dictatorship of the Bonapartist type. But for that it requires a number of years even in the event of a complete victory: a longer span of years in Germany than in Italy. It is clear that the possessing classes would prefer a more economical path, that is, the path of Schleicher and not of Hitler, not to speak of the fact that Schleicher himself prefers it that way.

The fact that the basis for the existence of the Papen government is rooted in the neutralisation of the irreconcilable camps in no way signifies, of course, that the forces of the revolutionary proletariat and of the reactionary petty bourgeoisie weigh equally on the scales of history. The whole question shifts here onto the field of politics. Through the mechanism of the Iron Front the Social Democracy paralyses the proletariat. By the policy of brainless ultimatism the Stalinist bureaucracy blocks the revolutionary way out for the workers. With correct leadership of the proletariat, fascism would be exterminated without difficulty and not a chink could remain open for Bonapartism. Unfortunately that is not the situation. The paralysed strength of the proletariat has assumed the deceptive form of the 'strength' of the Bonapartist clique. Therein lies the political formula of the present day.

The Papen government is the featureless point of intersection of great historical forces. Its independent weight is next to nil. Therefore it can do nothing but take fright at its own gesticulations and grow dizzy at the vacuum unfolding on all sides of it. Thus and only thus can it be explained that in the deeds of the government up to now there have been two parts of cowardice to one part of audacity. In Prussia, that is, with the Social Democracy, the government played a sure game: it knew that these gentlemen would offer no resistance. But after it had dissolved the Reichstag, it announced new elections and did not dare to postpone them. After proclaiming the state of martial law, it hastened to explain: this is only in order to facilitate the capitulation without a struggle of the Social-Democratic leaders.

However, isn't there a Reichswehr? We are not inclined to forget it. Engels defined the state as armed bodies of men with material accessories in the form of prisons, etc. With respect to the present governmental power, it can even be said that only the Reichswehr really exists. But the Reichswehr seems by no means a submissive and reliable instrument in the hands of that group of people at whose head stands Papen. As a matter of fact, the government is rather a sort of political commission of the Reichswehr.

But for all its preponderance over the government, the Reichswehr nevertheless cannot lay claim to any independent political role. A hundred thousand soldiers, no matter how cohesive and steeled they may be (which is still to be tested), are incapable of commanding a nation of 65 million torn by the most profound social antagonisms. The Reichswehr represents only one element in the interplay of forces, and not the decisive one.

In its fashion, the new Reichswehr reflects rather well the political situation in the country that has led to the Bonapartist experiment. The parliament without a majority, with irreconcilable wings, offers an obvious and irrefutable argument in favour of *dictatorship*. Once more the limits of democracy emerge in all their obviousness. Where it is a question of the foundations of society itself, it is not parliamentary arithmetic that decides. What decides is the struggle.

We shall not undertake to counsel from afar what road the attempts at forming a government will take in the next days. Our hypotheses would come tardily in any case, and besides, it is not the possible transitional forms and combinations which decide the question. A bloc of the right wing with the Centre would signify the 'legalisation' of a seizure of power by the National Socialists, that is, the most suitable cloak for the fascist coup d'état. What relationships would develop in the early days between Hitler, Schleicher and the Centre leaders[15] is more important for them than it is for the German people. Politically, all the conceivable combinations with Hitler signify the dissolution of bureaucracy, courts, police and army into fascism.

If it is assumed that the Centre will not agree to a coalition in which it would have to pay by a rupture with its own workers for the role of a brake on Hitler's locomotive – then in this case only the open extra-parliamentary road remains. A combination without the Centre would more easily and speedily insure the predominance of the National Socialists. If the latter do not immediately unite with Papen and at the same time do not pass over to an immediate assault, then the Bonapartist character of the government will have to emerge more sharply: Schleicher would have his 'hundred days'… without the preceding Napoleonic years.

Hundred days – no, we are figuring far too generously. The Reichswehr does not decide. Schleicher does not suffice. The extra-parliamentary dictatorship of the Junkers[16] and the magnates of financial capital can only be assured by the method of a wearisome and relentless civil war. Will Hitler be able to fulfil this task? That depends not only upon the evil will of fascism, but also upon the revolutionary will of the proletariat.

---

15 Referring to leaders of the Catholic Centre Party.

16 Members of the landed nobility in Prussia and subsequently Germany.

## *Bourgeoisie, petty bourgeoisie and proletariat*

Any serious analysis of the political situation must take as its point of departure the mutual relations among the three classes: the bourgeoisie, the petty bourgeoisie (including the peasantry) and the proletariat.

The economically powerful big bourgeoisie, in itself, constitutes an infinitesimal minority of the nation. To enforce its domination, it must ensure a definite mutual relationship with the petty bourgeoisie and, through its mediation, with the proletariat.

To understand the dialectics of these interrelations, we must distinguish three historical stages: the dawn of capitalist development when the bourgeoisie required revolutionary methods to solve its tasks; the period of bloom and maturity of the capitalist regime, when the bourgeoisie endowed its domination with orderly, pacific, conservative, democratic forms; finally the decline of capitalism, when the bourgeoisie is forced to resort to methods of civil war against the proletariat to protect its right of exploitation.

The political programmes characteristic of these three stages: *Jacobinism*,[17] reformist *democracy* (Social Democracy included) and *fascism*, are basically programmes of petty-bourgeois currents. This fact alone, more than anything else, shows of what tremendous – rather, of what decisive – importance the self-determination of the petty-bourgeois masses of the people is for the whole fate of bourgeois society.

Nevertheless, the relationship between the bourgeoisie and its basic social support, the petty bourgeoisie, does not at all rest upon reciprocal confidence and pacific collaboration. In its mass, the petty bourgeoisie is an exploited and oppressed class. It regards the bourgeoisie with envy and often with hatred. The bourgeoisie, on the other hand, while utilising the support of the petty bourgeoisie, distrusts the latter, for it very correctly fears its tendency to break down the barriers set up for it from above.

While they were laying out and clearing the road for bourgeois development the Jacobins engaged, at every step, in sharp clashes

---

17 The Jacobins were the radical wing of the French Revolution 1789-93, who fought for bourgeois-democratic demands against the old aristocratic and feudal order.

with the bourgeoisie. They served it in intransigent struggle against it. After they had fulfilled their limited historical role, the Jacobins fell, for the rule of capital was predetermined.

For a whole series of stages, the bourgeoisie asserted its power under the form of parliamentary democracy. But again, not peacefully and not voluntarily. The bourgeoisie was mortally afraid of universal suffrage. But in the long run it succeeded, with the aid of a combination of repressions and concessions, with the threat of starvation coupled with measures of reform, in subordinating within the framework of formal democracy not only the old petty bourgeoisie, but in considerable measure also the proletariat by means of the new petty bourgeoisie – the labour bureaucracy. In August 1914 the imperialist bourgeoisie was able, by means of parliamentary democracy, to lead millions of workers and peasants to the slaughter.

But precisely with the war there begins the distinct decline of capitalism and above all of its democratic form of domination. It is now no longer a matter of new reforms and aims, but of cutting down and abolishing the old ones. Therewith the bourgeoisie comes into conflict not only with the institutions of proletarian democracy (trade unions and political parties) but also with parliamentary democracy, within the framework of which the workers' organisations arose. Hence the campaign against 'Marxism' on the one hand and against democratic parliamentarism on the other.

But just as the summits of the liberal bourgeoisie in their time were unable, by their own force alone, to get rid of feudalism, monarchy and the church, so the magnates of finance capital are unable, by *their* force alone, to cope with the proletariat. They need the support of the petty bourgeoisie. For this purpose, it must be whipped up, put on its feet mobilised, armed. But this method has its dangers. While it makes use of fascism, the bourgeoisie nevertheless fears it. Piłsudski[18]

18 Józef Piłsudski was a Polish nationalist. He was the leader of the Polish Socialist Party (PSP), which, despite the name, was a bourgeois-nationalist party, as opposed to the internationalist party, the Social Democracy of the Kingdom of Poland and Lithuania (SDKPiL), which counted Rosa Luxemburg among

was forced in May 1926 to save bourgeois society by a coup d'état directed against the traditional parties of the Polish bourgeoisie. The matter went so far that the official leader of the Polish Communist Party, Warski,[19] who came over from Rosa Luxemburg not to Lenin, but to Stalin, took the coup d'état of Piłsudski to be the road of the "revolutionary democratic dictatorship" and called upon the workers to support Piłsudski.

At the session of the Polish Commission of the Executive Committee of the Comintern on 2 July 1926, the author of these lines said on the subject of the events in Poland:

> ... the movement he [Piłsudski] headed was petty bourgeois, a 'plebeian' means of solving the pressing problems of capitalist society in process of decline and destruction. Here there is a direct parallel with Italian fascism...
>
> These two currents undoubtedly have common features: their shock troops are recruited [...] among the petty bourgeoisie; both Piłsudski and Mussolini operated by extra-parliamentary, nakedly violent means, by the methods of civil war; both of them aimed not at overthrowing bourgeois society, but at saving it. Having raised the petty-bourgeois masses to their feet they both clashed openly with the big bourgeoisie after coming to power. Here a historical generalisation involuntarily comes to mind: one is forced to recall Marx's definition of Jacobinism as a plebeian means of dealing with the feudal enemies of the bourgeoisie. That was in the epoch of the *rise* of the bourgeoisie. It must be said that now, in the epoch of the *decline* of bourgeois society, the bourgeoisie once again has need of a 'plebeian' means of solving its problems – which are no longer progressive but rather, thoroughly reactionary. In this sense, then, fascism contains a reactionary caricature of Jacobinism...

---

its leaders. He was Prime Minister of Poland 1918-22. He led the coup against the government in May 1926 and established himself as the head of the military dictatorship.

19 Adolf Warski was a Polish Marxist who co-founded the SDKPiL and the Communist Party of Poland (KPP). He was executed in 1938 during the Great Purge.

> The bourgeoisie in decline is incapable of maintaining itself in power with the methods and means of its own creation – the parliamentary state. It needs fascism as a weapon of self-defence, at least at the most critical moments. The bourgeoisie does not like the 'plebeian' means of solving its problems. It had an extremely hostile attitude toward Jacobinism which cleared a path in blood for the development of bourgeois society. The fascists are immeasurably closer to the bourgeois in decline than the Jacobins were to the bourgeoisie on the rise. But the established bourgeoisie does not like the fascist means of solving its problems either, for the shocks and disturbances, although in the interests of bourgeois society, involve dangers for it as well. This is the source of the antagonism between fascism and the traditional parties of the bourgeoisie…
>
> The big bourgeoisie dislikes this method, much as a man with a swollen jaw dislikes having his teeth pulled. The respectable circles of bourgeois society viewed with hatred the services of the dentist Piłsudski, but in the end, they gave in to the inevitable, to be sure, with threats of resistance and much haggling and wrangling over the price. And lo, the petty bourgeoisie's idol of yesterday has been transformed into the gendarme of capital!

To this attempt at defining the historical place of fascism as the political replacement for the Social Democracy, there was counterposed the theory of social fascism. At first it could appear as a pretentious, blustering, but harmless stupidity. Subsequent events have shown what a pernicious influence the Stalinist theory actually exercised on the entire development of the Communist International.

Does it follow from the historical role of Jacobinism, of democracy and of fascism that the petty bourgeoisie is condemned to remain a tool in the hands of capital to the end of its days? If things were so, then the dictatorship of the proletariat would be impossible in a number of countries in which the petty bourgeoisie constitutes the majority of the nation; and more than that, it would be rendered extremely difficult in other countries in which the petty bourgeoisie represents an important minority. Fortunately, things are not so. The experience of the Paris Commune[20] first showed, at least within the limits of one city, just as the experience of the October Revolution has shown after it on a much larger scale and over an incomparably longer period, that the alliance of the petty bourgeoisie and the big bourgeoisie is not indissoluble. Since the petty bourgeoisie is incapable of an *independent* policy (that is also why the petty-bourgeois 'democratic dictatorship' is unrealisable) no choice is left for it other than that between the bourgeoisie and the proletariat.

In the epoch of the rise, the sprouting and blooming of capitalism, the petty bourgeoisie, despite acute outbreaks of discontent, generally marched obediently in the capitalist harness. Nor could it do anything else. But under the conditions of capitalist disintegration and the impasse in the economic situation, the petty bourgeoisie strives, seeks and attempts to tear itself loose from the fetters of the old masters and rulers of society. It is quite capable of linking its fate with that of the proletariat. For that, only one thing is needed: the petty bourgeoisie must acquire faith in the ability of the proletariat to lead society onto a new road. The proletariat can inspire this faith only by its strength, by the firmness of its actions, by a skilful offensive against the enemy, by the success of its revolutionary policy.

But woe if the revolutionary party does not measure up to the situation! The daily struggle of the proletariat sharpens the instability of bourgeois society. The strikes and the political disturbances aggravate the economic situation of the country. The petty bourgeoisie could reconcile itself temporarily to the growing privations, if it came through experience to the conviction that the proletariat is in a position to lead it onto a new road. But if the revolutionary party, in spite of a class struggle becoming incessantly more accentuated, proves time and again to be incapable of uniting the working class behind it if it vacillates, becomes confused,

20 In 1871, the workers of Paris rose up and established the Paris Commune. It was the first living example of a workers' state. Nine weeks after the Commune was established, the French army overran the city and brutally executed the Communards.

contradicts itself, then the petty bourgeoisie loses patience and begins to look upon the revolutionary workers as those responsible for its own misery. All the bourgeois parties, including the Social Democracy, turn its thoughts in this very direction. When the social crisis takes on an intolerable acuteness, a particular party appears on the scene with the direct aim of agitating the petty bourgeoisie to a white heat and of directing its hatred and its despair against the proletariat. In Germany, this historic function is fulfilled by National Socialism, a broad current whose ideology is composed of all the putrid vapours of decomposing bourgeois society.

The principal political responsibility for the growth of fascism rests, of course, on the shoulders of the Social Democracy. Ever since the imperialist war, the labours of this party have been reduced to uprooting from the consciousness of the proletariat the idea of an independent policy, to implanting within it the belief in the eternity of capitalism, and to forcing it to its knees time and again before the decadent bourgeoisie. The petty bourgeoisie can follow the worker only when it sees in him the new chief. The Social Democracy teaches the worker to be a lackey. The petty bourgeoisie will not follow a lackey. The policy of reformism deprives the proletariat of the possibility of leading the plebeian masses of the petty bourgeoisie and thereby converts the latter into cannon fodder for fascism.

The political question, however, is not settled for us with the responsibility of the Social Democracy. Ever since the beginning of the war we have denounced this party as the agency of the imperialist bourgeoisie within the ranks of the proletariat. Out of this new orientation of the revolutionary Marxists arose the Third International. Its task consisted in uniting the proletariat under the banner of the revolution and thereby securing for it the directing influence over the oppressed masses of the petty bourgeoisie in the towns and the countryside.

The postwar period, in Germany more than anywhere else, was an epoch of economic hopelessness and civil war. The international conditions as well as the domestic ones pushed the country peremptorily on the road to socialism. Every step of the

Social Democracy revealed its decadence and its impotence, the reactionary import of its politics, the venality of its leaders. What other conditions are needed for the development of the Communist Party? And yet, after the first few years of significant successes, German communism entered into an era of vacillations, zigzags, alternate turns to opportunism and adventurism. The centrist bureaucracy has systematically weakened the proletarian vanguard and prevented it from bringing the class under its leadership. Thus it has robbed the proletariat as a whole of the possibility of leading behind it the oppressed masses of the petty bourgeoisie. The Stalinist bureaucracy bears the direct and immediate responsibility for the growth of fascism before the proletarian vanguard.

## *An alliance of Social Democracy with fascism or a struggle between them?*

To understand the interrelationship of the classes in the form of a schema, fixed once and for all, is comparatively simple. The evaluation of the concrete relations between the classes in every given situation is immeasurably more difficult.

The German big bourgeoisie is at present vacillating – a condition which the big bourgeoisie, in general, very rarely experiences. One part has definitely come to be convinced of the inevitability of the fascist path and would like to accelerate the operation. The other part hopes to become master of the situation with the aid of a Bonapartist military police dictatorship. No one in this camp desires a return to the Weimar 'democracy'.

The petty bourgeoisie is split up. National Socialism, which has united the overwhelming majority of the intermediate classes under its banner, wants to take the whole power into its own hands. The democratic wing of the petty bourgeoisie, which still has millions of workers behind it, wants a return to democracy according to the Ebertian model.[21] In the meantime, it is prepared

21 Friedrich Ebert was the leader of the SPD. He oversaw the crushing of the January 1919 insurrection of the Berlin workers and became the first President of the Weimar Republic.

to support the Bonapartist dictatorship at least passively. The Social Democracy figures as follows: under the pressure of the Nazis, the Papen-Schleicher government will be forced to establish a balance by strengthening its left wing; meanwhile, the crisis will perhaps subside; the petty bourgeoisie will perhaps sober up; capitalism will perhaps decrease its frantic pressure upon the working class – and with the aid of God everything will once again be in order.

The Bonapartist clique actually does not want the complete victory of fascism. It would not by any means be opposed to exploiting the support of the Social Democracy within certain bounds. But for this purpose it would have to 'tolerate' the workers' organisations, which is conceivable only if, at least to a certain extent, the legal existence of the Communist Party is to be allowed. Moreover, support of the military dictatorship by the Social Democracy would push the workers irresistibly into the ranks of Communism. By seeking a means of support against the brown[22] devil, the government would very soon become subject to the blows of the red Beelzebub.

The official Communist press declares that the toleration of Brüning by the Social Democracy paved the road for Papen and that the semi-toleration of Papen will accelerate the arrival of Hitler. That is entirely correct. Within these limits, there are no differences of opinion between ourselves and the Stalinists. But this precisely signifies that in times of social crisis the politics of reformism no longer turns against the masses alone but against itself. In this process the critical moment has just now arrived.

Hitler tolerates Schleicher. The Social Democracy does not oppose Papen. If this situation could really be assured for a long period of time, then the Social Democracy would become transformed into the left wing of Bonapartism and leave to fascism the role of the right wing. Theoretically, it is not, of course, excluded that the present unprecedented crisis of German capitalism will lead to no conclusive solution, i.e. will end with neither the victory of the proletariat nor

22 Referring to the *Sturmabteilung* (SA, Storm troopers), the paramilitary wing of the NSDAP. Its members were colloquially called Brownshirts, referring to the colour of their uniform.

the triumph of the fascist counter-revolution. *If* the Communist Party continues its policy of stupid ultimatism and thereby saves the Social Democracy from inevitable collapse; *if* Hitler does not in the near future decide upon a coup d'état and thereby initiate the inevitable disintegration within his own ranks; *if* the economic conjuncture takes an upward turn before Schleicher falls – then the Bonapartist combination of Article 48 of the Weimar Constitution, of the Reichswehr, the semi-oppositional Social Democracy and semi-oppositional fascism could perhaps maintain itself (until a new social outburst which is to be expected in any case).

But offhand, we are still far from such a happy fulfilment of the conditions that form the subject of Social-Democratic daydreams. Such a thing is by no means assured. Even the Stalinists hardly believe in the power of resistance or the durability of the Papen-Schleicher regime. All signs point to the breakup of the Wels-Schleicher-Hitler triangle even before it has begun to take shape.

But perhaps it will be replaced by a Hitler-Wels combination? According to Stalin they are "twins, not antipodes".[23] Let us assume that the Social Democracy would, without fearing its own workers, want to sell its toleration to Hitler. But Hitler does not need this commodity: he needs not the toleration but the abolition of the Social Democracy. The Hitler government can only accomplish its task by breaking the resistance of the proletariat and by removing all the possible organs of its resistance. Therein lies the historical role of fascism.

The Stalinists confine themselves to a purely psychological, or more exactly, to a purely moral evaluation of those cowardly and avaricious petty bourgeois who lead the Social Democracy. Can we actually assume that these inveterate traitors would separate themselves from the bourgeoisie and oppose it? Such an idealist method has very little in common with Marxism, which proceeds not from what people think about themselves or what they desire

---

23 Stalin, 'Concerning the International Situation', *Works*, Vol. 6, p. 294. This speech of Stalin from 1924 was quoted frequently by the communist parties between 1928-32.

but from the conditions in which they are placed and from the changes which these conditions will undergo.

The Social Democracy supports the bourgeois regime, not for the profits of the coal, steel and other magnates, but for the sake of those gains which it itself can obtain as a party, in the shape of its numerically great and powerful apparatus. To be sure, fascism in no way threatens the bourgeois regime, for the defence of which the Social Democracy exists. But fascism endangers that role which the Social Democracy fulfils in the bourgeois regime and the income which the Social Democracy derives from playing its role. Even though the Stalinists forget this side of the matter, the Social Democracy itself does not for one moment lose sight of the mortal danger with which a victory of fascism threatens *it* – not the bourgeoisie, but it – the Social Democracy.

About three years ago, when we pointed out that the point of departure in the coming political crisis in Austria and in Germany would in all probability be fixed by the incompatibility of Social Democracy and fascism; when, on this basis, we rejected the theory of social fascism, which was not disclosing but concealing the approaching conflict; when we called attention to the possibility that the Social Democracy, and a significant part of its apparatus along with it, would be forced by the march of events into a struggle against fascism and that this would be a favourable point of departure for the Communist Party for a further attack, a great many communists – not only hired functionaries, but even quite honest revolutionists – accused us of... "idealising" the Social Democracy. Nothing remained but to shrug our shoulders. It is hard to dispute with people whose thought stops there where the question first begins for a Marxist.

In conversations, I often cited the following example: the Jewish bourgeoisie in tsarist Russia represented an extremely frightened and demoralised part of the entire Russian bourgeoisie. And yet, insofar as the pogroms of the Black Hundreds,[24] which were in the main directed against the Jewish poor, also hit the bourgeoisie,

24 The Black Hundreds were reactionary terrorist bands in Russia, loyal to the tsar, responsible for state-sanctioned pogroms against Jews and social-democrats.

the latter was forced to defend itself. To be sure, it did not show any remarkable bravery on this field either. But due to the danger hanging over their heads, the liberal Jewish bourgeoisie, for example, collected considerable sums for the arming of revolutionary workers and students. In this manner, a temporary practical agreement was arrived at between the most revolutionary workers, who were prepared to fight with guns in hand, and the most frightened group of the bourgeoisie, which had got into a scrape.

Last year I wrote that in the struggle against fascism the communists were duty-bound to come to a practical agreement not only with the devil and his grandmother, but even with Grzesinski.[25] This sentence made its way through the entire Stalinist world press. Was better proof needed of the 'social fascism' of the Left Opposition? Many comrades had warned me in advance: "They are going to seize on this phrase." I answered them: "It has been written so they will seize on it. Just let them seize upon this hot iron and burn their fingers. The blockheads must get their lesson."

The course of the struggle has led to Papen acquainting Grzesinski with the inside of a jail. Did this episode follow from the theory of social fascism and from the prognoses of the Stalinist bureaucracy? No, it occurred in complete contradiction of the latter. Our evaluation of the situation, however, had such an eventuality in view and had assigned a definite place for it.

But the Social Democracy this time, too, avoided the struggle, some Stalinist will object. Yes, it did avoid it. Whoever expected the Social Democracy to go beyond the urging of its leaders and take up the struggle independently, and at that under conditions in which even the Communist Party showed itself incapable of struggle, naturally had to experience disappointment. We did not expect such miracles. Therefore we could not lay ourselves open to any 'disappointments' about the Social Democracy.

---

25 Albert Grzesinski was a member of the SPD and Minister of the Interior of Prussia from 1926-30. After this, he was the police chief of Berlin and responsible for the suppression of communist rallies. During the Hindenburg-Papen coup of 20 July 1932, he ensured the police offered little to no resistance.

Grzesinski has not become transformed into a revolutionary tiger; that we will readily grant. But nevertheless, there is quite a difference between a situation in which Grzesinski, sitting in his fortress, sends out police detachments for the safeguarding of 'democracy' against revolutionary workers, and a situation in which the Bonapartist saviour of capitalism puts Grzesinski himself in jail, is there not? And are we not to take this difference into account politically; are we not to take advantage of it?

Let us turn back to the example cited above: it is not hard to grasp the difference between a Jewish manufacturer who tips the tsarist policeman to beat down the strikers, and the same manufacturer who turns over money to the strikers of yesterday to obtain arms against the pogromists. The bourgeois remains the same. But from the change in the situation there results a change in relations. The Bolsheviks conducted the strike against the manufacturer. Later on, they took money from the same manufacturer for the struggle against the pogroms. That did not, naturally, prevent the workers, when their hour had come, from turning their arms against the bourgeoisie.

Does all that has been said mean that the Social Democracy as a whole will fight against fascism? To this we reply: part of the social-democratic functionaries will undoubtedly go over to the fascists; a considerable section will creep under their beds in the hour of danger. The working masses also will not fight in their entirety. To guess in advance what part of the social-democratic workers will be drawn into the struggle and when, and what part of the apparatus they will take along with them, is altogether impossible. That depends upon many circumstances, among them the position of the Communist Party. The policy of the united front has as its task to separate those who want to fight from those who do not; to push forward those who vacillate; and finally, to compromise the capitulationist leaders in the eyes of the workers, to consolidate the workers' fighting capacity.

How much time has been lost – aimlessly, senselessly, shamefully! How much could have been achieved, even in the last two years alone! Was it not clear in advance that monopoly capital and its fascist army would drive the Social Democracy with fists and blackjacks onto the road of opposition and self-defence? This prognosis should have been displayed before the entire working class, the initiative should have been taken for the united front and this initiative should have been kept firmly in our hands at every new stage. It was not necessary to shout or scream; it was possible to play quietly with a sure hand. It would have sufficed to formulate, in a clear-cut manner, the inevitability of every next step of the enemy and to set up a practical programme for a united front, without exaggerations and without haggling, but also without weakness and without concessions. How high the Communist Party would stand today if it had assimilated the ABCs of Leninist policy and applied it with the necessary perseverance!

## *Thälmann's 'twenty-one mistakes'*

In the middle of July appeared a pamphlet with Thälmann's answers to twenty-one questions by social-democratic workers on how the 'red united front' is to be created. The pamphlet begins with the words: "Mightily the anti-fascist united front rushes ahead!" On 20 July the Communist Party called upon the workers to come out in a political strike. The appeal met with no response. Thus within five days was the tragic abyss revealed between bureaucratic rhetoric and political reality.

The party received 5.3 million votes in the elections of 31 July. By trumpeting forth this result as a tremendous victory, the party showed how greatly the defeats have diminished its claims and hopes. In the first balloting for the presidential election, on 13 March, the party received almost 5 million votes. In the course of four-and-a-half months – and what months! – it therefore gained barely 300,000 votes. The communist press repeated hundreds of times in March that the number of votes would have been incomparably larger had it been a Reichstag election: in a presidential election, hundreds of thousands of sympathisers deemed it superfluous to lose any time over a 'platonic' demonstration. If this March commentary is taken into consideration – and it deserves to be taken into consideration – it follows that the party has practically not grown at all in the last four-and-a-half months.

In April, the Social Democracy elected Hindenburg, who thereupon carried out a coup d'état aimed directly against it. One would think that this fact alone ought to have sufficed to convulse the structure of reformism to its very foundations. Add to this the further aggravation of the crisis with all its frightful consequences. Finally, on 20 July, eleven days before the elections, the Social Democracy drew its tail miserably between its legs at the coup d'état of the federal president it elected. In such periods, revolutionary parties grow feverishly. Whatever the Social Democracy, forced into a steel vice, may yet undertake to do, it must drive the workers away from it to the left. But instead of striding forward with seven-league boots, communism marks time, vacillates, is on the retreat and after each step forward it takes half a step backward. To exult over a victory only because the Communist Party suffered no loss of votes on 31 July, is to lose the sense of reality entirely.

In order to understand why and how the revolutionary party condemns itself to a debasing impotence under exceptionally favourable political conditions, one must read Thälmann's answers to the social-democratic workers. A wearisome and unpleasant job, but it may enlighten one on what is taking place in the minds of the Stalinist leaders.

To the question: "How do the communists evaluate the character of the Papen government?", Thälmann gives several mutually contradictory replies. He begins with a reference to "the danger of the immediate establishment of the fascist dictatorship". Then it follows that it does not yet exist? He speaks with complete accuracy of the government members as "representatives of trust capital, of the generals and of Junkerdom". A minute later he says about the same government: "this fascist cabinet", and concludes his reply with the assertion that: "the Papen government ... has set itself the aim of the immediate establishment of the fascist dictatorship."

By disregarding the social and political distinctions between *Bonapartism*, that is, the regime of 'civil peace' resting upon military-police dictatorship, and *fascism*, that is, the regime of open civil war against the proletariat, Thälmann deprives himself in advance of the possibility of understanding what is taking place before his very eyes. If Papen's cabinet is a fascist cabinet, then what fascist 'danger' is he talking about? If the workers will believe Thälmann that Papen sets himself the aim (!) of establishing the fascist dictatorship, then the probable conflict between Hitler and Papen-Schleicher will catch the party napping just as the conflict between Papen and Otto Braun[26] did in its time.

To the question: "Is the Communist Party of Germany sincere about the united front?" Thälmann naturally answers affirmatively, and for proof he refers to the fact that the Communists do not go hat in hand to Hindenburg and Papen. "No, we put the question of the struggle, of the struggle against the whole system, against capitalism. And here lies the kernel of the *sincerity* of our united front."

Thälmann manifestly does not understand what it is all about. The social-democratic workers remain social-democrats precisely because they still believe in the gradual, reformist road to the transformation of capitalism into socialism. Since they know that the communists stand for the revolutionary overthrow of capitalism, the social-democratic workers ask: "Do you sincerely propose the united front to us?" To this Thälmann replies: "Naturally, sincerely, for with us it is a question of overthrowing the whole capitalist system."

Of course we don't dream of concealing anything from the social-democratic workers. Nevertheless, one must know the measure of things and preserve the political proportions. A skilled propagandist should have answered in the following manner: "You put your stakes on democracy; we believe that the only way out lies in the revolution. Yet we cannot and we do not want to make the revolution without you. Hitler is now the common foe. After the victory over him we

---

26 Otto Braun was the SPD Minister-President of Prussia from 1925. In the July 1932 coup, he was removed by President Hindenburg, along with Carl Severing.

shall draw the balance together with you and see where the road ahead actually leads."

The audience in the Thälmann pamphlet, peculiar as this may seem at first sight, not only listens forbearingly to the speaker but even agrees with him many times. The secret of their forbearance, however, rests upon the fact that Thälmann's partners in the conversation not only belong to the 'Anti-fascist Action'[27] but also call for the casting of votes for the Communist Party. They are *former* Social-Democrats who have gone over to the side of communism. Such recruits can only be welcomed. But what is deceptive in the whole affair is that a conversation with workers who have broken with the social-democracy is palmed off as a conversation with the social-democratic mass. This cheap masquerade is highly characteristic of the whole present-day policy of Thälmann and co.!

At any rate, the former social-democrats put questions which actually agitate the social-democratic mass. "Is the Anti-fascist Action a front organisation of the Communist Party?" they ask. Thälmann replies: "No!" The proof? The Anti-fascist Action "is no organisation but a mass movement." As if it were not just the task of the Communist Party to organise the mass movement. Still better is the second argument: the Anti-fascist Action is non-partisan, for (!) it directs itself against the capitalist state: "Karl Marx, in dealing with the lessons of the Paris Commune, already placed in the foreground in all sharpness, as the task of the working class, the question of smashing the bourgeois state apparatus." O hapless quotation! For what the social-democrats want, regardless of Marx, is to perfect the bourgeois state, but not to smash it. They are not communists, but reformists. Despite his intentions, Thälmann proves just the thing he would like to refute – the party character of the Anti-fascist Action.

The official leader of the Communist Party obviously understands neither the situation nor the political thought of the

27 Anti-fascist Action (Antifaschistische Aktion) was a short-lived organisation founded by the KPD in 1932 which aimed to work with social-democratic workers to mount an armed resistance to the fascists.

social-democratic workers. He does not understand what purpose the united front serves. With every one of his sentences, he delivers weapons to the reformist leaders and drives the social-democratic workers to them.

The impossibility of any kind of joint step with the Social Democracy is demonstrated by Thälmann in the following manner:

> In this connection we [?] must clearly recognise that the Social Democracy, even when it today mimics a sham opposition, will *at no moment* give up its actual thoughts of coalition and its compacts with the fascist bourgeoisie.

Even if this were right, there would nevertheless remain the task of proving it to the social-democratic workers through experience. However, it is also false in essence. If the Social-Democratic leaders do not want to abandon compacts with the bourgeoisie, the fascist bourgeoisie does, however, abandon compacts with the Social Democracy. And this fact may become decisive for the fate of the Social Democracy. In the passage of power from Papen to Hitler, the bourgeoisie will in no way be able to spare the Social Democracy. The civil war has its laws. The reign of the fascist terror will and can only mean the abolition of the Social Democracy. Mussolini began with precisely that, so as to be able all the more unrestrainedly to crush the revolutionary workers. In any event, the 'social fascist' cherishes his skin. The communist united-front policy at the present time must proceed from the concern of the Social Democracy for its own hide. That will be the most realistic policy and at the same time the most revolutionary in its consequences.

But if the Social Democracy will "at no moment" separate itself from the fascist bourgeoisie (although Matteotti[28] 'separated' himself from Mussolini), do not the social-democratic workers who want to take part in the Anti-fascist Action have to leave their party? So runs one question.

---

28 Giacomo Matteotti was an Italian Socialist and member of the Italian parliament. In 1924, two years after Mussolini's rise to power, Matteotti spoke in Parliament denouncing the fascists. Eleven days later, they kidnapped and killed him.

To this Thälmann replies:

> For us communists it is a matter of course that social-democratic or Reichsbanner[29] workers may take part in the Anti-fascist Action *without* having to leave their party.

To show himself free from sectarianism, Thälmann adds:

> If you were to stream into it by the millions, in a serried front, we would greet it with joy, even if a lack of clarity still exists in your minds, in our opinion, about certain questions of estimating the Social Democratic Party of Germany.

Golden words! We consider your party to be fascist, you consider it to be democratic, but let's not dispute over petty matters. It suffices for you to come to us "by the millions" without leaving your fascist party. "Lack of clarity about certain questions" cannot constitute an obstacle. But alas, the lack of clarity in the heads of the all-powerful bureaucrats is an obstacle at every step.

To give depth to the question, Thälmann proceeds to say: "We do not put the question as between parties, but on a class basis." Like Seydewitz,[30] Thälmann is prepared to renounce party interests in the interests of the class. The misfortune lies in this, that for a Marxist there cannot be such a contrast. Were not its programme the scientific formulation of the interests of the working class, the party would not be worth a penny.

Only, along with the crude mistake in principle, Thälmann's words contain also a practical absurdity. How is it possible not to put the question of relations between parties when that is just where the very essence of the question lies? Millions of workers follow the Social Democracy. Other millions – the Communist Party. To the social-democratic workers who ask how we shall today achieve *joint* actions between *your* party and *ours* against fascism, Thälmann

29 Reichsbanner Schwarz-Rot-Gold (Black-Red-Gold Banner of the Reich, abbreviated to Reichsbanner) was a paramilitary organisation of the SPD, later subsumed into the Iron Front.

30 Max Seydewitz was a member of the SPD in the Reichstag. He was later expelled from the SPD and formed the SAPD in 1931, which advocated a united front.

answers: "On a class and not a party basis" stream toward us by the millions. Isn't this the most wretched bombast?

"We communists", continues Thälmann, "do not want unity at any price." We cannot, in the interest of unity with the Social Democracy, "disavow the class content of our policy [...] and renounce strikes, struggles of the unemployed, actions of the tenants and revolutionary mass defence." The agreement on definite practical actions is misconstrued into an absurd *unity* with the Social Democracy. Out of the indispensability of the final revolutionary assault of *tomorrow*, is deduced the impermissibility of joint strike or self-defence actions for *today*. Whoever can see rhyme or reason in Thälmann's thoughts deserves a prize.

Thälmann's listeners insist: "Is an alliance of the KPD and the SPD possible in the struggle against the Papen government and against fascism?" Thälmann mentions two or three facts as evidence that the Social Democracy does not fight against fascism and concludes:

> Every SPD comrade will say we are right when we say that an alliance between the KPD and the SPD is impossible on the basis of these facts and also for reasons of principle. [!]

The bureaucrat again assumes the thing that should be proved. Ultimatism acquires a particularly ludicrous character as soon as Thälmann replies to the question of the united front with organisations which embrace millions of workers. The social-democrats must acknowledge that an agreement with their party is impossible because it is fascist. Can Wels and Leipart[31] be rendered a better service?

> We communists, who reject any accord with the SPD leaders [...] repeatedly declare that we are at all times ready for the antifascist struggle with the militant social-democratic and Reichsbanner comrades and with the lower [?] militant organisations.

31 Theodore Leipart was a German trade union official, Chairman of the ADGB – the Allgemeiner Deutscher Gewerkschaftsbund (General German Trades Union Federation) – and a leading member of various international trade union organisations.

Where do the lower organisations stop? And what is to be done if the lower organisations submit to the discipline of the upper, and propose that the negotiations shall be begun with the latter? Finally, between the lower and the upper there are intermediate stories. And can one prophesy where the dividing line will be between those who want to fight and those who dodge the struggle? This can be determined only in action and not by anticipatory appraisals. What sense is there in binding oneself hand and foot?

In *Die Rote Fahne* of 29 July, in a report of a Reichsbanner meeting, the noteworthy words of a social-democratic company commander are mentioned:

> The will to an anti-fascist united front exists in the masses. If the leaders fail to take it into account, then I will go to the united front over their heads.

The communist paper reproduces these words without comment. Yet they contain the key to the whole tactic of the united front. The social democrat wants to fight against the fascists in common with the communists. He is already in doubt about the goodwill of his leaders. If the leaders refuse, says he, then I shall go over their heads. Social democrats similarly disposed can be counted by the dozens, hundreds, thousands, millions. It is the task of the Communist Party to really show them whether or not the Social-Democratic leaders want to fight. This can be demonstrated only through experience, through a new, fresh experience, in a new situation. This experience will not be gained at one blow. The Social-Democratic leaders must be subjected to a test: in the factory and workshop, in town and country, in the whole nation, today and tomorrow. We must repeat our proposal, put it in a new form, from a new angle, adapted to the new situation.

But Thälmann will have none of it. On the basis of the "differences in *principle* shown to exist between the KPD and the SPD we reject negotiations from the top with the SPD." This shattering argument is repeated by Thälmann several times. But if there were no 'antagonisms in principle' then there would be no two parties. And if there were no two parties, there would be no question of the united front. Thälmann wants to prove far too much. Less – would be better.

Did not the founding of the RGO,[32] ask the workers, signify "a splitting of the organised working class?" No, replies Thälmann, and as proof he cites Engels' letter of 1895 against the aesthetic-sentimental philanthropists. Who is treacherously handing Thälmann such quotations? The RGO is created in the spirit of unity and not of schism. Also, the worker is in no case to leave his trade-union organisation in order to join the RGO. On the contrary, it were better if the RGO members remained in the trade unions in order to carry on oppositional work therein. Thälmann's words may sound convincing to communists who have set themselves the task of fighting against the Social-Democratic leadership. But as an answer to social-democratic workers, who are concerned with trade-union unity, Thälmann's words sound like a mockery.

"Why have you left our trade unions and organised yourselves separately?" ask the social-democratic workers.

"If you want to enter our separate organisation in order to fight against the Social-Democratic leadership, we do not demand that you leave the trade unions", Thälmann replies. An appropriate reply, right on the head of the nail!

"Is there democracy within the KPD?", ask the workers, passing over to another theme. Thälmann replies in the affirmative. Absolutely! But he immediately adds unexpectedly:

> In legality as well as in illegality, most particularly in the latter, the party must be on guard against spies, provocateurs and police agents.

This interpolation is not made accidentally. The latest doctrine, proclaimed throughout the world in the brochure of a mysterious Büchner, justifies the strangulation of democracy in the interest of the struggle against spies. Whoever protests against the autocracy of the Stalinist bureaucracy must be declared a suspicious character at the

32 The Revolutionäre Gewerkschafts Opposition (Revolutionary Union Opposition) was set up by the KPD, composed of members from other unions who had been expelled due to their political activity.

very least. The police agents and provocateurs of every country revel with enthusiasm over this theory. They will hound Oppositionists louder than anyone else: this may divert attention from themselves and enable them to fish in troubled waters.

The flourishing of democracy is also demonstrated, according to Thälmann, by the fact that "the problems are dealt with at world congresses and conferences of the ECCI." The speaker fails to report when the last world congress took place. We will call it to mind: in July 1928, more than four years ago! Apparently no noteworthy questions have arisen since then. Why, let it be asked in passing, doesn't Thälmann himself convoke an extraordinary German party convention to resolve the questions upon which the fate of the German proletariat depends? Certainly not because of an excess of party democracy.

So runs page after page. Thälmann replies to twenty-one questions. Every reply a mistake. In sum, twenty-one mistakes, not counting the small and secondary ones. And they are numerous.

Thälmann relates that the Bolsheviks broke with the Mensheviks in 1903. In reality, the split first took place in 1912. But even that did not prevent the February Revolution in 1917 from finding united Bolshevik and Menshevik organisations over a large part of the country. As late as the beginning of April, Stalin came out for the unification of the Bolsheviks with Tsereteli's party[33] – *not the united front but the fusion of the parties!* This was prevented only by Lenin's arrival.

Thälmann says that the Bolsheviks dispersed the Constituent Assembly in 1917. In reality this occurred at the beginning of 1918. Thälmann is not at all familiar with the history of the Russian Revolution and the Bolshevik Party.

Far worse, however, is the fact that he does not grasp the foundations of the Bolshevik tactic. In his 'theoretical' articles, he even dares to dispute the fact that the Bolsheviks concluded an agreement with the Mensheviks and Socialist-Revolutionaries

---

33 Irakli Tsereteli was a leading Menshevik. He was a minister of the Provisional Government of Russia in 1917.

against Kornilov.[34] As proof, he adduces quotations shoved under his door by somebody or other, which have nothing to do with the matter. But he forgets to answer the questions: were there Committees for the Defence of the People throughout the land during the Kornilov putsch? Did they direct the struggle against Kornilov? Did representatives of the Bolsheviks, Mensheviks and Socialist-Revolutionaries belong to these committees? Yes, yes, yes. Were the Mensheviks and Socialist-Revolutionaries in power at that time? Did they persecute the Bolsheviks as agents of the German general staff? Were thousands of Bolsheviks confined to prisons? Did Lenin hide in illegality? Yes, yes, yes. What quotations can refute these historical facts?

Let Thälmann appeal to his heart's content to Manuilsky,[35] Lozovsky,[36] and Stalin himself (if the latter ever opens his mouth). But let him leave in peace Leninism and the history of the Russian Revolution: for him they are books sealed with seven seals.

In conclusion one must throw into relief still another question, which stands by itself: it concerns Versailles. The social-democratic workers ask if the Communist Party isn't making political concessions to National Socialism. In his reply, Thälmann continues to defend the slogan of 'national emancipation' and to place it on the same plane with the slogan of social emancipation. The reparations – what is left of them now – are just as important to Thälmann as private ownership of the means of production. One could say this policy was contrived uniquely to divert the attention of the workers from the basic problem, to weaken the blow against capitalism and to compel one to seek the principal foe and author of poverty on the

34 Lavr Kornilov was a Russian general who in August 1917 marched his troops on St. Petersburg in an attempt to overthrow the Provisional Government. In response, 25,000 armed workers joined the fight against Kornilov, spearheaded by the Bolsheviks. The coup collapsed within three days.

35 Dmitry Manuilsky was a Bolshevik, who became a follower of Stalin and Secretary of the ECCI from December 1926 until its dissolution in 1943.

36 Solomon Lozovsky was a Bolshevik, became a high-ranking Stalinist official in the bureaucracy. He was General Secretary of the Red International of Trade Unions (Profintern).

other side of the frontier. However, now more than ever before, "the main enemy is at home!"[37] Schleicher expressed this idea even more coarsely: before anything else, he declared on the radio on 26 July, we must "put an end to the dirty swine at home!" This soldier's formula is very good. We pick it up willingly. Every communist must firmly adopt it as his own. While the Nazis divert attention to Versailles, the communist workers must retort to them with Schleicher's words: no, before anything else we must put an end to the dirty swine at home!

## *The checking of the Stalin-Thälmann policy against their own experience*

Tactics are tested in the most critical and crucial moments. The strength of Bolshevism rested upon this, that its slogans and methods found their supreme confirmation as soon as the course of events demanded bold decisions. What value have principles which must be renounced as soon as the situation assumes a serious character?

Realistic policy bases itself upon the natural development of the class struggle. Sectarian policy endeavours to prescribe artificial regulations for the class struggle. The revolutionary situation signifies the highest accentuation of the class struggle. Just because of that, the realistic policy of Marxism, in the revolutionary situation, exercises a powerful force of attraction upon the mass. The sectarian policy, on the contrary, becomes all the weaker the more mighty is the thrust of events. The Blanquists[38] and Proudhonists,[39] taken by surprise by the events of the Paris Commune, did the opposite of what they had constantly preached. During the Russian Revolution, the anarchists were forced to recognise the soviets, that is, the organs of power. And so on without end.

37 Referring to Karl Liebknecht's famous leaflet agitating against the First World War, entitled 'The Main Enemy is at Home!'.

38 Blanquism, named after the nineteenth century French socialist Louis Auguste Blanqui, refers to the theory that a revolution can be carried out through a coup led by a small group of conspirators.

39 Proudhonism refers to the anarchist ideas of Pierre-Joseph Proudhon, who argued against any form of government or state, and instead called for society to be run on the basis of worker's cooperatives.

The Comintern supports itself upon the masses who were won over in the past by Marxism and fused together by the authority of the October Revolution. But the policy of the present leading Stalin faction seeks to command the class struggle instead of investing it with political expression. This is the essential feature of *bureaucratism*, and in this it coincides with *sectarianism*, from which it distinguishes itself sharply in other features. Thanks to the strong apparatus, to the material means of the Soviet state and to the authority of the October Revolution, the Stalinist bureaucracy has been able, in comparatively calm periods, to impose for some time artificial restraints upon the proletarian vanguard. But to the degree that the class struggle is condensed into civil war, the bureaucratic prescriptions come into increasing collision with unrelenting reality. Faced with sharp turns in the situation, the arrogant and inflated bureaucracy easily lands in a muddle. If it cannot command, it capitulates. The policy of the Thälmann Central Committee in recent months will someday be studied as a model of the most pitiful and miserable brainlessness.

Since the 'third period' it has been considered inviolable that there could be no talk about agreements with the Social Democracy. It was not only inadmissible to assume the initiative in the united front, as the Third and Fourth World Congresses had taught – but even proposals for common actions emanating from the Social Democracy had to be rejected. The reformist leaders are "sufficiently exposed". The experience of the past is sufficient. Instead of pursuing politics, the masses must be told history. To turn to the reformists with proposals means to acknowledge them capable of fighting.

That alone would be social fascism, etc. Such was the deafening intonation of the ultraleftist barrel organ in the last three or four years. But then: in the Prussian Landtag, the communist fraction proposed on 22 June, unexpected by all and by itself, an agreement with the Social Democracy and even with the Centre. The same thing was repeated in Hessen. In the face of the danger that the presidium of the Landtag might fall into the hands of the Nazis, all the consecrated principles flew to the devil. Isn't this astounding? And isn't it humiliating?

To explain these goat-leaps, however, is not so difficult. As is known, many superficial liberals and radicals continue to joke all their lives about religion and celestial powers, only to call for a priest when they face death or serious illness. So also in politics. The mark of centrism is opportunism. Under the influence of external circumstances (tradition, mass pressure, political competition), centrism is at certain times compelled to make a parade of radicalism. For this purpose it must overcome itself, violate its political nature. By spurring itself on with all its strength, it not infrequently lands at the extreme limit of formal radicalism. But hardly does the hour of serious danger strike than the true nature of centrism breaks out to the surface. In so delicate a question as the defence of the Soviet Union, the Stalinist bureaucracy always built much more upon the bourgeois pacifists, British trade-union bureaucrats and French Radicals than upon the revolutionary movement of the proletariat. Scarcely did an external danger approach than the Stalinists promptly sacrificed not only their ultraleftist phrases but also the vital interests of the international revolution – in the name of amity with uncertain and false 'friends' of the genus of lawyers, writers and simple drawing room heroes. United front from above? Under no circumstances! At the same time, however, the Top Commissar for Ambiguous Affairs, Münzenberg[40] by name, went tugging at the coat-tails of all sorts of liberal jabberers and radical scribblers 'for the defence of the USSR'.

The Stalinist bureaucracy in Germany, as in every other country – except the Soviet Union – is extremely dissatisfied with the compromising leadership of Barbusse[41] in the affair of the Anti-

40 Wilhelm Münzenberg was a KPD member and Member of the Reichstag. He vacillated between ultra-leftism and reformism. He ended up expelled from the KPD in 1936. He then went on to lead anti-fascist resistance among German émigrés in Paris. He was found strangled to death in the south of Nazi-occupied France after escaping an internment camp in 1940.

41 Henri Barbusse was a French writer and member of the Communist Party.

war Congress.[42] On this field, Thälmann, Foster,[43] and others would prefer to be radical. Yet in their own national affairs, every one of them proceeds according to the same model as the Moscow authorities: at the approach of a serious danger they cast off the inflated, falsified radicalism in order to reveal their true, that is, their opportunistic nature.

Was the initiative of the communist Landtag fraction, as such, false and inadmissible? We don't think so. The Bolsheviks more than once proposed to the Mensheviks and Socialist-Revolutionaries in 1917: "Take the power, we will support you against the bourgeoisie if it should resist." Compromises are admissible and, under certain conditions, obligatory. The whole question lies in what aim the compromise shall serve; how it looks to the masses; what its limits are. To confine the compromise to the Landtag or the Reichstag, to regard as an independent aim whether the president will be a social-democrat or a Catholic democrat instead of a fascist, means to sink completely into parliamentary cretinism. The situation is completely different when the party sets itself the task of the systematic and planned struggle for the social-democratic workers on the basis of the united front policy. A parliamentary agreement against fascist predominance in the presidium, etc., would in this case constitute merely one component part of the extra-parliamentary fighting agreement against fascism. Naturally, the Communist Party would prefer to resolve the whole question at one blow outside of parliament, but preferences alone are not sufficient where the forces are lacking. The social-democratic workers have demonstrated their faith in the magic power of the

42 Münzenburg founded the World Committee Against War and Fascism, an international organisation sponsored by the Comintern. It was launched in August 1932, at the World Congress Against Imperialist War, held in Amsterdam with over 2,000 delegates, including communists, pacifists, reformists and liberals. Barbusse was a founding member of the committee and played a leading role in organising the congress. The committee itself included prominent individuals, such as Bertrand Russell, Upton Sinclair and Albert Einstein.

43 William Z Foster was General Secretary of the Communist Party of the USA from 1929-32 and later from 1945-47.

31 July vote.[44] It is from this fact that we must proceed. The former mistakes of the Communist Party (Prussian referendum,[45] and so on) facilitated extraordinarily well the sabotage of the united front practiced by the reformist leaders. A technical parliamentary agreement – or even just the proposal for such an agreement – must help free the Communist Party from the accusation that it is collaborating with the fascists against the Social Democracy. This is no independent action, but solely the clearing of the road to a fighting agreement or at least to the struggle for a fighting agreement of the mass organisations.

The difference between the two lines is entirely obvious. The joint struggle with the social-democratic organisations can – and in its unfolding it must – assume a revolutionary character. The possibility for an approach to the social-democratic masses can and must be paid for, under certain conditions, even with parliamentary agreements at the top. But for a Bolshevik, this is merely the *admission* price. The Stalinist bureaucracy acts in the opposite manner: it not only rejects fighting agreements, but still worse, it maliciously destroys those agreements which arise from below. At the same time, it proposes to the Social-Democratic deputies a parliamentary accord. This means that at the moment of danger it declares its own ultraleftist theory and praxis to be worthless; yet it is replaced not with the policy of revolutionary Marxism but with an unprincipled parliamentary combination in the spirit of the 'lesser evil'.

---

44 On 31 July 1932 a federal election was held in Germany, following the dissolution of the Reichstag by President Hindenburg. The election led to a dramatic increase for the NSDAP, who received 37.4 per cent of the votes, becoming the largest party in the Reichstag. The SPD share dropped to 21.6 per cent, whilst the KPD share increased slightly from 13.1 to 14.3 per cent. The Papen Government was not immediately ousted, but dissolved on 12 September after it was defeated in a vote on the emergency powers it relied on to survive. It was replaced in December with the Schleicher cabinet.

45 In 1931, a referendum was held to dissolve the Prussian Landtag. Various right-wing groups, including the NSDAP supported the referendum. The KPD supported it in spite of opposition from local party leaders. The referendum failed after a boycott by the opposition led to it failing to meet the required 50 per cent turnout.

We will indeed be told the Prussian and Hessian episodes were a mistake of the deputies and were made good again by the Central Committee. In the first place, a decision so important in principle should not have been taken without the Central Committee: the mistake falls back completely upon the latter as well; in the second place: explain how that the 'steel-hard', 'consistent', 'Bolshevik' policy, after months of blustering and screeching, of polemic, of vilification and expulsions, at once gives way at the critical moment to an opportunist 'mistake'?

But the matter is not confined to the Landtag. Thälmann-Remmele have absolutely renounced themselves and their own school on a much more important and critical question. On the eve of 20 July, the Central Committee of the Communist Party adopted the following decision:

> The Communist Party, before the proletarian public, addresses to the SPD, to the ADGB and to the AfA-Bund[46] the question if they are prepared to carry out, together with the Communist Party, a general strike for the proletarian demands.

This decision, so important and unexpected, was made public by the Central Committee in its circular letter of 26 July without any commentary. Can a more annihilating judgment be made of its whole preceding policy? The approach to the reformist summits with the proposal of joint actions was but yesterday declared to be social fascist and counter-revolutionary. Because of this question communists were expelled. On this ground the struggle against 'Trotskyism' was conducted. How then was this Central Committee suddenly able, at one stroke, on the eve of 20 July, to bow before what it had the day before banished? And to what tragic state has the bureaucracy brought the party when the Central Committee could dare to come before it with its amazing decision without explaining or justifying it!

---

46 The General Federation of Free Employees (*Allgemeiner freier Angestelltenbund*, abbreviated AfA-Bund) was an amalgamation of social-democratic trade unions of technical and administrative workers.

The policy is tested upon such turns. The Central Committee of the German Communist Party in reality demonstrated to the whole world on the eve of 20 July: "*Up to this moment our course was good for nothing.*" An involuntary but completely correct admission. Unfortunately, even the proposal of 20 July, which overthrew the preceding policy, could in no case yield a positive result. An appeal to the summits – independently of the present answer of these summits – can become of revolutionary significance only when it has been previously prepared from below, that is, when it is based upon the whole policy in its totality. But the Stalinist bureaucracy repeated to the social-democratic workers, day in and day out: "We communists reject any connection with the SPD leaders" (see Thälmann's answers in the preceding section). The unprepared, unexpected, unmotivated proposal of 20 July was suitable only for exposing the communist leadership by revealing its inconsistency, lack of seriousness, inclination to panic and adventuristic leaps.

The policy of the centrist bureaucracy helps the adversary at every step. Even when the mighty pressure of events drives a hundred thousand new workers under the communist banner, it takes place in spite of the Stalin-Thälmann policy. Precisely because of this the future of the party is in no way assured.

## *What they say in Prague about the united front*

"When the Communist International made a united front with the Social-Democratic leaders in 1926", wrote the central organ of the Czechoslovakian Communist Party, *Rude Pravo*, on 27 February 1932, allegedly in the name of a worker-correspondent "from the bench":

> ... it did this in order to expose them before the masses of supporters, and at that time Trotsky was terribly opposed to it. Now, when the Social Democracy has so discredited itself by its countless betrayals of the workers' struggles, Trotsky proposes the united front with its leaders [...]

> Trotsky is today against the Anglo-Russian Committee of 1926,[47] but for any sort of Anglo-Russian Committee of 1932.

These lines lead us right to the heart of the question. In 1926, the Comintern sought to "expose" the reformist leaders with the aid of the united front policy, and that was right. But since then the Social Democracy has "discredited" itself. Before whom? There are still more workers following it than follow the Communist Party. This is sad but true. The problem of exposing the reformist leaders thus remains unsolved. If the method of the united front was good in 1926, why should it be bad in 1932?

"Trotsky is for an Anglo-Russian Committee of 1932, against the Anglo-Russian Committee of 1926." In 1926, the united front was concluded only at the top, between the leaders of the Soviet trade unions and the British trade unionists, not in the name of definite practical actions of the masses separated from each other by state frontiers and social conditions, but upon the basis of a friendly-diplomatic, pacifist-evasive 'platform'. During the miners' strike, and later the general strike, the Anglo-Russian Committee could not even come together, for the 'allies' pulled in two opposite directions: the Soviet trade unions strove to assist the strikers, the British trade unionists sought to break the strike. The substantial contributions collected by the Russian workers were rejected by the General Council[48] as "damned Russian gold". Only after the strike had been finally betrayed and broken did the Anglo-Russian Committee come together again to the scheduled banquet to exchange small talk. Thus did the policy of the Anglo-Russian Committee serve to cover up the reformist strike-breakers before the working masses.

---

47 The Anglo-Russian Trade Union Committee was established in April 1925 as a committee to promote collaboration between Soviet and British trade unions. In the General Strike of 1926, it tied the hands of the communists, who muted their criticism of the leadership of the strike in order not to antagonise British members of the committee.

48 Referring to the leading body of the Trade Union Congress (TUC), the national federation of trade unions in Britain.

At the present time we are speaking of something quite different. In Germany the social-democratic and the communist workers stand on the same ground, before the same danger. They mingle with each other in factories, in trade unions, at the unemployment registries, etc. It is not a question here of a verbal 'platform' of the leaders, but of thoroughly concrete tasks which are calculated to draw the mass organisations directly into the struggle.

The united front policy on a national scale is ten times harder than on a local scale. The united front policy on an international scale is a hundred times harder than on a national scale. To unite with the British reformists around so general a slogan as "defence of the USSR" or "defence of the Chinese Revolution" is to talk the blue out of the sky. In Germany, on the contrary, there is the immediate danger of the destruction of the workers' organisations, the social-democratic included. To expect the Social Democracy to fight for the defence of the Soviet Union against the German bourgeoisie would be an illusion. But we certainly can expect that the Social Democracy will fight for the defence of its mandates, its meetings, periodicals, treasuries and finally for its own head.

Only, even in Germany we in no way advocate lapsing into a united-front fetishism. An agreement is an agreement. It remains in effect so long as it serves the practical goal for which it was concluded. If the reformists begin to curb or to sabotage the movement the communists must always put to themselves the question: is it not time to tear up the agreement and to lead the masses further under our own banner? Such a policy is not an easy one. But who has ever argued that to lead the proletariat to victory is a simple task? By counterposing the year 1926 to the year 1932, *Rude Pravo* has demonstrated only its lack of comprehension of what occurred six years ago as well as of what is happening today.

The 'worker-correspondent' from the imaginary bench also turns his attention to the example I gave of the agreement of the Bolsheviks with the Mensheviks and Socialist-Revolutionaries.

> All that time, [he writes] Kerensky[49] really fought for a certain time against Kornilov and at the same time helped the proletariat smash Kornilov. That the German Social Democracy today does not fight against fascism is evident to any little child.

Thälmann, who in no way resembles a 'little child', contends that an agreement of the Russian Bolsheviks with the Mensheviks and Socialist-Revolutionaries never even existed. *Rude Pravo,* as we see, pursues a different course. The agreement it does not deny. But according to its conception, the agreement was justified by this: that Kerensky really fought against Kornilov, in contradistinction to the Social Democracy, which is preparing the road to power for fascism.

The idealisation of Kerensky here is quite astounding. When did Kerensky begin to fight against Kornilov? At the very moment when Kornilov swung the Cossack's sabre over Kerensky's own head, that is, on the eve of 26 August 1917. On the previous day, Kerensky was still in a direct conspiracy with Kornilov, with the aim of jointly crushing the Petrograd workers and soldiers. If Kerensky began to 'fight' against Kornilov or, more correctly, to offer no resistance for a time to the fight against Kornilov, then it was only because the Bolsheviks left him no other alternative. That Kornilov and Kerensky, both of them conspirators, broke with each other and came into open conflict, was to a certain extent a surprise. That it would have to come to a collision between German fascism and the Social Democracy, could and should have been foreseen, if only on the basis of the Italian and Polish experiences. Why could an agreement with Kerensky against Kornilov have been concluded, and why is it forbidden to preach, to fight for, to advocate and to prepare an agreement with the social-democratic mass organisations? Why must such agreements be destroyed wherever they have come into being? That, however, is just how Thälmann and co. proceed.

---

49 Alexander Kerensky was a lawyer and a nominal member of the Socialist-Revolutionary Party (SRs). He was head of the Provisional Government of Russia from July 1917 until the October Revolution.

*Rude Pravo* naturally pounced ravenously upon my words that an agreement on fighting actions may be made with the devil, with his grandmother and even with Noske[50] and Grzesinski.

> "Look, communist workers, [writes the paper] you've got to come to terms with Grzesinski who has already shot so many of your comrades-in-arms. Come to an agreement with him for he is to fight together with you against the fascists, with whom he hobnobs at banquets and on the boards of directors of factories and banks."

The whole question is shifted here onto the plane of spurious sentimentality. Such an objection is worthy of an anarchist an old Russian Left Socialist-Revolutionary, a 'revolutionary pacifist', or of Münzenberg himself. There isn't a glimmer of Marxism in it.

First of all: is it correct that Grzesinski is a workers' hangman? Absolutely correct. But wasn't Kerensky a hangman of the workers and peasants in far greater measure than Grzesinski? Nevertheless, *Rude Pravo* approves, after the fact, the practical agreement with Kerensky.

To support the hangman in every action directed against the workers is a crime, if not treachery: that is just what the alliance of Stalin with Chiang Kai-shek consisted of. But if this same Chinese hangman were to find himself engaged tomorrow in a war with the Japanese imperialists, then practical fighting agreements of the Chinese workers with the hangman Chiang Kai-shek would be quite permissible and even – a duty.

Did Grzesinski hobnob with the fascists at banquets? I do not know, but I'm quite prepared to grant it. Only, Grzesinski was subsequently obliged to sit in the Berlin prison, not in the name of socialism, it is true, but only because he was loath to give up his warm seat to the Bonapartists and the fascists. Had the Communist Party openly declared at least a year ago: against the fascist assassins we are prepared to fight jointly even with Grzesinski; had it invested

50 Gustav Noske was a right-wing SPD leader, and was put in charge of the armed forces by the Provisional Government in December 1918. He led the violent suppression of the January 1919 uprising and he was responsible for the execution of Rosa Luxemburg and Karl Liebknecht.

this formula with a fighting character, developed it in speeches and articles, brought it into the depths of the masses – Grzesinski would have been unable to defend before the masses his capitulation in July with references to the sabotage of the Communist Party. He would either have had to go along with this or that active step or else expose himself hopelessly in the eyes of his own workers. Isn't this clear?

To be sure, even if Grzesinski were drawn into the struggle by the logic of his situation and the pressure of the masses, he would be an extremely unreliable, a thoroughly perfidious ally. His principal thought would be to pass over as quickly as possible from struggle or half-struggle to an agreement with the capitalists. But the masses set into motion, even the social-democratic masses, do not come to a halt as easily as do outraged police chiefs. The rapprochement of the social-democratic and the communist workers in the process of the struggle would offer the Communist Party leaders a far broader possibility for influencing the social-democratic workers, especially in face of the common danger. And that is precisely the final aim of the united front.

To reduce the whole policy of the proletariat to agreements with the reformist organisations or, still worse, to the abstract slogan of 'unity', is something that only spineless centrists of the stripe of the SAP[51] can do. For the Marxists, the united front policy is merely one of the methods in the course of the class struggle. Under certain conditions this method becomes completely useless; it would be absurd to want to conclude an agreement with the reformists to achieve the socialist upheaval. But there are conditions under which the rejection of the united front may ruin the revolutionary party for many decades to come. That is the situation in Germany at the present time.

The policy of the united front on the international scale, as we have said above, faces even more difficulties and dangers, for there the formulation of the practical tasks and the organisation of control by the masses is harder. That is so above all in the question of the

51 The Socialist Worker's Party of Germany (SAPD) was a centrist party formed in 1931.

struggle against war. The prospects of joint actions are far slighter here, the possibilities of subterfuge and deception by the reformists and pacifists are far greater. By this, of course, we do not contend that the united front in this field is out of the question. On the contrary, we demanded that the Comintern should turn directly and immediately to the Second and the Amsterdam Internationals[52] with the proposal for a joint antiwar congress. It would then have been the task of the Comintern to work out the most concrete possible obligations, applicable to the various countries and differing circumstances. Were the Social Democracy compelled to agree to such a congress, the problem of war, providing there were a correct policy on our side, could be driven into its ranks like a sharp wedge.

The first premise for this: utmost clarity, political as well as organisational. There is involved an agreement of proletarian, million-membered organisations, which are today still divided by deep antagonisms in principle. No ambiguous intermediaries, no diplomatic masqueradings and hollow pacifist formulas!

The Comintern, however, found it proper this time also to act counter to the ABCs of Marxism: while it refused to enter into open negotiations with the reformist Internationals, it opened up negotiations behind the scenes with Friedrich Adler[53] through the medium... of the pacifist literary gentleman and first-class muddlehead, Henri Barbusse. As a result of this policy, Barbusse gathered together in Amsterdam half-hidden communist or 'related', 'sympathising' organisations and groups, together with the pacifist freelancers of all countries. The most honest and sincere among the latter – and they are the minority – can each say for himself:

---

52 The International Federation of Trade Unions (IFTU), known as the Amsterdam International, was a reformist trade union organisation affiliated to the Second International.

53 Friedrich Adler, son of leading Austrian social-democrat Victor Adler, was an anti-war Social-Democrat, who in desperation assassinated the Austro-Hungarian head of government. After the war, he became a leading member of Austrian Social Democracy, and briefly led the centrist Two-and-a-half International, only to become the General Secretary of the Second international after its reconstitution in 1923.

"Me and my confusion." Who needed this masquerade, this bazaar of intellectualistic conceit, this Münzenbergerie, which turns into downright political charlatanry?

But let us return to Prague. Five months after the appearance of the article discussed above, the same journal printed the article of one of the party leaders, Klement Gottwald,[54] which bears the character of an appeal to the Czechoslovakian workers of the different tendencies to make fighting agreements. The fascist danger menaces all of Central Europe: the onslaught of the reaction can be beaten off only by the unity of the proletariat; no time should be lost; it is already 'five minutes to midnight'. The appeal is very passionately written. In vain, however, does Gottwald swear, following Seydewitz and Thälmann, that he is not pursuing the interests of the party but the interests of the class: such a contrast is absolutely improper in the mouth of a Marxist. Gottwald stigmatises the sabotage of the Social-Democratic leaders. It is needless to say that the truth here is entirely on his side. Unfortunately, the author says nothing direct about the policy of the Central Committee of the German Communist Party: evidently he is not resolved upon defending it, but does not yet dare to criticise it. Gottwald himself, nevertheless, goes into the painful question, not resolutely, it is true, but still fairly correctly. After he has called upon the workers of the various tendencies to come to an agreement in the factories, Gottwald writes:

> Many of you may perhaps say: Unite there 'at the top', we 'below' will get together pretty easily. We believe [continues the author] that the most important thing is for the workers to agree 'below'. And as for the leaders – we have already said that we combine even with the devil if only it is directed against the rulers and in the interests of the workers. And we say to you openly, if your leaders give up their alliance with the bourgeoisie for even a single instant, proceed in reality against the rulers even in one question – we will greet it and support them in it.

Almost everything necessary is said here, and almost the way it should be said. Gottwald did not even forget to mention the devil,

54 Klement Gottwald was the Chairman of the Czechoslovak Communist Party.

whose name the editorial board of *Rude Pravo* printed five months before in pious indignation. Gottwald did indeed omit the devil's grandmother. But God be with her; for the sake of the united front, we are ready to sacrifice her. Perhaps Gottwald would be prepared, for his part, to console the offended old dame by turning over for her disposal the article from *Rude Pravo* of 27 February, together with the inkwell 'worker correspondent'.

Gottwald's political considerations, let us hope, are applicable not only to Czechoslovakia but also to Germany. And that is just how it should have been said. On the other hand, neither in Berlin nor in Prague can the party leadership confine itself to the bald declaration of its readiness for a united front with the Social Democracy, but must demonstrate this readiness in deeds, enterprisingly, in a Bolshevik manner, by means of quite definite practical proposals and actions. That is just what we demand.

Gottwald's article, thanks to the fact that it rings with a realistic and not an ultimatist tone, instantly found an echo among the social-democratic workers. On 31 July there appeared in *Rude Pravo* a letter, among others, from an unemployed printer who had recently returned from a visit to Germany. The letter bears the imprint of a worker-democrat who is undoubtedly afflicted with the prejudices of reformism. All the more important is it to pay attention to how the policy of the German Communist Party reflects itself in his consciousness.

> When in the spring of last year, [thus writes the printer] comrade Breitscheid[55] directed to the Communist Party the appeal to begin joint actions with the Social Democracy, he evoked in the *Rote Fahne* a veritable storm of indignation. So the social-democratic workers said to themselves: "Now we know how serious are the intentions of the communists on the united front."

Here you have the genuine voice of a worker. Such a voice contributes more to the solution of the question than dozens of articles by

55 Rudolf Breitscheid was a SPD deputy in the Reichstag. He fled Germany in 1933, but was arrested in 1941. He died in 1944 at Buchenwald concentration camp.

unprincipled pen-pushers. As a matter of fact, Breitscheid did not propose any united front. He only frightened the bourgeoisie with the possibility of joint actions with the communists. Had the Central Committee of the Communist Party promptly put the question right on the edge of the knife, the Social Democratic Party leadership would have been pushed into a difficult position. But the Central Committee of the Communist Party hastened, as always, to put itself into a difficult position. In the pamphlet *What Next?* I happened to write on Breitscheid's speech:

> Isn't it self-evident that Breitscheid's diplomatic and equivocal offer should have been grabbed with both hands; and that from one's own side, one should have submitted a concrete, carefully detailed and practical programme for a joint struggle against fascism and demanded joint sessions of the executives of both parties, with the participation of the executives of the Free Trade Unions? Simultaneously, one should have carried this same programme energetically down through all the layers of both parties and of the masses.

By spurning the trial balloon of the reformist leaders, the Central Committee of the Communist Party transformed in the minds of the workers the ambiguous assertion of Breitscheid into a direct united front proposal and prompted the social-democratic workers to the conclusion: "*Our people* want joint actions, but the *communists* are sabotaging." Can one imagine a more stupid and inappropriate policy? Could Breitscheid's manoeuvre be better supported? The letter from the Prague printer demonstrates with remarkable plainness that with Thälmann's aid, Breitscheid completely attained his goal.

*Rude Pravo* endeavours to perceive contradiction and confusion in the fact that in one case we reject an agreement, but in another, we acknowledge it and deem it necessary to determine anew each time the scope, the slogans and the methods of the agreement. *Rude Pravo* does not understand that in politics, as in all other serious fields, one must know well: *what, when, where* and *how*. Also it cannot hurt to understand: *why*.

In *The Third International After Lenin*, written four years ago, we set down a few elementary rules for the united front policy. We consider it worthwhile to recall them here:

> The possibility of betrayal is always contained in reformism. But this does not mean to say that reformism and betrayal are one and the same thing at every moment. Not quite. Temporary agreements may be made with the reformists whenever they take a step forward. But to maintain a bloc with them when, frightened by the development of a movement they commit treason, is equivalent to criminal toleration of traitors and a veiling of betrayal. [...]
>
> The most important best established, and most unalterable rule to apply in every manoeuvre reads: you must never dare to merge, mix, or combine your own party organisation with an alien one, even though the latter be most 'sympathetic' today. Undertake no such steps as lead directly or indirectly, openly or maskedly, to the subordination of your party to other parties, or to organisations of other classes, or constrict the freedom of your own agitation, or your responsibility, even if only in part, for the political line of other parties. You shall not mix up the banners, let alone kneel before another banner.[56]

Today, after the experience with the Barbusse Congress, we would add still another rule:

> 'Agreements should be reached only openly, before the eyes of the masses, from party to party, from organisation to organisation. You shall not avail yourself of equivocal middlemen. You shall not palm off diplomatic affairs with bourgeois pacifists as a proletarian united front.'

## *The class struggle in the light of the economic cycle*

If we have insistently demanded that a distinction be made between fascism and Bonapartism, it has not been out of theoretical pedantry. Names are used to distinguish between concepts; concepts, in politics, in turn serve to distinguish among real forces. The smashing of fascism would leave no room for Bonapartism

56 Trotsky, *The Third International After Lenin*, Pioneer, 1957, pp. 129, 140.

and, it is to be hoped, would mean the direct introduction to the social revolution.

Only – the proletariat is not armed for the revolution. The reciprocal relations between Social Democracy and the Bonapartist government on the one hand, and between Bonapartism and fascism on the other – while they do not decide the fundamental questions – distinguish by what roads and in what tempo the struggle between the proletariat and the fascist counter-revolution will be prepared. The contradictions between Schleicher, Hitler and Wels, in the given situation, render more difficult the victory of fascism, and open for the Communist Party a new credit, the most valuable of all – a credit in time.

"Fascism will come to power by the cold method." We have heard this more than once from the Stalinist theoreticians. This formula means that the fascists will come to power legally, peacefully, through a coalition – without needing an open upheaval. Events have already refuted this prognosis. The Papen government came to power through a coup d'état, and it complemented it with a coup d'état in Prussia. Even if we assume that a coalition between the Nazis and the Centre would overthrow the Bonapartist Papen government with 'constitutional methods', in and of itself this still decides nothing. Between the peaceful assumption of power by Hitler and the establishment of the fascist regime there still lies a long way. A coalition would only facilitate the coup d'état, but not replace it. Along with the final abolition of the Weimar Constitution there would still remain the most important task – the abolition of the organs of proletarian democracy. From this point of view, what does the "cold method" mean? Nothing other than the lack of resistance on the part of the workers. Papen's Bonapartist coup d'état remained in fact unpunished. Will Hitler's fascist upheaval also remain unpunished? It is precisely around this question that, consciously or unconsciously, the guessing about the "cold method" turns.

If the Communist Party represented an overwhelming force, and if the proletariat were to march forward for the immediate seizure of power, all the contradictions in the camp of the possessing classes would temporarily be wiped out – fascists, Bonapartists and democrats would stand in one front against the proletarian revolution. But this is not the case. The weaknesses of the Communist Party and the division of the proletariat permit the possessing classes and the parties which serve them to carry their contradictions out into the open. Only by supporting itself on these contradictions will the Communist Party be able to strengthen itself.

But perhaps fascism in highly industrialised Germany will altogether decide not to validate its claims for full power? Undoubtedly, the German proletariat is incomparably more numerous and potentially stronger than the Italian. Although fascism in Germany represents a more numerous and better organised camp than in Italy at the corresponding period, still the task of liquidating 'Marxism' must appear both difficult and risky to the German fascists. In addition, it is not excluded that Hitler's political peak has already been passed. The all too long period of waiting and the new barrier on its road in the shape of Bonapartism, undoubtedly weakens fascism, intensifies its internal frictions and might materially weaken its pressure. But here we enter a domain of tendencies which at the present moment cannot be calculated in advance. Only the living struggle can answer these questions. To build in advance on the assumption that National Socialism will inevitably stop halfway would be most frivolous.

The theory of the "cold method", carried to its conclusion, is not in the least better than the theory of social fascism; more accurately, it only represents the obverse of that theory. The contradictions among the constituents of the enemy's camp are in both cases completely neglected, the successive stages of the process blurred. The Communist Party is left completely on the side. Not for nothing was the theoretician of the 'cold method', Hirsch,[57] at the same time the theoretician of social fascism.

The political crisis of the country develops on the foundation of the economic crisis. But economy too is not immovable. If

57 Werner Hirsch was the joint Editor-in-Chief of the central organ of the KPD, *Die Rote Fahne* from 1928. He became secretary to Thälmann in 1932 and the two were arrested together in 1933. After spending some time in Nazi concentration camps, he was released, which led to accusations of being a 'Trotskyist Gestapo-agent'. He died in one of Stalin's prisons in 1941.

yesterday we were obliged to say that the cyclical crisis only sharpens the fundamental, organic crisis of the capitalist system, so today we must recall that the general decline of capitalism does not exclude cyclical fluctuations. The present crisis will not last forever. The hopes of the capitalist world for a turn in the crisis are exaggerated to the utmost, but not groundless. The question of the struggle of political forces must be incorporated into the economic perspectives. Papen's programme makes this all the more impossible to postpone, since the programme starts from the assumption of an approaching economic improvement.

The industrial revival steps on the scene for everyone to see as soon as it expresses itself in the form of growing turnover of goods, rising production, increased number of employed workers. But it does not begin in that way. The revival is preceded by preparatory processes in the field of money circulation and of credit. The capital invested in unprofitable undertakings and branches of industry must be released and receive the form of liquid money which seeks investment. The market, freed of its fatty deposits, growths and swellings, must show a real demand. The entrepreneurs must gain confidence in the market and in each other. On the other hand, the 'confidence' of which the world press speaks so much must be spurred on, not only by economic, but also by political factors (reparations, war debts, disarmament-rearmament, etc.).

A rise in the turnover of goods, in production, in the number of employed workers, is nowhere to be seen as yet; on the contrary, the decline continues. As for the processes preparatory to a turn in the crisis, they have obviously fulfilled the greater part of the tasks assigned to them. Many signs really permit us to assume that the moment of turn in the economic cycle has drawn close, if it is not immediately before us. That is the estimation, seen on a world scale.

But we must draw a distinction between the creditor countries (the United States, Britain, France) and the debtor countries, or more accurately the bankrupt countries; the first place in the latter group is occupied by Germany. Germany has no liquid capital. Its economy can receive an impetus only through an influx of capital from outside. But a country which is not in condition to pay its old debts receives no loans. In any case, before the creditors open their money-bags they must be convinced that Germany is again in condition to export a greater amount than it needs to import; the difference has to serve to cover the debts. The demand for German goods is to be expected primarily from the agrarian countries, in the first instance from south-eastern Europe. The agrarian countries, for their part, depend on the demand of the industrial countries for raw materials and foodstuffs. Germany will therefore be forced to wait; the stream of life will first have to flow through the series of its capitalist competitors and its agrarian partners before it affects Germany's own economic performance.

But the German bourgeoisie cannot wait. Still less can the Bonapartist clique wait. While it promises not to touch the stability of the currency, the Papen government is introducing a material inflation. Together with speeches on the rebirth of economic liberalism, it assumes the administrative disposition over the economic cycle; in the name of the freedom of private initiative it subordinates the taxpayers directly to the capitalist entrepreneurs.

The axis around which the government programme turns is the hope of a nearby turn in the crisis. If this does not take place soon, the 2 billion[58] will evaporate like two drops of water on a red-hot stove. Papen's plan has immeasurably more of a gambling, speculative character than the bullish movement which is currently taking place on the New York Stock Exchange. In any case, the consequences of a collapse of the Bonapartist gamble will be far more catastrophic.

The most immediate and tangible result of the gap between the plans of the government and the actual movement of the market will consist in the slipping of the mark. The social evils, increased by inflation, will assume an intolerable character. The bankruptcy of the Papen economic programme will demand its replacement by another and more effective programme. Which one? Obviously,

58 The Papen government gave the German capitalists 2 billion marks as a stimulus.

the programme of fascism. Once the attempt to force a recovery through Bonapartist therapy has failed, it must be tried with fascist surgery. Social Democracy in the meantime will make 'left' gestures and fall to pieces. The Communist Party, if it does not put obstacles in its own way, will grow. All in all, this will mean a revolutionary situation. The question of the prospects for victory under these circumstances is three-fourths a question of communist strategy.

But the revolutionary party must also be prepared for another prospect, that of a quicker appearance of a turn in the crisis. Let us assume that the Schleicher-Papen government were to succeed in maintaining itself until the beginning of a revival in commerce and industry. Would it be saved thereby? No, the beginning of an upward movement in business would mean the certain end of Bonapartism and might even mean more.

The forces of the German proletariat are not exhausted. But they have been undermined by sacrifices, defeats and disappointments, beginning with 1914; by the systematic betrayals of the Social Democracy, by the discredit which the Communist Party has heaped upon itself. Six or seven million unemployed are a heavy load dragging on the feet of the proletariat. The emergency decrees of Brüning and Papen have found no resistance. The coup d'état of 20 July has remained unpunished.

We can predict with full assurance that an upward turn in the cycle would give a powerful impetus to the activity of the proletariat at present in decline. At the moment when the factory stops discharging workers and takes on new ones, the self-confidence of the workers is strengthened; they are once again necessary. The compressed springs begin to expand again. Workers always enter into the struggle for the reconquest of lost positions more easily than for the conquest of new ones. And the German workers have lost too much. Neither emergency decrees nor the use of the Reichswehr will be able to liquidate mass strikes which develop on the wave of the upturn. The Bonapartist regime, which is able to maintain itself only through the 'social truce', will be the first victim of the upturn in the cycle.

A growth of strike struggles is already to be observed in various countries (Belgium, Britain, Poland, in part in the United States, but not Germany). An evaluation of the mass strikes now developing, in the light of the worldwide economic cycle, is not an easy task. Statistics are inevitably slow to reveal fluctuations in the business cycle. The revival must become a fact before it can be registered. The workers usually sense the revival of economic life earlier than the statisticians. New orders or even the expectation of new orders, reorganisation of enterprises for expansion of production or at least the interruption of the discharge of workers, immediately increase the powers of resistance and the demands of the workers. The defensive strike of the textile workers in Lancashire was unquestionably called forth by a certain upturn in the textile industry. As for the Belgian strike, it is obviously taking place on the basis of the still deepening crisis of the coal mining industry. The transitional and critical character of the present phase of the world economic cycle corresponds to the variety of the economic impulses which are the basis of the most recent strikes. But in general, the growth of the mass movement rather tends to indicate the existence of an upward trend which is about to become perceptible. In any case, a real revival of economic activity, even in its first stages, will call forth a broad upsurge of the mass struggle.

The ruling classes of all countries expect miracles from the industrial upswing; the speculation in stocks which has already broken out is a proof of this. If capitalism were really to enter upon the phase of a new prosperity or even of a gradual but persistent rise, this would naturally involve the stabilisation of capitalism, accompanied by a weakening of fascism and a simultaneous reinforcement of reformism. But there is not the least ground for the hope or fear that the economic revival, which in and of itself is inevitable, will be able to overcome the general tendencies of decay in world economy and in European economy in particular. If pre-war capitalism developed under the formula of expanded production of goods, present-day capitalism, with all its cyclical fluctuations, represents an expanded production of misery and of catastrophes.

The new economic cycle will entail the inevitable readjustment of forces within the individual countries as well as within the capitalist camp as a whole, predominantly toward America and away from Europe. But within a very short time it will confront the capitalist world with insoluble contradictions and condemn it to new and still more frightful convulsions.

Without the risk of error, we can make the following prognosis: the economic revival will suffice to strengthen the self-confidence of the workers and give a new impetus to their struggle, but it will in no way suffice to give capitalism, and particularly European capitalism, the possibility of rebirth.

The practical conquests which the new cyclical upturn in declining capitalism will open to the workers' movement will necessarily bear a most limited character. Will German capitalism, at the height of the new revival in economic activity, be able to restore those conditions for the working class which existed before the present crisis? Everything compels us to answer this question in advance with "No." All the more quickly will the awakened mass movement have to strike out along the political road.

Even the very first step of the industrial revival will be most dangerous for Social Democracy. The workers will throw themselves into struggle to win back what they have lost. The leaders of the Social Democracy will again base their hopes on the restoration of the 'normal' order. Their main consideration will be the restoration of their fitness to join a coalition government. Leaders and masses will pull in opposite directions. In order to exploit to the limit the new crisis of reformism, the communists need a correct orientation in the cyclical changes and the preparation sufficiently ahead of time of a practical programme of action, beginning first of all with the losses suffered by the workers during the years of crisis. The transition from economic struggles to political ones will constitute an especially suitable moment for the strengthening of the power and influence of the revolutionary proletarian party.

But success in this field as in others can be achieved only under one condition – the correct application of the policy of the united front.

For the Communist Party of Germany this means, before anything else: an end to the present policy of sitting between two stools in the trade-union field; a firm course toward the Free Trade Unions,[59] drawing the present cadres of the RGO into their ranks; the opening of a systematic struggle for influence on the shop councils by means of the trade unions; and the preparation of a broad campaign under the slogan of workers' control of production.

## *The road to socialism*

Kautsky[60] and Hilferding,[61] among others, have declared more than once in recent years that they never shared the theory of the collapse of capitalism which the revisionists once ascribed to the Marxists and which the Kautskyists themselves now frequently attribute to the communists.

The Bernsteinians[62] outlined two perspectives: one, unreal, allegedly orthodox 'Marxist', according to which in the long run, under the influence of the internal contradictions of capitalism, its mechanical collapse was supposed to take place; and the second, 'realistic', according to which a gradual evolution from capitalism to socialism was to be accomplished. Antithetical as these two schemas

59 The Free Trade Unions refers to those trade unions that were affiliated to the social-democratic ADGB.

60 Karl Kautsky was one of the leading theoreticians of the German Social-Democratic Party (SPD) and the Second International. After the outbreak of the First World War, he rejected a revolutionary position and instead opposed the war on pacifist grounds. Together with Hugo Haase, Eduard Bernstein and others, he formed the minority break-away centrist USPD in 1917. When the majority of the USPD merged with the KPD, he joined the minority that returned to the SPD.

61 Rudolf Hilferding was an Austrian economist and social-democrat. He opposed the war and joined the USPD in 1918. When the USPD split, he joined the minority that returned to the SPD. In 1930-31 he defended the deflationary austerity programme of the Brüning government with pseudo-Marxist language.

62 Eduard Bernstein was a leading theoretician of the SPD. In 1896, he published a series of articles entitled 'Problems of Socialism' in the party's theoretical journal *Neue Zeit*, in which he broke with Marxism and advocated the peaceful, gradual transformation of society. The publication of these articles and the failure of the SPD leadership to reply led to a sharp polemic in the Second International.

may be at first glance, they are nevertheless united by a common trait: the absence of the revolutionary factor. While they disavowed the caricature of the automatic collapse of capitalism attributed to them, the Marxists demonstrated that, under the influence of the sharpening class struggle, the proletariat would carry through the revolution long before the objective contradictions of capitalism could lead to its automatic collapse.

This dispute was carried on as long ago as the end of the last century. It must however be acknowledged that the capitalist reality since the war approached, in a certain respect, much closer to the Bernsteinian caricature of Marxism than anyone might ever have assumed – least of all the revisionists themselves, since they had only portrayed the spectre of the collapse in order to bring out its unreality. Nevertheless, capitalism proves in actuality to be closer to automatic decay the more delayed is the revolutionary intervention of the proletariat in the destiny of society.

The most important component of the theory of collapse was the theory of pauperisation. The Marxists contended, with some prudence, that the sharpening of social contradictions need not signify unconditionally an absolute drop in the standard of living of the masses. But in reality, it is precisely this latter process which is unfolding. Wherein could the collapse of capitalism express itself more acutely than in chronic unemployment and the destruction of social insurance, that is, the refusal of the social order to feed its own slaves?

The opportunistic brakes in the working class have proved to be powerful enough to grant the elemental forces of outlived capitalism additional decades of life. As a result, it is not the idyll of the peaceful transformation of capitalism into socialism which has taken place, but a state of affairs infinitely closer to social decay.

The reformists sought for a long time to shift the responsibility for the present state of society onto the war. But in the first place, the war did not create the destructive tendencies of capitalism, but only brought them to the surface and accelerated them; secondly, the war would have been unable to accomplish its work of destruction without the political support of reformism; thirdly, the hopeless contradictions of capitalism are preparing new wars from various sides. Reformism will be unable to shift the historical responsibility from itself. By paralysing and curbing the revolutionary energy of the proletariat, the international Social Democracy invests the process of the capitalist collapse with the blindest, most unbridled, catastrophic and bloody forms.

Of course, one cannot speak of a realisation of the revisionist caricature of Marxism except conditionally, in applying it to some given historical period. The way out of decaying capitalism, however, will be found, even if after a great delay, not upon the road of the automatic collapse but upon the revolutionary road.

The present crisis has swept aside with a final flourish of the broom the remnants of the reformist utopias. Opportunist practice at the present time possesses no theoretical covering whatsoever. For in the long run it is pretty much a matter of indifference to Wels, Hilferding, Grzesinski and Noske how many catastrophes will still hurtle down upon the heads of the masses of the people, if only their own interests remain immune. Only, the point is that the crisis of the bourgeois regime strikes at the reformist leaders, too.

"Act, state, intervene!" the Social Democracy still cried a short while ago, as it fell back before fascism. And the state acted: Otto Braun and Severing were kicked into the street.[63] Now, wrote the *Vorwärts*,[64] everybody must recognise the advantages of democracy over the regime of dictatorship. Yes, democracy has substantial advantages, reflected Grzesinski while he made the acquaintance of prison from the inside.

From this experience resulted the conclusion: "It is time to proceed to socialisation!" Tarnow,[65] yesterday still a doctor of capitalism, suddenly decided to become its gravedigger. Now, when capitalism has turned the reformist ministers, police chiefs and lord

63 Referring to the 20 July coup, when Braun and Severing were removed from their positions as Prussian Prime Minister and Minister of the Interior respectively.

64 *Vorwärts* (*Forwards*) was the daily newspaper of the SPD.

65 Fritz Tarnow was a Reichstag deputy for the SPD.

lieutenants into unemployed, it has manifestly exhausted itself. Wels writes a programmatic article, "The hour of socialism has struck!" There only remains for Schleicher to rob the deputies of their salary and the former ministers of their pension – and Hilferding will write a study on the historic role of the general strike. The 'left turn' of the Social-Democratic leaders startles one with its stupidity and deceitfulness. This by no means signifies, however, that the manoeuvre is condemned in advance to failure. This party, laden with crimes, still stands at the head of millions. It will not fall of its own accord. One must know how to overthrow it.

The Communist Party will declare that the Wels-Tarnow course towards socialism is a new form of mass deception, and that will be correct. It will relate the history of the social-democratic 'socialisations' of the last fourteen years. That will be useful. But it is insufficient: history, even the most recent, cannot take the place of active politics.

Tarnow seeks to reduce the question of the revolutionary or the reformist road to socialism to the simple question of the 'tempo' of the transformations. Deeper a theoretician cannot sink. The tempo of socialist transformations depends in reality upon the state of the productive forces of the country, its culture, the extent of the overhead imposed upon it for defence, etc. But socialist transformations, the speedy as well as the slow, are possible only if at the summits of society stands a class interested in socialism, and at the head of this class a party which does not dupe the exploited, and which is always ready to suppress the resistance of the exploiters. We must explain to the workers that precisely in that consists the regime of the *dictatorship of the proletariat.*

Only, even this does not suffice. Once it is a question of the burning problems of the world proletarian one should not – as the Comintern does – forget the fact of the existence of the Soviet Union. With regard to Germany, the task today does not lie in beginning socialist construction for the first time, but in tying together Germany's productive forces, its culture, its technical and organisational genius with the socialist construction already in process in the Soviet Union.

The German Communist Party confines itself to the mere eulogising of Soviet successes, and in this connection commits gross and dangerous exaggerations. But it is completely incapable of linking together the socialist construction in the USSR, its enormous experiences and valuable achievements, with the tasks of the proletarian revolution in Germany. The Stalinist bureaucracy, for its part, is least of all in a position to render the German Communist Party any assistance in this highly important matter: its perspectives are limited to one single country.

The incoherent and cowardly state-capitalistic projects of the Social Democracy must be countered with *a general plan for the joint socialist construction of the USSR and Germany.* Nobody demands that a detailed plan should be worked out instantly. A preliminary rough draft suffices. Foundation pillars are necessary. This plan must be made the object of action as speedily as possible by every organisation of the German working class, primarily of its trade unions.

The progressive forces among the German technicians, statisticians and economists must be drawn into this action. The discussions about planned economy so widespread in Germany, reflecting the hopelessness of German capitalism, remain purely academic, bureaucratic, lifeless, pedantic. The communist vanguard alone is capable of lifting the treatment of the question out of the vicious circle.

Socialist construction is already in progress – to continue this work a bridge must be thrown over the state frontiers. Here is the first plan: study it, improve it, make it concrete! Workers, elect special planning commissions, charge them with entering into liaison with the trade unions and economic organs of the Soviets. On the basis of the German trade unions, the factory councils and other labour organisations, create a central planning commission which has the job of liaison with the Gosplan[66] of the USSR. Draw into this work German engineers, organisers, economists!

66 The State Planning Committee of the USSR (Gosplan) was responsible for the central planning of the economy.

This is the only correct approach to the question of planned economy, today, in the year 1932, after fifteen years of existence of the Soviets, after fourteen years of convulsions in the German capitalist republic.

Nothing is easier than to ridicule the social-democratic bureaucracy, beginning with Wels, who has struck up a Song of Solomon to socialism. Yet it must not be forgotten that the reformist workers have a thoroughly serious attitude to the question of socialism. One must have a serious attitude to the reformist workers. Here the problem of the united front rises up once again in its full scope.

If the Social Democracy sets itself the task (only in words, we know), not to save capitalism but to build up socialism, then it must seek an agreement not with the Centre but with the communists. Will the Communist Party reject such an agreement? By no means. On the contrary, it will itself propose such an agreement, demand it before the masses as a redemption of the just-signed socialist promissory note.

The attack of the Communist Party upon the Social Democracy must proceed at the present time along three lines. The task of demolishing fascism retains all its acuteness. The decisive battle of the proletariat against fascism will signal the simultaneous collision with the Bonapartist state apparatus. This makes the *general strike* an indispensable fighting weapon. It must be prepared. A special general strike plan must be worked out, that is, a plan for the mobilisation of the forces to carry it out. Proceeding from this plan, a mass campaign must be unfolded, on the basis of which an agreement for carrying out the general strike under well-defined political conditions may be proposed to the Social Democracy. Repeated and made concrete at every new stage, this proposal will lead in the process of its development to the creation of the soviets *as the highest organs of the united front.*

That Papen's economic plan, which has now become law, brings the German proletariat unprecedented poverty, is recognised in words also by the leaders of the Social Democracy and the trade unions. In the press, they express themselves with a vehemence they have not voiced for a long time. Between their words and their deeds lies an abyss; we know that very well – but we must understand how to pin them down to their word. *A system of joint measures of struggle must be elaborated against the regime of emergency decrees and Bonapartism.* This struggle imposed upon the proletariat by the whole situation cannot, by its very nature, be conducted within the framework of democracy. A situation where Hitler possesses an army of 400,000 men, Papen-Schleicher, besides the Reichswehr, the semi-private Stahlhelm[67] army of 200,000 men, the bourgeois democracy the half-tolerated Reichsbanner army, the Communist Party the proscribed Red Front army[68] – such a situation by itself lays bare the problem of the state as a problem of power. A better revolutionary school cannot be imagined!

The Communist Party must say to the working class: Schleicher is not to be overthrown by any parliamentary game. If the Social Democracy wants to set to work to overthrow the Bonapartist government with other means, the Communist Party is ready to aid the Social Democracy with all its strength. At the same time, the communists obligate themselves in advance to use no violent methods against a social-democratic government insofar as the latter bases itself upon the majority of the working class and insofar as it guarantees the Communist Party the freedom of agitation and organisation. Such a way of putting the question will be comprehensible to every social-democratic and non-party worker.

The third line, finally, is *the fight for socialism.* Here too the iron must be forged while it is hot and the Social Democracy pressed to the wall with a concrete plan of collaboration with the USSR. What is necessary on this point has already been said above.

Naturally, these sectors of struggle, which are of varying significance in the complete strategical perspective, are not separated from each other, but rather overlap and merge. The political crisis of society demands the combining of the partial questions with the general questions: precisely therein lies the essence of the revolutionary situation.

67 Der Stahlhelm (The Steel Helmet) was an armed veterans organisation affiliated to the German National People's Party (DNVP), a right-wing monarchist party.

68 Roter Frontkämpferbund (The Red Front Fighter's League, RFB) was a paramilitary organisation affiliated to the KPD.

## *The only road*

Can it be expected that the Central Committee of the Communist Party will independently accomplish a turn to the right road? Its whole past demonstrates that it is incapable of doing this.

Hardly had it begun to rectify itself than the apparatus saw before it the perspective of 'Trotskyism'. If Thälmann himself did not grasp it immediately, then he was told from Moscow that the 'part' must be sacrificed for the sake of the 'whole', that is, the interests of the German revolution for the sake of the interests of the Stalinist apparatus. The abashed attempts to revise the policy were once more withdrawn. The bureaucratic reaction triumphed again all along the line.

It is not of course, a matter of Thälmann. Were the present-day Comintern to give its sections the possibility of living, of thinking and of developing themselves, they would long ago, in the last fifteen years, have been able to select their own leading cadres. But the bureaucracy erected instead a system of appointed leaders and their support by means of artificial ballyhoo. Thälmann is a product of this system and at the same time its victim.

The cadres, paralysed in their development, weaken the party. They supplement their inadequacy with repressions. The vacillations and the uncertainty of the party are inexorably transmitted to the class as a whole. The masses cannot be summoned to bold actions when the party itself is robbed of revolutionary determination.

Even if Thälmann were to receive tomorrow a telegram from Manuilsky on the necessity of a turn to the path of the united front policy, the new zigzag at the top would bring little good. The leadership is too compromised. A correct policy demands a healthy regime. Party democracy, at present a plaything of the bureaucracy, must rise again as a reality. The party must become a party; then the masses will believe it. Practically, this means to put upon the order of the day *an extraordinary party convention* and *an extraordinary congress of the Comintern.*

The party convention must naturally be preceded by a thorough discussion. All apparatus barriers must be razed. Every party organisation, every nucleus has the right to call to its meetings and listen to every communist, member of the party or expelled from it if it considers this necessary for the working out of its opinion. The press must be put at the service of the discussion; adequate space must be allotted daily for critical articles in every party paper. Special press commissions, elected at mass meetings of the party members, must see to it that the papers serve the party and not the bureaucracy.

The discussion, it is true, will require no little time and energy. The apparatus will argue: how can the party permit itself the 'luxury of discussion' at such a critical period? The bureaucratic saviours believe that under difficult conditions the party must shut up. The Marxists, on the contrary, believe that the more difficult the situation, the more important the independent role of the party.

The leadership of the Bolshevik Party enjoyed, in 1917, a very great esteem. And notwithstanding this, a series of deep-going party discussions took place throughout the year 1917. On the eve of the October overturn the whole party debated passionately which of the two sections of the Central Committee was right: the majority, which was for the uprising, or the minority, which was against the uprising. Expulsions, and repressions in general, were nowhere to be seen, in spite of the differences of opinion. Into these discussions were drawn the non-party masses. In Petrograd, a meeting of non-party working women dispatched a delegation to the Central Committee in order to support the majority in it. To be sure, the discussion required time. But in return for that, there grew out of the open discussion, without threats, lies and falsifications, the general, indomitable certainty of the correctness of the policy, that is, that which alone makes possible the victory.

What course will things take in Germany? Will the small wheel of the Opposition succeed in turning the large party wheel in time? That is how the question stands now. Pessimistic voices are often raised. In the various communist groupings, in the party itself, as well as in the periphery, there are not a few elements who say to themselves: in every important question the Left Opposition has a correct stand. But it is weak. Its cadres are small in number and politically inexperienced. Can such an organisation, with a small weekly paper (*Die Permanente Revolution*)[69] successfully counterpose itself to the mighty Comintern machine?

The lessons of events are stronger than the Stalinist bureaucracy. We want to be the interpreters of these lessons to the communist masses. Therein lies our historic role as a faction. We do not demand, as do Seydewitz and co., that the revolutionary proletariat should believe us on credit. We allot ourselves a more modest role: we propose our assistance to the communist vanguard in the elaboration of the correct line. For this work we are gathering and training our own cadres. This stage of preparation may not be jumped over. Every new stage of struggle will push to our side those in the proletariat who reflect the most and are most critical.

The revolutionary party begins with an idea, a programme, which is aimed against the most powerful apparatus of class society. It is not the cadre that creates the idea, but the idea that creates the cadre. Fear of the power of the apparatus is one of the most conspicuous features of that specific opportunism which the Stalinist bureaucracy cultivates. Marxist criticism is stronger than any and every apparatus.

The organisational forms which the further evolution of the Left Opposition will assume, depend upon many circumstances: the momentum of the historical blows, the degree of the power of resistance of the Stalin bureaucracy, the activity of the rank and file communists, the energy of the Opposition itself. But the principles and methods we fight for have been tested by the greatest events in world history, by the victories as well as by the defeats. They will make their way.

The successes of the Opposition in every country, Germany included, are indisputable and manifest. But they are developing slower than many of us expected. We may regret this, but we do not need be surprised at it. Every communist who begins to listen to the Left Opposition is cynically given the choice by the bureaucracy:

69 *Die Permanente Revolution* was the weekly newspaper of the German Left Oppositionists in the early 1930s.

either go along with the baiting of 'Trotskyism' or else be kicked out of the ranks of the Comintern. For the party official, it is a question of position and wages: the Stalinist apparatus plays this key to perfection. But immeasurably more important are the thousands of rank-and-file communists who are torn between their devotion to the ideas of communism and the threatened expulsion from the ranks of the Comintern. That is why there are in the ranks of the official Communist Party a great number of partial, intimidated or concealed oppositionists.

This extraordinary combination of historical conditions sufficiently explains the slow organisational growth of the Left Opposition. At the same time, in spite of this slowness, the spiritual life of the Comintern revolves, today more than ever before around the struggle against 'Trotskyism'. The theoretical periodicals and theoretical newspaper articles of the CPSU,[70] as well as the other sections of the Comintern are chiefly devoted to the struggle against the Left Opposition, now openly, now maskedly. Still more symptomatic in significance is that mad organisational baiting which the apparatus pursues against the Opposition: disruption of its meetings by blackjack methods; employment of all sorts of other physical violence; behind-the-scenes agreements with bourgeois pacifists, French Radicals[71] and Freemasons against the 'Trotskyists'; the dissemination of envenomed calumnies from the Stalinist centre, etc., etc.

The Stalinists perceive much more directly and know better than the Oppositionists to what extent our ideas are undermining the pillars of their apparatus. The methods of self-defence of the Stalinist faction, however, have a double-edged character. Up to a certain moment, they have an intimidating effect. But at the same time, they prepare a mass reaction against the system of falsity and violence.

When, in July 1917, the government of the Mensheviks and the Socialist-Revolutionaries branded the Bolsheviks as agents of

70 The Communist Party of the Soviet Union.

71 The Republican, Radical and Radical-Socialist Party, founded in 1901, was a petty-bourgeois reformist party.

the German Staff, this despicable measure succeeded at first in exercising a strong influence upon the soldiers, the peasants and the backward strata of workers. But when all the further events clearly confirmed how right the Bolsheviks had been, the masses began to say to themselves: so they deliberately slandered the Leninists, they basely incited against them, only because they were right? And the feeling of suspicion against the Bolsheviks was converted into a feeling of warm devotion and love for them. Although under different conditions, this very complex process is taking place now too. By means of a monstrous accumulation of calumnies and repressions, the Stalinist bureaucracy has undeniably succeeded for a period of time in intimidating the rank and file party members; at the same time, it is preparing for the Bolshevik-Leninists an enormous rehabilitation in the eyes of the revolutionary masses. At the present time, there can no longer be the slightest doubt on this score.

Yes, today we are still weak. The Communist Party still has masses, but already it has neither doctrine nor strategic orientation. The Left Opposition has already worked out its Marxist orientation, but as yet it has no masses. The remaining groups of the 'Left' camp possess neither the one nor the other. Hopelessly the Leninbund[72] pines away, thinking to substitute the individual fantasies and whims of Urbahns[73] for a serious principled policy. The Brandlerites, in spite of their apparatus cadre, are descending step by step; small tactical recipes cannot replace a revolutionary-strategical position. The SAP has put up its candidacy for the revolutionary leadership of the proletariat. Baseless pretension! Even the most serious representatives of this 'party' do not overstep, as Fritz Sternberg's latest book shows, the barriers of Left Centrism. The more assiduously they seek to create an 'independent' doctrine the more they reveal themselves to be disciples of Thalheimer. But this school is as hopeless as a corpse.

---

72 The Leninbund was a communist organisation founded in April 1928 by members of the KPD including Fischer and Maslow, who were expelled during Thälmann's purge of the left of the party..

73 Hugo Urbahns was a member of the KPD and founder of the Leninbund.

A new historical party cannot arise simply because a number of old social-democrats have convinced themselves, very belatedly, of the counter-revolutionary character of the Ebert-Wels policy. A new party can just as little be improvised by a group of communists who have as yet done nothing to warrant their claim to proletarian leadership. For a new party to arise, it is on the one hand necessary to have great historical events, which would break the backbone of the old parties, and on the other hand, a position in principle worked out and cadres tested, in the experience of events.

While we are fighting with all our strength for the rebirth of the Comintern and the continuity of its further development, we are least of all inclined to any fetishism of form. The feat of the proletarian world revolution stands, for us, above the organisational fate of the Comintern. Should the worst variant materialise; should the present official parties, despite all our efforts, be led to a collapse by the Stalinist bureaucracy; should it mean in a certain sense to begin all over again, then the New International will trade its genealogy from the ideas and cadres of the Communist Left Opposition.

And that is why the short-term 'pessimism' and 'optimism' are not applicable to the work which we are carrying through. It stands above the separate stages, the partial defeats and victories. Our policy is a policy of long range.

## *Afterword*

The present brochure, whose different parts were written at different times, had already been finished when a telegram from Berlin brought the news of the conflict of the overwhelming majority of the Reichstag with the Papen government and consequently with the Reich President. We expect to follow the concrete development of subsequent events in the columns of *Die Permanente Revolution*. Here we wish only to emphasise some general conclusions, which seemed to be open to criticism when we began the brochure and which, thanks to the testimony of facts, have since become incontestable.

1. The *Bonapartist* character of the Schleicher-Papen government has been completely disclosed by its isolated position in the Reichstag. The agrarian-capitalist circles which stand directly behind the presidential government constitute an incomparably smaller percentage of the German nation than the percentage of votes given for Papen in the Reichstag.

2. The antagonism between Papen and Hitler is the antagonism between the agrarian-capitalist leadership and the reactionary petty bourgeoisie. Just as once the liberal bourgeoisie used the revolutionary movement of the petty bourgeoisie, but employed every means to keep it from seizing the power, so the monopolistic bourgeoisie is prepared to reward Hitler as its lackey, but not as its master. Without compelling necessity it will not turn over the full power to fascism.

3. The fact that the various fractions of the grand, middle and petty bourgeoisie are carrying on an open struggle for power, without avoiding a most dangerous conflict, proves that the bourgeoisie does not see itself as being immediately threatened by the proletariat. Not only the Nazis and the Centre, but also the leaders of the Social Democracy have dared enter on a *struggle for the constitution* only in the firm confidence that it will not change into a *revolutionary struggle*.

4. The only party whose vote against Papen was dictated by revolutionary purposes is the *Communist Party*. But it is a long way from revolutionary purposes to revolutionary achievements.

5. The logic of events is such that the struggle for 'parliament' and for 'democracy' becomes for every social-democratic worker a question of *power*. Therein lies the main content of the whole conflict from the standpoint of the revolution. The question of power is the question of the revolutionary unity in action of the proletariat. The policy of the united front toward the Social Democracy must be prepared in the very near future to render possible, on the basis of proletarian democratic representation, the creation of class organs of struggle, i.e. of *workers' soviets*.

6. In view of the gifts to capitalists and the monstrous attack on the standard of living of the proletariat, the Communist Party must set up the slogan of *workers' control of production.*

7. The fractions of the possessing classes can afford to quarrel among themselves only because the revolutionary party is weak. The revolutionary party could become immeasurably stronger if it would correctly exploit the quarrels among the possessing classes. For this it is necessary to know how to distinguish the various fractions according to their social composition, but not to throw them all into one heap. The theory of 'social fascism' which has completely and finally been bankrupted, must at last be thrown out as worthless junk.

# *The Tragedy of the German Proletariat*

## *The German Workers Will Rise Again – Stalinism, Never!*

Written 14 March 1933

Editors note: In February 1933, the Reichstag building was set on fire by the SA. Hitler, now appointed Chancellor by Hindenburg, used this as a pretence with which to attack the Communists in particular, passing the Reichstag Fire Decree.

* * *

The most powerful proletariat of Europe, measured by its place in production, its social weight and the strength of its organisations, has manifested no resistance since Hitler's coming to power and his first violent attacks against the workers' organisations. This is the fact from which to proceed in subsequent strategic calculations.

It would be patently stupid to believe that the future evolution of Germany will follow the Italian road; that Hitler will strengthen his domination step by step without serious resistance; that German fascism will enjoy long years of domination. No, the further fate of

National Socialism will have to be deduced from an analysis of the German and international conditions, and not from purely historical analogies. But this much is already evident: if from September 1930 onwards we demanded of the Communist International a short-range policy in Germany, then it is necessary now to work out a long-range policy. Before *decisive* battles will become possible, the proletarian vanguard will have to reorient itself; that is to say, it will have to understand what has happened, assign the responsibility for the great historical defeat, trace out the new road, and thus regain confidence in itself.

The criminal role of the Social Democracy requires no commentary: the Comintern was created fourteen years ago precisely in order to snatch the proletariat from the demoralizing influence of the Social Democracy. If it has not succeeded up to now, if the German proletariat found itself impotent, disarmed and paralysed at the moment of its greatest historic test, the direct and immediate blame falls upon the leadership of the post-Leninist Comintern. That is the first conclusion which ought to be drawn immediately.

Under the treacherous blows of the Stalinist bureaucracy, the Left Opposition maintained its fidelity to the official party to the very end. The Bolshevik-Leninists now share the fate of all the other communist organisations: the militants of our cadres are arrested, our publications forbidden, our literature confiscated. Hitler even hurried to suspend the *Bulletin of the Opposition*[1] appearing in the Russian language. But if, together with the whole proletarian vanguard, the Bolshevik-Leninists bear the consequences of the first serious victory of fascism, they cannot and will not bear even a shadow of the responsibility for the official policy of the Comintern.

Since 1923, that is, since the beginning of the struggle against the Left Opposition, the Stalinist leadership, although indirectly, assisted the Social Democracy with all its strength to derail, to befuddle, to enfeeble the German proletariat: it restrained and hindered the workers when the conditions dictated a courageous revolutionary

1 The *Bulletin of the Opposition* was the paper of the Left Opposition, published from 1929-41.

offensive; it proclaimed the approach of the revolutionary situation when it had already passed; it worked up agreements with petty-bourgeois phrase-mongers and windbags; it limped impotently at the tail of the Social Democracy under cover of the policy of the united front; it proclaimed the 'third period' and the struggle for the conquest of the streets under conditions of political ebb and the weakness of the Communist Party; it replaced the serious struggle by leaps, adventures or parades; it isolated the communists from the mass trade unions; it identified the Social Democracy with fascism and rejected the united front with the mass workers' organisations in face of the aggressive bands of the National Socialists; it sabotaged the slightest initiative for the united front for local defence, at the same time it systematically deceived the workers as to the real relationship of forces, distorted the facts, passed off friends as enemies and enemies as friends – and drew the noose tighter and tighter around the neck of the party, not permitting it to breathe freely any longer, nor to speak, nor to think.

Out of the vast literature devoted to the question of fascism it is enough to refer to the speech of Thälmann, official leader of the German Communist Party, who, at the plenum of the Executive Committee of the Communist International in April 1931, denounced the 'pessimists', that is, those who knew how to foresee, in the following terms:

> We have not allowed the moods of panic to rout us [...] We have soberly and firmly established the fact that 14 September [1930][2] was in a certain sense Hitler's best day, and that afterwards will come not better days but worse. This evaluation which we made of the development of this party is confirmed by the events [...] Today, the fascists have no reasons for laughing.

Referring to the creation of defence groups by the Social Democracy, Thälmann demonstrated in the same speech that these groups differ in no respect from the shock troops of the National Socialists and that both of them are likewise preparing to annihilate Communism.

---

2 The fifth Reichstag elections, where the Nazis won 107 seats, a major increase on the twelve seats they won in 1928.

Today, Thälmann is under arrest. Faced with triumphant reaction, the Bolshevik-Leninists are in the same ranks as Thälmann. But the policy of Thälmann is the policy of Stalin, that is, the official policy of the Comintern. It is precisely this policy which is the cause of the complete demoralisation of the party at the moment of danger, when the leaders lose their heads, when the party members, unaccustomed to thinking, fall prostrate, when the principal historic positions are surrendered without a fight. A false political theory bears within itself its own punishment. The strength and the obstinacy of the apparatus only augment the dimensions of the catastrophe.

Having surrendered to the enemy everything that could be surrendered in such a short space of time, the Stalinists are trying to rectify the past by means of convulsive acts, which only more brightly illuminate the whole chain of crimes committed by them. Now that the press of the Communist Party is stifled, now the apparatus is destroyed, now the bloody pennant of fascism waves with impunity over the Karl Liebknecht House,[3] the Executive Committee of the Comintern is starting out on the road of the united front not only from below but also from above. The new zigzag, sharper than all that preceded it, has not, however, been effected on the impulse of the ECCI itself, the Stalinist bureaucracy has abandoned the initiative to the Second International. The latter has succeeded in taking hold of the weapon of the united front of which it has been in mortal dread until now. To the extent that it is possible to speak of political advantages under the conditions of a panicky retreat, they are to be found exclusively on the side of reformism. Forced to reply to a direct question, the Stalinist bureaucracy chose the worst way: it does not reject an entente of the two Internationals, but neither does it accept it; it plays hide-and-seek. It has come to such a lack of self-confidence, to such degradation, that it no longer dares to show itself to the world proletariat face to face with the leaders of the Second International, the branded agents of the bourgeoisie, the electors of Hindenburg who blazed the trail of fascism.

3 Karl Liebknecht Haus in Berlin held the offices of the KPD.

In a special appeal of the ECCI on 5 March, 'To the Workers of All Countries', the Stalinists do not say a word about social fascism as the main enemy. They no longer speak about the great discovery of their leader: "The Social Democracy and fascism are not antipodes but twins."[4] They no longer insist on saying that the struggle against fascism demands *as a preliminary* the defeat of the Social Democracy. They do not breathe a word about the inadmissibility of the united front from above. On the contrary, they carefully enumerate those cases in the past where the Stalinist bureaucracy, unexpectedly for the workers and for itself, found itself forced to improvise proposals for the united front to the reformist summits. Thus do artificial, false and charlatanesque theories founder in the fury of the historical tempest.

"Taking into account the peculiarities of each country" and the impossibility, which allegedly flows from them, of organising the united front on an international scale (the struggle against 'exceptionalism', that is, the theory of the right-wingers on national peculiarities, is suddenly forgotten), the Stalinist bureaucracy recommends to the national Communist Parties that they address proposals for a united front to the "Central Committees of the Social Democratic Parties". Only yesterday this was proclaimed a capitulation to social fascism! Thus do all the great lessons of Stalinism for the last four years fly under the table into the waste-basket. Thus is a whole political system reduced to dust.

Matters do not rest there: having just declared the impossibility of generating the conditions for a united front on the international arena, the ECCI immediately forgets it and no more than twenty lines further on formulates the conditions under which the united front is admissible and acceptable in all countries, in spite of the difference in national conditions. The retreat before fascism is followed by a panic-stricken retreat from the theoretical commandments of Stalinism. Chips and fragments of ideas and principles are thrown out along the road like so much ballast.

---

4 Stalin, 'Concerning the International Situation', *Works*, Vol. 6, p. 294.

The conditions for the united front put forward by the Comintern for all the countries (committees of action against fascism, demonstrations and strikes against wage reductions) present nothing new. On the contrary, they are the schematised and bureaucratised reproduction of the slogans that the Left Opposition formulated much more clearly and concretely two and a half years ago, for which it was registered in the camp of social fascism. The united front on such a basis could have yielded decisive results in Germany; but for that, it would have had to be carried out in time. Time is an important factor in politics.

What is therefore the practical value now of the proposals of the ECCI? For Germany, it is minimal. The policy of the united front assumes a 'front', that is, stabilised positions and a centralised leadership. The Left Opposition put forward the conditions for the united front back then as conditions for an *active defence*, with the perspective of passing over to the offensive. Now, the German proletariat has been reduced to a state of *disorderly retreat*, without even rearguard battles. In this situation, voluntary unions of communist and social-democratic workers can and will be realised for various episodic tasks, but the systematic construction of the united front is inevitably thrust back for the indefinite future. There must be no illusions on this score.

About eighteen months ago, we wrote that the key to the situation is in the hands of the German Communist Party. The Stalinist bureaucracy has now let this key fall from its hands. Great events outside of the will of the party will be necessary to give the workers the possibility of drawing up short, of fortifying themselves, of rebuilding their ranks and of passing over to an active defence. We have no way of knowing with precision when this will occur. Perhaps much quicker than the triumphant counter-revolution hopes. But in any case, it is not those who issued the manifesto of the ECCI who will direct the policy of the united front in Germany.

If the central position has been surrendered, one must fortify the approaches; one must prepare bases for a future assault from all sides. In Germany, this preparation implies the critical elucidation of the past, maintaining the spirits of the vanguard fighters, rallying them and organising rearguard combats wherever possible – in anticipation of the moment when the various fighting groups will draw together into a great army. This preparation implies at the same time defending the proletarian positions in the countries closely connected with Germany or located near it: in Austria, Czechoslovakia, Poland, the Baltic countries, Scandinavia, Belgium, Holland, France and Switzerland. Fascist Germany must be surrounded by a powerful circle of proletarian fortifications. Without ceasing for an instant the attempts to halt the disorderly retreat of the German workers, it is necessary to create fortified proletarian positions around the frontiers of Germany for the struggle against fascism.

In the first place comes Austria, which is immediately threatened by the fascist cataclysm. One can say with confidence that if the Austrian proletariat were to seize power now and transform its country into a revolutionary battleground, Austria would become for the revolution of the German proletariat what Piedmont[5] was for the revolution of the Italian bourgeoisie. It cannot be predicted how far the Austrian proletariat, pushed forward by the events but paralysed by the reformist bureaucracy, will advance along this road. The task of communism is to help the events, overcoming Austro-Marxism.[6] The policy of the united front is one of the means. The conditions which the manifesto of the ECCI takes over so tardily from the Left Opposition thus retain all their force.

However, the policy of the united front contains not only advantages but also dangers. It easily gives birth to combinations between leaders behind the back of the masses, to a passive adaptation to the ally, to opportunist vacillations. It is possible to ward off these dangers only if there exist two express guarantees: the maintenance of full freedom of criticism of the ally and the re-establishment of full

5 The Italian bourgeoisie based its struggle for Italian unification, the *risorgimento*, from the region of Piedmont.

6 Austro-Marxism refers to the revisionist ideas put forward by the leaders of the Austrian Social Democracy, attempting to cover their reformism through the use of Marxist phraseology.

freedom of criticism within the ranks of one's own party. To refuse to criticise one's allies leads directly and immediately to capitulation to reformism. The policy of the united front in the absence of party democracy, that is, without control of the apparatus by the party, leaves the leaders a free hand for opportunist experiments, the inevitable complements of adventurist experiments.

How has the ECCI acted in this case? Dozens of times the Left Opposition predicted that under the blows of events, the Stalinists would be forced to repudiate their ultra-leftism and that, placing themselves on the road of the united front they would begin to commit all the opportunist treasons which they attributed to us only yesterday. This time, too, the prediction has been realised literally.

In making a dizzying swing towards the position of the united front the ECCI tramples on the fundamental guarantees which alone can assure a revolutionary content to the policy of the united front. The Stalinists take into consideration and accept the hypocritical-diplomatic demands of the reformists for so-called mutual non-aggression. Breaking with all the traditions of Marxism and of Bolshevism, they recommend to the communist parties, in case a united front is realised, that they "abandon all attacks against the social-democratic organisations during the joint action." That's just what it says. "To abandon all attacks [!] upon the Social Democracy" (what a shameful formula!) means to abandon the freedom of political criticism, that is, a basic function of the revolutionary party.

The capitulation is called for not by practical necessity but by a panicky state of mind. The reformists come and will come to an agreement to the extent that the pressure of events and the pressure of the masses force them to do so. The demand for 'non-aggression' is blackmail, that is, the attempt of the reformist leaders to extort an auxiliary advantage. To submit to blackmail means to build the united front upon rotten foundations and to give the reformist businessmen the possibility of blowing it up under some arbitrary pretext or other.

Criticism in general, all the more so under the conditions of a united front should of course correspond to the real relations and observe the necessary proportions. The absurdities about 'social fascism' must be refuted. That is a concession not to the Social Democracy, but to Marxism. It is not for the treachery of 1918 but for its evil work in 1933 that the ally must be criticised. But criticism, like political life itself, of which criticism is the voice, cannot be halted for an hour. If the communists' disclosures correspond to reality, they serve the purposes of the united front pushing forward the temporary ally and, what is more important giving a revolutionary education to the whole proletariat. To abandon this fundamental duty is the first stage in that shameful and criminal policy which Stalin foisted upon the Chinese communists with regard to the Kuomintang.

Matters stand no better with regard to the second guarantee. Having renounced criticism of the Social Democracy, the Stalinist apparatus does not even think of giving the right of criticism to the members of its own party. The turn itself is accomplished, as usual, by way of a bureaucratic revelation. Not a single national congress, no international congress, nor even a plenum of the ECCI; no preparation in the press of the party, no analysis of the policy of the past. And there is nothing astounding in this. At the very first steps in the discussion in the party, each thinking worker would ask the functionaries: Why have the Bolshevik-Leninists been expelled from all the sections and why are they subjected in the Soviet Union to arrests, to deportation and to firing squads? Is it only because they dig deeper and see further? The Stalinist bureaucracy cannot permit such a conclusion. It is capable of any flip-flops or somersaults, but to present itself honestly before the workers face to face with the Bolshevik-Leninists – that's something it cannot and does not dare to do. Thus in the struggle for self-preservation, the Stalinist apparatus vitiates its new turn by making it suspect beforehand in the view not only of the social-democratic workers but also of the communists.

The publication of the manifesto of the ECCI is accompanied by yet another circumstance, extraneous to the question we are examining, but which throws an exceedingly glaring light on the present position of the Comintern and on the attitude of the leading Stalinist groups towards it. In *Pravda* of 6 March, the manifesto is published not as a direct and open appeal of the ECCI situated in Moscow – as was always the case – but as the translation of a document from *L'Humanité*,[7] transmitted from Paris by the telegraphic agency TASS.

What a stupid and humiliating ruse! After all the successes, after the realisation of the first Five Year Plan, after the 'disappearance of the classes', after the 'entry into socialism', the Stalinist bureaucracy no longer dares to publish in its own name the manifesto of the Executive Committee of the Communist International. That is its real relationship to the Comintern and that is how confident it is on the international arena.

The manifesto is not the sole reply to the initiative of the Second International. Through the intermediary of paper organisations – the revolutionary trade union oppositions (RGOs) of Germany and Poland, the Anti-fascist Alliance and the so-called Italian General Confederation of Labour[8] – the Comintern is convening for the month of April a 'Pan-European Workers' Anti-fascist Congress'. The list of those invited, as is proper, is confused and vast: factories (they say "factories", although by the efforts of Stalin-Lozovsky the communists have been ousted from practically all the factories in the world), local labour organisations, revolutionary, reformist, Catholic, belonging to a party or not, sports, anti-fascist and peasant organisations. And more: "We wish also to invite all those individuals who are really [!] fighting for the cause of the workers." Having compromised for a long time the cause of the masses, the strategists appeal to the 'individuals', to those hermits who have found no place in the ranks of the masses but who, just the same, "are really fighting

7 *L'Humanité* was a daily newspaper founded in 1904. It began as the paper of the French Section of the Second International (SFIO), before becoming the paper of the French Communist Party (PCF).

8 The General Confederation of Labour was an underground Communist trade union organisation and a forerunner of today's CGIL.

for the cause of the workers". Barbusse and General Schoenaich[9] will once more be mobilised to save Europe from Hitler.

Here we have a ready-made libretto for one of those charlatan presentations with which the Stalinists are in the habit of masking their impotence. What has the Amsterdam bloc of centrists and the pacifists accomplished in the struggle against the aggression of the Japanese bandits in China? Nothing. Out of respect for Stalinist 'neutrality', the pacifists have not even issued a manifesto of protest. Now a new edition of the Amsterdam Congress is being prepared, not against war but against fascism. What will the anti-fascist bloc of vacated 'factories' and impotent 'individuals' do? Nothing. It will issue a hollow manifesto, if, as a matter of fact things go as far this time as the holding of a congress.

The propensity for individuals has two faces: opportunistic and adventurist. The Russian Socialist-Revolutionaries in the old days extended the right hand to the liberals and held a bomb in the left hand. The experience of the last ten years attests that after every great defeat provoked or at least aggravated by the policy of the Comintern, the Stalinist bureaucracy invariably sought to refurbish its reputation with the aid of some grandiose adventure or other (Estonia, Bulgaria, Canton).[10] Doesn't this danger exist now too? In any case, we deem it necessary to raise a voice of warning. Adventures that aim to replace the action of the paralysed masses disorganise the masses still more and aggravate the catastrophe.

The conditions of the present world situation, as well as the conditions of each country in particular, are just as deadly for the Social Democracy as they are favourable for the revolutionary party. But the Stalinist bureaucracy has succeeded in converting the crisis of capitalism and of reformism into a crisis of communism.

---

9 Major General Paul von Schoenaich was a cavalry commander in the First World War, but became a pacifist after the war. He signed a manifesto against compulsory military service in 1926 with Albert Einstein and Bertrand Russell, and was the president of the German Peace Society 1929-33.

10 This is a reference to the attempted insurrections in Estonia in 1924, Bulgaria in 1923 and Guangzhou in 1927, launched under pressure from the Comintern, despite conditions being unfavourable.

That is the sum total of ten years of uncontrolled command by the epigones.

Hypocrites will be found to say: the Opposition is criticizing a party which has fallen into the hands of the executioner. Blackguards will add: the Opposition is helping the executioner. By combining a specious sentimentalism with venomous falsehood, the Stalinists will endeavour to hide the Central Committee behind the apparatus, the apparatus behind the party, to eliminate the question of responsibility for the catastrophe, for the false strategy, for the disastrous regime, for the criminal leadership: *that* means helping the executioners of today and tomorrow.

The policy of the Stalinist bureaucracy in China was no less disastrous than it is now in Germany. But there, the affair took place behind the back of the world proletariat, under conditions which were incomprehensible to it. The critical voice of the Opposition hardly reached beyond the Soviet Union to the workers of the other countries. The Stalinist apparatus went practically unpunished for the Chinese experience. In Germany, it is entirely different. All the stages of the drama developed before the world proletariat. At each stage, the Opposition raised its voice. The whole course of development was announced in advance. The Stalinist bureaucracy slandered the Opposition, imputed to it ideas and plans alien to it; expelled all those who dared to speak of the united front; helped the social-democratic bureaucracy demolish the united local defence committees; cut the workers off from the slightest possibility of setting out on the road of the mass struggle; disorganised the vanguard; paralysed the proletariat. Thus, by opposing a united front of defence with the Social Democracy, the Stalinists found themselves with the latter in a united front of panic and of capitulation.

And now, already standing just short of ruin, the leadership of the Comintern fears light and criticism more than anything else. Let the world revolution perish, but long live vain prestige! The bankrupts sow confusion, bury the evidence and cover their tracks. The fact that the Communist Party of Germany lost 'only' 1.2

million votes at the first blow – with a general rise in the number of voters of 3 to 4 million – is proclaimed by *Pravda* as an "enormous political victory". In the same way, in 1924, Stalin proclaimed as an 'enormous victory' the fact that the workers in Germany, who were retreating without battle, had still given the Communist Party 3.6 million votes. If the proletariat, deceived and disarmed by both apparatuses, has this time given the Communist Party almost 5 million votes, this signifies only that they would have given it twice or three times that number had they trusted its leadership. They would have raised it to power had it shown itself capable of taking and holding power. But it gave the proletariat nothing, save confusion, zigzags, defeats and calamities.

Yes, 5 million communists still succeeded in reaching the ballot box, one by one. But in the factories and on the streets, there are none. They are disconcerted, dispersed, demoralised. They have been broken away from independence under the yoke of the apparatus. The bureaucratic terror of Stalinism paralysed their willpower before the turn came for the terror of the fascist bands.

It must be said clearly, plainly, openly: Stalinism in Germany has had its 4 August.[11] Henceforth, the advanced workers will only speak of the period of the domination of the Stalinist bureaucracy with a burning sense of shame, with words of hatred and curses. The official German Communist Party is doomed. From now on it will only decompose, crumble and melt into the void. German Communism can be reborn only on a new basis and with a new leadership.

The law of uneven development acts also upon the fate of Stalinism. In the various countries, it finds itself in different stages of decomposition. To what degree the tragic experience of Germany will serve as a stimulus to the rebirth of the other sections of the Comintern, the future will show. In Germany in any case the swan song of the Stalinist bureaucracy has been sung. The German proletariat will rise again, Stalinism – never. Under the terrible

11 On 4 August 1914, the SPD voted in the Reichstag for the war credits, thereby backing the German bourgeoisie and monarchy in the First World War. This triggered the collapse of the Second International.

blows of the enemy, the advanced German workers will have to build up a new party. The Bolshevik-Leninists will give all their forces to this work.

# *What is National Socialism?*

Written 10 June 1933

Naive minds think that the office of kingship lodges in the king himself, in his ermine cloak and his crown, in his flesh and bones. As a matter of fact, the office of kingship is an interrelation between people. The king is king only because the interests and prejudices of millions of people are refracted through his person. When the flood of development sweeps away these interrelations, then the king appears to be only a washed-out man with a flabby lower lip. He who was once called Alfonso XIII[1] could discourse upon this from fresh impressions.

The leader by will of the people differs from the leader by will of God in that the former is compelled to clear the road for himself or, at any rate, to assist the conjuncture of events in discovering him. Nevertheless, the leader is always a relation between people, the individual supply to meet the collective demand. The controversy over Hitler's personality becomes the sharper the more the secret of his success is sought in himself. In the meantime, another political figure would be difficult to find that is in the same measure the focus of anonymous historic forces. Not every exasperated petty bourgeois could have become Hitler, but a particle of Hitler is lodged in every exasperated petty bourgeois.

1 King Alfonso XIII was the King of Spain, until the Second Spanish Republic was proclaimed in 1931.

The rapid growth of German capitalism prior to the First World War by no means signified a simple destruction of the middle classes. Although it ruined some layers of the petty bourgeoisie, it created others anew: around the factories – artisans and shopkeepers; within the factories – technicians and executives. But while preserving themselves and even growing numerically – the old and the new petty bourgeoisie compose a little less than one-half of the German nation – the middle classes have lost the last shadow of independence. They live on the periphery of large-scale industry and the banking system, and they live off the crumbs from the table of the monopolies and cartels and off the spiritual alms of their theorists and professional politicians.

The defeat in 1918 raised a wall in the path of German imperialism. External dynamics changed to internal. The war passed over into revolution. Social Democracy, which aided the Hohenzollerns in bringing the war to its tragic conclusion, did not permit the proletariat to bring the revolution to its conclusion. The Weimar democracy spent fourteen years finding interminable excuses for its own existence. The Communist Party called the workers to a new revolution but proved incapable of leading it. The German proletariat passed through the rise and collapse of war, revolution, parliamentarism and pseudo-Bolshevism. At the time when the old parties of the bourgeoisie had drained themselves to the dregs, the dynamic power of the working class also found itself sapped.

The postwar chaos hit the artisans, the peddlers and the civil employees no less cruelly than the workers. The economic crisis in agriculture was ruining the peasantry. The decay of the middle strata did not mean that they were made into proletarians, inasmuch as the proletariat itself was casting out a gigantic army of chronically unemployed. The pauperisation of the petty bourgeoisie, barely covered by ties and socks of artificial silk, eroded all official creeds and first of all the doctrine of democratic parliamentarism.

The multiplicity of parties, the icy fever of elections, the interminable changes of ministries aggravated the social crisis by creating a kaleidoscope of barren political combinations. In the atmosphere brought to white heat by war, defeat, reparations, inflation, occupation of the Ruhr, crisis, need and despair – the petty bourgeoisie rose up against all the old parties that had bamboozled it. The sharp grievances of small proprietors never out of bankruptcy, of their university sons without posts and clients, of their daughters without dowries and suitors, demanded order and an iron hand.

The banner of National Socialism was raised by upstarts from the lower and middle commanding ranks of the old army. Decorated with medals for distinguished service, commissioned and non-commissioned officers could not believe that their heroism and sufferings for the fatherland had not only come to naught, but also gave them no special claims to gratitude. Hence their hatred of the revolution and the proletariat. At the same time, they did not want to reconcile themselves to being sent by the bankers, industrialists and ministers back to the modest posts of bookkeepers, engineers, postal clerks and schoolteachers. Hence their 'socialism'. At the Yser and under Verdun they had learned to risk themselves and others, and to speak the language of command, which powerfully overawed the petty bourgeois behind the lines. Thus these people became leaders.

At the start of his political career, Hitler stood out only because of his big temperament, a voice much louder than others and an intellectual mediocrity much more self-assured. He did not bring into the movement any ready-made programme, if one disregards the insulted soldier's thirst for vengeance. Hitler began with grievances and complaints about the Versailles terms, the high cost of living, the lack of respect for a meritorious non-commissioned officer and the plots of bankers and journalists of the Mosaic persuasion.[2] There were in the country plenty of ruined and drowning people with scars and fresh bruises. They all wanted to thump with their fists on the table. This Hitler could do better than others. True, he knew not how to cure the evil. But his harangues resounded, now like commands and now like prayers addressed to inexorable fate. Doomed classes, like those fatally ill, never tire of making variations on their plaints

2 I.e. Jewish people, in reference to Moses.

nor of listening to consolations. Hitler's speeches were all attuned to this pitch. Sentimental formlessness, absence of disciplined thought, ignorance along with gaudy erudition – all these minuses turned into pluses. They supplied him with the possibility of uniting all types of dissatisfaction in the beggar's bowl of National Socialism, and of leading the mass in the direction in which it pushed him. In the mind of the agitator was preserved, from among his early improvisations, whatever had met with approbation. His political thoughts were the fruits of oratorical acoustics. That is how the selection of slogans went on. That is how the programme was consolidated. That is how the 'leader' took shape out of the raw material.

Mussolini from the very beginning reacted more consciously to social materials than Hitler, to whom the police mysticism of a Metternich[3] is much closer than the political algebra of Machiavelli.[4] Mussolini is mentally bolder and more cynical. It may be said that the Roman atheist only utilises religion as he does the police and the courts, while his Berlin colleague really believes in the infallibility of the Church of Rome. During the time when the future Italian dictator considered Marx as 'our common immortal teacher', he defended not unskillfully the theory which sees in the life of contemporary society first of all the reciprocal action of two classes, the bourgeoisie and the proletariat. True, Mussolini wrote in 1914, there lie between them very numerous intermediate layers which seemingly form:

> ... a joining web of the human collective [... but] during periods of crisis, the intermediate classes gravitate, depending upon their interests and ideas, to one or the other of the basic classes.

3 Klemens von Metternich was Foreign Minister and later Chancellor of the Austrian Empire. He utilised spy networks, censorship and other means to suppress the democratic aspirations of the peoples of the Empire. He was ousted and forced into exile in Britain during the Revolution of 1848.

4 Niccolò Machiavelli was a Florentine diplomat and historian, who pioneered a more scientific approach to history and political theory in the early sixteenth century. Highly influential, particularly amongst republican and later materialist philosophers, his work was banned by the Catholic Church, allegedly for its promotion of evil and deceit. As a consequence, a cynical and scheming approach to politics is referred to as 'Machiavellian', even today.

A very important generalisation! Just as scientific medicine equips one with the possibility not only of curing the sick but of sending the healthy to meet their forefathers by the shortest route, so the scientific analysis of class relations, predestined by its creator for the mobilisation of the proletariat, enabled Mussolini, after he had jumped into the opposing camp, to mobilise the middle classes against the proletariat. Hitler accomplished the same feat in translating the methodology of fascism into the language of German mysticism.

The bonfires which burn the impious literature of Marxism light up brilliantly the class nature of National Socialism. While the Nazis acted as a party and not as a state power, they did not quite find an approach to the working class. On the other side, the big bourgeoisie, even those who supported Hitler with money, did not consider his party theirs. The national 'renaissance' leaned wholly upon the middle classes, the most backward part of the nation, the heavy ballast of history. Political art consisted in fusing the petty bourgeoisie into oneness through its common hostility to the proletariat. What must be done in order to improve things? First of all, throttle those who are underneath. Impotent before big capital, the petty bourgeoisie hopes in the future to regain its social dignity through the ruin of the workers.

The Nazis call their overturn by the usurped title of revolution. As a matter of fact, in Germany as well as in Italy, fascism leaves the social system untouched. Taken by itself, Hitler's overturn has no right even to the name counter-revolution. But it cannot be viewed as an isolated event; it is the conclusion of a cycle of shocks which began in Germany in 1918. The November Revolution, which gave the power to the workers' and peasants' soviets, was proletarian in its fundamental tendencies. But the party that stood at the head of the proletariat returned the power to the bourgeoisie. In this sense the Social Democracy opened the era of counter-revolution before the revolution could bring its work to completion. However, so long as the bourgeoisie depended upon the Social Democracy, and consequently upon the workers, the regime retained elements of compromise. All the same, the international and the internal situation of German capitalism left no more room for concessions. As Social Democracy saved the bourgeoisie from the proletarian revolution, fascism came in its turn to liberate the bourgeoisie from the Social Democracy. Hitler's coup is only the final link in the chain of counter-revolutionary shifts.

The petty bourgeois is hostile to the idea of development, for development goes immutably against him; progress has brought him nothing except irredeemable debts. National Socialism rejects not only Marxism but Darwinism. The Nazis curse materialism because the victories of technology over nature have signified the triumph of large capital over small. The leaders of the movement are liquidating 'intellectualism' because they themselves possess second- and third-rate intellects, and above all because their historic role does not permit them to pursue a single thought to its conclusion. The petty bourgeois needs a higher authority, which stands above matter and above history, and which is safeguarded from competition, inflation, crisis and the auction block. To evolution, materialist thought and rationalism – of the twentieth, nineteenth and eighteenth centuries – is counterposed in his mind national idealism as the source of heroic inspiration. Hitler's nation is the mythological shadow of the petty bourgeoisie itself, a pathetic delirium of a thousand-year Reich.

In order to raise it above history, the nation is given the support of the race. History is viewed as the emanation of the race. The qualities of the race are construed without relation to changing social conditions. Rejecting 'economic thought' as base, National Socialism descends a stage lower: from economic materialism it appeals to zoologic materialism.

The theory of race, specially created, it seems, for some pretentious self-educated individual seeking a universal key to all the secrets of life, appears particularly melancholy in the light of the history of ideas. In order to create the religion of pure German blood, Hitler was obliged to borrow at second hand the ideas of racism from a

Frenchman, Count Gobineau,[5] a diplomat and a literary dilettante. Hitler found the political methodology ready-made in Italy, where Mussolini had borrowed largely from the Marxist theory of the class struggle. Marxism itself is the fruit of union among German philosophy, French history and British economics. To investigate retrospectively the genealogy of ideas, even those most reactionary and muddleheaded, is to leave not a trace of racism standing.

The immense poverty of National Socialist philosophy did not, of course, hinder the academic sciences from entering Hitler's wake with all sails unfurled, once his victory was sufficiently plain. For the majority of the professorial rabble, the years of the Weimar regime were periods of riot and alarm. Historians, economists, jurists and philosophers were lost in guesswork as to which of the contending criteria of truth was right – that is, which of the camps would turn out in the end the master of the situation. The fascist dictatorship eliminates the doubts of the Fausts and the vacillations of the Hamlets of the university rostrums. Coming out of the twilight of parliamentary relativity, knowledge once again enters into the kingdom of absolutes. Einstein has been obliged to pitch his tent outside the boundaries of Germany.

On the plane of politics, racism is a vapid and bombastic variety of chauvinism in alliance with phrenology. As the ruined nobility sought solace in the gentility of its blood, so the pauperised petty bourgeoisie befuddles itself with fairy tales concerning the special superiorities of its race. Worthy of attention is the fact that the leaders of National Socialism are not native Germans but interlopers from Austria, like Hitler himself, from the former Baltic provinces of the tsar's empire, like Rosenberg;[6] and from colonial countries, like Hess,[7] who is Hitler's present alternate for the party leadership. A barbarous din of nationalisms on the frontiers of civilisation was required in order to

---

5 Arthur de Gobineau was a French aristocrat who argued that the Germanic 'Aryan' race was superior to others and was the basis of European civilisation from ancient Greece to his day.

6 Alfred Rosenberg was a leading Nazi theoretician, born in present-day Estonia, then part of the Russian Empire.

7 Rudolf Hess was Deputy Führer of the Nazi Party from 1933-41.

instil into its 'leaders' those ideas which later found response in the hearts of the most barbarous classes in Germany.

'Personality and class – liberalism and Marxism – are evil. The nation – is good.' But at the threshold of private property this philosophy is turned inside out. Salvation lies only in personal private property. The idea of national property is the spawn of Bolshevism. Deifying the nation, the petty bourgeois does not want to give it anything. On the contrary, he expects the nation to endow him with property and to safeguard him from the worker and the process-server. Unfortunately, the Third Reich will bestow nothing upon the petty bourgeois except new taxes.

In the sphere of modern economy, international in its ties and anonymous in its methods, the principle of race seems unearthed from a medieval graveyard. The Nazis set out with concessions beforehand; the purity of race, which must be certified in the kingdom of the spirit by a passport, must be demonstrated in the sphere of economy chiefly by efficiency. Under contemporary conditions this means competitive capacity. Through the back door, racism returns to economic liberalism, freed from political liberties.

Nationalism in economy comes down in practice to impotent though savage outbursts of antisemitism. The Nazis abstract the usurious or banking capital from the modern economic system because it is of the spirit of evil; and, as is well known, it is precisely in this sphere that the Jewish bourgeoisie occupies an important position. Bowing down before capitalism as a whole, the petty bourgeois declares war against the evil spirit of gain in the guise of the Polish Jew in a long-skirted caftan and usually without a cent in his pocket. The pogrom becomes the supreme evidence of racial superiority.

The programme with which National Socialism came to power reminds one very much – alas – of a Jewish department store in an obscure province. What won't you find here – cheap in price and in quality still lower! Recollections of the 'happy' days of free competition, and hazy evocations of the stability of class society; hopes for the regeneration of the colonial empire, and dreams of a shut-in economy; phrases about a return from Roman law back to the Germanic, and pleas for an American moratorium; an envious hostility to inequality in the person of a proprietor in an automobile, and animal fear of equality in the person of a worker in a cap and without a collar; the frenzy of nationalism, and the fear of world creditors… all the refuse of international political thought has gone to fill up the spiritual treasury of the new Germanic Messianism.

Fascism has opened up the depths of society for politics. Today, not only in peasant homes but also in city skyscrapers, there lives alongside of the twentieth century the tenth or the thirteenth. A hundred million people use electricity and still believe in the magic power of signs and exorcisms. The Pope of Rome broadcasts over the radio about the miraculous transformation of water into wine. Movie stars go to mediums. Aviators who pilot miraculous mechanisms created by man's genius wear amulets on their sweaters. What inexhaustible reserves they possess of darkness, ignorance and savagery! Despair has raised them to their feet, fascism has given them a banner. Everything that should have been eliminated from the national organism in the form of cultural excrement in the course of the normal development of society has now come gushing out from the throat; capitalist society is puking up the undigested barbarism. Such is the physiology of National Socialism.

German fascism, like Italian fascism, raised itself to power on the backs of the petty bourgeoisie, which it turned into a battering ram against the organisations of the working class and the institutions of democracy. But fascism in power is least of all the rule of the petty bourgeoisie. On the contrary, it is the most ruthless dictatorship of monopoly capital. Mussolini is right: the middle classes are incapable of independent policies. During periods of great crisis they are called upon to reduce to absurdity the policies of one of the two basic classes. Fascism succeeded in putting them at the service of capital. Such slogans as state control of trusts and the elimination of unearned income were thrown overboard immediately upon the assumption of power. Instead, the particularism of German 'lands' leaning upon the peculiarities of the petty bourgeoisie gave way to capitalist-police centralism. Every success of the internal and foreign policies of National Socialism will inevitably mean the further crushing of small capital by large.

The programme of petty-bourgeois illusions is not discarded; it is simply torn away from reality, and dissolved in ritualistic acts. The unification of all classes reduces itself to semi-symbolic compulsory labour and to the confiscation of the labour holiday of May Day for the 'benefit of the people'. The preservation of the Gothic script as opposed to the Latin is a symbolic revenge for the yoke of the world market. The dependence upon the international bankers, Jews among their number, is not eased an iota, wherefore it is forbidden to slaughter animals according to the Talmudic ritual. If the road to heaven is paved with good intentions, then the avenues of the Third Reich are paved with symbols.

Reducing the programme of petty-bourgeois illusions to a naked bureaucratic masquerade, National Socialism raises itself over the nation as the worst form of imperialism. Absolutely vain are hopes that Hitler's government will fail today or tomorrow, a victim of its internal inconsistency. The Nazis required the programme in order to assume power; but power serves Hitler not at all for the purpose of fulfilling the programme. His tasks are assigned him by monopoly capital. The compulsory concentration of all forces and resources of the people in the interests of imperialism – the true historic mission of the fascist dictatorship – means preparation for war; and this task, in its turn, brooks no internal resistance and leads to a further mechanical concentration of power. Fascism cannot be reformed or retired from service. It can only be overthrown. The political orbit of the regime leans upon the alternative, war or revolution.

* * *

## *Postscript*

The first anniversary of the Nazi dictatorship is approaching. All the tendencies of the regime have had time to take on a clear and distinct character. The 'socialist' revolution pictured by the petty-bourgeois masses as a necessary supplement to the national revolution is officially liquidated and condemned. The brotherhood of classes found its culmination in the fact that on a day especially appointed by the government, the haves renounced the *hors d'oeuvre* and dessert in favour of the have-nots. The struggle against unemployment is reduced to the cutting of semi-starvation doles in two. The rest is the task of uniformed statistics. 'Planned' autarky is simply a new stage of economic disintegration.

The more impotent the police regime of the Nazi is in the field of national economy, the more it is forced to transfer its efforts to the field of foreign policy. This corresponds fully to the inner dynamics of German capitalism, aggressive through and through. The sudden turn of the Nazi leaders to peaceful declarations could deceive only utter simpletons. What other method remains at Hitler's disposal to transfer the responsibility for internal distresses to external enemies and to accumulate under the press of the dictatorship the explosive force of nationalism? This part of the programme, outlined openly even prior to the Nazi's assumption of power, is now being fulfilled with iron logic before the eyes of the world. The date of the new European catastrophe will be determined by the time necessary for the arming of Germany. It is not a question of months, but neither is it a question of decades. It will be but a few years before Europe is again plunged into a war, unless Hitler is forestalled in time by the inner forces of Germany.

# *German Bonapartism*

Written 30 October 1932

The elections to the Reichstag put the 'presidential' government to a new critical test. It is useful, therefore, to remind ourselves of its social and political nature. It is precisely through the analysis of such concrete and, at first glance, 'sudden' political phenomena as the government of Papen-Schleicher, that the Marxist method reveals its invaluable advantages.

At one time we defined the 'presidential' government as a species of Bonapartism. It would be incorrect to see in this definition the chance outcome of a desire to find a familiar name for an unfamiliar phenomenon. The decline of capitalist society places Bonapartism – side by side with fascism and coupled with it – again on the order of the day. Previously we have characterized the government of Brüning as a Bonapartist one. Then, in retrospect, we narrowed the definition to a half, or pre-Bonapartist one.

What did other communists and in general 'left' groups say in this connection? To await an attempt at a scientific definition of a new political phenomenon from the present leadership of the Comintern would of course be naive, not to say foolish. The Stalinists simply place Papen in the fascist camp. If Wels and Hitler are 'twins', then such a trifle as Papen is altogether not worth breaking one's head about. This is the same political literature that Marx called 'vulgarian' and which he taught us to despise. In reality fascism represents one of the two main camps of civil war. Stretching his arm to power, Hitler first of all demanded the relinquishing of the street to him for seventy-two hours. Hindenburg refused this. The task of Papen-Schleicher: to avoid civil war by amicably disciplining the National Socialists and chaining the proletariat to police fetters. The very possibility of such a regime is determined by the relative weakness of the proletariat

The SAP rids itself of the question of the Papen government as well as of other questions by means of general phrases. The Brandlerites preserved silence on our definition as long as the matter concerned Brüning, that is, the incubation period of Bonapartism. When, however, the Marxist characterisation of Bonapartism confirmed itself fully in the theory and practice of the presidential government the Brandlerites came out with their criticism: the wise owl of Thalheimer takes flight in the late hours of the night.

The Stuttgart *Arbeitertribüne* teaches us that Bonapartism, raising the military-police apparatus over the bourgeoisie in order to defend its class domination against its own political parties, must be supported by the peasantry and must use methods of Social Democracy. Papen is not supported by the peasantry and does not introduce a pseudo-radical program. Therefore, our attempt to define the government of Papen as Bonapartism "does not fit at all." This is severe but superficial.

How do the Brandlerites themselves define the government of Papen? In the same issue of the *Arbeitertribüne* there are very timely announcements of the lecture of Brandler on the subject: *Junker-monarchical, fascist or proletarian dictatorship?* In this triad the regime of Papen is presented as a Junker-monarchist dictatorship. This is most worthy of the *Vorwärts* and of vulgar democrats in general. That titled German Bonapartists make some sort of little private presents to the Junkers is obvious. That these gentlemen are inclined to a monarchistic turn of mind is also known. But it is purest liberal nonsense that the essence of the presidential regime is Junker monarchism.

Such terms as *liberalism, Bonapartism, fascism* have the character of generalisations. Historical phenomena never repeat themselves completely. It would not have been difficult to prove that even the government of Napoleon III,[1] compared with the regime of Napoleon I,[2] was not 'Bonapartist' – not only because Napoleon himself was a doubtful Bonaparte by blood, but also because his relations to the classes, especially to the peasantry and to the lumpenproletariat were not at all the same as those of Napoleon I. Moreover, classical Bonapartism grew out of the epoch of gigantic war victories, which the Second Empire did not know at all. But if we should look for the repetition of all the traits of Bonapartism, we will find that Bonapartism is a one-time, unique occurrence, i.e. that Bonapartism in general does not exist, but that there once was a general named Bonaparte born in Corsica. The case is no different with liberalism and with all other generalised terms of history. When one speaks by analogy of Bonapartism, it is necessary to state precisely which of its traits found their fullest expression under present historical conditions.

Present-day German Bonapartism has a very complex and, so to speak, combined character. The government of Papen would have been impossible without fascism. But fascism is not in power. And the government of Papen is not fascism. On the other hand, the government of Papen, at any rate in its present form, would have been impossible without Hindenburg who, in spite of the final prostration of Germany in the war, stands for the great victories of Germany and symbolizes the army in the memory of the popular masses. The second election of Hindenburg had all the characteristics of a *plebiscite*. Many millions of workers, petty bourgeois and peasants (Social Democracy and Centre) voted for Hindenburg. They did

1 Charles-Louis Napoleon Bonaparte was the nephew of Napoleon I. He took power in 1848, before becoming the second Emperor of the French. He ruled until 1870, when he was deposed in the revolutionary crisis following the defeat in the Franco-Prussian war.

2 Napoleon Bonaparte was a French general who came to power after the great French Revolution of 1789-99, before being ousted from power in 1815 by the victors of the Napoleonic Wars.

not see in him any one political program. They wanted first of all to avoid civil war, and raised Hindenburg on their shoulders as a super-arbiter, as an arbitration judge of the nation. But precisely this is the most important function of Bonapartism: raising itself over the two struggling camps in order to preserve property and order. It suppresses civil war, or precedes it or does not allow it to rekindle. Speaking of Papen, we cannot forget Hindenburg, on whom rests the sanction of the Social Democracy. The combined character of German Bonapartism expressed itself in the fact that the demagogic work of catching the masses for Hindenburg was performed by two big, independent parties: the Social Democracy and National Socialism. If they are both astonished at the results of their work, that does not change the matter one whit.

The Social Democracy asserts that fascism is the product of communism. This is correct insofar as there would have been no necessity at all for fascism without the sharpening of the class struggle, without the revolutionary proletariat without the crisis of capitalist society. The flunkeyish theory of Wels-Hilferding-Otto Bauer has no other meaning. Yes, fascism is a reaction of bourgeois society to the threat of proletarian revolution. But precisely because this threat is not an imminent one today, the ruling classes make an attempt to get along without a civil war through the medium of a Bonapartist dictatorship.

Objecting to our characterisation of the government of Hindenburg-Papen-Schleicher, the Brandlerites refer to Marx and express thereby an ironic hope that his authority may also have weight with us. It is difficult to deceive oneself more pathetically. The fact is that Marx and Engels wrote not only of the Bonapartism of the two Bonapartes, but also of other species. Beginning, it seems, with the year 1864, they more than once likened the 'national' regime of Bismarck[3] to French Bonapartism. And this in spite of the fact that Bismarck was not a

3 Otto von Bismarck, the 'Iron Chancellor', was a German aristocrat and Minister-President of Prussia under Kaiser Wilhelm I from 1862 who oversaw German unification in a series of wars between 1863-71. He was removed by Wilhelm II in 1890, after repression failed to stem the growth of German Social Democracy.

pseudo-radical demagogue and, so far as we know, was not supported by the peasantry. The Iron Chancellor was not raised to power as the result of a plebiscite, but was duly appointed by his legitimate and hereditary king. And nevertheless Marx and Engels are right. Bismarck made use in a Bonapartist fashion of the antagonism between the propertied classes and the rising proletariat overcoming in this way the antagonism within the two propertied classes, between the Junkerdom and the bourgeoisie and raised a military-police apparatus over the nation. The policy of Bismarck is that very tradition to which the 'theoreticians' of present German Bonapartism refer. True, Bismarck solved in his fashion the problem of German unity, of the external greatness of Germany. Papen however so far only promises to obtain for Germany 'equality' on the international arena. Not a small difference! But we were not trying to prove that the Bonapartism of Papen is of the same calibre as the Bonapartism of Bismarck. Napoleon III was also only a parody of his pretended uncle.

The reference to Marx, as we have seen, has an obviously imprudent character. That Thalheimer does not understand the dialectics of Marxism we suspected long ago. But we must admit we thought that at least he knew the texts of Marx and Engels. We take this opportunity to correct our mistake.

Our characterisation of the presidential government rejected by the Brandlerites, received a very brilliant confirmation from a completely unexpected and in its way highly 'authoritative' source. With regard to the dissolution of the 'five-day' Reichstag, *DAZ* (*Deutsche Allgemeine Zeitung*, organ of heavy industry) quoted in a long article on 28 August the work of Marx, *The Eighteenth Brumaire of Louis Bonaparte* – for what purpose? No more and no less than to support the historical and political right of the president to put his boot on the neck of popular representation. The organ of heavy industry risked at a difficult moment drinking from the poisoned wells of Marxism. With a remarkable adroitness the paper takes from the immortal pamphlet a long quotation explaining how and why the French president as the incarnation of the 'nation' obtained a preponderance over the split-up parliament. The same article in the *DAZ* reminds us most opportunely of how, in the spring of 1890, Bismarck developed a plan for a most suitable governmental change. Napoleon III and Bismarck as forerunners of presidential government are called by their right name by the Berlin newspaper, which – in August at least – played the role of an official organ.

To quote *The Eighteenth Brumaire of Louis Bonaparte* in reference to the '20 July of Papen' is of course very risky, since Marx characterised the regime of Napoleon in the most acid terms as the regime of adventurists, crooks and pimps. As a matter of fact, the *DAZ* could be liable to punishment for a malicious slander of the government. But if we should leave aside this incidental inconvenience, there remains nevertheless the indubitable fact that historic instinct brought the *DAZ* to the proper place. Unfortunately one cannot say the same of the theoretical wisdom of Thalheimer.

The Bonapartism of the era of the decline of capitalism differs utterly from the Bonapartism of the era of the ascension of bourgeois society. German Bonapartism is not supported directly by the petty bourgeoisie of the country and village, and this is not accidental. Precisely therefore, we wrote at one time of the weakness of the government of Papen, which holds on only by the neutralisation of two camps: the proletariat and the fascists.

But behind Papen stand the great landowners, finance capitalists, generals – so rejoin other 'Marxists'. Do not the propertied classes in themselves represent a great force? This argument proves once more that it is much easier to understand class relations in their general sociological outline than in a concrete historical form. Yes, immediately behind Papen stand the propertied heights and they only: precisely therein is contained the cause of his weakness.

Under the conditions of present-day capitalism, a government which would not be the agency of finance capital is in general impossible. But of all possible agencies, the government of Papen is the least stable one. If the ruling classes could rule directly, they would have no need either of parliamentarism, or of Social Democracy, or of fascism. The government of Papen exposes finance capital too clearly, leaving it without even the sacred fig-leaf ordered by the Prussian Commissioner Bracht.[4] Just because the extra-party 'national' government is in fact able to speak only in the name of the social heights, capital is ever more careful not to identify itself with the government of Papen. The *DAZ* wants to find support for the presidential government in the National Socialist masses, and in the language of ultimatums demands of Papen a bloc with Hitler, which means capitulation to him.

In evaluating the 'strength' of the presidential government we must not forget the fact that if finance capital stands behind Papen, this does not at all mean that it falls together with him. Finance capital has innumerably more possibilities than Hindenburg-Papen-Schleicher. In case of the sharpening of contradictions there remains the reserve of pure fascism. In case of the softening of contradictions, they will manoeuvre until the time when the proletariat puts its knee on their chests. For how long Papen will manoeuvre, the near future will show.

These lines will appear in the press when the new elections to the Reichstag shall already have gone by. The Bonapartist nature of the 'anti-French' government of Papen will inevitably reveal itself with a new force, but also its weakness. We will take this up again in due time.

4 Franz Bracht was a Centre Party politician, appointed Deputy Commissioner of the Interior of Prussia after the 20 July coup. In that position he decreed a shoot-to-kill policy on Berlin tram strikers, and that women's gowns must 'decently' cover their rear.

# *Part 2: France*

## *Writings by Leon Trotsky*

*July 1934 – July 1936*

# *Bonapartism and Fascism*

Written 15 July 1934

The vast practical importance of a correct theoretical orientation is most strikingly manifested in a period of acute social conflict or rapid political shifts, of abrupt changes in the situation. In such periods, political *conceptions* and *generalisations* are rapidly used up, and require either a complete replacement (which is easier) or their concretisation, precision or partial rectification (which is harder). It is in just such periods that all sorts of *transitional, intermediate* situations and combinations arise, as a matter of necessity, which upset the customary patterns and doubly require a sustained theoretical attention. In a word, if in the pacific and 'organic' period (before the war) one could still live on the revenue from a few ready-made abstractions, in our time each new event forcefully brings home the most important law of the dialectic: *The truth is always concrete.*

The Stalinist theory of fascism indubitably represents one of the most tragic examples of the injurious practical consequences that can follow from the substitution of the dialectical analysis of reality, in its every concrete phase, in all its transitional stages, that is, in its gradual changes as well as in its revolutionary (or counter-revolutionary) leaps, by abstract categories formulated upon the basis of a partial and insufficient historical experience (or a narrow and insufficient view of the whole). The Stalinists adopted the idea that in the contemporary period, finance capital cannot accommodate itself to parliamentary democracy and is obliged to resort to fascism. From this idea, absolutely correct within certain limits, they draw in a purely deductive, formally logical manner the same conclusions for all the countries and for all stages of development. To them, Primo de Rivera, Mussolini, Chiang Kai-shek, Masaryk,[1] Brüning, Dollfuss,[2] Piłsudski, the Serbian King Alexander,[3] Severing, MacDonald,[4] etc., were the representatives of fascism. In doing this, they forgot:

a. That in the past, too, capitalism never accommodated itself to 'pure' democracy, now supplementing it with a regime of open repression, now substituting one for it;
b. That 'pure' finance capitalism nowhere exists;
c. That even while occupying a dominant position, finance capital does not act within a void and is obliged to reckon with the other strata of the bourgeoisie and with the resistance of the oppressed classes;
d. That, finally, between parliamentary democracy and the fascist regime a series of transitional forms, one after another, inevitably interposes itself, now 'peaceably', now by civil war. And each one of these transitional forms, if we want to go forward and not be flung to the rear, demands a correct theoretical appraisal and a corresponding policy of the proletariat.

---

1 Tomáš Masaryk was a bourgeois liberal and first Prime Minister of Czechoslovakia.

2 Engelbert Dollfuss was the right-wing Chancellor of Austria from 1932-34. He was killed in a failed coup attempt by pro-German Nazis in July 1934.

3 King Alexander I Karađorđević was the Serbian king of the Kingdom of Serbs, Croats and Slovenes. He renamed this state the Kingdom of Yugoslavia and acted as an absolute monarch in 1929, dissolving the constitution and National Assembly.

4 James Ramsay MacDonald was a Scottish Labour politician and member of the ILP. A pacifist during the war, he became the first Labour Prime Minister in 1924. During his second term as Prime Minister (1929-35), he entered into a coalition with the Conservative Party to vote through austerity measures, splitting the Labour Party parliamentary group in the process.

On the basis of the German experience, the Bolshevik-Leninists recorded for the first time the transitional governmental form (even though it could and should already have been established on the basis of Italy) which we called Bonapartism (the Brüning, Papen, Schleicher governments). In a more precise and more developed form, we subsequently observed the Bonapartist regime in Austria. The determinism of this transitional form has become patent, naturally not in the fatalistic but in the dialectical sense, that is, for the countries and periods where fascism, with growing success, without encountering a victorious resistance of the proletariat, attacked the positions of parliamentary democracy in order thereupon to strangle the proletariat.

During the period of Brüning-Schleicher, Manuilsky-Kuusinen proclaimed: "Fascism is already here"; the theory of the intermediate, Bonapartist stage they declared to be an attempt to paint over and mask fascism in order to make easier for the Social Democracy the policy of the 'lesser evil'. At that time the social-democrats were called 'social fascists', and the 'left' Social Democrats of the Zyromsky-Marceau Pivert-Just[5] type passed – after the 'Trotskyists' – for the most dangerous social fascists. All this has changed now. With regard to present-day France, the Stalinists do not dare to repeat: 'fascism is already here'; on the contrary, they have accepted the policy of the united front, which they rejected yesterday, in order to prevent the victory of fascism in France. They have found themselves compelled to distinguish the Doumergue regime[6] from the fascist regime.

5 Jean Zyromsky was the leader of the left-wing Bataille Socialiste tendency in the French Socialist Party in the late 1920s and early 1930s. It advocated for a planned economy and convergence with the Communist Party. In 1935 he became an enthusiastic advocate for the Popular Front and unity with the Communist Party. Marceau Pivert belonged to the same tendency until he broke with them and formed the centrist Gauche Revolutionnaire.
Claude Just was a member of SFIO's National Council and a leader of the Comite d'Action Socialiste et Revolutionnaire tendency.

6 Gaston Doumergue was a Radical deputy and President of France from 1924-31. In February 1934, following the attempted fascist coup, he replaced Édouard Daladier as premier, promising a 'strong' government and a constitutional reform that would restrict democratic liberties. When he lost the confidence of the Radicals, his government fell in November 1934.

But they have arrived at this distinction as empiricists and not as Marxists. They do not even attempt to give a scientific definition of the Doumergue regime. He who operates in the domain of theory with abstract categories is condemned to capitulate blindly to facts. And yet it is precisely in France that the passage from parliamentarism to Bonapartism (or more exactly, the first stage of this passage) has taken on a particularly striking and demonstrative character. It suffices to recall that the Doumergue government appeared on the scene between the rehearsal of the civil war by the fascists (6 February [1934]) and the general strike of the proletariat (12 February). As soon as the irreconcilable camps had taken up their fighting positions at the poles of capitalist society, it wasn't long before it became clear that the adding machine of parliamentarism lost all importance. It is true that the Doumergue government like the Brüning-Schleicher governments in their day, appears at first glance to govern with the assent of parliament. But it is a parliament which has abdicated, a parliament which knows that in case of resistance the government would dispense with it. Thanks to the relative equilibrium between the camp of counter-revolution which attacks and the camp of the revolution which defends itself, thanks to their temporary mutual neutralisation, the axis of power has been raised above the classes and above their parliamentary representation. It was necessary to seek the head of the government outside of parliament and 'outside the parties'. The head of the government has called two generals to his aid. This trinity has supported itself on its right and its left by symmetrically arranged parliamentary hostages. The government does not appear as an executive organ of the parliamentary majority, but as a judge-arbiter between two camps in struggle.

A government which raises itself above the nation is not, however, suspended in air. The true axis of the present government passes through the police, the bureaucracy, the military clique. It is a military-police dictatorship with which we are confronted, barely concealed with the decorations of parliamentarism. But a government of the sabre as the judge arbiter of the nation – that's just what *Bonapartism* is.

The sabre by itself has no independent programme. It is the instrument of 'order'. It is summoned to safeguard what exists. Raising itself *politically* above the classes, Bonapartism, like its predecessor Caesarism, for that matter, represents *in the social sense*, always and at all epochs, the government of the strongest and firmest part of the exploiters; consequently, present-day Bonapartism can be nothing else than the government of finance capital which directs, inspires and corrupts the summits of the bureaucracy, the police, the officers' caste and the press.

The 'constitutional reform' about which so much has been said in the course of recent months, has as its sole task the adaptation of the state institutions to the exigencies and conveniences of the Bonapartist government. Finance capital is seeking legal paths that would give it the possibility of each time imposing upon the nation the most suitable judge-arbiter with the forced assent of the quasi-parliament. It is evident that the Doumergue government is not the ideal of a 'strong government'. More suitable candidates for a Bonaparte exist in reserve. New experiences and combinations are possible in this domain if the future course of the class struggle is to leave them enough time.

In prognosticating, we are obliged to repeat what the Bolshevik-Leninists said at one time about Germany: the political chances of present French Bonapartism are not great; its stability is determined by the temporary and at bottom unsteady equilibrium between the camps of the proletariat and fascism. The relation of forces of these two camps must change rapidly, in part under the influence of the economic conjuncture, principally in dependence upon the quality of the proletarian vanguard's policy. The collision between these two camps is inevitable. The timescale of the process will be calculated in months and not in years. A stable regime could be established only after the collision, depending upon the results.

Fascism in power, like Bonapartism, can only be the government of finance capital. In this *social* sense, it is indistinguishable not only from Bonapartism but even from parliamentary democracy. Each time, the Stalinists made this discovery all over again, forgetting that *social* questions resolve themselves in the domain of the *political*. The strength of finance capital does not reside in its ability to establish a government of any kind and at any time, according to its wish; it does not possess this faculty. Its strength resides in the fact that every non-proletarian government is forced to serve finance capital; or better yet, that finance capital possesses the possibility of substituting for each one of its systems of domination that decays, another system corresponding better to the changed conditions. However, the passage from one system to another signifies the *political* crisis which, with the concourse of the activity of the revolutionary proletariat may be transformed into a social danger to the bourgeoisie. The passage of parliamentary democracy to Bonapartism itself was accompanied in France by an effervescence of civil war. The perspective of the passage from Bonapartism to fascism is pregnant with infinitely more formidable disturbances and consequently also revolutionary possibilities.

Up to yesterday, the Stalinists considered that our 'main mistake' was to see in fascism the petty bourgeoisie and not finance capital. In this case too they put abstract categories in place of the dialectics of the classes. Fascism is a specific means of mobilising and organising the petty bourgeoisie in the social interests of finance capital. During the democratic regime capital inevitably attempted to inoculate the workers with confidence in the reformist and pacifist petty bourgeoisie. The passage to fascism, on the contrary, is inconceivable without the preceding permeation of the petty bourgeoisie with hatred of the proletariat. The domination of one and the same superclass, finance capital, rests in these two systems upon directly opposite relations of oppressed classes.

The political mobilisation of the petty bourgeoisie against the proletariat, however, is inconceivable without that social demagogy which means playing with fire for the big bourgeoisie. The danger to 'order' of the unleashed petty-bourgeois reaction, has just been confirmed by the recent events in Germany. That is why, while supporting and actively financing reactionary banditry, in the form of one of its wings, the French bourgeoisie seeks not to push matters to the point of the political victory of fascism, aiming only at the establishment of a 'strong' power which, in the last analysis, is to discipline the two extreme camps.

What has been said sufficiently demonstrates how important it is to distinguish the Bonapartist form of power from the fascist form. Yet it would be unpardonable to fall into the opposite extreme, that is, to convert Bonapartism and fascism into two logically incompatible categories. Just as Bonapartism begins by combining the parliamentary regime with fascism, so triumphant fascism finds itself forced not only to enter into a bloc with the Bonapartists, but what is more, to draw closer internally to the Bonapartist system. The prolonged domination of finance capital by means of reactionary social demagogy and petty-bourgeois terror is impossible. Having arrived in power, the fascist chiefs are forced to muzzle the masses who follow them by means of the state apparatus. By the same token, they lose the support of broad masses of the petty bourgeoisie. A small part of it is assimilated by the bureaucratic apparatus. Another sinks into indifference. A third, under various banners, passes into opposition. But while losing its social mass base, by resting upon the bureaucratic apparatus and oscillating between the classes, fascism is regenerated into Bonapartism. Here, too, the gradual evolution is cut into by violent and sanguinary episodes. Differing from pre-fascist or *preventive Bonapartism* (Giolitti,[7] Brüning-Schleicher, Doumergue, etc.) which reflects the extremely unstable and short-lived equilibrium between the belligerent camps, *Bonapartism of fascist origin* (Mussolini, Hitler, etc.), which grew out of the destruction, the disillusionment and the demoralisation of the two camps of the masses, distinguishes itself by its much greater stability.

The question 'fascism or Bonapartism?' has engendered certain differences on the subject of the Piłsudski regime among our Polish comrades. The very possibility of such differences testifies best to the fact that we are dealing not with inflexible logical categories but

7 Giovanni Giolitti was Mussolini's predecessor as Italian Premier, serving as Prime Minister of Italy four times between 1892 and 1921.

with living social formations which represent extremely pronounced peculiarities in different countries and at different stages.

Piłsudski came to power at the end of an insurrection based upon a mass movement of the petty bourgeoisie and aimed *directly* at the domination of the traditional bourgeois parties in the name of the 'strong state'; this is a fascist trait characteristic of the movement and of the regime. But the specific political weight, that is, the mass of Polish fascism was much weaker than that of Italian fascism in its time and still more than that of German fascism; to a much greater degree, Piłsudski had to make use of the methods of military conspiracy and to put the question of the workers' organisations in a much more circumspect manner. It suffices to recall that Piłsudski's coup d'état took place with the sympathy and the support of the Polish party of the Stalinists. The growing hostility of the Ukrainian and Jewish petty bourgeoisie towards the Piłsudski regime made it, in turn, more difficult for him to launch a general attack upon the working class.

As a result of such a situation, the oscillation between the classes and the national parts of the classes occupied and still occupies with Piłsudski a much greater place, and mass terror a much smaller place, than in the corresponding periods with Mussolini or Hitler; there is the Bonapartist element in the Piłsudski regime. Nevertheless, it would be patently false to compare Piłsudski to Giolitti or to Schleicher and to look forward to his being relieved by a new Polish Mussolini or Hitler. It is methodologically false to form an image of some 'ideal' fascism and to oppose it to this real fascist regime which has grown up, with all its peculiarities and contradictions, upon the terrain of the relationship of classes and nationalities in the Polish state. Will Piłsudski be able to lead the action of destruction of the proletarian organisations to the very end? – and the logic of the situation drives him inevitably on this path – that does not depend upon the formal definition of 'fascism as such', but upon the true relationship of forces, the dynamics of the political processes taking place in the masses, the strategy of the proletarian vanguard, finally, the course of events in Western Europe and above all in France.

History may successfully inscribe the fact that Polish fascism was overthrown and reduced to dust before it succeeded in finding for itself a 'totalitarian' form of expression.

We said above that Bonapartism of fascist origin is incomparably more stable than the preventive Bonapartist experiments to which the big bourgeoisie resorts in the hope of avoiding fascist bloodletting. Nevertheless, it is still more important – from the theoretical and practical point of view – to emphasise that *the very fact of the regeneration of fascism into Bonapartism signifies the beginning of its end.* How long a time the withering away of fascism will last, and at what moment its malady will turn into agony, depends upon many internal and external causes. But the fact that the counter-revolutionary activity of the petty bourgeoisie is quenched, that it is disillusioned, that it is disintegrating and that its attack upon the proletariat is weakening, opens up new revolutionary possibilities. All history shows that it is impossible to keep the proletariat enchained with the aid merely of the police apparatus. It is true that the experience of Italy shows that the psychological heritage of the enormous catastrophe experienced maintains itself among the working class much longer than the relationship between the forces which engendered the catastrophe. But the psychological inertia of the defeat is but a precarious prop. It can crumble at a single blow under the impact of a powerful convulsion. Such a convulsion – for Italy, Germany, Austria and other countries – could be the success of the struggle of the French proletariat.

The revolutionary key to the situation in Europe and in the entire world is now above all in France!

# *Whither France?*

Written 9 November 1934

Editor's note: Exiled by Stalin from the Soviet Union in 1929, Trotsky was living in France in 1934. *Whither France?* is a pamphlet compiling eight articles written over two and a half years, beginning on 6 February 1934.

On that day, several thousand armed fascists and royalists imposed upon the country the reactionary government of Doumergue, under whose protection the fascist bands continued to grow and arm themselves. The workers responded with a massive strike wave in June 1934.

Due to the nature of the pamphlet covering events as they happened, many points are repeated, and so only select articles are present in this volume.

The French events occurred in the context of the developments not only in Germany but also of the early stages of the Spanish Civil War. After the signing of the Franco-Soviet pact, the French Popular Front government bowed to pressure from the Stalinists to expel Trotsky from France. He found refuge in Norway, until he was deported from there to Mexico in December 1936.

* * *

In these pages we wish to explain to the advanced workers the fate of France in the years to come. For us, France is neither the Bourse,[1] nor the banks, nor the trusts, nor the government, nor the state, nor the church – all these are the oppressors of France – it is the working class and the exploited peasantry.

## *The collapse of bourgeois democracy*

After the war a series of brilliantly victorious revolutions occurred in Russia, Germany, Austria-Hungary and later in Spain. But it was only in Russia that the proletariat took full power into its hands, expropriated its exploiters and knew how to create and maintain a workers' state. Everywhere else the proletariat, despite its victory, stopped half way because of the mistakes of its leadership. As a result, power slipped from its hands, shifted from left to right and fell prey to fascism. In a series of other countries power passed into the hands of a military dictatorship. Nowhere were the parliaments capable of reconciling class contradictions and assuring the peaceful development of events. Conflicts were solved arms in hand.

The French people for a long time thought that fascism had nothing whatever to do with them. They had a republic in which all questions were dealt with by the sovereign people through the exercise of universal suffrage. But on 6 February 1934, several thousand fascists and royalists, armed with revolvers, clubs and razors, imposed upon the country the reactionary government of Doumergue, under whose protection the fascist bands continue to grow and arm themselves. What does tomorrow hold?

Of course, in France, as in certain other European countries (England, Belgium, Holland, Switzerland, the Scandinavian countries), there still exist parliaments, elections, democratic liberties, or their remnants. But in all these countries the class struggle is sharpening, just as it did previously in Italy and Germany. Whoever consoles himself with the phrase "France is not Germany"

1 The Paris Stock Exchange.

is hopeless. In all countries the same historic laws operate, the laws of capitalist decline. If the means of production remain in the hands of a small number of capitalists, there is no way out for society. It is condemned to go from crisis to crisis, from need to misery, from bad to worse. In the various countries the decrepitude and disintegration of capitalism are expressed in diverse forms and at unequal rhythms. But the basic features of the process are the same everywhere. *The bourgeoisie is leading its society to complete bankruptcy.* It is capable of assuring the people neither bread nor peace. *This is precisely why it cannot any longer tolerate the democratic order.* It is forced to smash the workers by the use of physical violence. The discontent of the workers and peasants, however, cannot be brought to an end by the police alone. Moreover, it is often impossible to make the army march against the people. It begins by disintegrating and ends with the passage of a large section of the soldiers over to the people's side. That is why finance capital is obliged to create special armed bands, trained to fight the workers just as certain breeds of dog are trained to hunt game. The historic function of fascism is to smash the working class, destroy its organisations and stifle political liberties when the capitalists find themselves unable to govern and dominate with the help of democratic machinery.

The fascists find their human material mainly in the petty bourgeoisie. The latter has been entirely ruined by big capital. There is no way out for it in the present social order, but it knows of no other. Its dissatisfaction, indignation and despair are diverted by the fascists away from big capital and against the workers. It may be said that fascism is the act of placing the petty bourgeoisie at the disposal of its most bitter enemies. In this way, big capital ruins the middle classes and then with the help of hired fascist demagogues incites the despairing petty bourgeois against the worker. The bourgeois regime can be preserved only by such murderous means as these. For how long? Until it is overthrown by proletarian revolution.

## *The beginning of Bonapartism in France*

In France, the movement from democracy toward fascism is only in its first stage. Parliament exists, but it no longer has the powers it once had and it will never retrieve them. The parliamentary majority, mortally frightened after 6 February, called to power Doumergue, the saviour, the arbiter. His government holds itself above parliament. It bases itself not on the 'democratically' elected majority but directly and immediately upon the bureaucratic apparatus, the police and the army. This is precisely why Doumergue can permit no liberty for the civil servants or in general for employees of the state. He needs a docile and disciplined bureaucratic apparatus on whose summit he can maintain himself without danger of falling. The parliamentary majority, scared of the fascists and the 'common front', is forced to bow before Doumergue.

At the present time much is being written about the forthcoming 'reform' of the constitution, on the right to dissolve the Chamber of Deputies, etc. All these questions have only a juridical interest. In the political sense, the question is already solved. Reform has been accomplished without the trip to Versailles. The appearance on the arena of armed fascist bands has enabled finance capital to raise itself above parliament. In this consists now the essence of the French constitution. All else is illusion, phraseology or conscious dupery.

The present role of Doumergue (like that of his possible successors, of the type of Tardieu)[2] is nothing new. It is a role analogous to that played, in different circumstances, by Napoleon I and Napoleon III. The essence of Bonapartism consists in this: basing itself on the struggle of two camps, it 'saves' the 'nation' with the help of a bureaucratic-military dictatorship. Napoleon I represented the Bonapartism of the bourgeoisie's impetuous youth. The Bonapartism of Napoleon III developed when the bourgeoisie was already slightly bald. In the person of Doumergue we meet the senile Bonapartism of capitalist decline.

2 André Tardieu was a conservative politician who served three short terms as Prime Minister of France.

The Doumergue government represents the first step of the passage from parliamentarianism to Bonapartism. To keep his balance, Doumergue needs at his right hand the fascist and other bands which brought him to power. To demand of him that he dissolve the Patriotic Youth,[3] the Croix de Feu,[4] the Camelots du Roi,[5] etc. – not on paper but in reality – is to demand that he cut off the branch upon which he rests.

Temporary oscillations to one side or the other are, of course, possible. Thus, a premature fascist offensive might provoke a certain shift to the 'left' at the top of the government. Doumergue would temporarily give way not to Tardieu but to Herriot.[6] But in the first place, no one has ever said that the fascists would attempt a premature coup d'état. Secondly, a temporary shift to the left at the top would not change the general course of development. It would only postpone the showdown.

There is no longer any path back to a peaceful democracy. Events are leading inevitably and irresistibly to a conflict between the proletariat and fascism.

## *Will Bonapartism last long?*

How long can the present transitional Bonapartist regime stand? Or in other words: how much time has the proletariat to prepare itself for the decisive battle? To this question it is impossible, naturally, to give an exact reply. But certain factors can be established for the purposes of evaluating the tempo at which the whole process is developing. For this the foremost element is the question of the immediate fate of the *Radical Party.*

3 The Jeunesses Patriotes (Young Patriots) was a far-right league recruited mostly from university students, financed by industrialists, founded in 1924.

4 The Croix de Feu (Cross of Fire) was a French fascist movement led by Colonel François de La Rocque. It was the leading force in the February riots of 1934.

5 The Fédération nationale des Camelots du Roi (The National Federation of the King's Camelots) was a far-right youth organisation belonging to the French militant royalist movement Action Française. It was active 1908-36.

6 Édouard Herriot was a member of the Radicals, Prime Minister of France and led the Cartel des Gauches, a reformist alliance between the Radicals, the SFIO and other smaller reformist parties.

The very appearance of the present Bonapartist regime links it, as we have said, to the beginning of a civil war between the extreme political camps. It finds its principal material support in the police and the army. But it also has a political support on the left – the Radical Socialist Party. The base of this mass party is in the petty bourgeoisie of town and country. Its summit is occupied by 'democratic' agents of the big bourgeoisie of town and country who have given the people occasional small reforms and, more often, democratic phrases, who have saved it daily (in words) from reaction and clericalism, but who, in all important questions, have carried out the policy of big capital.

Under the threat of fascism, and still more under the threat of the proletariat, the Radical-Socialists have found themselves obliged to pass from the camp of parliamentary 'democracy' over to the camp of Bonapartism. Like the camel under its driver's whip, Radicalism gets down on its four knees to let capitalist reaction sit between its humps. Without the political support of the Radicals, the Doumergue government would at the present moment be impossible.

If the political evolution of France is compared with that of Germany, the Doumergue government and its possible successors correspond to the Brüning, Papen and Schleicher governments which filled in the gap between Weimar and Hitler. There is, however, a difference which, politically, *can* assume enormous importance. German Bonapartism came upon the scene when the democratic parties had collapsed and the Nazis were growing at a prodigious rate. The three Bonapartist governments in Germany, having a very feeble base of their own, were balanced on the tight rope stretched across the abyss between two hostile camps – *the proletariat and fascism.* All three of these governments fell quickly. The camp of the proletariat was split and unprepared for the struggle, disoriented, duped and betrayed by its leaders. The Nazis were able to take power almost without a struggle.

French fascism does not yet represent a mass force. On the other hand, Bonapartism finds support, neither sure nor very stable but nevertheless a mass support, in the Radicals. Between these two facts there is an inner link. By the social character of its base, Radicalism is the party of the petty bourgeoisie. Fascism can only become a mass force by conquering the petty bourgeoisie. In other words, *fascism can develop in France above all at the expense of the Radicals.* This process is already under way, although still in its early stages.

## *The role of the Radical Party*

The last district elections gave results which could and should have been anticipated. The flanks, i.e. the reactionaries and the workers' bloc, gained, and the centre, i.e. the Radicals, lost. But gains and losses are still negligible. If it were a question of parliamentary elections, these phenomena would have undoubtedly taken on much more considerable dimensions. The displacements which have been noted have for us an importance not in themselves but only as symptoms of changes in the consciousness of the masses.

They show that the petty-bourgeois centre has already begun to give way to the two extreme camps. That means that the remnants of the parliamentary regime are going to be increasingly eaten away. The extreme camps are going to grow. Clashes between them are approaching. It is not difficult to understand that this process is absolutely inescapable.

The Radical Party is the party with whose aid the big bourgeoisie preserves the hopes of the petty bourgeoisie in a progressive and peaceful improvement of its situation. This role of the Radicals was possible only so long as the economic situation of the petty bourgeoisie remained supportable and tolerable, so long as mass ruin was averted, so long as the petty bourgeoisie retained its hope in the future. To be sure, the programme of the Radicals has always remained on paper. They have brought about no serious social reform on behalf of the toilers nor could they have done so. It was not permitted by the big bourgeoisie which holds on to all the real levers of power, the banks and the Bourse, the press, the higher officials, key diplomats and the general staff.

From time to time the Radicals handed out petty alms to their clientele, especially on a provincial scale, and, with the help of these handouts, preserved the illusions of the popular masses. Thus it went until the last crisis. It has now become clear to the most backward peasant that it is not a matter of an ordinary, passing crisis, of which there were not a few before the war, but of a crisis of the whole social system. It calls for bold, decisive measures. What ones? The peasant does not know. No one has told him what he should have been told.

Capitalism has brought the means of production to such a level that they are paralysed by the misery of the popular masses, ruined by the self-same capitalism. The whole system has thereby begun to decline, decompose and rot. Capitalism not only cannot give the toilers new social reforms, nor even petty alms, it is forced to take back what it once gave. All of Europe has entered an era of economic and political counter-reforms. The policy of despoiling and suffocating the masses stems not from the caprices of the reaction but from the decomposition of the capitalist system. That is the fundamental fact which must be assimilated by every worker if he is not to be duped by hollow phrases.

That is precisely why the democratic reformist parties are disintegrating and losing their forces one after another throughout Europe. The same fate also awaits the French Radicals. Only fools can think that the capitulation of Daladier or the treason of Herriot[7] in the face of the worst reaction results from fortuitous, temporary causes or from the lack of character in these two lamentable leaders. No! Great political phenomena always have profound social causes. The decline of the democratic parties is a universal phenomenon whose causes rest in the disintegration of capitalism itself. The big bourgeoisie says to the Radicals: “Now is no time for joking. If you do not stop flirting with the socialists and coyly promising the people mountains and miracles, I will call in the fascists. Understand that 6 February was only a first warning!” After which, the Radical camel gets down on his four knees. There is nothing else he can do.

7 Édouard Daladier was a member of the Radicals and Prime Minister from 1933 to 9 February 1934, when he resigned and handed power to Doumergue after the 6 February riots. Herriot took up the role of Minister of State in the Doumergue cabinet.

But Radicalism will not find its salvation along that road. Linking its fate in the eyes of the people to the fate of the reaction, it inevitably hastens its own end. The loss of votes and mandates in the district elections is only a beginning. The process of the collapse of the Radical Party will unfold with increasing speed. The whole question is to know in whose favour this inevitable and irresistible collapse will take place – in favour of the proletarian revolution or fascism.

Will it be revolutionary socialism or fascist reaction which will first offer the middle classes, boldly and broadly, the most convincing programme and, what is the most important, win their confidence by demonstrating in words and deeds its ability to smash every obstacle on the road to a better future?

On this question depends the fate of France for many years to come. Not only of France, but of all Europe. Not only of Europe, but of the entire world.

## *The 'middle classes', the Radical Party and fascism*

Since the victory of the Nazis in Germany there has been much talk in the parties and groups of the French 'left' of the necessity for staying close to the 'middle classes' to bar the road to fascism. The fraction of Renaudel[8] and co. split from the Socialist Party for the particular purpose of drawing near to the Radicals. But at the moment that Renaudel, who lives on the ideas of 1848, extended both hands to Herriot, the latter had both his engaged, the one by Tardieu, the other by Louis Marin.[9]

From this, however, it does not at all follow that the working class can turn its back on the petty bourgeoisie, leaving it to its fate. Oh, no! To approach the peasants and the petty bourgeoisie of the cities, to draw them to our side, is the necessary condition of the success of the struggle against fascism, not to speak of the conquest of power.

8 Pierre Renaudel was a reformist and member of the SFIO as well as wartime editor of *L'Humanité*. He was expelled from the SFIO in 1933, and formed the Socialist Party of France – Jean Jaurès Union (PSdF).

9 Louis Marin was a French minister in Doumergue's government and a right-wing republican.

Only the problem must be correctly posed, and for that it is necessary to understand clearly the nature of the 'middle classes'. Nothing is more dangerous in politics, especially in a critical period, than to repeat general formulas without examining their social content.

Contemporary society is composed of three classes: the big bourgeoisie, the proletariat and the 'middle classes', or the petty bourgeoisie. The relations among these three classes determine in the final analysis the political situation in the country. The fundamental classes of society are the big bourgeoisie and the proletariat. Only these two classes can have a clear, consistent, independent policy of their own. The petty bourgeoisie is distinguished by its economic dependence and its social heterogeneity. Its upper stratum is linked directly to the big bourgeoisie. Its lower stratum merges with the proletariat and even falls to the status of lumpenproletariat. In accordance with its economic situation, the petty bourgeoisie can have no policy of its own. It always oscillates between the capitalists and the workers. Its own upper stratum pushes it to the right; its lower strata, oppressed and exploited, are capable in certain conditions of turning sharply to the left. These contradictory relations among the different strata of the 'middle classes' always determine the confused and thoroughly bankrupt policy of the Radicals, their vacillations between the cartel with the socialists to calm the base, and the national bloc with the capitalist reaction to save the bourgeoisie. *The final decomposition of Radicalism begins when the big bourgeoisie, itself in an impasse, permits it to vacillate no longer.*

The petty bourgeoisie, the ruined masses of city and country, begins to lose patience. It assumes an attitude more and more hostile towards its own upper stratum. It becomes convinced of the bankruptcy and the perfidy of its political leadership. The poor peasant, the artisan, the petty merchant become convinced that an abyss separates them from all these mayors, all these lawyers and political businessmen of the type of Herriot, Daladier, Chautemps[10] and co., who by their mode of life and their conceptions are big bourgeois. It is precisely

10 Camille Chautemps was a member of the Radicals, a Freemason and was Prime Minister three times.

this disillusionment of the petty bourgeoisie, its impatience, its despair, that fascism exploits. Its agitators stigmatise and execrate the parliamentary democracy which supports careerists and grafters but gives nothing to the toilers. These demagogues shake their fists at the bankers, the big merchants and the capitalists. Their words and gestures correspond to the feelings of the small proprietors caught in a blind alley. The fascists show boldness, go out into the streets, attack the police and attempt to drive out parliament by force. That makes an impression on the despairing petty bourgeois. He says to himself:

> The Radicals, among whom there are too many swindlers, have definitely sold themselves to the bankers; the socialists have promised for a long time to abolish exploitation but they never pass from words to deeds, the communists one cannot understand at all – today it is one thing tomorrow another; let's see if the fascists cannot save us.

## *Must the 'middle classes' inevitably go over to fascism?*

Renaudel, Frossard[11] and their similars imagine that the petty bourgeoisie is attached above all to democracy, wherefore it is necessary to hang on to the coat tails of the Radicals. What monstrous confusion! Democracy is only a political form. The petty bourgeoisie is not concerned with the shell but with the kernel. It wants to save itself from misery and ruin. If democracy proves impotent – then to the devil with democracy! Every petty bourgeois reasons or feels this way.

The principal social and political source of fascism is in the growing revolt of the lower petty bourgeoisie against its own, 'educated' upper layers in the municipalities, the districts and in parliament. To this must be added the hatred of the crisis-shattered intellectual youth for the lawyers, the deputies and the *parvenu* ministers. Here also the lower petty-bourgeois intellectuals rebel against those above them.

11 Ludovic-Oscar Frossard was an SFIO pacifist during the war, becoming General Secretary of the SFIO, until the formation of the Communist Party, where he again served as General Secretary until 1922. He left the party in 1923 and rejoined the SFIO, becoming a deputy in 1928. He ended his political career as minister in the Pétain government.

Does this mean that the passage of the petty bourgeoisie to fascism is inevitable and inescapable? No, such a conclusion would be shameful fatalism.

What is really inevitable and inescapable is the doom of Radicalism and all the political groupings which link themselves to its fate.

Under conditions of capitalist decline there is no longer any place for a party of democratic reforms and 'peaceful' progress. Whatever path events take in France, Radicalism will disappear from the scene, rejected and dishonoured by the petty bourgeoisie which it has definitely betrayed.

Every conscious worker will become convinced by the experience of every passing day that our prediction corresponds to reality. New elections will bring defeats for the Radicals. Whole sections will cut away one after another, the popular masses below and groups of frightened careerists above. Departures, splits, betrayals will follow uninterruptedly. No manoeuvre nor any bloc will save the Radical Party. It will draw into the abyss with it the 'party' of Renaudel-Déat[12] and co. The end of the Radical Party is the inevitable result of the fact that bourgeois society can no longer overcome its difficulties with the help of so-called democratic methods. The split between the base of the petty bourgeoisie and its summit is inevitable.

But that does not at all mean that the masses who follow Radicalism must *inevitably* place their hopes in fascism. Certainly the most demoralised section, the most declassed and the most avid of the youth of the middle classes have already made their choice in that direction. It is out of this reservoir particularly that the fascist bands are taking form. But the basic masses of city and country have not yet made their choice. They hesitate before a great decision. It is precisely because they are hesitating that they still continue, although already without confidence, to vote for the Radicals. This situation of hesitation, of irresolution, will not, however, last for years, but for months.

12 Marcel Déat was a member of the SFIO. Elected deputy in 1932, he was prominent in the right-wing 'Neosocialists' tendency and was expelled in 1933, where he joined Renaudel in the PSdF.

Political developments in the coming period will move at a febrile rhythm. The petty bourgeoisie will reject the demagogy of fascism only if it puts its faith in the reality of another road. That other road is the road of proletarian revolution.

## *Is it true that the petty bourgeoisie fears revolution?*

Parliamentary cretins who consider themselves connoisseurs of the people like to repeat: "One must not frighten the middle classes with revolution. They do not like extremes". In this general form this affirmation is absolutely false. Naturally, the petty proprietor prefers order so long as business is going well and so long as he hopes that tomorrow it will go better.

But when this hope is lost, he is easily enraged and is ready to give himself over to the most extreme measures. Otherwise, how could he have overthrown the democratic state and brought fascism to power in Italy and Germany? The despairing petty bourgeois sees in fascism, above all, a fighting force against big capital, and believes that, unlike the working-class parties which deal only in words, fascism will use force to establish more 'justice'. They understand that one cannot forgo the use of force.

It is false, thrice false, to affirm that the present petty bourgeoisie is not going to the working-class parties because it fears 'extreme measures'. Quite the contrary. The lower petty bourgeoisie, its great masses, only see in the working-class parties parliamentary machines. They do not believe in their strength, nor in their capacity to struggle, nor in their readiness this time to conduct the struggle to the end.

And if this is so, is it worth the trouble to replace Radicalism by its parliamentary confrères on the left? That is how the semi-expropriated, ruined and discontented proprietor reasons or feels. Without an understanding of this psychology of the peasants, the artisans, the employees, the petty functionaries, etc., – a psychology which flows from the social crisis – it is impossible to elaborate a correct policy. The petty bourgeoisie is economically dependent and politically atomised. That is why it cannot conduct an independent policy. It needs a 'leader' who inspires it with confidence. This individual or collective leadership, i.e. a personage or party, can be given to it by one or the other of the fundamental classes – either the big bourgeoisie or the proletariat. Fascism unites and arms the scattered masses. Out of human dust it organises combat detachments. It thus gives the petty bourgeoisie the illusion of being an independent force. It begins to imagine that it will really command the state. It is not surprising that these illusions and hopes turn the head of the petty bourgeoisie!

But the petty bourgeoisie can also find a leader in the proletariat. This was demonstrated in Russia and partially in Spain. In Italy, in Germany and in Austria the petty bourgeoisie gravitated in this direction. But the parties of the proletariat did not rise to their historic task.

To bring the petty bourgeoisie to its side, the proletariat must win its confidence. And for that it must have confidence in its own strength.

It must have a clear programme of action and must be ready to struggle for power by all possible means. Tempered by its revolutionary party for a decisive and pitiless struggle, the proletariat says to the peasants and petty bourgeoisie of the cities:

> We are struggling for power. Here is our programme. We are ready to discuss with you changes in this programme. We will employ violence only against big capital and its lackeys, but with you toilers, we desire to conclude an alliance on the basis of a given programme.

The peasants will understand such language. Only, they must have faith in the capacity of the proletariat to seize power.

But for that it is necessary to purge the united front of all equivocation, of all indecision, of all hollow phrases. It is necessary to understand the situation and to place oneself seriously on the revolutionary road.

## *An alliance with the Radicals would be an alliance against the middle class*

Renaudel, Frossard and their similars seriously imagine that an alliance with the Radicals is an alliance with the 'middle classes' and consequently a barrier against fascism. These men see nothing but parliamentary shadows. They ignore the real evolution of the masses and chase after the 'Radical Party' which has outlived itself and which in the meantime turns its back on them. They think that in an era of great social crisis an alliance of classes set in motion can be replaced by a bloc with a parliamentary clique that is compromised and doomed to extinction. A real alliance of the proletariat and the middle classes is not a question of parliamentary statistics but of revolutionary dynamics.

This alliance must be created and forged in the struggle. The whole meaning of the present political situation resides in the fact that the despairing petty bourgeoisie is beginning to break from the yoke of parliamentary discipline and from the tutelage of the conservative 'radical' clique which has always fooled the people, and which has now definitely betrayed it. To join in this situation with the Radicals means to condemn oneself to the scorn of the masses, and to push the petty bourgeoisie into the embrace of fascism as the sole saviour.

The working-class party must occupy itself not with a hopeless effort to save the party of the bankrupts. It must, on the contrary, with all its strength, accelerate the process of liberation of the masses from Radical influence. The more zeal and the more boldness it applies to this task, the more surely and rapidly will it prepare a real alliance of the working class with the petty bourgeoisie. It is necessary to place oneself at their head and not at their tail. History is working quickly. Woe to him who lags behind!

When Frossard denies the right of the Socialist Party to expose, weaken and speed the disintegration of the Radical Party, he comes forward not as a socialist but as a conservative Radical. Only that party has the right to historical existence which believes in its own programme and strives to rally the whole people to its banner. Otherwise it is not a party but a parliamentary coterie, a clique of careerists. It is not only the right but the elementary duty of the proletarian party to free the toiling masses from the fatal influence of the bourgeoisie. This historic task takes on a particular sharpness at the present time, for the Radicals are more than ever striving to cover up the reaction, to lull and dupe the people and in this way prepare for the victory of fascism. And the left Radicals? They capitulate to Herriot, just as Herriot capitulates to Tardieu.

Frossard would have the alliance of the Socialists and the Radicals end in a government of the 'left' which will dissolve the fascist organisations and save the republic. It is difficult to imagine a more monstrous amalgam of democratic illusions and police cynicism. When we say – we speak of this in more detail below – that *what is needed is a workers' militia*, Frossard and his satellites object: "Against fascism one must fight not with physical but with ideological means". When we say only a bold mobilisation of the masses, which is only possible in a struggle against Radicalism, is capable of mining the ground under fascism, the same gentlemen reply to us: "No, only the police government of Daladier-Frossard can save us."

What pitiful prattle! For the Radicals have held the power, and if they voluntarily ceded it to Doumergue, it was not because they lacked the aid of Frossard but because they feared fascism, because they feared the big bourgeoisie which threatened it with royalist razors and because they feared still more the proletariat which was beginning to marshal itself against fascism. To cap it all, Frossard himself, taking fright at the alarm of the Radicals, advised Daladier to capitulate.

If one supposes for an instant – an obviously unlikely hypothesis – that the Radicals had consented to break the alliance with Doumergue for the alliance with Frossard, the fascist bands, this time with the direct collaboration of the police, would have come into the streets trebly numerous and the Radicals, together with Frossard, would have immediately crawled under the tables or hidden themselves in their ministerial toilets.

But let us make one more fantastic hypothesis: the police of Daladier-Frossard 'disarm the fascists'. Does that settle the question? And who will disarm the same police, who with the right hand will give back to the fascists what they will have taken from them with the left? The comedy of disarmament by the police will only have caused the authority of the fascists to increase as fighters against the capitalist state. Blows against the fascist gangs can prove effective only to the extent that these gangs are at the same time politically isolated.

Meanwhile, the hypothetical government of Daladier-Frossard would give nothing either to the workers or to the petty-bourgeois masses because it would be unable to attack the foundations of private property, and without expropriation of the banks, the great commercial enterprises, the key branches of industry and transport, without foreign trade monopoly and without a series of other profound measures, there is no possible way of coming to the aid of the peasant, the artisan, the petty merchant. By its passivity, its impotence, its lies, the government of Daladier-Frossard would provoke a tempest of revolt in the petty bourgeoisie, and would push it definitely on the road to fascism, if this government were possible. It is necessary to recognize, however, that Frossard is not alone. The same day (24 October) on which the moderate Zyromsky came out in *Le Populaire*[13] against the attempt of Frossard to revive the cartel, Cachin[14] spoke up in *L'Humanité* to defend the idea of a bloc with the Radical Socialists. He, Cachin, greeted with enthusiasm the fact that the Radicals had declared for the "disarmament of the fascists".

Certainly, the Radicals declared themselves for the disarmament of everyone – workers' organisations included. Certainly, in the hands of a Bonapartist state, such a measure would be directed especially against the workers. Certainly, the 'disarmed' fascists would receive on the morrow double their arms, not without the aid of the police. But why trouble with sombre reflections? Every man needs to hope. So there is Cachin travelling in the footsteps of Wels and Otto Bauer who also in their time sought salvation in the disarmament to be effected by the police of Brüning and Dollfuss.

13 *Le Populaire* (*The Popular*) was a weekly propaganda journal affiliated to the SFIO.

14 Marcel Cachin was a leading member of the Communist Party and editor of *l'Humanite* from 1918-58, first under the SFIO, then the Communist Party.

Executing the latest turn of 180 degrees, Cachin identifies the Radicals with the middle classes. He sees oppressed peasants only through the prism of Radicalism. The alliance with the petty toiling proprietors is represented by him only in the form of a bloc with the parliamentary careerists who are at last beginning to lose the confidence of the petty proprietors.

Instead of nourishing and fanning the nascent revolt of the peasant and the artisan against the 'democratic' exploiters and guiding this revolt in the direction of an alliance with the proletariat, Cachin is preparing to support the bankrupt Radicals with the authority of the 'common front', and thus to drive the revolt of the most exploited petty bourgeoisie along the road of fascism.

Theoretical sloppiness always takes cruel vengeance in revolutionary politics. 'Anti-fascism', like fascism, are for the Stalinists not concrete conceptions, but two great empty sacks into which they stuff anything that comes into their hands. For them Doumergue is a fascist just as before that Daladier was also for them a fascist. In point of fact, Doumergue is a capitalist exploiter of the fascist wing of the petty bourgeoisie just as Herriot is an exploiter of the radical petty bourgeoisie. At the present time these two systems combine in the Bonapartist regime. Doumergue is also, after his fashion, an 'anti-fascist', since he prefers a military and police dictatorship of big capital to a civil war whose issue is always uncertain. For fear of fascism and still more for fear of the proletariat, the 'anti-fascist' Daladier joins with Doumergue. But the regime of Doumergue is inconceivable without the existence of the fascist gangs. An elementary Marxist analysis thus shows the utter futility of the idea of an alliance with the Radicals against fascism!

The Radicals themselves will take pains to show in action how fantastic and reactionary are the political day dreams of Frossard and Cachin.

## *The workers' militia and its opponents*

To struggle, it is necessary to conserve and strengthen the instrument and the means of struggle – organisations, the press, meetings, etc.

Fascism threatens all of that directly and immediately. It is still too weak for the direct struggle for power but it is strong enough to attempt to beat down the working-class organisations bit by bit, to temper its bands in its attacks and to spread dismay and lack of confidence in their forces in the ranks of the workers.

Fascism finds unconscious helpers in all those who say that the 'physical struggle' is impermissible or hopeless, and demand of Doumergue the disarmament of his fascist guard. Nothing is so dangerous for the proletariat, especially in the present situation, than the sugared poison of false hopes. Nothing increases the insolence of the fascists so much as 'flabby pacifism' on the part of the workers' organisations. Nothing destroys the confidence of the middle classes in the working class as temporising, passivity and the absence of the will to struggle.

*Le Populaire* and especially *L'Humanité* write every day: "The united front is a barrier against fascism"; "the united front will not permit"; "the fascists will not dare"; etc. These are phrases. It is necessary to say squarely to the workers, socialists and communists: do not allow yourselves to be lulled by the phrases of superficial and irresponsible journalists and orators. It is a question of our heads and the future of socialism. It is not that we deny the importance of the united front. We demanded it when the leaders of both parties were against it. The united front opens up numerous possibilities but nothing more. In itself, the united front decides nothing. Only the struggle of the masses decides. The united front will reveal its value when communist detachments will come to the help of socialist detachments and vice versa in the case of an attack by the fascist bands against *Le Populaire* or L'Humanité. But for that, proletarian combat detachments must exist and be educated, trained and armed. And if there is not an organisation of defence, i.e. a workers' militia, *Le Populaire* and *L'Humanité* will be able to write as many articles as they like on the omnipotence of the united front but the two papers will find themselves defenceless before the first well-prepared attack of the fascists.

We propose to make a critical study of the 'arguments' and the 'theories' of the opponents of the workers' militia who are very numerous and influential in the two working-class parties.

"We need mass self-defence and not the militia", we are often told. But what is this "mass self-defence" without combat organisations, without specialised cadres, without arms? To give over the defence against fascism to unorganised and unprepared masses left to themselves would be to play a role incomparably lower than the role of Pontius Pilate. To deny the role of the militia is to deny the role of the vanguard. Then why a party? Without the support of the masses, the militia is nothing. But without organised combat detachments, the most heroic masses will be smashed bit by bit by the fascist gangs. It is nonsense to counterpose the militia to self-defence. The militia is an organ of self-defence.

"To call for the organisation of a militia", say some opponents who, to be sure, are the least serious and honest, "is to engage in provocation". This is not an argument but an insult. If the necessity for the defence of the workers' organisations flows from the whole situation, how then can one not call for the creation of the militia? Perhaps they mean to say that the creation of a militia 'provokes' fascist attacks and government repression. In that case this is an absolutely reactionary argument. Liberalism has always said to the workers that by their class struggle they 'provoke' the reaction.

The reformists repeated this accusation against the Marxists, the Mensheviks against the Bolsheviks. These accusations reduced themselves, in the final analysis, to the profound thought that if the oppressed do not baulk, the oppressors will not be obliged to beat them. This is the philosophy of Tolstoy and Gandhi but never that of Marx and Lenin. If *L'Humanité* wants hereafter to develop the doctrine of 'non-resistance to evil by violence', it should take for its symbol not the hammer and sickle, emblem of the October Revolution, but the pious goat which provides Gandhi with his milk.

'But the arming of the workers is only opportune in a revolutionary situation, which does not yet exist.'

This profound argument means that the workers must permit themselves to be slaughtered until the situation becomes revolutionary. Those who yesterday preached the 'third period' do not want to see what is going on before their eyes. The question of arms itself has only come forward because the 'peaceful', 'normal', 'democratic' situation has given way to a stormy, critical and unstable situation which can transform itself into a revolutionary as well as a counter-revolutionary situation.

This alternative depends above all on whether the advanced workers will allow themselves to be attacked with impunity and defeated bit by bit or will reply to every blow by two of their own, arousing the courage of the oppressed and uniting them around their banner. A revolutionary situation does not fall from the skies. It takes form with the active participation of the revolutionary class and its party.

The French Stalinists now argue that the militia did not safeguard the German proletariat from defeat. Only yesterday they completely denied any defeat in Germany and asserted that the policy of the German Stalinists was correct from beginning to end. Today they see the entire evil in the German workers' militia (*Rote Front*). Thus from one error, they fall into a diametrically opposite one no less monstrous. The militia in itself does not settle the question. *A correct policy is necessary.* Meanwhile the policy of Stalinism in Germany ("social fascism is the chief enemy", the split of the trade unions, the flirtation with nationalism, putschism) fatally led to the isolation of the proletarian vanguard and to its shipwreck. With an utterly worthless strategy no militia could have saved the situation.

It is nonsense to say that in itself the organisation of the militia leads to adventures, provokes the enemy, replaces the political struggle by physical struggle, etc. In all these phrases there is nothing but political cowardice.

The militia, as the strong organisation of the vanguard, is in fact the surest defence against adventures, against individual terrorism, against bloody spontaneous explosions.

The militia is at the same time the only serious way of reducing to a minimum the civil war which fascism imposes upon the proletariat. Let the workers, despite the absence of a 'revolutionary situation', occasionally correct the 'papa's son' patriots in their own way and the recruitment of new fascist bands will become incomparably more difficult.

But here the strategists, tangled in their own reasoning, bring forward against us still more stupefying arguments. We quote textually:

> If we reply to the revolver shots of the fascists with other revolver shots, [writes *L'Humanité* of 23 October 1934] we lose sight of the fact that fascism is the product of the capitalist regime and that in fighting against fascism it is the entire system which we face.

It is difficult to accumulate in a few lines greater confusion of more errors. It is impossible to defend oneself against the fascists because they are "a product of the capitalist regime". That means we have to renounce the whole struggle, for all contemporary social evils are "products of the capitalist system".

When the fascists kill a revolutionist or burn down the building of a proletarian newspaper, the workers' are to sigh philosophically: "Alas! Murders and arson are products of the capitalist system", and go home with easy consciences. Fatalist prostration is substituted for the militant theory of Marx, to the sole advantage of the class enemy. The ruin of the petty bourgeoisie is, of course, the product of capitalism. The growth of the fascist bands is, in turn, a product of the ruin of the petty bourgeoisie. But on the other hand, the increase in the misery and the revolt of the proletariat are also products of the sharpening of the class struggle. Why, then, for the 'Marxists' of *L'Humanité* are the fascist bands the legitimate product of capitalism and the workers' militia the illegitimate product of the Trotskyists? It is impossible to make head or tail of this.

"We have to deal with the whole system", we are told. How? Over the heads of human beings? The fascists in the different countries began with their revolvers and ended by destroying the whole 'system' of workers' organisations. How else to check the armed offensive of the enemy if not by an armed defence in order, in our turn, to go over to the offensive?

*L'Humanité* now admits defence in words, but only in the form of 'mass self-defence'. The militia is harmful because, you see, it divides the combat detachments from the masses. But why then are there independent armed detachments among the fascists who are not cut off from the reactionary masses but who, on the contrary, arouse the courage and embolden the masses by their well-organised attacks? Or perhaps the proletarian mass is inferior in combative quality to the declassed petty bourgeoisie?

Hopelessly tangled, *L'Humanité* finally begins to hesitate: it appears that mass self-defence requires the creation of special "self-defence groups". In the place of the rejected militia special groups or detachments are proposed. It would seem at first sight that there is a difference only in the name. Certainly the name proposed by *L'Humanité* means nothing. One can speak of "mass self-defence" but it is impossible to speak of "self-defence groups" since the purpose of the groups is not to defend themselves but the workers' organisations. However, it is of course not a question of the name. The "self-defence groups", according to *L'Humanité*, must renounce the use of arms in order not to fall into "putschism". These sages treat the working class like an infant who must not be allowed to hold a razor in his hands. Razors, moreover, are the monopoly, as we know, of the Camelots du Roi, who are a legitimate 'product of capitalism' and who with the aid of razors have overthrown the 'system' of democracy. In any case, how are the 'self-defence groups' going to defend themselves against the fascist revolvers? "Ideologically", of course. In other words: they can only hide themselves. Not having what they require in their hands, they will have to seek 'self-defence' in their feet. And the fascists will in the meanwhile sack the workers' organisations with impunity. But if the proletariat suffers a terrible defeat, it will at any rate not have been guilty of 'putschism'. This fraudulent chatter, parading under the banner of 'Bolshevism' arouses only disgust and loathing.

During the 'third period' of happy memory, when the strategists of *L'Humanité* were afflicted with barricade delirium, 'conquered' the streets every day and stamped as 'social fascist' everyone who did not share their extravagances, we predicted: "The moment these gentlemen burn the tips of their fingers, they will become the worst opportunists." That prediction has now been completely confirmed. At a time when, within the Socialist Party, the movement in favour of the militia is growing and strengthening, the leaders of the so-called Communist Party run for the hose to cool down the desire of the advanced workers to organise themselves in fighting columns. Could one imagine a more demoralising or more damning work than this?

## *A workers' militia must be built*

In the ranks of the Socialist Party sometimes this objection is heard: "A militia must be formed but there is no need of shouting about it." One can only congratulate comrades who wish to protect the practical side of the business from inquisitive eyes and ears. But it would be much too naive to think that a militia could be created unseen and secretly within four walls. We need tens and later hundreds of thousands of fighters. They will come only if millions of men and women workers and behind them the peasants, understand the necessity for the militia and create around the volunteers an atmosphere of ardent sympathy and active support. Conspiratorial care can and must envelop only the *technical* aspect of the matter. The *political* campaign must be openly developed, in meetings, factories, in the streets and on the public squares.

The fundamental cadres of the militia must be the factory workers grouped according to their place of work, known to each other and able to protect their combat detachments against the provocations of enemy agents far more easily and more surely than the most elevated bureaucrats. Conspirative general staffs without an open mobilisation of the masses will at the moment of danger remain impotently suspended in mid-air. Every working-class organisation has to plunge into the job. In this question there can be no line of demarcation between the working-class parties and the trade unions.

Hand in hand they must mobilise the masses. The success of the people's militia will then be fully assured.

"But where are the workers going to get arms?" object the sober 'realists' – that is to say, frightened philistines – "the enemy has rifles, cannon, tanks, gas and aircraft. The workers have a few hundred revolvers and pocket knives".

In this objection everything is piled up to frighten the workers. On the one hand, our sages identify the arms of the fascists with the armament of the state. On the other, they turn towards the state and demand that it disarm the fascists. Remarkable logic! In fact their position is false in both cases. In France the fascists are still far from controlling the state. On 6 February they entered into armed conflict with the state police. That is why it is false to speak of cannon and tanks when it is a matter of the *immediate* armed struggle against the fascists. The fascists, of course, are richer than we. It is easier for them to buy arms. But the workers are more numerous, more determined, more devoted, when they are conscious of a firm revolutionary leadership.

In addition to other sources, the workers can arm themselves at the expense of the fascists by systematically disarming them.

This is now one of the most serious forms of the struggle against fascism. When workers' arsenals will begin to stock up at the expense of the fascist arms depots, the banks and trusts will be more prudent in financing the armament of their murderous guards. It would even be possible in this case – *but in this case only* – that the alarmed authorities would really begin to prevent the arming of the fascists in order not to provide an additional source of arms for the workers. We have known for a long time that only a revolutionary tactic engenders, as a by-product, 'reforms' or concessions from the government.

But how to disarm the fascists? Naturally, it is impossible to do so with newspaper articles alone. Fighting squads must be created. An intelligence service must be established. Thousands of informers and friendly helpers will volunteer from all sides when they realise that the business has been seriously undertaken by us. It requires a will to proletarian action.

But the arms of the fascists are of course not the only source. In France there are more than one million organised workers. Generally speaking, this number is small. But it is entirely sufficient to make a beginning in the organisation of a workers' militia. If the parties and unions armed only a tenth of their members, that would already be a force of 100,000 men. There is no doubt whatever that the number of volunteers who would come forward on the morrow of a 'united front' appeal for a workers' militia would far exceed that number. The contributions of the parties and unions, collections and voluntary subscriptions would within a month or two make it possible to assure the arming of 100,000 to 200,000 working-class fighters. The fascist rabble would immediately sink its tail between its legs. The whole perspective of development would become incomparably more favourable.

To invoke the absence of arms or other objective reasons to explain why no attempt has been made up to now to create a militia, is to fool oneself and others. The principal obstacle – one can say the only obstacle – has its roots in the conservative and passive character of the leaders of the workers' organisations. The sceptics who are the leaders do not believe in the strength of the proletariat. They put their hope in all sorts of miracles from above instead of giving a revolutionary outlet to the energies pulsing below. The Socialist workers must compel their leaders to pass over immediately to the creation of the workers' militia or else give way to younger, fresher forces.

## *The arming of the proletariat*

A strike is inconceivable without propaganda and without agitation. It is also inconceivable without pickets who, when they can, use persuasion, but when obliged, use force. The strike is the most elementary form of the class struggle which always combines, in varying proportions, 'ideological' methods with physical methods. The struggle against fascism is basically a political struggle which needs a militia just as the strike needs pickets. Basically, the picket is the embryo of the workers' militia. He who thinks of renouncing 'physical' struggle must renounce all struggle, for the spirit does not live without flesh.

Following the splendid phrase of the great military theoretician, Clausewitz, "war is the continuation of politics by other means". This definition also fully applies to civil war. Physical struggle is only 'another means' of the political struggle. It is impermissible to oppose one to the other since it is impossible to check at will the political struggle when it transforms itself, by force of inner necessity, into a physical struggle.

The duty of a revolutionary party is to foresee in time the inescapability of the transformation of politics into open armed conflict, and with all its forces to prepare for that moment just as the ruling classes are preparing.

The militia detachments for defence against fascism are the first step on the road to the arming of the proletariat, not the last. Our slogan is: "*Arm the proletariat and the revolutionary peasants.*"

The workers' militia must in the final analysis embrace all the toilers. To fulfil this program *completely* would be possible only in a workers' state into whose hands would pass all the means of production and consequently also all the means of destruction, i.e. all the arms and the factories which produce them.

However, it is impossible to arrive at a workers' state with empty hands. Only political invalids like Renaudel can speak of a peaceful, constitutional road to socialism. The constitutional road is cut by trenches held by the fascist bands. There are not a few trenches before us. The bourgeoisie will not hesitate to resort to a dozen coups d'état aided by the police and the army, to prevent the proletariat from coming to power.

A workers' socialist state can be created only by a victorious revolution.

Every revolution is prepared by the march of economic and political development, but it is always decided by open armed conflicts between hostile classes. A revolutionary victory can become possible only as a result of long political agitation, a lengthy period of education and organisation of the masses.

But the armed conflict itself must likewise be prepared long in advance.

The advanced workers must know that they will have to fight and win a death struggle. They must reach out for arms, as a guarantee of their emancipation.

In an era as critical as the present, the party of the revolution must unceasingly preach to the workers the need for arming themselves and must do everything to assure the arming, at least, of the proletarian vanguard. Without this, victory is impossible.

The most recent electoral victories of the British Labour Party do not at all invalidate what is said above. Even if we were to allow that the next parliamentary elections will give the Labour Party an absolute majority, which is not assured in any case; if we were further to allow that the party would actually take the road of socialist transformations – which is scarcely probable – it would immediately meet with such fierce resistance from the House of Lords, the king, the banks, the stock market, the bureaucracy, the press, that a split in its ranks would become inevitable, and the left, more radical wing would become a parliamentary minority. Simultaneously the fascist movement would acquire an unprecedented sweep. Alarmed by the municipal elections, the British bourgeoisie is no doubt already actively preparing for an extra-parliamentary struggle actively while the tops of the Labour Party lull the proletariat with the successes and are compelled, unfortunately, to see the British events through the rosy spectacles of Jean Longuet.[15] In point of fact, the less the leaders of the Labour Party prepare for it, the more cruel will be the civil war forced upon the proletariat by the British bourgeoisie.

"But where will you get arms for the whole proletariat?" object once more the sceptics who mistake their own inner futility for an objective impossibility. They forgot that the same question has been posed before every revolution in history. And despite everything, victorious revolutions mark important stages in the development of humanity.

---

15 Jean Longuet was a deputy for the SFIO during the war who opposed joining the Communist International and joined the right-wing split of the party in 1920. He was a deputy once more from 1932-38. He also was the grandson of Karl Marx.

The proletariat produces arms, transports them, erects the buildings in which they are kept, defends these buildings against itself, serves in the army and creates all its equipment. It is neither locks nor walls which separate the proletariat from arms, but the habit of submission, the hypnosis of class domination and nationalist poison.

It is sufficient to destroy these psychological walls – and no wall of stone will stand in the way. It is enough that the proletariat should want arms – and it will find them. The task of the revolutionary party is to awaken this desire and to facilitate its realisation.

But here Frossard and hundreds of frightened parliamentarians, journalists and trade-union officials, advance their last argument, the weightiest:

> Can serious men in general place their hopes in the success of physical struggle after the recent tragic experiences in Austria and Spain?[16] Think of present-day technique, tanks, gas, aircraft!!

This argument only shows that a number of 'serious men' not only want to learn nothing but in their fear even forgot what little they ever learned.

The history of the last twenty years demonstrates with particular clarity that the fundamental problems in the relations among classes, as among nations, are settled by physical force. The pacifists have long hoped that the growth of military technique would make war impossible. The philistines have repeated for decades that the growth of military technique would make revolution impossible. However, wars and revolutions continue. Never have there been so many revolutions, including victorious revolutions, as there have been since the last war which uncovered all the might of military technique.

Frossard and co. offer old clichés as though they were the latest discoveries, invoking instead of automatic rifles and machine guns, tanks and bombing planes. We reply: behind each machine there are men who are linked not only by technical but by social and political

16 This refers to the defeated uprisings in 1934 of miners of Asturias against the right-wing CEDA government in Spain, and of workers in Vienna against the reactionary Dollfuss government.

bonds. When historic development poses before society an unpostponable revolutionary task as a question of life or death, when there exists a progressive class with whose victory is joined the salvation of society – then the development itself of the political struggle opens up before the revolutionary class the most varied possibilities – as much to paralyse the military force of the enemy as to win it over, at least partially. In the mind of a philistine these possibilities always appear as 'lucky accidents' which will never be repeated. In fact, in the most unexpected but fundamentally natural combinations, possibilities of every sort open up in every great, i.e. truly popular, revolution. But despite everything victory does not come of itself.

To utilise the favourable possibilities it is necessary to have a revolutionary will, an iron determination to conquer, a bold and perspicacious leadership. *L'Humanité* agrees in words with the slogan of "arming the workers" but only to renounce it in deeds. At the present time, according to this paper, it is inadmissible to advance a slogan which is only opportune "in a full revolutionary crisis". It is dangerous to load your rifle, says the 'too-prudent' hunter, so long as the game remains invisible. But when the game puts in an appearance it is a little too late to load the rifle. Do the strategists of *L'Humanité* really think that in "the full revolutionary crisis" they will be able without any preparation to mobilise and arm the proletariat? To secure a large quantity of arms, one needs a certain quantity on hand. One needs military cadres. One needs the invincible desire of the masses to secure arms. One needs uninterrupted preparatory work not only in the gymnasiums but in indissoluble connection with the daily struggle of the masses. This means:

*It is necessary immediately to build the militia and at the same time to carry on propaganda for the general armament of the revolutionary workers and peasants.*

## *"But the defeats in Austria and Spain…"*

The impotence of parliamentarianism in the conditions of the crisis of the whole capitalist system is so obvious that the vulgar democrats in the camp of the workers (Renaudel, Frossard and their imitators) do not find a single argument to defend their petrified prejudices. All the more readily do they seize upon every defeat and every failure suffered along the revolutionary road. The development of their thought is this: if pure parliamentarianism offers no way out, armed struggle does no better. The defeats of the proletarian insurrections in Austria and in Spain are now, of course, their choice argument. In fact, in their criticism of the revolutionary method the theoretical and political bankruptcy of the vulgar democrats appears still more clearly than in their defence of the methods of rotting bourgeois democracy.

No one has said that the revolutionary method automatically assures victory. What is decisive is not the method in itself but its correct application, the Marxist orientation in events, powerful organisation, the confidence of the masses won through long experience, a perspicacious and bold leadership. The issue of every struggle depends upon the moment and conditions of the conflict and the relation of forces. Marxism is quite far from the thought that armed conflict is the only revolutionary method, or a panacea, good under all conditions. Marxism in general knows no fetishes, neither parliamentary nor insurrectional. There is a time and place for everything. There is one thing that one can say at the beginning:

On the parliamentary road the socialist proletariat nowhere and never conquered power nor ever even as yet has drawn close to it.

The governments of Scheidemann,[17] Hermann Müller,[18] MacDonald, had nothing in common with socialism. The bourgeoisie permitted the social democrats and Labourites to come to power only on condition that they defend capitalism against its enemies. They scrupulously fulfilled this condition. Purely parliamentary, anti-revolutionary socialism nowhere and never resulted in a socialist ministry. It did succeed in producing loathsome renegades who

17 Philipp Scheidemann was a member of the 1918-19 SPD government alongside Friedrich Ebert and Gustav Noske, in the cabinet that strangled the November 1918 Revolution.

18 Herman Müller was an SPD politician and served as Chancellor twice, in 1920 and 1928-30.

exploited the workers' party to carve out cabinet careers – Millerand, Briand, Viviani, Laval, Paul-Boncour, Marquet.[19]

On the other hand, historical experience shows that the revolutionary method can lead to the conquest of power by the proletariat – in Russia in 1917, in Germany and Austria in 1918, in Spain in 1930. In Russia there was a powerful Bolshevik Party which prepared for the revolution over a long period of years and knew solidly how to take over power.

The reformist parties of Germany, Austria and Spain did not prepare the revolution, did not lead it, but suffered it.

Frightened by the power which had come into their hands against their own will, they benevolently handed it over to the bourgeoisie. In this way they undermined the confidence of the proletariat in itself and, further, the confidence of the petty bourgeoisie in the proletariat. They prepared the conditions for the growth of fascist reaction and fell victims to it.

Civil war, we have said, following Clausewitz, is a continuation of politics but by other means. This means that the result of the civil war depends for one-fourth, not to say one-tenth, upon the development of the civil war itself, its technical means, its purely military leadership, and for three-fourths, if not for nine-tenths, on the political preparation.

Of what does this political preparation consist? It is in the revolutionary cohesion of the masses, in their liberation from servile hopes in the clemency, generosity and loyalty of 'democratic slave-owners', in the education of revolutionary cadres who know how to defy official public opinion and who know how to display towards the bourgeoisie one-tenth the implacability which the bourgeoisie displays towards the toilers. Without this temper, civil war when conditions force it – *and they always end by forcing it* – will take place under conditions most unfavourable for the proletariat, will depend upon many hazards and then, even in case of military victory, power can escape the hands of the proletariat.

19 These were all former 'socialist' deputies and ministers who had gone over to the bourgeois parties.

Whoever does not foresee that the class struggle leads inevitably to armed conflict is blind. But he is no less blind who fails to see behind this armed conflict and its outcome the whole previous policy of the classes in struggle.

What was defeated in Austria was not the method of insurrection but Austro-Marxism and in Spain unprincipled parliamentary reformism.

In 1918, the Austrian Social Democracy handed over to the bourgeoisie, behind the back of the proletariat, the power which the latter had won. In 1927, it not only turned away in cowardly fashion from the proletarian insurrection which had every chance of victory, but led the workers' Schutzbund[20] against the insurgent masses. Thus it prepared the victory of Dollfuss. Bauer and co. said: "We desire peaceful evolution but if the enemy loses his head and attacks us, then..."

This formula appeared very 'wise' and very 'realistic'. Unfortunately, it is on this Austro-Marxist model that Marceau Pivert also constructs his reasoning: 'If – then'. In fact, this formula is a snare for the workers. It lulls them and deceives them. 'If' means that the forms of the struggle depend upon the goodwill of the bourgeoisie and not upon the absolute irreconcilability of class interests. 'If' means that *if* we are wise, prudent, conciliatory, the bourgeoisie will be loyal and everything will proceed peacefully.

Running after the phantom 'if', Otto Bauer and the other leaders of the Austrian Social Democracy passively retreated before the reaction, ceded one position after another, demoralised the masses, retreated again, until they found themselves in the final impasse. There on the last redoubt they accepted battle and lost it.

In Spain events took a different course but the causes of the defeat were basically the same. The Socialist Party, like the Russian Socialist-Revolutionaries and Mensheviks, shared power with the republican bourgeoisie to prevent the workers and peasants from carrying the revolution to its conclusion. For two years the Socialists in power

20 The Republikanischer Schutzbund was an Austrian paramilitary organisation established in 1923 by the Social Democratic Workers' Party of Austria.

helped the bourgeoisie disembarrass itself of the masses by crumbs of national, social and agrarian reforms. Against the most revolutionary strata of the people, the Socialists used repression.

The result was twofold. Anarcho-syndicalism, which would have melted like wax in the heat of revolution had the workers' party pursued a correct course, was strengthened and drew around it the militant layers of the proletariat. At the other pole, social-catholic demagogy succeeded in skilfully exploiting the discontent of the masses with the bourgeois-socialist government.

When the Socialist Party was sufficiently compromised, the bourgeoisie drove it from power and took over the offensive on the whole front. The Socialist Party had to defend itself under the most unfavourable conditions which had been prepared for it by its own previous policy. The bourgeoisie already had a mass support at the right. The anarcho-syndicalist leaders, who during the course of the revolution committed all the mistakes typical of these professional confusionists, refused to support the insurrection led by the traitor 'politicians'. The movement did not take on a general character but remained sporadic. The government directed its blows at the scattered sections of the workers. The civil war forced by the reaction ended in the defeat of the proletariat.

From the Spanish experience it is not difficult to draw conclusions against socialist participation in a bourgeois government. The conclusion itself is indisputable but utterly insufficient. The alleged 'radicalism' of Austro-Marxism is in no sense any better than Spanish ministerialism. The difference between them is technical, not political. Both waited for the bourgeoisie to give them 'loyalty' for 'loyalty'. Both led the proletariat to catastrophe.

In Spain as in Austria it was not revolutionary methods which were defeated but opportunist methods in a revolutionary situation. It is not the same thing!

We shall not stop here on the policy of the Communist International in Austria and in Spain. We refer the reader to the files of *La Vérité*[21] and a series of pamphlets of recent years. In

21 *La Vérité* (*The Truth*) was the weekly newspaper of the French Left Oppositionists.

an exceptionally favourable situation the Austrian and Spanish Communist Parties, fettered by the theory of the 'third period' and 'social fascism', etc., found themselves doomed to complete isolation. Compromising the methods of revolution by the authority of 'Moscow' they barred, thereby, the road to a truly Marxist, truly Bolshevik policy. The fundamental faculty of revolution is to submit to a rapid and pitiless examination all doctrines and all methods. The punishment almost immediately follows the crime.

The responsibility of the Communist International for the defeats of the proletariat in Germany, Austria and in Spain is incommensurable. It is not sufficient to carry out a 'revolutionary' policy (in words). A *correct* policy is needed. No one has yet found any other secret of victory.

## *The united front and the struggle for power*

We have already said that the united front of the Socialist and Communist Parties embodies immense possibilities. If only it wants it seriously, it will tomorrow become master in France. But the will must be there.

The fact that Jouhaux[22] and, in general, the bureaucracy of the CGT remain *outside* the united front preserving their 'independence' seems to contradict what we say. But that is only at first sight. In an epoch of great tasks and great dangers which bring the masses to their feet, the barriers between the political and trade-union organisations of the proletariat disappear. The workers want to know how to save themselves from capital, and they are scarcely concerned with the 'independence' of Jouhaux from proletarian policy (on bourgeois policy Jouhaux is, alas, quite dependent). If the proletarian vanguard represented in the united front correctly treads the path of struggle, all the obstacles established by the trade-union bureaucracy will be overthrown by the living torrent of the proletariat. The key to the situation is now in the united front. If it does not use this key, it will play the lamentable role which would

22 Léon Jouhaux was General Secretary of the General Confederation of Labour from 1909-47.

inevitably have been played by the united front of the Mensheviks and Socialist-Revolutionaries in Russia in 1917, if the Bolsheviks had not prevented them from doing so.

We shall not speak of the Socialist and Communist Parties in particular because both have renounced their independence in favour of the united front. As soon as the two working-class parties, which sharply competed in the past, renounced mutual criticism and the winning of adherents from each other, by that alone they ceased to exist as distinct parties. To invoke 'principled differences' which remain, changes nothing. As soon as principled differences are not manifested openly and actively, at a moment as laden with responsibility as the present, they cease thereby to exist politically. They are like treasure which rests on the bottom of the ocean. We do not predict whether the common work will end in fusion but for the present period, which is of decisive importance for the destiny of France, the united front operates like an incomplete party constructed on the federalist principle.

What does the united front want? Until now it has not told the masses. The struggle against fascism? But until now the united front has not explained *how* it proposes to fight against fascism. Besides, a purely defensive bloc against fascism could only suffice if in everything else the two parties preserved complete independence. But no, we have a united front which embraces almost the entire public activity of the two parties and excludes their reciprocal struggle to win the majority of the proletariat. From this situation all the consequences must be drawn. The first and the most important is the struggle for power. The aim of the united front can be only a government of the united front, i.e. a Socialist-Communist government, a Blum-Cachin[23] ministry.

This must be said openly. If the united front takes itself seriously – and it is only on this condition that the popular masses will take it seriously – it cannot divest itself of the slogan of conquest of power. By what means? By every means which leads to that end.

23 André Léon Blum was the leader of the SFIO in the 1920s and 1930s. He would go on to become Prime Minister of France from 1936-37, in 1938 and briefly in 1946.

The united front does not renounce parliamentary struggle but it utilises parliament above all to unmask its impotence and to explain to the people that the present government has an extra-parliamentary base and that it can be overthrown only by a powerful mass movement.

The struggle for power means the utilisation of all the possibilities provided by the semi-parliamentary Bonapartist regime to overthrow this regime by a revolutionary push, to replace the bourgeois state by a workers' state.

The last district elections showed an increase in the socialist and especially the communist vote. In itself this fact settles nothing. The German Communist Party on the eve of its collapse had an incomparably more striking increase of votes. New, broad strata of the oppressed are driven to the left by the whole situation, independently even of the policy of the extreme parties. The French Communist Party gained more votes because by tradition it remains, despite its present conservative policy, the 'extreme left'. The masses showed by this their tendency to give the working-class parties an impulsion *to the left*, for the masses are infinitely more to the left than their parties. Further testimony of this is the revolutionary spirit of the socialist youth. It must not be forgotten that the youth is the sensitive barometer of the whole class and its vanguard!

If the united front does not emerge from passivity or, worse still, if it enters upon an unworthy romance with the Radicals, then to the 'left' of the united front, Anarchists, Anarcho-syndicalists and other similar groupings of political disintegration will be strengthened. At the same time apathy, precursor of catastrophe, will make headway.

On the other hand, the united front, assuring its rear and its flanks against the fascist bands, opens up a *broad political offensive under the slogan of conquest of power.* It will awaken an echo so powerful as to exceed the most optimistic expectations.

Only hollow charlatans for whom great mass movements shall always remain a book sealed with seven seals can fail to understand this.

## *Not a programme of passivity, but a programme of revolution*

The struggle for power must begin with the fundamental idea that if opposition to further aggravation of the situation of the masses under capitalism is still possible, no real improvement of their situation is conceivable without a revolutionary invasion of the right of capitalist property. The political campaign of the united front must base itself upon a well-elaborated *transition programme*, i.e. on a system of measures which with a workers' and peasants' government can assure the transition from capitalism to socialism.

Now a programme is needed not to ease the conscience but to guide revolutionary action. What is a programme worth if it remains a dead letter? The Belgian Workers' Party, for example, adopted the pompous plan of de Man[24] with all its 'nationalisations'. But what sense was there in it when the party did not lift its little finger to realise it? Programs of fascism are fantastic, false, demagogic. But fascism carries on a fierce struggle for power. Socialism can advance the most scientific programme but its value will be equal to zero if the vanguard of the proletariat does not unfold a bold struggle to capture the state. The social crisis in its political expression is the crisis of power. The old master of society is bankrupt. A new master is needed.

If the revolutionary proletariat does not take power, fascism will inevitably take it!

A programme of transitional demands for 'the middle classes' can naturally assume great importance if this programme corresponds, on the one hand, to the real needs of the middle classes, and on the other, to the demands of the development towards socialism. But once more the centre of gravity does not exist now in a special programme. The middle classes have seen many programs. What they need is confidence that the programme will be realised. The moment the peasant says: "This time it seems that the working-class parties will not retreat" – the cause of socialism is won.

24 Henri de Man was a leading figure in the Belgian Labour Party. Like the Neosocialists in France, he advocated planning to end economic depression.

But for that it is necessary to show in action that we are firmly prepared to smash every obstacle in our path.

There is no need of inventing means of struggle. They are provided by the whole history of the world working-class movement.

A concentrated campaign in the working-class press pounding steadily on the same key; real socialist speeches from the tribune of parliament, not by tame deputies but by leaders of the people; the utilisation of every electoral campaign for revolutionary purposes; repeated meetings to which the masses come not merely to hear the speakers but to get the slogans and directives of the hour; the creation and strengthening of the workers' militia; well-organised demonstrations driving the reactionary bands from the streets; protest strikes; an open campaign for the unification and enlargement of the trade-union ranks under the banner of resolute class struggle; stubborn, carefully calculated activity to win the army over to the cause of the people; broader strikes; more powerful demonstrations; the general strike of toilers of town and country; a general offensive against the Bonapartist government for the workers' and peasants' power.

There is still time to prepare for victory. Fascism has not yet become a mass movement. The inevitable decomposition of Radicalism will mean, however, the narrowing of the base of Bonapartism, the growth of the two extreme camps and the approach of the showdown. It is not a question of years but of months. The length of this period is not fixed by anyone but depends upon the struggle of living forces and above all upon the policy of the proletariat and its united front.

The potential forces of the revolution exceed by far the forces of fascism and in general of the whole united reaction. Sceptics who think that all is lost must be pitilessly driven out of the workers' ranks. From the depths of the masses come vibrant echoes to every bold word, every truly revolutionary slogan. The masses want the struggle.

It is not the spirit of combination among parliamentarians and journalists, but the legitimate and creative hatred of the oppressed for the oppressors which is today the single most progressive factor in history. It is necessary to turn to the masses, toward their deepest layers. It is necessary to appeal to their passions and to their reason. It is necessary to reject the false 'prudence' which is a synonym for cowardice and which, at great historical turning points, amounts to treason. The united front must take for its motto the formula of Danton: "*De l'audace, toujours de l'audace, et encore de l'audace.*"[25] To understand the situation fully and to draw from it all the practical conclusions, boldly and without fear and to the end, is to assure the victory of socialism.

25 "Audacity, more audacity, and ever more audacity."

# *France at the Turning Point*

Written 26 March 1936

Editor's note: This article, 'France at the Turning Point', was written as the introduction to a 1936 edition of Trotsky's book *Terrorism and Communism.*

* * *

This book is devoted to elucidating the methods of the revolutionary policies of the proletariat in our epoch. The presentation is polemical in nature, like the revolutionary policy itself. Once the masses have been won, the polemic against the ruling class turns, at a certain stage, into revolution.

Revolutionary policy has its theoretical basis in a clear understanding of the class nature of modern society, of its state, its laws and its ideology. The bourgeoisie operates with abstractions ('nation', 'fatherland', 'democracy') in order to cover up thereby the exploiting character of its rule. *Le Temps,*[1] one of the most venal newspapers on the terrestrial globe, gives daily lectures to the popular masses of France on patriotism and altruism. Meanwhile, it is a secret to nobody that the altruism of *Le Temps* itself is on the market at fixed international rates.

The first step of revolutionary politics is the exposure of bourgeois fictions which poison the consciousness of the masses. These fictions

1 *Le Temps* (*The Times*) was a daily Parisian newspaper.

acquire a particularly malignant character when amalgamated with the ideas of 'socialism' and 'revolution'. Today, more than ever before, the tone in the workers' organisations of France is being set by the manufacturers of such amalgams.

The first edition of this book played a certain role in the formative stages of the French Communist Party. At that time considerable evidence of this came to the author's notice, and, incidentally, it is not difficult to find traces of it in *L'Humanité* up to the year 1924. During the twelve years that have since elapsed, a radical recasting of values took place in the Communist International – after a number of feverish zigzags. Suffice to mention that this work is listed today among the proscribed books. In their ideas and methods, the present leaders of the French Communist Party (we are compelled to retain this name which is in complete variance with reality) do not differ in any principle from Kautsky, against whom our work was originally directed. They are only infinitely more ignorant and cynical. The relapse into reformism and patriotism that Cachin and co. are now living through might itself have served as a sufficient justification for a new edition of this book. However, more serious motives exist: they are rooted in the profound pre-revolutionary crisis which is convulsing the regime of the Third Republic.

* * *

After a lapse of eighteen years, the author of this book has had the occasion to spend two years in France (1933-35); to be sure, only as an observer in the provinces, who, moreover, found himself under constant police surveillance. During this time, in the Isère Department, where the writer had to live, a minor and quite banal routine episode occurred, which, however, provides the key to French politics as a whole. In a hospital, owned by the Comité des Forges,[2] a young worker, about to undergo a serious operation, took the liberty to read the revolutionary press (or, to be more precise, the press which he innocently accepted as revolutionary, namely: *L'Humanité*). The hospital delivered an ultimatum to the careless

2 The Comité des Forges (Foundry Committee) was an organisation of iron and steel foundry owners.

patient and, later, to four others who shared his sympathies: either they must renounce receiving the undesirable publications or they would be immediately thrown out into the street. Of course it availed the patients nothing to argue that clerical-reactionary propaganda was being carried on quite openly in, the hospital. Inasmuch as only ordinary workers were concerned, who had neither mandates as deputies nor ministerial portfolios to risk, but only their health and lives, the ultimatum proved ineffectual. Five sick men, one of whom was scheduled for an operation, were ejected from the hospital. Grenoble at that time was a Socialist municipality, headed by Doctor Martin, one of those conservative bourgeois who generally set the tone in the Socialist Party, and whose consummate representative is Léon Blum. The ejected workers sought a champion in the mayor. In vain. Despite all entreaties, letters and intercessions they failed even to obtain an interview. They then turned to the local left newspaper *Dépêche*,[3] in which Radicals and Socialists composed an indivisible cartel. Upon learning that the matter involved the hospital of the Comité des Forges, the director of the newspaper refused point blank to intervene: anything your heart desires, except that! For a previous indiscretion in connection with this all-powerful organisation, *Dépêche* had already been deprived of an advertisement, and suffered a loss of 20,000 francs. In contrast to the proletarians, the director of the 'left' newspaper, like the mayor, stood to lose something. They therefore refused to engage in an unequal struggle, leaving the workers with their diseased intestines and kidneys to their fate.

Once every week or every fortnight, the Socialist mayor disturbs the dim recollections of his youth by delivering a speech on the superiorities of socialism over capitalism. During elections, *Dépêche* supports the mayor and his party. Everything is in order. The Comité des Forges maintains an attitude of liberal tolerance towards socialism of this sort, which does not do the least harm to the material interests of capitalism. By means of an advertisement of 20,000 francs per year (so cheaply are these gentlemen priced!), the feudalists of the

3 *La Dépêche de Toulouse* (*The Toulouse Dispatch*) was a left-leaning bourgeois paper.

heavy industry and banks keep a large cartel newspaper in actual subjection. And not the newspaper alone. The Comité des Forges apparently has arguments, both direct and indirect, weighty enough for Messrs. Mayors, Senators, Deputies, including the socialists. Entire official France is under the dictatorship of finance capital. In the Larousse dictionary this system is called a 'democratic republic'.

It seemed to the Messrs. left deputies and journalists, not only in the Isère but in all the departments of France, that there would be no end to their peaceful cohabitation with capitalist reaction. They were mistaken. Long corroded by dry rot, democracy suddenly felt the barrel of a gun at its temple. Just as the rearmament of Hitler – a coarse material fact – brought about a real upheaval in the relations between states, laying bare the vain and illusory nature of the so-called 'international law', just so did the arming of the gangs of Colonel de La Rocque[4] result in convulsing the internal relations of France, compelling all parties without exception to reform their ranks, to assume a different colouration and to effect regroupments.

* * *

Friedrich Engels once wrote that the state, including the democratic republic, consists of detachments of armed men in defence of property; everything else serves only to embellish or camouflage this fact. Eloquent champions of 'Law', like Herriot or Blum, always became incensed at such cynicism. But both Hitler and de La Rocque, each in his own domain, have once again demonstrated that Engels is correct.

Early in 1934, Daladier was the presiding minister by will of universal, equal, direct and secret suffrage. He walked around with national sovereignty in his pocket alongside of his handkerchief. But the moment that the detachments of de La Rocque, Maurras[5] and co. showed that they dared to shoot and to slash the tendons of the police horses, sovereign Daladier surrendered his post to a political invalid designated by the leaders of the armed detachments. This fact

4 Colonel François de La Rocque was the leader of the fascist Croix de Feu, a key component of the 6 February riots.

5 Charles Maurras was leader of the monarchist Action Française.

is of considerably greater importance than all the electoral statistics, and it cannot be erased from the pages of the most recent history of France, for it forecasts the future.

Assuredly, the course of the political life of a country cannot be altered by *every* group armed with revolvers, at any time. Only those armed detachments which are the organs of specific classes can play a decisive role under *certain* conditions. Colonel de La Rocque and his henchmen seek to ensure 'law and order' against convulsions. And inasmuch as law and order in France signify the rule of finance capital over the middle and petty bourgeoisie, and the rule of the bourgeoisie as a whole over the proletariat and the social strata closest to it, the detachments of de La Rocque are simply the armed pickets of finance capital.

This idea is not new. One can often run across it even in the pages of *Le Populaire* and *L'Humanité*, although, of course, they were not the original formulators of it. These publications, however, speak only half of the truth. The other and equally important half consists of the fact that Herriot and Daladier with their followers are also an agency of finance capital; otherwise the Radicals could not have been the ruling party in France for a period of decades. If we are not to play the game of hide and seek, we must say that de La Rocque and Daladier both serve one and the same master. This does not mean to say that either they themselves or their methods are identical. Quite the contrary. They fiercely war against each other, like two specialised agencies each of whom has its own special secret of salvation. Daladier promises to maintain order through the exercise of the self-same tricolour democracy. De La Rocque holds that outlived parliamentarianism must be swept away and replaced by an open military-police dictatorship. The political methods are antagonistic but the social aims they serve are the same. The historical basis of the antagonism between de La Rocque and Daladier – we use these names merely for the sake of simplicity in our presentation – is the decline of the capitalist system, its incurable crisis, its decay. Despite the constant triumphs of technology and the explosive successes achieved by individual branches of industry, capitalism as a whole acts as a brake upon the development of the productive forces, engendering an extreme instability in social and international relations. Parliamentary democracy is indissolubly bound up with the epoch of free competition and free international trade. The bourgeoisie was able to tolerate the freedom of strikes, of assembly and of the press only so long as the productive forces were mounting upwards, so long as the sales markets were being extended, the welfare of the popular masses, even if only partially, was rising and the capitalist nations were able to live and let live. It is otherwise now. If we exclude the Soviet Union, the imperialist epoch is characterised by the stagnation or decline of the national income, a chronic agrarian crisis and organic unemployment. These phenomena pertain internally to the present phase of capitalism just as gout and arteriosclerosis pertain to certain ages of man. To explain world economic chaos by the consequences of the last war is to lay bare a hopeless superficiality in the spirit of Caillaux,[6] Count Sforza[7] and the like. The war itself was nothing else than an attempt on the part of capitalist countries to unload the already impending crash upon the enemy's back. The attempt failed. The war only deepened the manifestations of collapse, which, in its subsequent development, prepares a new war.

Bad as French economic statistics are, and although they deliberately evade the problems of class contradictions, even these statistics are unable to cover up the manifestations of a direct social disintegration. Amid the general decline of the national income, amid the truly horrifying fall in the income of the peasants, amid the ruin of the little men in the cities and the growth of unemployment, the gigantic enterprises with a turnover above 100 to 200 million a year are doing a brilliant business. Finance capital is sucking the lifeblood from the veins of the French people, in the full sense of the term. Such is the social basis for the ideology and politics of 'national unity'.

---

6 Joseph Caillaux was a minister in various French governments in the 1920s and a member of the senate from 1925-44.

7 Count Carlo Sforza was an aristocrat, short-lived Italian foreign minister and Senator. Whilst in exile in Belgium he wrote a number of books about fascism.

Mitigations and flickers of better times are possible in the process of decline; they are even inevitable. They remain, however, purely episodic in character. The general tendency of our epoch imperiously drives France, in the wake of a number of other countries, to the alternative: either the proletariat must overthrow the utterly decayed bourgeois order, or capitalism, in the interests of self-preservation, must replace democracy with fascism. How long can fascism last? The answer to this question will be provided by the fate of Mussolini and Hitler.

The fascists fired their guns on 6 February 1934 at the direct orders of the Bourse, the banks and the trusts. From the self-same ruling summits, Daladier received the instruction to hand over power to Doumergue. And if the Radical premier capitulated – with the pusillanimity that is generally characteristic of the Radicals – it was precisely because he recognized his own master in the gangs of de La Rocque. In other words: sovereign Daladier surrendered power to Doumergue for the self-same reason that the director of *Dépêche* and the mayor of Grenoble refused to expose the abominable cruelty of the agents of the Comité des Forges.

However, the transition from democracy to fascism carries with it the danger of social upheavals. Thence arise the tactical vacillations and differences among the summits of the bourgeoisie. All the magnates of capital are in favour of further strengthening the armed detachments, which can serve as safety reserves in the hour of danger. But what place should be allotted to these detachments even today? Should they be permitted immediately to assume the offensive or should they still be held in reserve as a threat? – These questions remain unsolved as yet.

Finance capital no longer believes in the ability of the Radicals to lead the petty-bourgeois masses behind them, and by means of the pressure exercised by these masses to restrain the proletariat within the framework of 'democratic' discipline. But finance capital is likewise uncertain of the ability of the fascist organisations, which still lack a real mass base, to seize power and establish firm order.

The behind-the-scenes leaders have been instilled with the need for caution not by parliamentary eloquence but by the rage of the workers, by the attempt of the general strike, which, to be sure, was stifled at its very inception by the bureaucracy of Jouhaux and, later, by the local uprisings (Toulon, Brest). A slight curb was placed on the fascists, and the Radicals breathed just a bit easier. *Le Temps*, which had already rushed to offer its hand and heart in a number of articles to the 'young generation', discovered anew the superior merits of a liberal regime as the one most in harmony with French genius. Thus, the unstable, transitional, bastard regime was established, which harmonises not with the genius of France but with the decline of the Third Republic. What stands out most sharply in this regime are its Bonapartist traits: the independence of power from parties and programs, the liquidation of the parliamentary legislation by means of emergency powers, the rising of the government in the guise of an 'arbiter' above the struggling camps, i.e. factually above the nation. The ministries of Doumergue, Flandin,[8] Laval,[9] all three with the invariable participation of the compromised and abject Radicals, represented minor variations of one and the same theme. Upon the inauguration of the Sarraut[10] ministry, Léon Blum, whose perspicacity possesses two dimensions instead of three, proclaimed that: "The final effects of 6 February have been destroyed on the parliamentary plane." (*Le Populaire*, 2 February 1936). This is commonly known as cleaning the shadow of a carriage with the shadow of a brush. As if it is possible, in general, to abolish 'on the parliamentary plane' the pressure of the armed detachments of finance capital! As if Sarraut can escape feeling this pressure and not quake before it! In point of fact the Sarraut-Flandin government represents another variation of the self-same semi-parliamentary 'Bonapartism', only somewhat inclined to the 'Left'. Sarraut,

8 Pierre-Étienne Flandin was a conservative politician and succeeded Doumergue as Prime Minister in 1934.

9 Pierre Laval was a member of the SFIO until 1922. He served as an independent Senator from 1925. He served as Prime Minister 1931-32, and then succeeded Flandin after the Bouisson government lasted only a week.

10 Albert Sarraut was a Radical and Prime Minister of France after Laval in 1936.

himself, in replying to the charge of his having resorted to arbitrary measures gave the Chamber the best answer possible. Said Sarraut: "If my measures are arbitrary, it is because I aim to be an arbiter". This aphorism would not have sounded badly even on the lips of Napoleon III. Sarraut feels himself to be not the plenipotentiary of a certain party or a bloc of parties in power, as is in accordance with the rules of parliamentarianism, but an arbiter over classes and parties, as in accordance with the laws of Bonapartism.

* * *

The sharpening of the class struggle, and especially the open emergence of the armed gangs of reaction, caused a similar upheaval among the workers' organisations. The Socialist Party which had been peacefully performing the role of the spare wheel in the chariot of the Third Republic, found itself compelled to half-renounce its cartel tradition, and even to break with its own right wing (the Neos).[11] Concurrently, the Communists completed their evolution in just the opposite direction but on a scale infinitely more extensive. Over a period of several years these gentlemen had raved deliriously about barricades, conquering the streets and so on (their delirium, to be sure, remained primarily literary in nature). Now after 6 February 1934, realising that the situation had taken a serious turn, the specialists in barricades scurried to the right. The normal reflex action of the scared phrase-mongers coincided most propitiously with the new international orientation of Soviet diplomacy.

Oppressed by the danger threatening from Hitler's Germany, the policy of the Kremlin turned towards France. Status quo – in international relations! Status quo – in the internal relations of the French regime! Hopes for the social revolution? Chimeras! The leading circles in the Kremlin refer as a rule only with contempt to French Communism. One must hang on to what exists, lest things get worse. Parliamentary democracy in France is inconceivable without the Radicals: they must be supported by the Socialists. It is necessary to order the communists not to hinder the bloc between

11 The Neosocialists (Neos) were a right-wing split within the SFIO, led by Pierre Renaudel and Marcel Déat. They were expelled in 1933.

Blum and Herriot and, if possible, the Communists – themselves must join the bloc. No convulsions, no threats! Such is the course pursued by the Kremlin.

When Stalin renounces the world revolution, the bourgeois parties of France refuse to believe him. Needless caution! In politics, blind credulity is, of course, not a great virtue. But blind distrust is no better. One must know how to compare words with deeds and be able to recognize a general tendency of development over a period of years. The policy of Stalin, determined by the interests of the privileged Soviet bureaucracy, has become conservative through and through. The French bourgeoisie has ample reasons to place faith in Stalin. All the less reason for trust on the part of the French proletariat.

During the Trade Union Unity Congress at Toulouse, the 'Communist' Racamond[12] gave a truly immortal formula of the policy of the People's Front: "How to overcome the timidity of the Radical Party?" How to overcome the bourgeoisie's fear of the proletariat? Very simply: the terrible revolutionists must fling away the knife clenched between their teeth, they must put pomade on their hair and filch the smile of the most fascinating courtesan. The result will be Vaillant-Couturier[13] – latest model. Under the onset of the pomaded 'communists', who with all their strength pushed the leftward-moving socialists to the right, Blum had to change his course once again, fortunately, in the accustomed direction. Thus arose the People's Front – the society for insuring Radical bankrupts at the expense of the capital of the working-class organisations.

Radicalism is inseparable from Freemasonry. When we say this, we have said everything. During the debate in the Chamber of Deputies on the fascist leagues, Mr. Xavier Vallat[14] recalled that Trotsky had once 'prohibited' French communists from participating in masonic lodges. Mr. Jammy Schmidt, a high

12 Julien Racamond was a leader of the Communist trade union confederation, CGTU, and represented it at the unification congress with the CGT.

13 Paul Vaillant-Couturier was a journalist, writer, member of the Communist Party of France's Central Committee and editor of *L'Humanité*.

14 Xavier Vallat was an antisemitic, independent and right-wing deputy.

authority in this field, we believe, immediately explained this edict by the incompatibility between despotic Bolshevism and the 'free spirit'. We shall not enter into a dispute over this point with the Radical deputy. But we still consider that a labour representative who seeks inspiration or solace in the vapid masonic cult of class collaboration is undeserving of the slightest trust. It was not accidental that the cartel was supplemented by the extensive participation of the socialists in the mummery of the lodges. Now the time has come for the repentant communists also to don the aprons! Incidentally, the newly converted pupils will be able to serve the old masters of the cartel more comfortably in aprons.

But, we are told, not without indignation, the People's Front is not a cartel at all, but a mass movement. There is, of course, no lack of pompous definitions, but they do not change the nature of things. The job of the cartel always consisted in putting a brake upon the mass movement, directing it into the channels of class collaboration. This is precisely the job of the People's Front as well. The difference between them – and not an unimportant one – is that the traditional cartel was applied during the comparatively peaceful and stable epochs of the parliamentary regime. Now, however, when the masses are impatient and explosive, a more imposing brake is needed, with the participation of the 'Communists'. Joint meetings, parade processions, oaths, mixing the banners of the Commune and of Versailles,[15] noise, bedlam, demagogy – all these serve a single aim: to curb and demoralize the mass movement.

While justifying himself in the Chamber before the rights, Sarraut declared that his innocent concessions to the People's Front were nothing else than the *safety valve* of the regime. Such frankness may have seemed imprudent. But it was rewarded by violent applause from the benches of the extreme left. There was no reason, therefore, for Sarraut to be bashful. In any case, he succeeded, perhaps not quite consciously, in providing a classic definition of the People's

15 The Paris Commune of 1871 was the first workers' state in history. The Palace of Versailles was the former royal residence, which was the organising centre for bourgeois reaction against the Commune.

Front: a safety valve for the mass movement. M. Sarraut is in every way fortunate with his aphorisms!

* * *

Foreign policy is the continuation of home policy. Having entirely renounced the viewpoint of the proletariat, Blum, Cachin and co. adopt, under the screen of 'collective security' and 'international law', the viewpoint of national imperialism. They are preparing precisely the same policy of bootlicking which they had conducted in the years 1914 to 1918, adding only the phrase: "For the Defence of the USSR." Yet during the years 1918-23, when Soviet diplomacy was also obliged to veer considerably and to conclude a good many agreements, not a single one of the sections of the Communist International so much as even dared to think of a bloc with its own bourgeoisie! Is not this alone ample proof of the sincerity of Stalin's renunciation of the world revolution?

The self-same motives which impelled the present leaders of the Comintern to suckle at the paps of 'democracy' in its period of agony led them to discover the glorious image of the League of Nations,[16] when the death rattle was already emanating from it. Thus was created a common platform of foreign policy between the Radicals and the Soviet Union. The home programme of the People's Front is concocted of generalities which allow of as liberal an interpretation as does the Geneva covenant. The general meaning of the programme is to leave everything as of old. Meanwhile, the masses refuse to accept the old any longer: therein lies the gist of the political crisis.

Disarming the proletariat politically, the Blums, Paul Faures,[17] Cachins and Thorezes[18] are most concerned lest the workers arm themselves physically. The agitation of these gentlemen does not

16 A forerunner to the UN, the League of Nations was set up by Western Imperialist powers in 1920, in the aftermath of the First World War, ostensibly to guarantee 'peace'. It effectively collapsed with the outbreak of war in 1939.

17 Paul Faure was a leader of the Right wing of the SFIO and a government minister from 1936-38. He was expelled from the SFIO for collaborating with the Vichy regime.

18 Maurice Thorez was leader of the French Communist Party from 1930-64.

differ in any way from the preacher's sermons on the superiorities of moral principles. Engels, who taught that the problem of state power is the problem of armed detachments, and Marx who looked upon insurrection as an art, appear as medieval barbarians in the eyes of the present deputies, senators and mayors of the People's Front. For the one hundred and first time, *Populaire* prints a cartoon picturing a naked worker with the caption: "You will learn that our bare fists are more solid than all your blackjacks." What a splendid contempt for military technique! Even the Abyssinian Negus[19] holds more progressive views on this subject. The overturns in Italy, Germany and Austria apparently do not exist for these people. Will they cease singing paeans to 'bare fists' when de La Rocque claps handcuffs upon them? Sometimes one feels sorry that such an experience cannot be afforded privately to the Messrs. Leaders, without involving the masses!

From the standpoint of the bourgeois regime as a whole, the People's Front represents an episode in the competition between Radicalism and fascism for the attention and good graces of big capital. By their theatrical fraternisation with socialists and communists, the Radicals want to prove to the master that the situation of the regime is not as bad as the rights assert; that the threat of the revolution is not at all so great; that even Vaillant-Couturier has swapped his knife for a dog collar; that through the medium of the domesticated 'revolutionists' it is possible to discipline the working masses, and, consequently, to save the parliamentary system from shipwreck.

Not all the Radicals believe in this manoeuvre; the most solid and influential among them, headed by Herriot, prefer to take a watchful position. But in the last analysis they have nothing else to propose themselves. The crisis of parliamentarianism is first of all the crisis of the confidence of the voters in Radicalism. Until some method for rejuvenating capitalism is discovered, there is not and cannot be any recipe for the salvation of the Radical Party. The latter has only the choice between two variants of political doom. Even the

19 Referring to the Negus, or Emperor, of Ethiopia, Haile Sellassie.

relative success it may score during the coming elections can neither avert nor even long postpone its shipwreck.

The leaders of the Socialist Party, the most carefree politicians in France, do not burden themselves with the study of the sociology of the People's Front. No one can learn anything from the endless monologues of Léon Blum. As for the Communists, the latter, extremely proud of their initiative in the cause of collaboration with the bourgeoisie, picture the People's Front as *an alliance between the proletariat and the middle classes*. What a parody on Marxism! The Radical Party is not at all the party of the petty bourgeoisie. Nor is it a "bloc between the middle and the petty bourgeoisie" in accordance with the idiotic definition of the Moscow *Pravda*. The middle bourgeoisie exploits the petty bourgeoisie not only economically but also politically, and it itself is the agency of finance capital. To give the hierarchic political relations, based upon exploitation, the neutral name of 'bloc' is to make a mock of reality. A horseman is not a bloc between a man and a horse. If the party of Herriot-Daladier extends its roots deeply into the petty bourgeoisie, and in part even into the working masses, it does so only in order to lull and dupe them in the interests of the capitalist order. The Radicals are the democratic party of French imperialism – any other definition is a lie.

The crisis of the capitalist system disarms the Radicals, depriving them of their traditional implements for lulling the petty bourgeoisie. 'The middle classes' are beginning to sense, if not to understand, that it is impossible to save the situation through paltry reforms, that it is necessary to scrap audaciously the existing system. But Radicalism and audacity are as incompatible as fire and water. Fascism is fed above all by the growing lack of confidence of the petty bourgeoisie in Radicalism. One can say without fear of exaggeration that the political fate of France in the period immediately ahead will take shape depending largely upon the manner in which Radicalism is liquidated, and who will fall heir to its legacy, i.e. its influence over the petty bourgeoisie: fascism or the party of the proletariat.

* * *

The elementary axiom of Marxist strategy reads that the alliance between the proletariat and the little men of the city and country can be realised only in the irreconcilable struggle against the traditional parliamentary representation of the petty bourgeoisie. In order to attract the peasant to the side of the worker, it is necessary to tear the peasant away from the Radical politician, who subjects the peasant to finance capital. In contradistinction to this, the People's Front, the conspiracy between the labour bureaucracy and the worst political exploiters of the middle classes is capable only of killing the faith of the masses in the revolutionary road and of driving them into the arms of the fascist counter-revolution.

Unbelievable as it may seem, some cynics attempt to justify the policy of the People's Front by quoting Lenin, who if you please, proved that there is no getting along without 'compromises' and, in particular, without making agreements with other parties. It has become an established rule among the leaders of the present Comintern to make mock of Lenin: they trample underfoot all the teachings of the builder of the Bolshevik Party, and then they take a trip to Moscow to kneel before his mausoleum.

Lenin began his activities in tsarist Russia, where not only the proletariat, the peasantry and the intelligentsia but also wide circles of the bourgeoisie stood in opposition to the old regime. If the policy of the People's Front has any justification at all, one should imagine that it could be justified first of all in a country that has yet to achieve its bourgeois revolution. The Messrs. Falsifiers, however, would not do badly at all if they were to point out at what stage and under what conditions the Bolshevik Party ever built even a semblance of the People's Front in Russia? Let them strain their imagination and rummage among the historical documents!

The Bolsheviks did conclude practical agreements with the revolutionary petty-bourgeois organisations, for example, for joint illegal transport of revolutionary literature; sometimes to repulse the Black-Hundred gangs. During elections to the state Duma they did, under certain conditions, enter into electoral blocs with the Mensheviks or the Socialist-Revolutionaries, on the second ballot.

That is all. No common 'programs', no common and permanent institutions, no renunciation of the criticism of temporary allies. Such episodic agreements and compromises, confined strictly to practical aims – and Lenin never spoke of any other kind – have absolutely nothing in common with the People's Front which represents a conglomeration of heterogeneous organisations, a long term alliance between different classes, that are bound for an entire period – and what a period! – by a common programme and a common policy of parades, declamations and of throwing up smokescreens. The People's Front will fall to pieces at the first serious test, and deep fissures will open up in all of its component sections. The policy of the People's Front is the policy of betrayal.

The rule of Bolshevism on the question of blocs reads: *march separately, strike together!* The rule of the leaders of the present Comintern is: *march together in order to be smashed separately*. Let these gentlemen hold on to Stalin and Dimitrov, but leave Lenin in peace!

It is impossible to read without indignation the declarations of the bragging leaders who allege that the People's Front has 'saved' France from fascism. In point of fact, they mean only to say that the mutual encouragement 'saved' the scared heroes from their own exaggerated fears. For how long? Between Hitler's first uprising and his coming to power, a decade elapsed, which was marked by frequent ebbs and flows. At that time, the German Blums and Cachins also used to proclaim more than once their 'victory' over national socialism. We refused to believe them, and we were not mistaken. This experience, however, has taught the French cousins of Wels and Thälmann nothing. In Germany, to be sure, the communists did not participate in the People's Front, which united the Social Democracy with the bourgeois left and the Catholic centre ("the alliance between the proletariat and the middle classes"!). During that period the Comintern rejected even fighting agreements between working-class organisations against fascism. The results are quite well known. The warmest sympathy to Thälmann as the captive of executioners cannot deter us from saying that his policy, i.e. the policy of Stalin, did more for Hitler's victory than the policy of Hitler himself. Having turned itself inside out, the Comintern now applies in France the quite familiar policy of the German Social Democracy. Is it really so difficult to foresee its results?

The coming parliamentary elections, no matter what their outcome, will not *in themselves* bring any serious changes into the situation: the voters, in the final analysis, are confronted with the choice between an arbiter of the type of Laval and an arbiter of the type, Herriot-Daladier. But inasmuch as Herriot has peacefully collaborated with Laval, and Daladier has supported them both, the difference between them is entirely insignificant, if measured by the scale of the tasks set by history.

To pretend that Herriot-Daladier are capable of proclaiming war against the '200 families' who rule France is to dupe the people shamelessly. The 200 families do not hang suspended in mid-air but are the crown of the system of finance capital. To cope with the 200 families it is necessary to overthrow the economic and political regime, in the maintenance of which Herriot and Daladier are just as much interested as Flandin and de La Rocque. The issue here is not a struggle of the 'nation' against a handful of magnates as *L'Humanité* pictures it, but the struggle of the proletariat against the bourgeoisie. It is a question of the class struggle which can be resolved only by revolution. The strike-breaking conspiracy of the People's Front has become the chief obstacle on this road.

It is impossible to say in advance how much longer the semi-parliamentary, semi-Bonapartist ministries will continue to succeed one another in France and in general through what concrete stages the country will pass in the next period. This depends on the world and national economic cycle, upon the degree of stability of Italian and German fascism, upon the course of events in Spain and last – but not least in importance – upon the awareness and the activity of the advanced elements of the French proletariat. The *dénouement* can be brought closer by the convulsions of the franc. A closer collaboration between France and England can postpone it. In any case the death throes of 'democracy' may drag out much longer than the pre-fascist period of Brüning-Papen-Schleicher endured in Germany; but this does not stop it from being the death throes just the same. Democracy will be swept away. The only question is: by whom?

* * *

The struggle against the '200 families', against fascism and war, for peace, bread and freedom and other magnificent things is either a lie, or it is the struggle for the overthrow of capitalism. The toilers of France are faced with the problem of the revolutionary conquest of power not as a distant goal but as the task of the coming period. Meanwhile, the Socialist and Communist leaders not only renounce the revolutionary mobilisation of the proletariat, but resist it with all their strength. Fraternising with the bourgeoisie, they hound and expel the Bolsheviks. So greatly do they hate the revolution and dread it! Under these conditions, the worst role is played by those pseudo-revolutionists of the type of Marceau Pivert who promise to overthrow the bourgeoisie, but only with the permission of Léon Blum! The entire course of the French labour movement for the last twelve years has placed the task of creating a new revolutionary party on the order of the day.

To speculate whether events will allow 'sufficient' time for its formation is to engage in the most fruitless of all occupations. History has absolutely inexhaustible resources in the domain of different variants, historical forms, stages, accelerations and retardations. Under the influence of economic difficulties fascism may venture prematurely and suffer a defeat. This would imply a long respite. Contrariwise, it may occupy a temporising position too long and thereby increase the chances in favour of the revolutionary organisations. The People's Front may break up out of its own contradictions before fascism is able to engage in a general battle: this would signify a period of regroupments and splits in the parties of the working class, and a rapid fusion of the revolutionary vanguard. Spontaneous mass movements as in Toulon and Brest may attain a wide sweep and create a reliable fulcrum for the revolutionary lever.

Finally, even the victory of fascism in France, which is theoretically not excluded, does not mean that it will reign for 1,000 years as Hitler prophesies, or that it is even assured to endure as long as Mussolini has been able to maintain himself. The twilight of fascism, beginning with Italy or Germany, would quickly spread over France as well. To build a revolutionary party in this, the least favourable variant, is to bring nearer the hour of vengeance. The wiseacres who shy away from the un-postponable task with the words, "the conditions are not yet mature", merely reveal that they themselves have not matured for the conditions.

The Marxists of France, as well as those of the entire world, must, in a certain sense, begin at the beginning, but on an infinitely higher historical level than their predecessors. Progress is at first rendered extremely difficult by the fall of the Communist International, more infamous than the fall of the Social Democracy in 1914. The new cadres are being recruited slowly, in a cruel struggle against the united front of the reactionary and patriotic bureaucracy in the working class. On the other hand, these very difficulties, which did not descend upon the proletariat accidentally, constitute an important condition for the correct selection and the firm tempering of the first detachments of the new party and the new international.

Only a very tiny section of the cadres of the Comintern began its revolutionary education from the outset of the war, prior to the October Revolution. All these elements, almost without a single exception, are now outside the Communist International. The next oldest stratum joined the already victorious October Revolution. This was much easier. But only an insignificant portion has remained even of this second draft. The overwhelming majority of the present cadres of the Comintern adhered not to the Bolshevik programme, not to the revolutionary banner, but to the Soviet bureaucracy. These are not fighters but docile functionaries, adjutants, errand boys. It is by reason of this that the Third International is putrefying so infamously amid the historical situation so rich in great revolutionary possibilities.

The Fourth International rises on the shoulders of its three predecessors. It is subjected to blows from the front, the sides and the rear. Careerists, cowards, philistines have nothing to seek in our ranks. The percentage of sectarians and adventurists, inevitable at the beginning, is winnowed away as the movement grows. Let pedants and sceptics shrug their shoulders about 'small' organisations that issue 'small' papers and fling a challenge to the entire world. Serious revolutionists will pass contemptuously by the pedants and sceptics. The October Revolution also once began with its swaddling clothes.

The mighty Russian parties of Socialist-Revolutionaries and Mensheviks who made up the 'People's Front' with the Cadets, crumbled into dust in the course of a few months under the blows of a 'handful of fanatics' of Bolshevism. Subsequently the German Social Democracy, the German Communist Party and the Austrian Social Democracy died an ignoble death under the blows of fascism. The epoch which is drawing close for the European peoples will sweep out of the working class, without leaving a trace, all that is equivocal and rotten. All the Jouhauxs, Citrines,[20] Blums, Cachins, Vanderveldes[21] and Caballeros[22] are only phantoms. The sections of the Second and Third Internationals will ingloriously leave the stage one after another. A new regroupment in the workers' ranks is inevitable. Young revolutionary cadres will gain flesh and blood. Victory is conceivable only on the basis of the methods of Bolshevism, to the defence of which this volume is dedicated.

---

20 Walter Citrine was General Secretary of the British Trade Union Congress (TUC) and president of the International Federation of Trade Unions (IFTU).

21 Emile Vandervelde was a leader of the Belgian Workers' Party and President of the Second International during the First World War, and again from 1923-38.

22 Francisco Largo Caballero was a leader of the Spanish Socialist Workers Party.

# *The French Revolution Has Begun!*

Written 9 June 1936

Never has the radio seemed so precious as during these days. From a distant village in Norway[1] one can follow the pulse beats of the French revolution. Or rather, to put it more exactly, the reflection of these pulsations in the minds and voices of the Messrs. ministers, trade-union secretaries and other mortally terrified leaders.

To say 'French revolution' may seem exaggerated. Oh, no! This is no exaggeration. That is precisely how a revolution springs into being. Generally speaking, a revolution cannot come into being any other way. The French revolution has begun.

To be sure, Léon Jouhaux, tailing Léon Blum, keeps assuring the bourgeoisie that this is a purely economic movement within the rigid framework of the law. The strikers, indeed, are seizing factories for the duration of the strike, establishing control over the bosses and their staffs. But one may shut one's eyes to this deplorable 'detail'. On the whole, these are 'craft strikes, not political strikes', the Messrs. leaders keep repeating. Yet, under the influence of these

1 After signing the Franco-Soviet pact in 1934, the French government bowed to pressure from the Stalinists to expel Trotsky from France. He then found refuge in Norway, until he was deported from there to Mexico in December 1936.

'non-political' strikes the entire political situation in the country is being radically transformed. The government decides to act with haste it never thought of the night before. Indeed, according to Blum, true strength lay in patience! The capitalists are unexpectedly compliant. The entire counter-revolution bides its time behind the backs of Blum and Jouhaux. And this miracle is brought about entirely by 'craft' strikes. What then would have happened had the strikes been political?

Oh, no, the leaders are not telling the truth. The craft union embraces the workers of a single, isolated trade, separating them from other trades. Trade unionism and reactionary syndicalism bend all efforts to keep the working-class movement within the framework of crafts. Upon this, in fact, rests the dictatorship of the trade-union bureaucracy over the working class (the worst of all dictatorships!) while the Jouhaux-Racamond clique in turn slavishly depends upon the bourgeois state. The essence of the present movement consists precisely in that it is breaking through trade union, craft and local bounds, raising beyond them the demands, hopes and will of the whole proletariat. The movement takes on the character of an epidemic. The contagion spreads from factory to factory, from craft to craft, from district to district. All the layers of the working class seem to be giving echoing answers to a roll call. The metal workers begin – they are the vanguard. But the strength of the movement lies in the fact that just behind the vanguard follow the heavy reserves of the class, including the most backward trades, the rearguard, completely forgotten on weekdays by Messrs. parliamentarians and trade-union leaders. Not for nothing did *Le Peuple*[2] openly confess that the emergence of certain particularly low-paid categories of the Paris population came to it as a complete 'surprise'. Yet precisely in the depths of these most oppressed strata, inexhaustible springs of enthusiasm, selflessness and courage lie hidden. The very fact of their awakening is the infallible mark of the tidal wave. It is necessary to reach these layers at all costs!

2 *Le Peuple* (*The People*) was the paper of the CGT trade union federation.

Tearing loose from the craft and local bounds, the strike movement has become terrible not only for bourgeois society, but also for the workers' own parliamentary and trade-union representatives who are primarily concerned with closing their eyes to reality. Historical legend has it that Louis XVI,[3] upon asking: "What is this, mutiny?", was answered by one of his courtiers: "No, sire, this is revolution." Now to the question of the bourgeoisie: "Is this mutiny?" its courtiers are replying: "No, these are only craft strikes." In giving comfort to the capitalists, Blum and Jouhaux are comforting themselves. But words will not help. To be sure, when these lines appear in the press, the first wave may have subsided. Outwardly life may seem to be returning to its old channels. But this changes nothing. These are not craft strikes that have taken place. These are not just strikes. This is a strike. This is the open rallying of the oppressed against the oppressors. This is the classic beginning of revolution.

The entire past experience of the working class, the history of its exploitation, miseries, struggles and defeats, comes to life under the impact of events and rises up in the consciousness of every proletarian, even the most backward, and drives him into the common ranks. The entire class has been set in motion. This colossal mass cannot be stopped by words. The struggle must be consummated either in the greatest of victories or the most ghastly of defeats.

*Le Temps* has called the strike the "practice manoeuvres of the revolution". This is infinitely more serious than what is being said by Blum and Jouhaux. But even the definition given by *Le Temps* is incorrect, for it is in a certain sense exaggerated. Manoeuvres presuppose the existence of a command, a general staff, a plan. This does not exist in the strike. The leading centres of the working-class organisations, including those of the Communist Party, have been caught unawares. They are afraid, above all, lest the strike spoil all their blueprints. The radio relays a remarkable statement by Marcel Cachin: "We are all of us – we and the others – confronted by the fact of the strike." In other words, the strike is our common misfortune.

3 Louis XVI was the last King of France before he was deposed and guillotined in the French Revolution.

With such words the terrible senator persuades the capitalists to make concessions in order not to aggravate the situation. The parliamentarians and the trade-union secretaries, who are adapting themselves to the strike from the sidelines the sooner to extinguish it, stand in reality outside the strike, dangling in the air. They themselves do not know whether they will land feet or head-first. The awakened mass is still without a revolutionary staff.

The ruling class has a real staff. This staff is not at all identical with the Blum government, although it uses the latter very skilfully. Capitalist reaction is now playing a big and risky game, but playing ably. At the present moment it is playing the game of 'losers win'.

> 'Let us today concede all the unpleasant demands which have met with unanimous approval of Blum, Jouhaux and Daladier. It is a far cry from recognition in principle to realisation in action. There is the parliament, there is the senate, there is the chancery – all these are instruments of obstruction. The masses will show impatience and will attempt to exert greater pressure. Daladier will divorce Blum. Thorez will try to shy to the left. Blum and Jouhaux will part company with the masses. Then we shall make up for all the present concessions, and with interest.'

This is the reasoning of the real staff of the counter-revolution, the famous '200 families' and their hired strategists. They are acting in accordance with a plan. It would be light-minded to say that their plan is groundless. No, with the assistance of Blum, Jouhaux and Cachin, the counter-revolution *can* attain its goal.

The profound organic and genuinely revolutionary character of the strike wave is best of all characterised by the fact that the mass movement, though improvised, has acquired such vast scope and has exercised so great a political influence. This is the guarantee of the endurance of the movement, its stubbornness and the inevitability of a series of ever-rising waves. Without this, victory would be impossible. But all this is not enough for victory. As against the staff and the plan of the '200 families' there must be a staff and a plan of proletarian revolution. None as yet exists. But they can be created.

All the prerequisites and all the elements for a new crystallisation of the masses are at hand.

The sweep of the strike springs, we are told, from the 'hopes' in the People's Front government. This is only one-quarter of the truth and even less than that. If matters were really limited to *hopes* alone, the workers would not have run the risk of struggle. The strike expresses above all the *distrust* or the *half-trust* of the workers, if not in the good intentions of the government, then in its ability to overcome obstacles and to come to grips with its problems. The proletarians want to 'assist' the government, but in their own way, in the proletarian way. They still of course lack complete consciousness of their own strength. But it would be a gross distortion to portray matters as if the masses were guided only by pious 'hopes' in Blum. It is not easy for them to muster their thoughts while yoked to the old leaders who try to drive them as soon as possible back into the old rut of slavery and routine. Nevertheless, the French proletariat is not at the beginning of its history. The strike has everywhere and in every place pushed the most thoughtful and fearless workers to the fore. To them belongs the initiative. They are still acting cautiously, feeling the ground under their feet. The vanguard detachments are trying not to rush ahead so as not to isolate themselves. The echoing and re-echoing answers of the hindmost ranks to their call gives them new courage. The roll call of the class has become a trial self-mobilisation. The proletariat was itself in greatest need of this demonstration of its strength. The practical successes won, however precarious they may be, cannot fail to raise the self-confidence of the masses to an extraordinary degree, particularly among the most backward and oppressed strata.

That leaders have come forward in the industries and in the factories is the foremost conquest of the first wave. The elements of local and regional staffs have been created. The masses know them. They know one another. Real revolutionists will seek contact with them. Thus the first self-mobilisation of the masses has outlined and in part brought forward the first elements of revolutionary leadership. The strike has stirred, revitalised and regenerated the whole colossal class organism. The old organisational shell has by no means dropped away. On the contrary, it still retains its hold quite stubbornly. But under it the new skin is already visible.

We do not speak now of the rhythm of events, which will undoubtedly be accelerated. In this sphere only suppositions and guesses are possible as yet. The second wave, its duration, its sweep and its intensity will doubtless permit a much more concrete prognosis than can be made now. But one thing is clear in advance: the second wave will not have by far the peaceful, almost good-natured, spring-like character that the first has had. It will be more mature, more stubborn and harsh, for it will arise from the disillusionment of the masses in the practical results of the policies of the People's Front and their own initial venture. In the government a process of stratification will take place as well as in the parliamentary majority. The counter-revolution will immediately become more self-assured and brazen. Further easy successes cannot be expected by the masses. Faced with the danger of losing what seemed to have been won, faced with the growing resistance of the enemy and the confusion and indecision of the official leadership, the masses will feel the burning need of a programme, an organisation, a plan and a staff. For this we must prepare ourselves and the advanced workers. In the atmosphere of revolution the masses are swiftly re-educated, the cadres swiftly selected and tempered.

The revolutionary general staff cannot emerge from combinations at the top. The combat organisation would not be identical with the party even if there were a mass revolutionary party in France, for the movement is incomparably broader than the party. The organisation also cannot coincide with the trade unions for the unions embrace only an insignificant section of the class and are headed by an arch-reactionary bureaucracy. The new organisation must correspond to the nature of the movement itself. It must reflect the struggling masses. It must express their growing will. This is a question of the direct representation of the revolutionary class. Here it is not necessary to invent new forms. Historical precedents exist. The industries and factories will elect their deputies who will meet to elaborate, jointly, plans of struggle, and to provide the leadership. Nor is it necessary to invent the name for such an organisation; it is the *soviets of workers' deputies*.

The main section of the revolutionary workers is now following the Communist Party. In the past they have more than once cried: "Soviets Everywhere!" The majority of them undoubtedly accepted this slogan honestly and seriously. There was a time when we regarded this slogan as untimely. But now the situation has radically changed. The mighty collision of classes is heading towards a climax. Whoever vacillates, whoever loses time is a traitor. The choice lies between the greatest of all historical victories and the most ghastly of defeats. We must prepare for victory. "Soviets Everywhere"? Agreed. But it is time to pass from words to action.

# *Revolutionary Interlude in France*

Written 9 July 1936

We must repeat once again that the serious capitalist press like the Paris *Temps* or the London *Times* has made a much more correct and penetrating evaluation of the meaning of the June events in France and Belgium than has the press of the People's Front. While the socialist and communist official organs, tagging behind Blum, talk about the beginning of the "peaceful transformation of the social regime in France", the conservative press insists that in France a revolution has begun and that it will inevitably assume violent forms during the next stages. It would be a mistake to view this prognosis as solely or chiefly intended to frighten the property owners. The representatives of big capital are capable of following the social struggle very realistically. Contrariwise, petty-bourgeois politicians readily incline to accept their own desires for reality. Standing between the principal classes, finance capital and the proletariat, the Messrs. 'Reformers' propose that both of the opponents accept the middle course which they have greatly laboured to elaborate in the general staff of the People's Front, and which they themselves interpret differently. However, they will shortly have occasion to convince themselves that it is much easier to reconcile class contradictions in leading articles than in governmental activity, especially in the very heat of a social crisis.

In parliament an ironical charge has been hurled against Blum that he carried on negotiations concerning the demands of the strikers with representatives of the '200 families'. "And who else was there for me to negotiate with?", wittily replied the premier. In point of fact, if any negotiations are to be carried on with the bourgeoisie, then it is necessary to choose the real masters, those capable of deciding for themselves and of issuing orders to others. But in that case, it was pointless to have so noisily declared war against them! Within the framework of the bourgeois regime, its laws and mechanics, each one of the '200 families' is incomparably more powerful than the Blum government. The financial magnates represent the crown of the bourgeois system of France, while the Blum government, despite all its electoral successes, 'crowns' only a brief interlude between the two contending camps.

At the present moment, in the first half of July, it might superficially seem as if everything had more or less returned to normal. As a matter of fact, within the depths of the proletariat, as well as among the summits of the ruling classes, a well-nigh automatic preparation for a new conflict is now going on. The very essence of the matter lies in the fact that the reforms, very meagre as they are in substance, upon which the capitalists and the leaders of the labour organisations agreed in June, are not viable, because they are already beyond the powers of declining capitalism, taken as a whole. The financial oligarchy, which did a swimming business in the very heat of the crisis, could, of course, abide both with the forty-hour week, paid vacations and so on, but the hundreds of thousands of middle and petty entrepreneurs, upon whom finance capital leans and upon whose shoulders it now is loading the costs of its agreement with Blum, must either submit docilely to ruin or seek, in their turn, to load the costs of social reforms upon the workers and peasants, as consumers.

Blum, to be sure, had more than once expatiated in the Chamber and in the press upon the enticing prospect of a general economic revival and of a rapidly expanding turnover which will make it possible to lower considerably the general productive costs and therefore allow of increased expenditures for labour power without a rise in commodity prices. In point of fact such combined economic processes were frequently to be observed in the past. They mark the entire history of rising capitalism. The only trouble is that Blum is trying to project into the future what has irrevocably receded into the past. Politicians, subject to such an aberration, may call themselves socialists and even communists but they fix their eyes not ahead but behind them, and they are therefore a brake upon progress.

French capitalism, with its celebrated 'equilibrium' between agriculture and industry, entered into the stage of decline later than Italy and Germany but no less irresistibly. This is not a phrase from a revolutionary proclamation, but a statement of incontrovertible fact. The productive forces of France have outgrown the bounds of private property and the boundaries of the state. Governmental intervention on the foundations of a capitalist regime can be of assistance only in shifting the unprofitable expenditures of the decline from one class to another. Which class would that be? When the Socialist premier has to carry on negotiations about a 'more just' distribution of the national income, he is unable, as we have already learned, to find any worthy partners other than the representatives of the '200 families'. Holding in their hands all the basic levers of industry, credit and commerce, the financial magnates shift the costs of the agreement upon the 'middle classes', compelling them by reason of this very thing to enter into a struggle with the workers. In this now lies the crux of the situation.

The manufacturers and the merchants present their ledgers to the ministers and say: "We cannot do it." The government, calling to mind old textbooks of political economy, replies: "It is necessary to cut down the costs of production." But this is easier said than done. Moreover, in the given conditions, technological improvements would mean increased unemployment, and ultimately a deepening of the crisis. The workers, on their part, are protesting against the fact that the incipient increases in prices threaten to devour their conquests. The government issues orders to the prefects that they launch a campaign against the high cost of living. But the prefects know from long experience that it is much easier to lower the tone of an oppositionist paper than to lower the price of meat. The wave of mounting prices still lies ahead.

The small manufacturers, tradesmen and, in their way, the peasants will become more and more disillusioned with the People's Front, from which they expected immediate salvation far more directly and innocently than the workers. The fundamental political contradiction of the People's Front lies in the fact that the politicians of the Golden Mean at its head, in their fear of 'scaring' the middle classes, do not transgress the bounds of the old social regime, that is, the historic blind alley. Meanwhile, the so-called middle classes – not their summits, of course, but the lower ranks – sense the impasse at every step and are not at all afraid of bold decisions, but on the contrary demand them as a riddance from the noose. "Do not expect miracles from us!" the pedants in power keep repeating. But the gist of the matter lies precisely in the fact that without 'miracles', without heroic decisions, without a complete overturn in property relations – without the concentration of the banking system, of the basic branches of industry and of foreign trade in the hands of the state – there is no salvation for the petty bourgeoisie of the city and country. If the 'middle classes' in whose name the People's Front was expressly created are unable to find revolutionary audacity from the left, they will seek it on the right. The petty bourgeoisie is gripped by fever and must inevitably toss from side to side. Meanwhile, the big capitalists are confidently watching for such a turn as will make a beginning for fascism. Not only as a semi-military organisation of bourgeois papa's sons with automobiles and aeroplanes but as a real mass movement in France.

The workers in June exerted colossal pressure upon the ruling classes, but they did not carry it to its conclusion. They evinced their revolutionary might but also their weakness: the lack of a programme and of a leadership. All the props of capitalist society and all of its incurable ulcers remain intact. Now the period is unfolding of the preparations for a counter-pressure: repressions against the left agitators, the increasingly envenomed agitation on the part of the right agitators, experimentation with rising prices, mobilisations of manufacturers for mass lockouts. The trade unions of France which on the eve of the strike hardly numbered one million members are now approaching the five million mark. This unprecedented mass influx is indicative of the feelings that inspire the labour masses. There cannot even be talk that they will permit the costs of their own conquests to be loaded upon themselves without a struggle. The ministers and their official leaders are indefatigable in urging the workers to remain seated peacefully and not to hinder the government while it is working over the solution of problems. But inasmuch as the government, in the nature of things, is incapable of solving any problem whatever; inasmuch as the June concessions were gained thanks to the strike and not patient waiting; inasmuch as every new day will expose the bankruptcy of the government in the face of the developing counter-offensive of capital, these monotonous exhortations will soon lose their potency. The logic of the situation which flows from the June victory, or, rather, to put it more correctly, from the semi-fictitious character of this victory, will compel the workers to accept the challenge, to embark once again upon a struggle. Taking fright at this prospect, the government shifts to the right. Under the direct pressure of the Radical allies, but, in the last analysis, upon the demand of the '200 families', the socialist Minister of Internal Affairs announced in the Senate that no further occupations of factories, stores and farms by the strikers would be tolerated. A warning of this sort cannot, of course, put a halt to the struggle, but it is capable of making it infinitely more decisive and acute.

An absolutely objective analysis, which proceeds from facts and not desires, thus leads us to the conclusion that a new social conflict is being prepared from two sides, and that it must break out with an almost mechanical inevitability. It is not difficult, even at the present time, to define in general the nature of this conflict. During all revolutionary periods in history, two successive stages may be established which are closely linked together: first, the 'elemental' movement of the masses which catches the opponent off-guard and which extorts serious concessions, or, at any rate, promises; and then the ruling classes, sensing that the foundations of their rule are being threatened, prepare for their revenge. The semi-victorious masses evince impatience. The traditional left leaders, who, like the opponents, were caught unawares by the movement, hope to save the situation by means of conciliatory eloquence, and end by losing their influence. The masses are drawn into a new struggle almost leaderless, without a clear programme and without understanding the difficulties ahead. Such a conflict ineluctably arising from the first semi-victory of the masses has often led to their defeat – or semi-defeat. An exception to this rule will hardly be found in the history of revolutions. However, the difference (it is no slight one) lies in the fact that sometimes the defeat assumes the character of a rout: such for example were the June Days in 1848 in France, which put an end to the revolution; in other cases, however, the semi-defeat proves only a stage toward victory: such a role, for example, was played by the defeat of the Petrograd workers and soldiers in July 1917. It was precisely the July defeat that accelerated the rise of the Bolsheviks, who were not only able to estimate correctly the situation without any illusions or any embellishments but also did not break away from the masses during the most difficult days of failure, sacrifice and persecution.

Yes, the conservative press is making a sober analysis of the situation. Finance capital with its auxiliary political and military organs cold-bloodedly prepares for revenge. Among the summits of the People's Front there is nothing except confusion and internal strife. The left newspapers are smothered in moral preachments. The leaders choke with phrases. The ministers vie to show the Bourse that they are mature statesmen. Together, all this implies that the proletariat will be drawn into the impending conflict not only without the leadership of its traditional organisations, as was the case in June, but also against them. But there is no generally recognised new leadership in existence as yet. Under such conditions one could hardly count upon immediate victory. An attempt to probe into the future would rather lead one to the following alternative: either June days, 1848 or July Days, 1917. In other words: either a rout for many years to come, with the inevitable triumph of fascist reaction, or only a severe lesson on strategy as a result of which the working class will mature, renew its leadership and prepare the conditions for future victory. The French proletariat is no novice. It has behind it a great number of epoch-making struggles. True, the new generations have to learn each time from their own experience – but they do not begin from the beginning, nor do they learn everything all over again, but through an abbreviated course, as it were. The great tradition permeates the very marrow of the workers and facilitates the selection of the road. Already in June the anonymous leaders of the awakened class had found methods and forms of struggle with magnificent revolutionary tact. The molecular process of mass consciousness is not being suspended now for a single hour. All this enables us to conclude that the new layer of the leaders not only will remain true to the masses in the days of the inevitable and, probably, not far-distant conflict, but will also be able to lead the inadequately prepared army from the battle without a rout.

It is not true that the revolutionists in France are allegedly interested in precipitating the conflict, or 'artificially' provoking it. Only the dullest police minds are capable of thinking so. Marxist revolutionists see their duty in looking clearly into the face of reality and calling things by their names. To make a timely deduction from the objective situation concerning the perspectives of the second stage is to help the advanced workers not to be caught unawares, and to introduce as much clarity as possible into the consciousness of the struggling masses. In this consists at present the task of the serious political leadership.

# *Part 3: Europe After the War*

*Writings by Leon Trotsky & Ted Grant*

*August 1940 – June 1948*

# *Bonapartism, Fascism and War*

Dictated 20 August 1940

Editor's note: This is Trotsky's last article. He delivered these words into his dictaphone for future editing into an article. Later that day, a Stalinist agent, Ramón Mercader, made an assassination attempt on Trotsky's life. He died the following day in hospital at age sixty.

The following is a literal translation of his dictated notes.

* * *

In his very pretentious, very muddled and stupid article, Dwight Macdonald tries to represent us as holding the view that fascism is simply a repetition of Bonapartism. A greater piece of nonsense would be hard to invent. We have analysed fascism as it developed, throughout the various stages of its development and advanced to the forefront now one now another of its aspects. There is an element of Bonapartism in fascism. Without this element, namely, without the raising of state power above society owing to an extreme sharpening of the class struggle, fascism would have been impossible. But we pointed out from the very beginning that it was primarily a question of Bonapartism of the epoch of imperialist decline which is qualitatively different from Bonapartism of the epoch of bourgeois rise. At the next stage we separated out pure Bonapartism as the prologue to a fascist regime. Because in the case of pure Bonapartism the rule of a monarch is approximated and...

In post-war Italy the situation was profoundly revolutionary. The proletariat had every opportunity.

The Ministries of Brüning, Schleicher and the Presidency of Hindenburg in Germany, Pétain's[1] government in France, but they all have proved, or must prove, unstable. In the epoch of imperialist decline, a pure Bonapartist Bonapartism is completely inadequate; imperialism finds it indispensable to mobilise the petty bourgeoisie and to crush the proletariat under its weight. Imperialism is capable of fulfilling this task only in case the proletariat itself reveals its inability to conquer power, while the social crisis drives the petty bourgeoisie into a condition of paroxysm.

The sharpness of the social crisis arises from this, that with today's concentration of the means of production – i.e. the monopoly of trusts, the law of value – the market is already incapable of regulating economic relations. State intervention becomes an absolute necessity. Inasmuch as the proletariat...

The present war, as we have stated on more than one occasion, is a continuation of the last war. But a continuation does not signify a repetition. As a general rule, a continuation signifies a development, a deepening, a sharpening. Our policy, the policy of the revolutionary proletariat toward the second imperialist war, is a continuation of the policy elaborated during the last imperialist war, primarily under Lenin's leadership. But a continuation does not signify a repetition. In this case too, continuation signifies a development, a deepening and a sharpening.

## *We were caught unaware in 1914*

During the last war, not only the proletariat as a whole but also its vanguard and, in a certain sense, the vanguard of this vanguard, was caught unaware. The elaboration of the principles of revolutionary policy toward the war began at a time when the war was already in

1 Philippe Pétain was a French general who became the Prime Minister and Chief of the collaborationist Vichy government in 1940, after capitulating to Hitler.

full blaze and the military machine exercised unlimited rule. One year after the outbreak of the war, the small revolutionary minority was still compelled to accommodate itself to a centrist majority at the Zimmerwald Conference. Prior to the February Revolution and even afterwards, the revolutionary elements felt themselves to be not contenders for power but the extreme left opposition. Even Lenin relegated the socialist revolution to a more or less distant future. In 1915 or 1916 he wrote in Switzerland: (quotation).[2] If that is how Lenin viewed the situation, then there is hardly any need of talking about the others.

This political position of the extreme Left wing expressed itself most graphically on the question of the defence of the fatherland.

In 1915 Lenin referred in his writings to revolutionary wars which the victorious proletariat would have to wage. But it was a question of an indefinite historical perspective and not of tomorrow's task. The attention of the revolutionary wing was centred on the question of the defence of the capitalist fatherland. The revolutionists naturally replied to this question in the negative. This was entirely correct. But this purely negative answer served as the basis for propaganda and for training the cadres, but it could not win the masses who did not want a foreign conqueror. In Russia prior to the war, the Bolsheviks constituted four-fifths of the proletarian vanguard, that is, of the workers participating in political life (newspapers, elections, etc.). Following the February Revolution, the unlimited rule passed into the hands of defencists, the Mensheviks and the SRs. True enough, the Bolsheviks in the space of eight months conquered the overwhelming majority of the workers. But the decisive role in this conquest was played not by the refusal to defend the bourgeois fatherland but by the slogan: "All Power to the Soviets!" And only by this revolutionary slogan! The criticism of imperialism, its militarism, the renunciation of the defence of bourgeois democracy

2 "However, five, ten and even more years may pass before the socialist revolution begins." (Lenin, 'The Socialist Revolution and the Right of Nations to Self-Determination', January 1916, *Collected Works* (henceforth referred to as *LCW*), Vol. 22, Progress Publishers, 1974, p. 153.)

and so on could have never conquered the overwhelming majority of the people to the side of the Bolsheviks. In all other belligerent countries, with the exception of Russia, the revolutionary wing toward the end of the war all…

In so far as the proletariat proves incapable at a given stage of conquering power, imperialism begins regulating economic life with its own methods; the fascist party which becomes the state power is the political mechanism. The productive forces are in irreconcilable contradiction not only with private property but also with national state boundaries. Imperialism is the very expression of this contradiction. Imperialist capitalism seeks to solve this contradiction through an extension of boundaries, seizure of new territories and so on. The totalitarian state, subjecting all aspects of economic, political and cultural life to finance capital, is the instrument for creating a super-nationalist state, an imperialist empire, the rule over continents, the rule over the whole world.

All these traits of fascism we have analysed – each one by itself and all of them in their totality to the extent that they became manifest or came to the forefront.

## *The point at which fascism succeeds*

Both theoretical analysis as well as the rich historical experience of the last quarter of a century have demonstrated with equal force that fascism is each time the final link of a specific political cycle composed of the following: the gravest crisis of capitalist society; the growth of the radicalisation of the working class; the growth of sympathy toward the working class and a yearning for change on the part of the rural and urban petty bourgeoisie; the extreme confusion of the big bourgeoisie; its cowardly and treacherous manoeuvres aimed at avoiding the revolutionary climax; the exhaustion of the proletariat, growing confusion and indifference; the aggravation of the social crisis; the despair of the petty bourgeoisie, its yearning for change, the collective neurosis of the petty bourgeoisie, its readiness to believe in miracles, its readiness for violent measures, the growth of hostility towards the proletariat which has deceived its expectations. These are the premises for a swift formation of a fascist party and its victory.

It is quite self-evident that the radicalisation of the working class in the United States has passed only through its initial phases, almost exclusively in the sphere of the trade union movement (the CIO). The pre-war period, and then the war itself may temporarily interrupt this process of radicalisation, especially if a considerable number of workers are absorbed into war industry. But this interruption of the process of radicalisation cannot be of a long duration. The second stage of radicalisation will assume a more sharply expressive character. The problem of forming an independent labour party will be put on the order of the day. Our transitional demands will gain great popularity. On the other hand, the fascist, reactionary tendencies will withdraw to the background, assuming a defensive position, awaiting a more favourable moment. This is the nearest perspective. No occupation is more completely unworthy than that of speculating whether or not we shall succeed in creating a powerful revolutionary leader party. Ahead lies a favourable perspective, providing all the justification for revolutionary activism. It is necessary to utilise the opportunities which are opening up and to build the revolutionary party.

## *Problem of power posed to the workers*

The Second World War poses the question of change of regimes more imperiously, more urgently than did the first war. It is first and foremost a question of the political regime. The workers are aware that democracy is suffering shipwreck everywhere, and that they are threatened by fascism even in those countries where fascism is as yet non-existent. The bourgeoisie of the democratic countries will naturally utilise this dread of fascism on the part of the workers, but, on the other hand, the bankruptcy of democracies, their collapse, their painless transformation into reactionary dictatorships, compel the workers to pose before themselves the problem of power, render them responsive to the posing of the problem of power.

Reaction wields today such power as perhaps never before in the modern history of mankind. But it would be an inexcusable blunder to see only reaction. The historical process is a contradictory one. Under the cover of official reaction, profound processes are taking place among the masses who are accumulating experience and are becoming receptive to new political perspectives. The old conservative tradition of the democratic state, which was so powerful even during the era of the last imperialist war, exists today only as an extremely unstable survival. On the eve of the last war, the European workers had numerically powerful parties. But on the order of the day were put reforms, partial conquests, and not at all the conquest of power.

The American working class is still without a mass labour party even today. But the objective situation and the experience accumulated by the American workers can pose within a very brief period of time on the order of the day the question of the conquest of power. This perspective must be made the basis of our agitation. It is not merely a question of a position on capitalist militarism and of renouncing the defence of the bourgeois state, but of directly preparing for the conquest of power and the defence of the proletarian fatherland.

May not the Stalinists turn out at the head of a new revolutionary upsurge and may they not ruin the revolution as they did in Spain and previously in China? It is of course impermissible to consider that such a possibility is excluded, for example in France. The first wave of the revolution has often, or more correctly, always carried to the top those 'left' parties which have not managed to discredit themselves completely in the preceding period and which have an imposing political tradition behind them. Thus the February Revolution raised up the Mensheviks, the SRs, who were the opponents of the revolution on its very eve. Thus the German Revolution in November 1918 raised to power the Social Democrats who were the irreconcilable opponents of revolutionary uprisings.

Twelve years ago Trotsky wrote in an article published by *The New Republic*:[3]

3 *The New Republic* is a liberal American weekly magazine, at this time sympathetic to the USSR.

There is no epoch in human history so saturated with antagonisms as ours. Under a too high tension of class and international animosities, the 'fuses' of democracy 'blow out'. Hence the short-circuits of dictatorship. Naturally the weakest 'interrupters' are the first to give way. But the force of internal and world controversies does not weaken: it grows. It is doubtful if it is destined to calm down, given that the process has so far only taken hold of the periphery of the capitalist world. Gout begins in the little finger of a hand or in the big toe, but once on the way it goes right to the heart. (*The New Republic*, 22 May 1929.)

## *The American philistine protests*

This was written at a time when the entire bourgeois democracy in each country believed that fascism was possible only in the backward countries which had not yet graduated from the school of democracy. The editorial board of *The New Republic*, which at that period had not yet been touched with the blessings of the GPU,[4] accompanied Trotsky's article with one of its own. The article is so characteristic of the average American philistine that we shall quote from it the most interesting passages.

> In view of his personal misfortunes, the exiled Russian leader shows a remarkable power of detached analysis; but his detachment is that of the rigid Marxist, and seems to us to lack a realistic view of history – the very thing on which he prides himself. His notion that democracy is a fair-weather form of government, incapable of withstanding the storms of international or domestic controversy, can be supported (as he himself half admits) only by taking for your examples countries where democracy has never made more than the feeblest beginnings, and countries, moreover, in which the industrial revolution has hardly more than started.

Further on, the editorial board of *The New Republic* dismisses the instance of Kerensky's democracy in Soviet Russia and why it failed to withstand the test of class contradictions arid yielded place to a revolutionary perspective. The periodical sagely writes:

4 The State Political Directorate (GPU) was the internal police of the Soviet Union.

> Kerensky's weakness was an historic accident, which Trotsky cannot admit because there is no room in his mechanistic scheme for any such thing.

Just like Dwight Macdonald, *The New Republic* accused the Marxists of being unable to understand history realistically owing to their orthodox or mechanistic approach to political events. *The New Republic* was of the opinion that fascism is the product of the backwardness of capitalism and not its over-ripeness. In the opinion of that periodical which, I repeat, was the opinion of the overwhelming majority of average democratic philistines, fascism is the lot of backward bourgeois countries. The sage editorial board did not even take the trouble of thinking about the question of why it was the universal conviction in the nineteenth century that backward countries must develop along the road of democracy. In any case, in the old capitalist countries democracy came into its sights at a time when the level of their economic development was not above but below the economic development of modern Italy. And what is more, in that era democracy represented the main highway of historical development which was entered by all countries one by one, the backward ones following the more advanced, and sometimes ahead of them. Our era, on the contrary, is the era of democracy's collapse, and moreover, the collapse begins with the weaker links but gradually extends to those which appeared strong and impregnable. Thus the 'orthodox' or 'mechanistic', that is, the Marxist approach to events, enabled us to forecast the course of developments many years in advance. On the contrary, the 'realistic' approach of *The New Republic* represented the approach of a blind kitten. *The New Republic* followed up its critical attitude toward Marxism by falling under the influence of the most revolting caricature of Marxism, namely, Stalinism.

## *The newest crop of philistines*

Most of the philistines of the newest crop base their attacks on Marxism on the fact that contrary to Marx's prognosis fascism came instead of socialism. Nothing is more stupid and vulgar than this criticism. Marx demonstrated and proved that when capitalism reaches a certain level, the only way out for society lies in the socialisation of the means of production, i.e. socialism. He also demonstrated that in view of the class structure of society, the proletariat alone is capable of solving this task in an irreconcilable revolutionary struggle against the bourgeoisie. He further demonstrated that for the fulfilment of this task the proletariat needs a revolutionary party. All his life, Marx, and together with him and after him Engels ,and after them Lenin, waged an irreconcilable struggle against those traits in proletarian parties, socialist parties, which obstructed the solution of the revolutionary historical task. The irreconcilability of the struggle waged by Marx, Engels and Lenin against opportunism on the one side, and anarchism on the other, demonstrates that they did not at all underestimate this danger. In what did it consist? In this, that the opportunism of the summits of the working class, subject to the bourgeoisie's influence, could obstruct, slow down, make more difficult, postpone the fulfilment of the revolutionary task of the proletariat. It is precisely this condition of society that we are now observing. Fascism did not at all come 'instead' of socialism. Fascism is the continuation of capitalism, an attempt to perpetuate its existence by means of the most bestial and monstrous measures. Capitalism obtained an opportunity to resort to fascism only because the proletariat did not accomplish the socialist revolution in time. The proletariat was paralysed in the fulfilment of its task by the opportunist parties. The only thing that can be said is that there turned out to be more obstacles, more difficulties, more stages on the road of the revolutionary development of the proletariat than was foreseen by the founders of scientific socialism. Fascism and the series of imperialist wars constitute the terrible school in which the proletariat has to free itself of petty bourgeois traditions and superstitions, has to rid itself of opportunist, democratic and adventurist parties, has to hammer out and train the revolutionary vanguard and in this way prepare for the solving of the task apart from which there is not, and cannot be, any salvation for the development of mankind.

Eastman,[5] if you please, has come to the conclusion that the concentration of the means of production in the hands of the state endangers his 'freedom' and he has therefore decided to renounce socialism. This anecdote deserves being included in the text of a history of ideology. The socialisation of the means of production is the only solution to the economic problem at the given stage of mankind's development. The delay in solving this problem leads to the barbarism of fascism. All the intermediate solutions undertaken by the bourgeoisie with the help of the petty bourgeoisie have suffered a miserable and shameful fiasco. All this is absolutely uninteresting to Eastman. He noticed that his 'freedom' (freedom of muddling, freedom of indifferentism, freedom of passivity, freedom of literary dilettantism) was being threatened from various sides, and he decided immediately to apply his own measure: renounce socialism. Astonishingly enough, this decision exercised no influence either on Wall Street or on the policy of the trade unions. Life went its own way just as if Max Eastman had remained a socialist. It may be set down as a general rule that the more impotent is a petty-bourgeois radical, especially in the United States, the more...

## *Fascism has not conquered in France*

In France there is no fascism in the real sense of the term. The regime of the senile Marshal Pétain represents a senile form of Bonapartism of the epoch of imperialist decline. But this regime too proved possible only after the prolonged radicalisation of the French working class, which led to the explosion of June 1936, had failed to find a revolutionary way out. The Second and Third Internationals, the reactionary charlatanism of the 'People's Fronts', deceived and demoralised the working class. After five years of propaganda in

5 Max Eastman was a writer and for a period of time a Trotskyist. After a split opened up in the ranks of the American Trotskyists in the Socialist Worker's Party, Eastman resigned from the party and ended up as bourgeois commentator and conservative.

favour of an alliance of democracies and of collective security, after Stalin's sudden passage into Hitler's camp, the French working class proved caught unaware. The war provoked a terrible disorientation and the mood of passive defeatism, or to put it more correctly, the indifferentism of an impasse. From this web of circumstances arose first the unprecedented military catastrophe and then the despicable Pétain regime.

Precisely because Pétain's regime is senile Bonapartism, it contains no element of stability and can be overthrown by a revolutionary mass uprising much sooner than a fascist regime.

## *Especially important to US workers*

In every discussion of political topics the question invariably flares up: Shall we succeed in creating a strong party for the moment when the crisis comes? Might not fascism anticipate us? Isn't a fascist stage of development inevitable? The successes of fascism easily make people lose all perspective, lead them to forget the actual conditions which made the strengthening and the victory of fascism possible. Yet a clear understanding of these conditions is of special importance to the workers of the United States. We may set it down as an historical law: fascism was able to conquer only in those countries where the conservative labour parties prevented the proletariat from utilising the revolutionary situation and seizing power.

In Germany, two revolutionary situations were involved: 1918-19 and 1923-24. Even in 1929 a direct struggle for power on the part of the proletariat was still possible. In all these three cases the Social Democracy and the Comintern criminally and viciously disrupted the conquest of power and thereby placed society in an impasse. Only under these conditions and in this situation did the stormy rise of fascism and its gaining of power prove possible.

# *Democracy or Bonapartism in Europe*

## *A Reply to Pierre Frank*

Written August 1946

Editor's note: After the war and Trotsky's death, the forces of the Fourth International were in a new political situation. A debate opened up between the British section, the Revolutionary Communist Party (RCP), and the leadership of the international on a number of questions, including Bonapartism. Ted Grant, founder and leader of the RCP, wrote this reply to Pierre Frank, a leading member of the Fourth International, who made a number of theoretical and political mistakes in his article, 'Democracy or Bonapartism in Europe?', published in November 1945.

* * *

Lenin's aphorism that we live in an epoch of wars and revolutions – to which Trotsky added "and counter-revolutions" – has been amply demonstrated by the history of the last three decades. Few periods in history have been filled with such terrific convulsions and clashes between the nations and classes, and such kaleidoscopic changes and manipulations of the political regimes whereby finance capital maintains its domination over the peoples. Thus, it becomes doubly important for those who carry on the scientific teachings of Marxism, and who alone can lay claim to make a theoretical analysis of events, to keep a scrupulous and careful check on the changes which are taking place if they are correctly to orientate the advance guard and give guidance to the masses.

In criticising the barren conceptions of Stalinism, which identified all regimes to fascism at the time of the 'third period', Trotsky brilliantly characterised the essence of the epoch as one of *change and fluctuations*, in which generalisations would not suffice. Each stage must be *examined concretely* by the vanguard who could thus understand and interpret events and draw the correct practical conclusions for activity therefrom. He wrote:

> The vast importance of a correct theoretical orientation is most strikingly manifested in a period of acute social conflict, of rapid political shifts, of abrupt changes in the situation. In such periods, political *conceptions and generalisations* are rapidly used up and require either a complete replacement (which is easier) or their concretisation, precision and partial rectification (which is harder). It is in just such periods that all sorts of *transitional*, intermediate situations and combinations arise, as a matter of necessity, which upset the customary patterns and doubly require a sustained theoretical attention. In a word, if in the pacific and 'organic' period (before the war) one could still live on the revenue from a few ready-made abstractions, in our time each new event forcefully brings home the most important law of the dialectic: *the truth is always concrete.*[1]

Among the cadres of the Fourth International, there are comrades who have not sufficiently understood this lesson. They continue to live on the 'revenue from a few ready-made abstractions' instead of concretising or partially rectifying previous generalisations. An outstanding example of this is the article of Pierre Frank.

Frank attempts to equate all regimes in Western Europe to 'Bonapartism'. His generalisations go even further: he argues that there have been Bonapartist regimes in France since 1934; that it is impossible to have any but Bonapartist or fascist regimes until

1 Trotsky, 'Bonapartism and Fascism', 15 July 1934, in this volume, p. 145.

the coming to power of the proletariat in Europe. This, if you please, in the name of "the continuity of our political analysis for more than ten years of French history"! Such complacency reduces theory to formless abstractions and conceals inevitable and episodic errors, thus making them into a system. It has no place in the Fourth International.

Comrade Frank indiscriminately mixes the terms 'bourgeois democracy' with 'Bonapartism', not explaining the specific traits of either. He interchangeably speaks of "Bonapartism", "elements of Bonapartism", and he contrasts democratic liberties with "a regime which one can correctly define as democratic". Yet the reader has to seek in vain for a definition of his ideal 'democratic regime' as distinguished from the very real bourgeois democracy. He denies the existence of democratic regimes in Europe today because "there is literally no place for them".

## *Economic basis and political superstructure*

We will here repeat some elementary ideas of Marxism in order to arrive at the necessary clarity and understanding of the shifting processes and changes taking place in the regimes in Europe at the present time – at least in Western Europe. The Eastern half, dominated directly by the Stalinist bureaucracy, develops in a different direction and under different conditions.

*The political character of a regime* (Bonapartist, fascist, democratic) is basically determined by the relations between the classes in the nation, which vary at different stages. Its fundamental nature is determined, in the last analysis, by its *mode of production and property relations*, by its *class character*. Thus the regimes of Hitler and Roosevelt,[2] of Attlee and Mussolini, of Franco[3] and Gouin,[4]

2 Franklin D Roosevelt was President of the United States from 1933 until his death in 1945.

3 Francisco Franco was a Spanish General who overthrew the Second Spanish Republic in the Spanish Civil War and ruled Spain as a dictator from 1939 until his death in 1975.

4 Félix Gouin was Prime Minister of France and Chair of the Provisional Government of the French Republic from January to June 1946.

of Perón[5] and Salazar,[6] of de Valera[7] and Chiang Kai Shek are all governments of the capitalist class, for they rest upon the economy of capitalist exploitation. However, the *class nature* of these regimes does not exhaust the problem. We have to classify the instrument – which differs in each case – by which the bourgeoisie ensures its dominance and rule. The character of this rule is decided not only by the *subjective* wishes and needs of the finance capitalists, which remain but one factor in the process, but precisely by the objective-subjective inter-relations between the classes at a given stage, which has been predicated by the previous history and the development of the class struggle of the given country.

It is a vulgarisation of Marxism – vulgar materialism of the worst sort – to argue that the superstructure of a society is determined immediately by the development of its economy.

The disappearance of the economic basis on which the 'democracy' of the imperialists is based, does not immediately lead to the disappearance of the bourgeois democracy. It only prepares its collapse in the *long run*. Properly speaking, the development of capitalism into imperialism by the beginning of this century had already rendered outmoded the existence of bourgeois democracy. Yet we see that bourgeois democracy managed to maintain itself for decades after its economic base had disappeared.

That capitalism had outlived its historic functions was attested already by the first imperialist world war. But this did not, and could not by itself, lead to the overthrow of the capitalist system. The First World War led to favourable conditions for the overthrow of the bourgeoisie on a world scale. But the proletariat was prevented from carrying out its mission by the organisations of its own creation. The Social Democracy betrayed the revolution and saved the capitalist system from destruction. In the revolutionary epoch following the First World War, the bourgeoisie was compelled to lean on the Social Democracy for support, the only reliable prop they had to maintain

5 Juan Perón was President of Argentina from 1946-55.

6 António de Oliveira Salazar led the Portuguese dictatorship from 1932-68.

7 Éamon de Valera was the Taoiseach of the Republic of Ireland from 1937-48.

their rule. Where the bourgeoisie relied on such regimes based on Social Democracy, uniting repression against the revolutionary workers with reforms and half-reforms, these could only be characterised as regimes of 'bourgeois democracy.' Thus, Lenin and Trotsky characterised the counter-revolutionary regime in Germany in 1918, which was organised by Social Democracy, as a bourgeois-democratic regime.

It is ABC that the democratic liberties were gained in the struggle against the bourgeoisie over a period of a century; the right to vote had to be fought for and wrested from the bourgeoisie at a period of *ascending capitalism*, at the time of the blossoming of bourgeois democracy. Even in its heyday there was never an idyllic democratic state without police intervention and without brute force.

Yet even at this stage when capitalism was still an ascending economy, there were not only democratic regimes but Bonapartist regimes as well. In the classic land of Bonapartism, both Louis Napoleon, and Bonaparte himself came to power at a time when there was a veritable boom which lasted in the one case for two decades. According to Comrade Frank's conception there was no basis for Bonapartism; there should have only been bourgeois democracy. But we see the problem is not so simple.

And after Louis Napoleon, bourgeois democracy (with one or two threats of dictatorship – Boulangerism)[8] lasted for decades in France. According to Frank's mysterious conceptions, after Bonapartism – which means that the economic basis for democracy is gone – it is no longer possible for the bourgeoisie to have democracy, but... only Bonapartism.

It is difficult to understand why Comrade Frank stops at 1934 to trace Bonapartist regimes in France. If we follow his method logically we have had Bonapartism since the coup d'état of Louis Napoleon in 1851, or perhaps since the first Bonaparte!

8 Georges Ernest Boulanger was a French general and politician, who gained popularity after the defeat of the Franco-Prussian War with his revanchist ('revenge') movement, which attempted to provoke another war with Germany.

If there is a grain of sense in his case that the economic basis for reforms has disappeared, all that it proves is not automatically and consequently a regime of Bonapartism is posed, but that the democratic regime under such conditions will be of an extremely unstable character, afflicted with convulsions and crises, which must make way either for the revolutionary proletarian dictatorship or the open dictatorship of finance capital through Bonapartism or fascism.

Comrade Frank says the existence of democratic liberties does not suffice to make a democratic regime. A profound observation! What follows? The existence of Bonapartist measures does not make a regime Bonapartist either, Comrade Frank! This argument is about as profound as those of the 'bureaucratic collectivists' who argued that we had the intervention of the state in the economy in Germany under Hitler, in France under Blum, in America under Roosevelt (National Industrial Recovery Act), in Russia under Stalin... consequently all those regimes were the same. It is not the points of similarity only – all human societies have points of similarity, particularly different types of capitalist societies – it is the *decisive traits* which determine our definition of regimes.

## *Counter-revolution in a democratic form*

The British RCP has characterised the regimes in Western Europe (France, Belgium, Holland, Italy) as regimes of counter-revolution in a democratic form. Comrade Pierre Frank claims that the idea of 'democratic counter-revolution' is "devoid of all content". He would then be hard put to explain what the Weimar Republic organised by the Social Democracy in Germany was. He would be compelled to argue that what took place in Germany in 1918, was *not* the proletarian revolution which was betrayed by the 'counter-revolution in a democratic form' (by the undemocratic and bloody suppression of the January 1919 uprisings), but was a democratic revolution which overthrew the Kaiser and replaced his regime by one of 'pure' bourgeois democracy! The fact that this regime was ushered in by martial law and the conspiracy of the Social-Democratic leaders with the General Staff of the Reichswehr, the

Junkers and the bourgeoisie, validates entirely the conclusion of Lenin and Trotsky that there was a 'democratic' counter-revolution, with the bourgeoisie using the social-democrats as their agents.

In advance Trotsky foresaw and prepared theoretically for a similar situation with the collapse of fascism in Italy, when he wrote in a letter to the Italian comrades in 1930:

> Following the above comes the question of the 'transitional' period in Italy. At the very outset it is necessary to establish very clearly: transition from what to what? A period of transition from the bourgeois (or 'popular') revolution to the proletarian revolution is one thing. A period of transition from the fascist dictatorship to the proletarian dictatorship is another. If the first conception is envisaged, the question of the bourgeois revolution is posed in the first place and it is then a question of establishing the role of the proletariat in it. Only after that will the question of the transitional period toward a proletarian revolution be posed. If the second conception is envisaged, the question is then posed of a series of battles, disturbances, upsets in the situation, abrupt turns, constituting in their ensemble the different stages of the proletarian revolution. These stages may be many in number. But in no case can they contain within them a bourgeois revolution or its mysterious hybrid: the 'popular' revolution.
>
> Does this mean that Italy cannot for a certain time again become a parliamentary state or become a 'democratic republic'? I consider – in perfect agreement with you, I think – that this eventuality is not excluded. But then it will not be the fruit of a bourgeois revolution but the abortion of an insufficiently matured and premature proletarian revolution. In case of a profound revolutionary crisis and of mass battles in the course of which the proletarian vanguard will not have been in a position to take power, it may be that the bourgeoisie will reconstruct its power on 'democratic' bases.
>
> Can it be said, for example, that the present German republic constitutes a conquest of the bourgeois revolution? Such an assertion would be absurd. There was in Germany in 1918-19 a proletarian revolution which,

> deprived of leadership, was deceived, betrayed and crushed. But the bourgeois counter-revolution nevertheless found itself obliged to adapt itself to the circumstances resulting from this crushing of the proletarian revolution and to assume the form of a republic in the 'democratic' parliamentary form. Is the same – or about the same – eventuality excluded from Italy? No, it is not excluded. The enthronement of fascism was the result of the incompletion of the proletarian revolution in 1920. Only a new proletarian revolution can overturn fascism. If it should not be destined to triumph this time either (weakness of the Communist Party, manoeuvres and betrayals of the social democrats, the Freemasons, the Catholics), the 'transitional' state that the bourgeois counter-revolution would then be forced to set up in the ruins of its power in a fascist form, could be nothing else than a parliamentary and democratic state.[9]

Events in Italy have demonstrated the remarkable foresight of Trotsky. The bourgeoisie has been compelled to allow the jettisoning of the king and the Stalinist-socialist traitors have headed off the developing proletarian revolution into the channels of a 'parliamentary and democratic state'.[10] This of course, will not attain a stable base, but will be subject to crises and upheavals, movements on the part of the proletariat and counter-movements of monarchists and fascists. Would Frank now deny the correctness of Trotsky's conceptions and assert that we have had a Bonapartist state since the fall of Mussolini?

It is incomprehensible that Frank, in his argumentation, should refer to this very article of Trotsky's which puts forward precisely the opposite point of view. After fascism what? asks the Old Man and answers that, as a means of preventing the revolution in face of mass upsurge, the bourgeoisie will turn towards the establishment of a bourgeois democratic republic. We note in

9 Trotsky, 'Problems of the Italian Revolution', 14 May 1930, *Writings of Leon Trotsky, 1930*, Pathfinder Press, 1975, p. 220.

10 When the Allies liberated Rome in May 1944, they blocked any attempt by King Victor Emmanuel to return to the throne, contrary to their previous agreements, for fear of provoking a new uprising of the workers.

this connection that the immediate introduction of Bonapartism (allegedly because democracy has no economic base) was not even considered by Trotsky.

From this can be seen that what is really 'devoid of content' is the mechanical conception that counter-revolution can only manifest itself in the form of fascism or Bonapartism, i.e. military-police dictatorships.

The experience of history has shown, and events now unfolding in Europe demonstrate irrefutably, that the methods of the bourgeoisie in its struggle against the proletarian revolution vary widely and are not determined *a priori*. The bourgeoisie makes use of different methods, relies on different strata, depending on the class relation of forces in order to re-enforce or re-establish its rule.

Whether they can manoeuvre the Stalinists or manipulate their social-democratic, Bonapartist, or fascist agencies, or as sometimes happens, *use all forces simultaneously*, does not depend only on the subjective intentions of the ruling class, or on this or that adventurer, but on the objective conditions and the inter-relations between all the classes in the nation – bourgeoisie, petty bourgeoisie and proletariat, at any given time. To repeat mechanically the conclusion that the existence of finance capital is incompatible with bourgeois democracy in the contemporary period (which is indubitably correct within certain limits), and thus that all regimes must be Bonapartist, is to substitute abstract categories formulated on the basis of partial and insufficient historical experience, or a narrow and incomplete view of the process as a whole, for a dialectical analysis of events.

To understand the nature of the regimes in Western Europe today, we must know the background on which they evolved. The revolutionary movement of the masses following the First World War was paralysed and betrayed by the social democrats, *who alone were able to save capitalism from destruction under the banner of bourgeois democracy*. The bourgeoisie was compelled to rely on its social democratic agencies for mere survival.

The failure of the proletariat to take power could lead only to the further degeneration and decay of capitalism. The ruin of the petty bourgeoisie, which was shown no way out by the mass organisations of the proletariat, led to them becoming a tool of fascist reaction. Trapped by the intolerable crisis of their system in one country after another, through many transitions, the bourgeoisie turned in the direction of open and unbridled dictatorship.

The wave of revolution was followed by a wave of counter-revolution. In Italy, Germany and other countries, the bourgeoisie used the forces of the frenzied petty bourgeoisie to destroy the organisations of the proletariat. They were compelled at a later stage to turn on the petty bourgeoisie and transform themselves into Bonapartist regimes, i.e. *regimes resting directly on the support of the military-police apparatus rather than regimes with a mass basis.*

This could not solve the contradictions of the capitalist system on a national or international scale but inevitably led to the Second World War, in a frantic endeavour by the bourgeoisie to find a way out by a repartition of the world. But the Second World War, even more than the first, put at stake the whole existence of capitalism as a system. The bourgeoisie realised, with dread, that the unleashing of the war would release tremendous revolutionary energy from the depths of the masses and recreate the conditions favourable to the overthrow of capitalism on a continental scale.

The victories of the Nazis and the conquest of practically the whole of the continent of Europe had, as a by-product, the effect of temporarily destroying the mass basis of reaction throughout Europe. Reaction and the capitalist system rested directly on the bayonets of the Nazi fascist armies. The hated Quislings[11] played a purely auxiliary role. With the victories of the Red Army and the collapse of Hitler and Mussolini, the problem of the socialist revolution was posed on the order of the day throughout Europe. Reaction was without a strong base in the populations *and without a strong, stable, military-police apparatus*. The Allied armies could not be a stable prop for reaction and open military dictatorship for long.

11 A 'Quisling' being a collaborator with an occupying force, after the Norwegian Vidkun Quisling, who headed the collaborationist regime during the Nazi occupation of Norway.

In most of the European countries the bourgeoisie was faced with mass upsurge, *which they could not bridle with their own forces.*

Greece was the exception. Only after a civil war and a bloody war of intervention was it possible to install a semi-Bonapartist or Bonapartist regime, which is step-by-step attempting to impose a totalitarian regime in that country. The imperialists are aware of the impossibility of using such methods on a continental scale. In addition, in Greece the power of reaction had to be maintained at all costs for fear that this last outpost of British imperialism in the Balkan peninsula should, in common with the rest of the Balkans, fall under the sway of the Stalinist bureaucracy. But even here it was not possible to destroy completely the mass organisations of the proletariat.

Nothing saved the capitalist system in Western Europe except the betrayal of social democracy and Stalinism. When the bourgeoisie leans on its social-democratic and Stalinist agencies *for the purpose of counter-revolution*, what is the 'content' of that counter-revolution? Bonapartist, fascist, authoritarian? Of course not! Its content is that of a 'counter revolution in a democratic form'.

Of course, the bourgeoisie cannot stabilise itself for any length of time on the basis of the democratic counter-revolution. Where the revolution is stemmed by the lackeys of the bourgeoisie, the class forces do not stay suspended. After a period, which can be more or less protracted according to the economic and political developments internationally and within the given country, the bourgeoisie shifts to Bonapartist or fascist counter-revolution.

That is how events manifested themselves in Italy within two years of the ebbing of the revolutionary tide provoked by the First World War, and in Germany over a period of fifteen years. The change in class relationships reflected itself in the change in regimes through democracy, preventative Bonapartism, to fascism, pure Bonapartist military dictatorship.

Despite the further degeneration of its economic and political base, the failure of the workers once again to take power, destroy capitalist relations and organise society anew, has resulted in the establishment of bourgeois democratic governments in Italy, France and other countries, based upon the manipulation of the Stalinists and social democrats. To argue that counter-revolution or the rule of the bourgeoisie in the present period can only manifest itself in Bonapartism, fascism or Franco-type governments, is to abandon the Marxist appreciation of the processes in modern society. Taking into account the many factors involved in the history of the period, including the weakness of the Marxist current, it could have been, and was, predicted in advance what the developments in Western Europe would be. But the process can only be understood if one takes into account the real nature of democracy, Bonapartism, fascism, and not merely their outward forms.

## *Differing regimes in capitalist society*

The classic Bonapartism of the first Napoleon rose out of the bourgeois-democratic revolution in the period of the youth and vigour of capitalism. Bonapartism, *the rule of the sword over society*, represented a position where the state assumed a relative independence of the classes, balancing between the hostile classes and arbitrating between them. It remained, nevertheless, an instrument above all, of the big capitalists. Napoleon, by leaning on the support of the peasants, could maintain himself for a whole historical period because of the development of the productive forces in France at this period.

So with Napoleon the Little, who established his power in France in the coup d'état of 1851. Marx, in the *Eighteenth Brumaire*, described the position thus:

> … the State has gone back to its earliest form, in which the sword rules without shame and club law prevails. [Hardly a mirror of the regime of de Gaulle in France after the liberation! – *EG*].[12] Thus is the *coup de main* of February 1848 answered by the *coup de tête* of December 1851.

That is the essence of Bonapartism: naked, military-police dictatorship, the 'arbiter' with a sword. A regime which indicates that the antagonisms within society have become so great that the state machine, 'regulating' and 'ordering' these antagonisms, while

12 Interpolations in square brackets added by Edward (Ted) Grant are marked 'EG'.

remaining an instrument of the property owners, assumes a certain independence of all the classes. A 'national judge' concentrating power in his hands, personally 'arbitrates' the conflicts within the nation, playing off one class against another, nevertheless remaining a tool of the property owners. At the same time, we characterise as Bonapartist a regime where the basic class forces of bourgeoisie and proletariat more or less balance one another, thus allowing the state power to manoeuvre and balance the contending camps and again giving the state power a certain independence in relation to society as a whole.

However, there is a big difference between the role of Bonapartism in the period of capitalism's ascending phase and the period of its decline. We give two quotations from Trotsky explaining this difference with the utmost clarity, in *Germany: The Only Road*:

> In its time, we designated the Brüning government as *Bonapartism* ('caricature of Bonapartism'), that is, as a regime of the military police dictatorship. As soon as the struggle of two social strata – the haves and the have-nots, the exploiter and the exploited – reaches its highest tension, the conditions are given for the domination of bureaucracy, police, soldiery. The government becomes 'independent' of society. Let us once more recall: if two forks are stuck symmetrically into a cork, the latter can stand even on the head of a pin. That is precisely the scheme of Bonapartism. To be sure, such a government does not cease being the clerk of the property-owners. Yet the clerk sits on the back of the boss, rubs his neck raw and does not hesitate at times to dig his boots into his face.
>
> It might have been assumed that Brüning would hold on until the final solution. Yet, in the course of events, another link inserted itself: the Papen government. Were we to be exact, we should have to make a rectification of our old designation: the Brüning government was a pre-Bonapartist government. Brüning was only a precursor. In a perfected form, Bonapartism came upon the scene in the Papen-Schleicher government.[13]

13 Trotsky, *Germany: The Only Road*, 14 September 1932, in this volume, p. 41.

And further on:

> However, in spite of the appearance of concentrated forces, the Papen government *as such* is weaker yet than its predecessor. The Bonapartist regime can attain a comparatively stable and durable character only in the event that it brings a revolutionary epoch to a close; when the relationship of forces has already been tested in battles; when the revolutionary classes are already spent; while the possessing classes have not yet freed themselves from the fear; will not the morrow bring new convulsions? Without this basic condition, that is, without a preceding exhaustion of the mass energies in battles, a Bonapartist regime is in no position to develop.[14]

The Bonapartism at the stage of capitalism's rise, raising itself above society, suppressing and 'arbitrating' the open conflicts within it and regulating the class antagonisms, is strong and confident. Under the conditions of a powerful development of the productive forces, it attains a certain stability. But the Bonapartism of capitalism's decline is affected by senility. Rising out of the crisis of capitalist society, it cannot solve any of the problems with which it is faced. The main crisis of society, the conflict between the productive forces and private ownership and the national state, has become so great, the class antagonisms which it engenders, so tense, that this which alone allows the rise of senile Bonapartism, at the same time, as a consequence, makes it so weak and feeble that its whole structure is shaky and likely to be overthrown in the series of crises which confront it. It is this weakness of Bonapartism which leads to the bourgeoisie and military clique surrendering the power to fascism and unleashing the greedy bands of maddened petty bourgeoisie and lumpenproletariat against the proletariat and its class organisations.

The differing categories of regimes, though of vital importance for Marxist theory and practice, are not metaphysical abstractions, indicating a rigid, fixed and eternal differentiation between them.

There are so many factors involved, that it is necessary to examine each regime concretely before categorically defining its position.

14 Ibid, p. 43.

It is only necessary to point out that even within each rough category, widely differing regimes can be comprised. England with her feudal remnants (House of Lords and monarchy) and barbarous oppression of colonial peoples, is a 'democracy'. The Federal Republic of Switzerland, and France with its laws based on the *Code Napoleon*, the United States, Weimar Germany and Éire[15] – despite their wide differences, remain 'democracies'. What, then, is the dominating thread which places these regimes under one head?

Despite their diverse histories, which explains their different national peculiarities, *they all possess certain specific traits in common.* These are the traits which are decisive in determining the Marxist classification. All have independent workers' organisations: trade unions, parties, clubs, etc., with the rights which go with them. The right to strike, organise, the right to vote, free speech, press, etc. and the other rights which have been the by-product of the class struggle of the proletariat in the past. (Here we might add that the loss of this or that right would not, in itself, be decisive in our analysis of a regime. It is the totality of the relations which is the determining factor.) In one sense, the existence, *within capitalism*, of elements of the new society. Or, as explained by Trotsky in *Germany: What Next?* in answering the Stalinist ultra-lefts, *under the regime of the bourgeoisie there already exists the embryo of the rule of the working class in the form of the workers' organisations.*

Where these organisations exist and play a powerful role (in France and Italy they are stronger than they have ever been) the bourgeoisie rules through the leaders and top layers of these organisations. It is not without interest, as Lenin pointed out, that at a certain stage, the bourgeoisie even ruled through the Soviets, or more correctly, the Menshevik leadership of the Soviets.

Fascism, too, has its peculiarities. The regimes of Franco, Mussolini, Hitler and Piłsudski, all are comprised within this conception. Yet there are wide differences between them. What fundamentally unites the conception is the *complete destruction of all working-class organisations.* Yet even here we see that right up

15 The Irish name for the Republic of Ireland.

to the outbreak of the war, Polish fascism, far weaker than that of Germany and Italy, had not completely succeeded in destroying the workers' organisations and may have been overthrown before it finally succeeded in doing so.

Bonapartism too, shows a similar variety. Napoleon, Louis Napoleon, von Schleicher and Papen, and the fascist-regimes-become-Bonapartist – all were Bonapartist regimes. What is it that they have in common? The independence of the state, the concentration of power 'personally', resting directly and openly on the domination of the state machine through *the naked power of the military-police apparatus, 'rule by the sword'*. Whatever differences there may be between the regimes, the existence of workers' organisations with attenuated or limited rights in certain cases, they all have the above mentioned features in common. The specific peculiarities in each case would again be determined by the history of the country, the development of the social contradictions which made the development of Bonapartism possible, etc., etc.

Thus the weak and sterile Bonapartism of Pétain and von Schleicher in the epoch of capitalist decline resembled only as a caricature the vigorous and powerful regime established by Napoleon in its period of ascent. In the change from democracy to fascism, there must be one, perhaps many, transitional phases. Thus the path for Bonapartism is prepared by the division of the nation into two hostile camps – that of the fascist petit bourgeoisie and that of the organised working class. Nominally, the state power assumes an independence of both and the military-police regime established prepares the way for the handing of power to fascism. (The bourgeoisie prefers to rule through democratic means. Under the impact of crisis, however, they utilise the fascist gangs as a terrorist agency for pressure on the proletariat so that they can push through Bonapartist dictatorial measures. Only as a last resort do they reluctantly surrender power to the fascists.) At least that was the process in Italy and Germany. Depending on many factors, including the policy of the revolutionary party of the proletariat, events in Europe and elsewhere may develop on somewhat different lines, should reaction succeed in temporarily stabilising itself.

However, it is important to note that the regimes of Schleicher and Papen, of Pétain and General Sirovy in Czechoslovakia after Munich, *all developed directly* (through intermediate stages perhaps) *out of the regimes of bourgeois democracy.* The pre-Bonapartist, or even Bonapartist regimes, of Doumergue, Laval and Flandin prepared the way for the Popular Front in France, which in turn paved the way again for a development towards Bonapartism. To call the Popular Front under Blum 'Bonapartism', as does Comrade Frank in the citation which follows, can only cause immeasurable confusion in the ranks of the Fourth International:

> ... But the Bonapartism of declining capitalism can cloak itself in other costumes. In certain cases it is fairly difficult to recognise it, for example in the case of governments, of the left, even very much to the left, notably of the Popular Front type. There, Bonapartism is so outrageously varnished with a democratic sheen that many allow themselves to be taken in by it. [!]

In those words of Comrade Frank is the key to the confusion in the characterisation of regimes. It is easy to slip into such errors because in the same way as the embryo of a new form of society exists in the workers' organisations, so the possibility of Bonapartism is rooted in the structure of society under bourgeois democracy. Within every state there is reflected the antagonisms within society, even in the freest bourgeois democratic society. As Engels wrote in his book *The Origin of the Family, Private Property and the State*:

> The state is therefore by no means a power imposed on society from the outside; just as little is it the reality of the moral idea, the image and reality of reason, as Hegel asserted. Rather it is a product of society at a certain stage of development; it is the admission that this society has become entangled in an insoluble contradiction within itself, that it is cleft into irreconcilable antagonisms which it is powerless to dispel. But in order that these antagonisms, classes with conflicting economic

> interests, may not consume themselves and society in sterile struggle, a power apparently standing above society becomes necessary, whose purpose is to moderate the conflict and keep it within the bounds of 'order'; and this power arising out of society, but placing itself above it and increasingly separating itself from it, is the state.[16]

In the last analysis every state is based on naked force. The army officers, the general staff clique, the police and civil service bureaucracy, trained and selected to serve the interests of capitalism, provide the soil on which military plots and conspiracies thrive, given conditions of crisis and social ferment.

Pierre Frank confuses here the role of the state with Bonapartism. A democracy that was not based on force, that did not have an apparatus placing itself above society, has never existed and never will exist. But this does not make Bonapartism.

But because every state is based on armed bodies of men with its appendages in the form of prisons, courts, etc., and thus even under the fullest democratic regime we have the hidden dictatorship of capitalism, it does not follow that every repressive regime is necessarily Bonapartist. Repression and suppression of the rights of the workers under conditions of 'emergency' take place under every regime, including the democratic, when the basic interests of capital are threatened and till 'normal' conditions are restored – i.e. till the masses accept, without active rebellion, the yoke of capital. The bourgeoisie preserves an extreme flexibility, manipulating the regimes according to the resistance of the masses, the class forces, etc. Thanks to the betrayals of the workers' leaderships they are enabled to do this.

## *Prognosis in the light of events*

Whatever their original desires or wishes to impose Bonapartist regimes in Europe, Anglo-American imperialism soon saw the impossibility of this (apart from Greece) in the incalculable dangers which it would bring and in Western Europe swung over to democratic regimes, based on a disarmed proletariat.

16 Engels, *The Origin of the Family, Private Property and the State*, *Marx and Engels Collected Works*, Vol. 26, Lawrence and Wishart, 1973, p. 269.

Events in France and Western Europe have confirmed the incorrectness of the method of Pierre Frank. Everywhere in Western Europe since the 'liberation', the tendency has been for a steady movement towards bourgeois democracy and not towards greater and greater dictatorial regimes; towards an increase in democratic rights, not towards their limitation. *At a later stage this tendency will be reversed*, but at present the motion in Western Europe is towards bourgeois democratic regimes. Thus in Italy we have the establishment of the bourgeois democratic republic, trade unions, etc; in France we have elections, parties, trade unions, etc; in Belgium and Holland we have democratic elections. The swing of the masses towards socialism-communism is reflected in the fact that these parties have secured a greater percentage of the votes than at any time in history. In order to mobilise the petty bourgeois reaction as a counterpoise against them, the bourgeoisie, *at this stage*, is leaning not on fascist reaction (that is still well in reserve) *but on the Catholic and Christian parties basing themselves on parliamentary democracy.* This gives the bourgeoisie a breathing space to prepare at a later stage and under the necessary favourable conditions for a transition through Bonapartist regimes to totalitarian dictatorship.

It is clear that the position today is entirely different from the position in Germany and Italy before the victory of fascism, where mass parties of fascism were organised and the possibility of the state manoeuvring between the two mortally hostile camps was posed by the whole situation. Far from this, in Italy and France the Christian Democratic parties are collaborating with the workers' organisations in a typical coalition cabinet of bourgeois democracy. The bourgeoisie cannot do otherwise because of the danger of revolutionary disturbances on the part of the masses.

The situation is similar to that in Germany in the Weimar Republic. In order to stem the revolution, the bourgeoisie organised a coalition government of Social Democracy and the Catholic Centre.

Was this Bonapartism? Obviously not. But as a result of the policy of Social Democracy they were punished by the petty bourgeoisie swinging to reaction and a Bonapartist-monarchist attempt at a coup d'état in the Kapp Putsch[17] in 1920. As is well known, this attempted Bonapartist coup was defeated by the masses, where the communists and socialists participated in a general strike. The indignation of the workers, *owing to the correct propaganda of the Communist Party* in warning of this danger and forming a united front to beat it off, led to the workers in the Ruhr attempting the seizure of power. The reaction then joined together with the social democrats to crush this movement of the masses. This in its turn, paved the way for an uneasy and unstable regime of bourgeois democracy.

The false position on the nature of the regimes in Europe flows from an incorrect perspective. The American comrades argued that only Franco-type military dictatorships were possible in Europe after the victory of the allied imperialists. Pierre Frank approvingly quotes a wrong position taken by the International Secretariat (IS)[18] in 1940:

> If England should install de Gaulle in France tomorrow, his regime would not in the least be distinguished from that of the Bonapartist government of Pétain.

A trifle different, Comrade Frank! For the workers a decisive difference! It is true that the capitalist class continued to rule under de Gaulle as they did under Pétain. But to argue in 1946 that the regimes could not be distinguished is to fall into the sectarian stupidity of the Stalinists in Germany who couldn't distinguish between a capitalist regime leaning on the workers' organisations and the abolition of these organisations by fascism.

Pierre Frank's confusion is further exposed by his triumphant declaration that the Pétain regime was Bonapartist. Trotsky said that the Pétain regime was Bonapartist. But Frank just does not understand what Trotsky was driving at. In their period of decay and decline, Trotsky referred to the regimes of Hitler and Mussolini

17 On 13 March 1920, 12,000 troops entered Berlin in order to establish a military dictatorship and declare Wolfgang Kapp the new Chancellor of Germany.

18 The International Secretariat was the leading body of the Fourth International.

as Bonapartist regimes. The only difference between these regimes and that of Pétain was that *Pétain never had a mass base in the petty bourgeoisie*, like Hitler and Mussolini, and in that sense could not be called fascist, but Bonapartist. For this reason his regime was much weaker and could be more easily over-thrown by a movement of the masses. Pétain had to lean on foreign bayonets for his rule. Otherwise there is no difference between the regimes of Franco, Mussolini and Hitler in their decaying phases and that of Pétain.

Comrade Frank declares:

> … our most responsible International body has predicted that a simple substitution of gangs following a victory of the Allies would not signify a change in the nature of the political regime. We find ourselves in the presence of an evaluation on the historical scale based on positions which were defended for many years by the Fourth International against all other theories and cheap labels spread by the other tendencies and formations of the labour movement. If an error was committed it would be truly a considerable one and we would be urgently obliged to seek the reasons for it and correct it. As for ourselves, we don't believe that our organisation was in error on this point…

The statement of the IS made in 1940 was incorrect. We made the same mistake. Under the circumstances it was excusable. But to repeat in 1946 a mistake that was already clear by 1943 is inexcusable. A British Trotskyist resolution, written in 1943, in which we corrected ourselves, analysed the coming situation in Europe as follows:

> In the absence of experienced Trotskyist parties with roots and traditions among the masses, the first stages of the revolutionary struggles in Europe will most likely result in a period of Kerenskyism or Popular Frontism. This is already presaged by the initial struggles of the Italian workers and the repeated betrayals of Social Democracy and Stalinism.[19]

19 Main resolution at the National Conference of the Workers International League (WIL), October 1943. The WIL was the forerunner to the Revolutionary Communist Party, founded in 1944.

Events have demonstrated the correctness of this analysis. Instead of frankly facing up to an error in perspective, Frank flies in the face of reality and attempts to convert an error into a virtue.

Frank takes France as the keystone of his thesis. He surely must be lamenting this by now. Because it is France, above all, which has mirrored the process very clearly. France is the key to Europe and any mistakes on the nature of the French regime could be fatal for the young cadres of Trotskyism.

Let us examine the situation. Pierre Frank visualises the development as follows: Bonapartism since 1934, because, you see, the bourgeoisie could not afford bourgeois democracy; Pétain was Bonaparte: de Gaulle was Bonaparte; the Popular Front (Blum!) was Bonapartism; in fact, as the metaphysicians would say: 'in the twilight all cats are grey'. The thesis is that all were Bonaparte. It follows that Gouin is Bonaparte and the government which will follow also will be Bonapartist. If this madness should infect the French, our French Party will be in a sorry state. Happily, this danger apparently does not exist.

A Marxist appreciation would be somewhat different from that of Pierre Frank. What was the development of the regime – from what to what is it evolving? What is the position of the classes? What are the relations between the classes? A sober appreciation of the last two years will tell us that:

a. Here we have an unachieved proletarian revolution; result:

b. Unstable bourgeois democracy, assembly, elections, constituent, bourgeois-democratic constitution;

c. In this setting, a candidate Bonaparte.

The real power rests in the principal working-class parties. A would-be Hitler striving for power and a Hitler in power are not one and the same thing. A would-be Bonaparte like de Gaulle and a real Bonaparte wielding real personal power with the sword, are two different things. De Gaulle may yet be a French Franco, but one does not declare the enemy victorious before the decisive battle has begun.

Bonapartism in the modern epoch, by its very nature, must be a regime of transition: transition to fascism, transition to democracy, or even to proletarian revolution – a period of manoeuvring between the classes. That there are *elements of Bonapartism in the situation in Europe, goes without saying*. These elements can be transformed into the dominant ones, but only under certain conditions. If one declares a regime Bonapartist, then the specific features of the regime must be brought out. In spite of Pierre Frank's zealous endeavours to elevate de Gaulle into a position to which he only aspired, the 'Bonaparte' de Gaulle, measuring the relation of forces, was forced to retire sadly from the scene to await a more propitious moment.

There precisely is the nub of the question: it is necessary to answer Stalinist and socialist propaganda by warning that their policies inevitably bring the dangers of counter-revolution and Bonapartism: to warn of the threat of military-police dictatorship which hangs over the proletariat if it does not disperse the Bonapartist nests, composed of the cadres of the general staff, police and civil bureaucracy, and take power into its own hands.

Comrades must not make the mistake of the German communists who declared every regime in turn 'fascist' till in the end, by their lulling and confusing the advance guard, the real Hitler arrived. Of course, if Pierre Frank continues to repeat it long enough, no doubt reality will, in the end, coincide with his definition and we will have a Bonapartist regime in France and other countries in Europe. But for Marxists this is not good enough. We must painstakingly analyse and explain every change in government. In that way we can prepare for the events to come.

## *Was the Kerensky regime 'Bonapartist'?*

Scattered through his article, Frank refers to 'Bonapartist *a-la-Kerensky*', the Bonapartism of Kerensky, thus assuming that Bonapartism had in fact been established under the Kerensky regime – entirely unwarranted by a knowledge of the period.

Frank takes one or two conditional formulations of Lenin and Trotsky in relation to the Kerensky regime in Russia and tries to convert them into hard and fast definitions. In reality, the record speaks against him. It is significant to note that the chapter in *History of the Russian Revolution* to which he refers, is headed, not 'Bonapartism', but 'Kerensky and Kornilov – Elements of Bonapartism in the Russian Revolution'. Trotsky was always particularly careful on definitions and thus when he says 'elements', he does not mean the thing itself. And for very good reason. No doubt Kerensky would have *liked* to play the role of Bonaparte. The possibilities of Bonapartism were rooted in the situation. But Bonapartism was never achieved because the Bolshevik Party was strong and achieved the proletarian revolution, leaving no avenue for adventurers to take control. Many citations could be given to show the conditional nature of the characterisation of the Kerensky regime as Bonapartist. In the very section quoted by Comrade Frank, from which he abstracts the single sentence characterising Kerensky as 'the mathematical centre of Russian Bonapartism', Trotsky wrote:

> The two hostile camps invoked Kerensky, each seeing in him a part of itself, and both swearing fealty to him. Trotsky wrote while in prison:
>
> … led by politicians who are afraid of their own shadow, the Soviet did not dare take the power. The Cadet Party, representing all the propertied cliques, could not yet seize the power. It remained to find a great conciliator, a mediator, a court of arbitration.
>
> In a manifesto to the people issued by Kerensky in his own name, he declared: "I, as head of the government […] consider that I have no right to hesitate if the changes (in the structure of the government) […] increase my responsibility in the matters of supreme administration." *That is the unadulterated phraseology of Bonapartism. But nevertheless, although supported from both right and left it never got beyond phraseology.*[20]

Trotsky wrote this as a historian, soberly evaluating and weighing every word. And if one studies the works of Lenin conscientiously, even

20 Trotsky, *History of the Russian Revolution*, Vol. 3, Wellred Books, 2022, p. 663. Our emphasis.

though written in the heat of events, one cannot but see the falsity of Frank's position in confusing the germs with the disease. Lenin writes, for example, in his work 'Towards the Seizure of Power': "Kerensky's cabinet is indubitably the first step towards Bonapartism."[21]

Here can be seen the *conditional* character of what Lenin and Trotsky were talking about. In the very section of *The State and Revolution* quoted by Frank, in which Lenin refers to the Kerensky government as Bonapartist, the conditional character of this is shown by the paragraphs immediately following. In dealing with the state and all its forms in *an instrument for the exploitation of the Oppressed Class* (that is what the chapter is headed in which these references to Bonapartism occur, and that is what Lenin is dealing with), he goes on to say:

> In a democratic republic, Engels continues, "wealth wields its power indirectly, but all the more effectively", first, by means of "direct corruption of officials" (America); second, by means of the "alliance of the government with the stock exchange" (France and America).
>
> At the present time, imperialism and the domination of the banks have 'developed' to an unusually fine art both these methods of defending and asserting the omnipotence of wealth in democratic republics of all descriptions. Since, for instance, in the very first months of the Russian democratic republic, one might say during the honeymoon union of the 'Socialists' – Socialist-Revolutionaries and Mensheviks – joined in wedlock with the bourgeoisie.[22]

To clinch the matter, in a later section of the same pamphlet dealing with the same period, in contrasting a soviet to a parliamentary body, Lenin goes on to say:

> "A working, and not a parliamentary body" – this hits the vital spot of present-day parliamentarians and the parliamentary social-democratic 'lap-dogs'! Take any parliamentary country, from America to Switzerland, from France to England, Norway and so forth – the actual

21 Lenin, 'The Beginning of Bonapartism', *LCW*, Vol. 25, p. 224.
22 Ibid, p. 397.

> work of the 'state' there is done behind the scenes and is carried out by the departments, the offices and the staffs. Parliament itself is given up to talk for the special purpose of the fooling the 'common people'. *This is so true that even in the Russian Republic, a bourgeois democratic republic, all these aims of parliamentarism were immediately revealed, even before a real parliament was created...*[23]

We would have to reduce Lenin to a mass of stupid contradictions if we used the method of Pierre Frank. For him there is no real contradiction because he makes no real contradiction between bourgeois democracy and Bonapartism. If he carried this through he would have to argue that we had *both* bourgeois democracy and Bonapartism in France and his objection to the term 'bourgeois-democratic regime' becomes entirely incomprehensible.

Frank points to the fact that the British comrades have referred to the Labour government in Britain as a Kerensky regime and then proceeds to argue that this is incorrect because we have not a Bonapartist regime in this country:

> Since we here speak of the resolution of our English comrades let us note that it defines the new Labour government as 'Kerenskyism'. The Bonapartism, that they ignored, has found the means to insinuate itself into their document under a very special name. But we do not think the present Attlee government is Bonapartist *à la* Kerensky.

This merely serves to demonstrate that Frank has not understood the meaning of the Kerenskiad or of Bonapartism. The Kerenskiad is the last, or 'one before the last' left government before the proletarian revolution, or, we may add, the bourgeois counter-revolution. Under given conditions, the social tensions and sharp conflicts of the classes in such a period would tend to give rise to Bonapartist conspiracies and plots. That is precisely what happened in the Russian revolution, and that is why Lenin and Trotsky referred to the Bonapartist tendencies within the Kerensky regime. However, for Comrade Frank's benefit, this does not make a Kerensky regime

23 Ibid, p. 428, emphasis added.

a Bonapartist regime. Here perhaps we had better make haste to add, that in referring to the Labour government as a Kerensky government, this was not at all a finished evaluation, but an analogy which we invested with appropriate and necessary safeguards. To put the question beyond dispute, we quote from our resolution:

> At a later stage the most resolute section of the bourgeoisie will begin to seek a solution in a Royalist or military dictatorship on the lines of the Spanish Primo de Rivera, or some similar solution. Royalist or fascist bands under the guise of ex-servicemen's or 'patriotic' associations will begin to spring up.
>
> Events may speed up or slow down the processes but what is certain is the heightening of social tension and class hatreds. *The period of triumphant reaction has drawn to a close, a new revolutionary epoch opens up in Britain. With many ebbs and flows, with a greater or lesser speed, the revolution is beginning.* The Labour government is a Kerensky government. That does not mean that the tempo of development will match that of the events in Russia after March 1917, on the contrary, the revolution will probably assume a long drawn out character but it provides the background against which the mass revolutionary party will be built.

Fortunately, to put the position in its proper perspective, Trotsky gave a definition of Kerenskyism – (he didn't call it Bonapartism!) when he dealt with the false positions of the Comintern in relation to the Spanish revolution of 1931:

> We see that fascism [we may add Bonapartism – *EG*] does not at all represent the only means of the bourgeoisie in its struggle against the revolutionary masses. The regime existing in Spain today [a coalition government of the bourgeois republicans and Socialist Party similar to that in Italy and France today – *EG*], corresponds best to the conception of the Kerenskiad, that is, the last, (or 'one before the last') 'left' government which the bourgeoisie can only set up in its struggle against the revolution. But this kind of government does not necessarily signify weakness and prostration. In the absence of a strong revolutionary party of the proletariat, a combination of semi-reforms, left phrases and

> gestures still more to the left and reprisals, can prove to be of much more effective service to the bourgeoisie than fascism [we may add, naked military dictatorship – *EG*].[24]

Frank's hazy notions of democracy and Bonapartism can be seen in his references scattered throughout his article. To take a few examples:

> The use of democratic slogans – combined with transitional slogans is justified more precisely, *because the possibilities of a democratic regime are non-existent*...
>
> Precisely because *we do not generally have in Europe at the present time democratic regimes, because there is literally no place for them*...
>
> One must no more confuse the Bonapartism 'of the right' with fascism than the Bonapartism 'of the left' with democracy. We have seen that Bonapartism takes very different forms according to the conditions in which the two mortally opposed camps find themselves; *we maintain also that the existence of democratic liberties, even of very great democratic liberties, does not suffice to make a regime democratic.* The Bonapartists *à la* Kerensky, Popular Front [...] are even notorious for their flood of democratic liberty up to the point where capitalist society thereby even risks its balance and is in danger of capsizing. *Democratic liberties do not proceed, as in a regime which one can correctly define as democratic, from the existence of a margin for reform within capitalism, but on the contrary, from a situation of acute crisis*, the result of the absence of all margin or reforms. [...]
>
> *The regime of the Popular Front was not a democratic regime*; it contained within itself numerous elements of Bonapartism as we shall see further on.

The conception of democracy which is put forward by comrade Frank never existed in heaven or earth. It exists only in the idealistic norms of liberalism. *Always, democracy, i.e. bourgeois democracy, has been built on the framework of repression.* Every bourgeois constitution or regime contains its Article 48 as in the Weimar

24 Trotsky, 'Germany, the Key to the International Situation', 26 November 1931, *The Struggle Against Fascism in Germany*, Pathfinder, 1971, p. 115.

Constitution. The very existence of class society presupposes a regime of oppression. But only one who has abandoned Marxist discipline of thought and operates on the basis of metaphysical categories can equate democracy with Bonapartism, or for that matter with fascism. Though there are many points of similarity between these regimes, and elements of naked military rule in all these regimes in one degree or another. But quantity changes into quality. What dictates the nature of the regime is not this or that *element*, but its *basic features*. Democracy today can become Bonapartism tomorrow and be changed into fascism the next day. Fascism, as we have seen, can be transformed into democracy and the process repeated.

The Marxist method is not to lump all regimes indiscriminately together. That is the easy way, but it will lead to blunders and confusion. The Marxist method is to examine things in their process of change and evolution. To examine each government in turn, to establish its specific features and tendencies. To prepare for abrupt changes and transitions, which is the basic characteristic of our epoch, and thus to rectify and delimit, if necessary, our characterisations at each successive stage. The painful limitations of Pierre Frank's method (which he labels Marxism but is in reality impressionism) is summed up in his own words:

> The term 'Bonapartism' does not completely exhaust the characterisation of the regime, but it is indispensable to employ it in present day Europe, if one wishes to go forward with the least possible chance of error. Let us add finally that Marxism is not alone in the possession of such important general ideas: all the sciences do likewise. Thus chemists call bodies carbides which differ more widely from one another than the Bonapartism of Schleicher and that of Kerensky. And chemistry doesn't get along so badly either on that account. The contrary is true.

The Stalinists used the same method during the Third Period with lamentable results in Germany. Starting with a correct generalisation that all the parties from Social Democracy to fascism were agents of the capitalist class… they ended up by saying that, therefore… there was no difference between them – all were fascists of different varieties. For the scientist as for the Marxist, the problem begins where, for Frank, it ends. A chemist can classify certain bodies under a general heading of carbides. But a chemist who stopped at this definition would not get along so well! If, for example, on the basis that a chemist had defined silicon carbide (carborundum) and calcium carbide all under the same heading of 'carbides', one attempted to work an acetylene lamp on a bicycle with the former instead of the latter, some very sad results would occur. It would not be possible to light the path ahead. No more can Frank's method cast light on the nature of the regimes in Europe.

# *The Menace of Fascism*

## *What It Is and How to Fight It*

Written June 1948

Editor's note: Ted Grant wrote this pamphlet in 1948 as a propaganda tool in response to the regrouping of fascist elements in Britain after the war. Though this regrouping was short-lived, undercut by the post-war boom, the pamphlet remains a key text distilling the lessons from the struggle against fascism through the first half of the twentieth century.

* * *

### *Mosley's early supporters*

Only two years after the war allegedly fought to destroy fascism, the British fascists have commenced to regroup their forces. Throughout the country, cautiously and unobtrusively at first, but more and more boldly, the fascists have come into the open.

At first they emerged as local and separate organisations and adopted a host of names for reasons of expediency. The aim was clearly to prepare for unification at a later stage. Among the most important of these organisations were the British League of Ex-Servicemen and women; Mosley's Book Club and Discussion Group; the Union of

British Freedom; the Sons of St George (Derby); the Imperial Defence League (Manchester); the British Workers' Party of National Unity (Bristol); the Corporate Club (a student group at Oxford University).

These organisations are not short of money. Before the war the British Union of Fascists (BUF) had extensive funds at its disposal. The fascists had intimate links with big business. Mosley boasted that he had spent 96,000 of his own personal fortune "in support of my beliefs during my political life". On two occasions Mosley himself married into millionaire families. In 1920 he married Lady Cynthia Curzon, a daughter of the late Marquis Curzon of Kedleston and a granddaughter of Levi Zeigler Leiter, a Jewish Chicago millionaire. Lady Cynthia inherited 28,000 a year from her own family (there are two children of this marriage). After the death of his first wife a few years prior to the war, Mosley married again, this time, into the Guinness millions. His wife is the sister of the notorious Unity Mitford, friend of Hitler.

In the early days of the fascist movement, Mosley was enthusiastically backed by a number of prominent capitalist and military figures. True, later when Mosley became discredited and it was clear that the movement was not timely, many of them dropped away or fell into the background. Apart from the open members of the Fascist Party, a powerful club composed of members of the ruling class was formed to back the Blackshirts. In a pamphlet entitled 'Who Backs Mosley' published by *Labour Research*, some enlightening facts were revealed:

> On New Year's day 1934 was formed the January Club, whose object is to form a solid Blackshirt front. The chairman Sir John Squire, editor of the *London Mercury*, said that it was not a fascist organisation but admitted that "the members who belonged to all political parties were for the most part in sympathy with the fascist movement". (*The Times*, 22 March 1934.) The January Club held its dinners at the Savoy and the Hotel Splendide. *The Tatler* shows pictures of the club assemblies, distinguished by evening dress, wines, flowers and a general air of luxury. The leader is enjoying himself among his own class.

The members of this club were:

- Colonel Lord Middleton: A director of the Yorkshire Insurance Co., Malton Investment Trust, British Coal Refining Processes Ltd and three other companies. He owns about 15,000 acres of land and minerals in Nottinghamshire.
- General Sir Hubert De La Poer Gough, GCMG, KCB, KCVO: Commander of the Fifth Army 1916-18 and Chief of the Allied Mission to the Baltic, 1919 (Russian intervention), now director of Siemens Bros, Caxton Electric Development Ltd, Enfield Rolling Mills and two other companies.
- Air Commodore Chamier, CB, CMG, OBE, DSO: Late Indian Army. Now aviation consultant and agent to, and lately director of, Vickers Aviation Ltd.
- Vincent C Vickers: Director of the London Assurance Corporation and a large shareholder in Vickers Ltd.
- Lord Lloyd: Former Governor of Bombay.
- The Earl of Glasgow: Privy Councillor, brother-in-law to Sir Thomas Inskip, the Attorney General, who was responsible for the Sedition Bill in the House of Commons. The Earl owns Kelburn Castle, Ayrshire and about 2,500 acres.
- Major Natham: Liberal MP for NE Bethnal Green, a member of the Jewish Agency under the mandate for Palestine, Chairman of the Anglo-Chinese Finance and Trade Corporation.
- Ward Price, special correspondent to the *Daily Mail* and director of Associated Newspapers and *British Movietone News*.
- Wing Commander Sir Louis Grieg, KBE, CBO: RAF, partner in J and H Scrimageour, stockbrokers, director of Handley Page Ltd, an insurance company, and Gentleman Usher in Ordinary to the King.
- Lady Ravendale, Baroness, sister-in-law to Mosley and granddaughter to Levi Leiter.

- Count and Countess Paul Munster.
- Major Metcalfe, MVO, MC: Brother-in-law of Lady Cynthia Mosley and Lady Ravendale, late aide-de-camp to the Prince of Wales and the Commander in Chief in India.
- Sir Philip Magnus, Bart.: a leading Conservative.
- Sir Charles Petrie.
- Hon. JF Rennell Rodd: Heir to Baron Rennell and a partner in Morgan, Grenfell & Co.
- Ralph D Blumenfeld, Chairman of the *Daily Express*, formerly editor. He was once editor of the *Daily Mail*. He is the founder of the Anti-Socialist Union and a member of its Executive Committee.

It is significant that among the early supporters of Mosley are named a number of wealthy Jews. This was before Mosley adopted antisemitism as an indispensable means of rallying ignorant and backward supporters.

Mosley had the financial backing of fascists abroad. He received a subsidy of 60,000 a year from Mussolini. This has been confirmed by the discovery of documents in the archives in Rome dated 1935, and was revealed by Chuter Ede, the Home Secretary, in the House of Commons.

Mosley paid visits to Hitler and Mussolini and was in close touch with the Nazi leaders.

With the outbreak of the war, the Mosley movement declined. Like other fascist movements in Europe the BUF became an agent of German imperialism on whose victory they banked to assure their future. The British capitalists at war with German imperialism had no use for the fascists and were compelled to illegalise them as part of the ideological war against fascism. But Mosley was well protected in prison and pampered with many of the comforts to which he was accustomed, including the best foods, furniture and servants. As one of their class who had perhaps ventured too early, the British capitalists treated him solicitously with an eye to the future.

## *Are the British capitalists anti-fascist?*

The British capitalist class fought the war, not because they opposed fascism and what it represents, but in a desperate struggle against rival imperialisms for world markets, for sources of raw materials – for profit. Their victory has not brought and will not bring the end of fascism.

Throughout the world, the British ruling class has supported fascism and reaction against the progressive movements of the working class. Let us take but a few examples.

When Mussolini was subjecting the Italian working class to his castor oil 'treatments' and other bestial tortures, Churchill became deeply impressed with his "gentle and simple bearing". Speaking in Rome on 20 January 1927, Churchill found only praise for the fascists:

> I could not help being charmed, like so many other people have been, by Signor Mussolini's gentle and simple bearing and by his calm, detached poise in spite of so many burdens and dangers. Secondly, anyone could see that he thought of nothing but the lasting good, as he understood it, of the Italian people, and that no lesser interest was of the slightest consequence to him. If I had been an Italian I am sure that I should have been whole-heartedly with you from the start to finish in your triumphant struggle against the bestial appetites and passions of Leninism. I will, however, say a word on an international aspect of fascism. Externally, your movement has rendered service to the whole world. The great fear which has always beset every democratic leader or a working-class leader has been that of being undermined by someone more extreme than he. Italy has shown that there is a way of fighting the subversive forces which can rally the masses of the people, properly led, to value and wish to defend the honour and stability of civilised society. She has provided the necessary antidote to the Russian poison. Hereafter no great nation will be unprovided with an ultimate means of protection against the cancerous growth of Bolshevism.

Here the outspoken mouthpiece of British capitalism clearly indicates that in the last resort, faced with the revolutionary working class, the "nation" (the capitalists) will not be "unprovided"; it will always be able to imitate Mussolini and adopt the fascist method of rule over the workers.

In the struggle of China against Japanese imperialism, the British backed Japan because they saw in her victory a bulwark against the rising struggles of the masses in Asia. Mr LS Amery, then Secretary of State for India, a position which he held right up till 1945, said on 27 February 1933 in the House of Commons:

> I confess that I see no reason whatever why, either in act or in word, or in sympathy, we should go individually or intentionally against Japan in this matter. Japan has got a very powerful case based upon fundamental realities. Who is there among us to cast the first stone and to say that Japan ought not to have acted with the object of creating peace and order in Manchuria and defending herself against the continual aggression of vigorous Chinese nationalism? Our whole policy in India, our whole policy in Egypt, stand condemned if we condemn Japan.

The Nazis were aided and financed by the British ruling class. Hitler received the unqualified approval and support of British big business. Lloyd George, the 'Liberal', described Hitler as a 'bulwark' against Bolshevism. As early as February 1934, the British government published a memorandum which allowed for an immediate increase in all German arms. "The German claim to equality of rights in the matter of arms cannot be resisted and ought not to be resisted. You will have to face rearmament of Germany", declared the British Foreign Secretary, Sir John Simon, on 6 February 1934. Export to Germany of unwrought nickel, cotton waste (the basis for gun cotton), aircraft and tanks rose tremendously. When asked in March 1934 if Vickers Ltd were engaged in rearming Hitler's Germany, its chairman replied:

> I cannot give you an assurance in definite terms, but I can tell you that nothing is being done without complete sanction and approval of our own government. (Quoted by Henry Owen in *War is Terribly Profitable.*)

The big financiers and bankers openly advocated a policy of support and assistance for Hitler. A short time after he came to power, the

Governor of the Bank of England declared that loans to Hitler were justified as "an investment against Bolshevism".

Large loans were given to Hitler. His occupation of the Rhineland, the rearmament of Germany, the *anschluss* with Austria, the seizure of Czechoslovakia – all were supported by British capitalism. The reason: they feared a Nazi collapse and what might replace it. Just before the war, the British, through RS Hudson, then Secretary of the Department of Overseas Trade, made an offer of a loan of a billion pounds to conciliate the Nazis and prevent them from expanding at the expense of British imperialism while remaining a bastion against the German workers and against the working class throughout Europe.

Churchill looked upon the Nazis with unbounded approval. In the 1939 edition of Great Contemporaries, Winston Churchill wrote about Hitler's rise to power:

> The story of that struggle cannot be read without admiration for the courage, the perseverance, the vital force which enabled him to challenge, defy, conciliate, or overcome, all authorities or resistance which barred his path. I have always said that if Great Britain were defeated in war, I hoped we should find a Hitler to lead us back to our rightful position among the nations.

The same book by Churchill contains a venomous attack on Trotsky, who earns his bitter hatred as builder of the Red Army and one of the leaders of the October Revolution.

Lord Beaverbrook, writing in the *Daily Express* on 31 October 1938 said:

> We certainly credit Hitler with honesty and sincerity. We believe in his purpose stated over and over again, to seek an accommodation with us, and we accept to the full the implications of the Munich document.

This, of course, did not prevent him from holding ministerial office in the Coalition government in the 'war against fascism'.

In the Spanish Civil War, the British capitalists were in sympathy with Franco. Under the cover of so-called 'non-intervention' they assisted him to crush the Republic.

No reactionary anti-working class movement went unsupported and unaided by British capitalism. Only when the Nazis encroached on their preserves did they declare war in the name of 'anti-fascism'. But when the needs of their class are such that fascism becomes necessary, they will as readily turn to Mosley or some other fascist adventurer, just as the German capitalists turned to Hitler and the Italian to Mussolini. Today, the fascists are not necessary for the defence of their profits. But tomorrow...

## *What is fascism and how does it arise?*

Most important for anti-fascists and working people is an understanding of fascism and why it arises. Without such an understanding of fascism it is not possible to effectively combat and destroy it. And unless it is viewed from the angle of the class structure of capitalist society and the class forces at work, the workers cannot prepare themselves for the future struggle against any rising fascist movement.

Capitalism as a system of society developed out of the decay of feudalism. In the period of its rise, up to the outbreak of the First World War, it was a progressive system because it resulted in the development of the forces of production, i.e. the power of man over nature, and consequently raised the level of culture of mankind.

Despite crises, wealth increased and in the main capitalist countries, the standards and the culture of the masses rose. With the development of technique the increased productivity of labour resulted in a further expansion of industry at the expense of the older methods of production and with this a numerical increase of the working class.

During the past 100 years, in their fight against capitalism, the working class organised their own class organisations, the trade unions and labour parties. It must always be remembered that the rights of today – the right to withhold labour – to strike, to organise, the right of free speech and press and even the right to vote, were not handed down benevolently by the capitalist class: *these were won only after a bitter and ceaseless class struggle on the part of the workers.*

Before the First World War, the capitalists could still afford to give concessions from the enormous profits which the expansion of capitalism and imperialism brought them.

But capitalism inevitably brings in its train the concentration of capital and the growth of monopoly and of the combines. Because of the development of the world market, which is the historical function of the capitalist system, at a certain stage the capitalist nations inevitably and necessarily come into conflict with each other in the frantic endeavour to find and extend markets. The development of the productive forces expands more rapidly than the markets, outstrips the boundaries of the national state and private ownership of the means of production. It is this contradiction that led to the First World War, as it led to the second.

Capitalism in its last stages not only reduces the working class, which it cannot provide with any security in either employment or sustenance, to the state of pauperism; it ruins also the middle class – small shopkeepers and businessmen, professional people, white collar workers, small traders and all those strata of the population whose social position is lodged between the industrial working class and the capitalist class.

To combat the working class it is not possible for the capitalists to rely only on the old forces of repression embodied in the state machine. In modern conditions no state can last very long which does not, at least in its initial stages, possess a mass basis. A military police dictatorship does not serve the purpose. The capitalists find a way out in fascism which finds its mass support in the middle class on the basis of anti-capitalist demagogy. It is important to understand that fascism represents a mass movement: that of the disillusioned middle class.

The working class, in times of crisis, seek to express their aspirations and struggle through their existing organisations. Joined together by production, organised as a class in large factories and plants, the workers think in terms of a socialist solution to their problems. Their social position gives rise to a social consciousness.

The middle class, because of their position in society, wedged half-way between the capitalists and the workers, sway between these classes. If the working class cannot show a revolutionary way out for the middle class, the latter turns to the capitalist class and becomes the main pillar of support for the fascist movement.

With the increasing rivalry on the world market, unable to secure their position while the organisations of the working class exist, the capitalists seek a way out of the crisis by the destruction of these organisations, thereby depriving the workers of the weapons through which they defend their rights and conditions. As the crisis affects one country after another, the capitalists look to fascist movements to smash the working-class organisations and parties. Herein lies the function of fascism.

The difference between capitalist democracy and fascism is explained thus by Leon Trotsky:

> After fascism is victorious finance capital gathers into its hands as in a vice of steel, directly and immediately all the organs and institutions of sovereignty, the executive administrative and educational powers of the state: the entire state apparatus together with the army, the municipalities, the universities, the schools, the press, the trade unions and the co-operatives. When a state turns fascist it does not only mean that the forms and methods of government are changed in accordance with the patterns set by Mussolini – the changes in this sphere ultimately play a minor role but it means first of all for the most part, that the workers' organisations are annihilated; that the proletariat is reduced to an amorphous state and that a system of administration is created which penetrates deeply into the masses and which serves to frustrate the independent crystallisation of the proletariat. Therein precisely is the gist of fascism.[1]

## *Mussolini's rise to power*

Fascism first appeared in Italy. At the end of the great world war of 1914-18, the Italian ruling class became terrified at the revolutionary upsurge of the masses. The capitalist newspapers wrote that the workers and peasants of Italy were behaving as if Lenin and Trotsky were masters of Italy. A whole series of strike struggles took place –

1 Trotsky 'What Next? The Key Question for Germany', 1932, *The Struggle Against Fascism in Germany*, p. 155.

1,663 in 1919; 1,881 in 1920. The workers forced concessions and reforms; better wages; the eight-hour day; general recognition of the trade unions; and a voice in production through factory committees. In September 1920, when the industrialists resorted to a lock-out as a reply to the demand for increased wages, 600,000 Italian metal workers occupied the mills and carried on production themselves, through their own elected shop committees.

The peasantry too were affected by the general post-war revolutionary wave. They began the seizure of the land. The Liberal government was forced to give them the right to remain on the land they had spontaneously seized, on condition that they organised themselves into cooperatives. The agricultural labourers formed strong unions known as the 'Red Leagues'.

The capitalists and landowners were paralysed. Power was in the grasp of the working class. The ruling class manoeuvred in face of the onslaught of the masses, and began to seek a way out, planning a counter-offensive.

At the beginning of April 1919, in Genoa the big industrialists and landowners formed an alliance for the fight against 'Bolshevism'.

> This gathering [wrote Rossi, the anti-fascist later murdered by Mussolini's agents, in his book *La Naissance du Fascisme*] is the first step towards the reorganisation of capitalist forces to meet the threatening situation.

After the formation of national General Federation of Industry, and a General Federation of Agriculture, the capitalists commenced to subsidise the Fasci, or aimed hooligan bands of Benito Mussolini.

This band was a specially trained anti-labour militia whose object was to terrorise the workers and at that stage, to disrupt their organisations. These anti-labour leagues began, openly, to attack meetings of workers. In Milan, stronghold of the socialists, as early as 15 April 1919, a demonstration and march of socialists including women and children, was attacked by the Fasci who were armed with daggers and hand grenades. In groups of two or three dozens, they attacked peaceful demonstrations of workers all over Italy. On the same day as the Milan episode, the offices of the official Italian socialist paper, *Avanti!*, were sacked by the fascists. On 1 December 1919, the socialist deputies were attacked and beaten as they left the Houses of Parliament.

But the failure of the working class to take power enabled the capitalists to undermine the gains that the workers had made, and the aggravated crisis in Italy made the ruined middle class easy victims of fascist demagogy. Because of the smallness and unimportance of the Jewish population in Italy, antisemitism was not part of the arsenal of Italian fascism. Their demagogy centred on opposition to the trusts and support for the little man. To the thugs and adventurers in Mussolini's militia, were added desperate students, unemployed, professional people and middle-class recruits generally.

The revolutionary energies of the masses ebbed. The fascists, lavishly financed by the big industrialists and landowners, began a real offensive against the workers. In Bologna, centre of Emilia's 'Red Leagues', the municipal elections in November 1920, brought a victory for the Socialist Party. On 21 November, the Blackshirts attacked the town hall, and in the struggle a reactionary councillor was killed. (It appeared as if he had been killed by a fascist gunman.) This was the signal which the fascists had been awaiting. According to Gorgolini, one of Mussolini's supporters, this:

> ... opened the great fascist era. The law of brutal retaliation, atavistic and savage, reigned in the Peninsula. It was the will of the fascists.

In the villages, armed by the landowners and supplied with cars, the Blackshirts began punitive expeditions. Having wrecked the organisations of the workers in the villages, they now began to attack the workers in the towns. In 1921, in Trieste, Medina, Florence and elsewhere, the Blackshirts wrecked the Labour Exchanges and the offices of the Cooperative and Labour newspapers.

## *Backing of the capitalist state – police, law courts and army*

In their offensive against the working class the Blackshirt thugs had the full backing of the forces of the capitalist state machine. The police recruited for the fascists, urging the criminal elements to join them, on the promise of all sorts of benefits and immunities. While the police placed their cars at the disposal of the fascists, and while giving permits to them to bear arms, they persistently refused applications for arms by workers and peasants. A fascist student sent a jeering letter to a communist paper, in which he wrote:

> We have the police disarm you before we advance against you, not out of fear of you whom we despise, but because our blood is precious and should not be wasted against vile and base plebeians. (Rossi, *La Naissance du Fascisme.*)

Meanwhile, the 'impartial' courts of law, handed out 'centuries in prison sentences to the anti-fascists, and centuries of absolution for the guilty fascists.' (Gobetti, *La Revolution Liberale.*) In 1921, the Minister of Justice, Fera, "sent a communication to the magistrates asking them to forget about the cases involving fascist criminal acts." (Rosenberg, *Der Weltkampf des Fascismus.*)

The army, through its officer caste, backed the fascists to the hilt.

> General Badoglio, Chief of Staff of the Italian Army, sent a confidential circular to all commandants of military districts stating that the officers then being demobilised (there were about 60,000 of them) would be sent to the most important centres and required to join the fascists, which they would staff and direct. They would continue to receive four-fifths of their pay. Munitions from the State Arsenals came into the hands of the fascist bands, which were trained by officers on leave, or even on active service. Many officers knowing the sympathies of their superiors had been won over to fascism, openly adhered to the movement. Cases of collusion between the army and the Blackshirts grew more and more frequent. For instance, the *Fascio* of Trent broke a strike with the help of an infantry company, and the Bolzano *Fascio* was founded by officers of the 232nd Infantry. (Daniel Guerin, *Fascism and Big Business.*)

Within a short space of time, becoming bolder and bolder, the Blackshirts started a campaign to annihilate the workers' organisations.

Malaparte – a fascist 'theoretician' – related in his *Technique du Coup-d'État*, 1931, that:

> Thousands of armed men, sometimes fifteen or twenty thousand, poured into a city or villages borne rapidly in trucks from one province to another.

Daniel Guerin comments:

> Every day, they attacked the Labour Exchanges and the headquarters of cooperatives and working-class publications. In the beginning of August 1922, they seized the city halls of Milan and Leghorn which had socialist administrations, they burned the offices of the newspaper *Avanti!* in Milan, and *Lavoro* in Genoa; they occupied the port of Genoa, stronghold of the dockworkers' labour cooperatives. Such tactics gradually wore out and weakened the organised proletariat, depriving it of its means of action and support. The fascists only waited for the conquest of power to crush it once and for all.

How did the workers' organisations face up to this mortal threat to their very existence? Instead of explaining the nature of fascism to the workers and what it would mean to them if Mussolini came to power, the leaders persisted in deluding themselves and their followers *that the capitalist state would protect them from the menace of these lawless bands*. Guerin relates how:

> ... the socialist and union leaders obstinately refused to reply to fascism blow for blow, to arm and organise themselves in military fashion. "Fascism cannot in any case be conquered in an armed struggle, but only in a legal struggle", insisted *Battaglia Syndicale* for 29 January 1921. As they possessed contacts in the state apparatus, the socialists on several occasions were offered arms to protect themselves from the fascists. But they rejected these offers, saving that it was the duty of the state to protect the citizen against the armed attacks of other citizens. (Kurella, *Mussolini ohne Maske*, 1931.)

The socialists even went to the extent of signing a peace pact with Mussolini on 3 August 1921. This, on the initiative of the Liberal

Prime Minister and his statement that he desired to 'reconcile' the socialists and fascists. Turati,[2] leader of the socialists in Italy; appealed to Mussolini:

> I shall say to you only this: Let us really disarm!

The Blackshirts must have laughed to themselves. They utilised this position the better to prepare. They denounced the pact and redoubled their offensive against the workers' organisations.

The socialists pleaded to the state to take action against the fascists. And the state took action. *Raids were undertaken, not against the fascists, but against the workers and their organisations.*

Because of the failure of the socialists and trade union leaders, left-wing militants of various tendencies – revolutionary trade unionists, left-wing socialists, young communists, socialists and republicans, with a few ex-Army officers organised armed anti-fascist militias in 1921 on the initiative of Mingrino. They called themselves the 'Arditi del Popo'. They undertook this in the teeth of the opposition of the labour and trade union leaders. Unfortunately, the young and weak Communist Party adopted an ultra-left attitude towards the problem. They split away and organised their own 'Squadrons of Action'.

> The result was [writes Guerin] that when the Blackshirts undertook a 'punitive expedition' against a locality and attacked the headquarters of labour organisations or the 'red' municipalities, the militant workers were either incapable of resisting or offered an improvised, anarchic resistance that was generally ineffective. For the most part, the aggressor remained master of the field.

Guerin writes further:

> After a 'punitive expedition', the anti-fascists abstained from reprisals, respected the 'fascists' residences and launched no counter-attacks. They were satisfied with proclaiming 'general protest strikes'. But these strikes,

2 Filippo Turati was a long-standing leader of the Italian Socialist Party. He led the right wing of the party and was expelled in 1922, after having participated in coalition talks with the king. He went on to form a new party, the Unitary Socialist Party (PSU).

> intended to force the authorities to protect labour organisations against the fascist terror, resulted only in ridiculous parleys with the authorities who were in reality the accomplices of fascism. (Silone, *Der Fascismus*, 1934.) As these strikes were unaccompanied by direct action, they left the enemy's forces intact. On the other hand, the fascists profited by the strikes to redouble their violence. They protected 'scabs', served as strike-breakers themselves, and 'in that threatening vacuum a strike creates around itself, dealt swift and violent blows at the heart of the enemy organisations.' (Malaparte, *Technique du Coup d'État*, 1931.) *However on the rare occasions when the anti-fascists offered an organised resistance to fascism, they temporarily got the upper hand.* For instance, in Parma, in August 1922, the working-class population successfully checked a fascist attack in spite of the concentration of several thousand militiamen *because the defence was organised in accordance with military methods* under the direction of the Arditi del Popolo. (A Rossi, *La Naissance du Fascism*, 1938.)

As the intention of the fascists to seize power became more and more obvious, Turati, the socialist spokesman, appealed to the King in July, 1922, to "remind him that he is the supreme defender of the Constitution". Meanwhile, the capitalists had come to their own conclusions. Rossi writes of:

> ... some very lively conferences that took place between Mussolini and the heads of the General Federation of Industry, Sig. Benni and Olivetti. The chiefs of the Banking Association, who had paid out 20 million to finance the March on Rome,[3] the leaders of the Federation of Industry and the Federation of Agriculture, telegraphed Rome that, in their opinion, the only possible solution was a Mussolini government.

Senator Ettore Conti, a big power magnate, sent a similar telegram: "Mussolini was the candidate of the plutocracy and the trade associations."

Despite the fact that the fascists only had thirty-five deputies in the Italian Parliament out of about 600 or so, the king, obedient to the demands of the ruling classes, handed power to Mussolini.

3 On 28 October 1922, 60,000 fascists under Mussolini began their 'March on Rome'. During the march, the King, Victor Emmanuel III, handed power to Mussolini.

Even after the coup of Mussolini in 1922, the reformist leaders were incapable of drawing the lessons from their bitter experiences.

> The Italian Socialists, blind as ever, continued to cling to legality and the Constitution. In December, 1923, the Federation of Labour sent Mussolini a report of the atrocities committed by fascist bands and asked him to break with his own troops. (Buozzi and Nitti, *Fascisme et Syndicalisme*, 1930.)

The Socialist Party took the electoral campaign of April, 1924, very seriously; Turati even had a debate at Turin with a fascist in a hall where Blackshirts guarded the entrance. And when, after Matteotti's assassination, a wave of revolt swept over the peninsula, the socialists did not know how to exploit it.

> At the unique moment' [Nenni writes] for calling the workers into the streets for insurrection, the tactic prevailed of a legal struggle on the judicial and parliamentary plane.

As a gesture of protest, the opposition was satisfied not to appear in parliament, and, like the ancient plebeians, *they retired to the Aventine.*

> What are our opponents doing? [Mussolini] mocked in the chamber. Are they calling general strikes, or even partial strikes? Are they trying to provoke revolts in the army? Nothing of the sort. They restrict themselves to press campaigns. (Speech, July 1924.)
>
> The socialists launched the triple slogan: "Resignation of the Government, dissolution of the militia, new elections." They continued to display confidence in the King, whom they begged to break with Mussolini; they published, for his enlightenment, petition after petition. But the King disappointed them a second time. (Guerin, *Fascism and Big Business.*)

## *Conditions of life under Mussolini*

Once in power, Mussolini established the model totalitarian state. Having smashed the organisations of the workers, the way was prepared for a savage attack on the standards of the masses in the interests of Big Business. The main brunt of fascism was borne by the working class, against whom it is aimed above all. With their weapons of struggle broken, with the establishment of scab company unions, the conditions were created to drive down the wages and lower the standards of living of the workers. The labour unions were crushed. Shop stewards' representation in the factories was abolished. The right to strike ended. All union contracts were rendered void. The employer reigned supreme in the factories once again. He became at the same tune, the 'leader' of his employees. Any attempt to strike, any resistance to the wishes of the employer, was:

> ... punished with ferocious, penalties by the State. To challenge the employer was to challenge the full force of the State. In the words of the fascists: strikes are crimes 'against the social community'.

The anti-fascist Liberal, Gaetano Salvemini, an authority on Italy, who made a conscientious research into all aspects of life under fascism, basing himself on official fascist government sources, was enabled to show what fascism meant to the Italian people. In his book, *Under the Axe of Fascism*, he revealed that from the very beginning of the Mussolini regime the conditions of the people deteriorated, especially of the unfortunate workers and small peasants. In times of 'prosperity' as well as during the depths of the slump of 1929-33, there were steady cuts in wages. The hours of work were steadily lengthened without any increase in overtime pay, while the cost of living increased. Giving extensive details of cuts in wages from 1922 right up till 1935, despite all the efforts of the regime to conceal this from the outside world, he shows how the consumption of the necessities of life steadily decreased.

In the year 1922, with a population of 38,800,000 the consumption of tobacco was 279,000 quintals;[4] by 1932, it had fallen to 245,000 quintals. The consumption of coffee was 472,000 quintals in 1922 and fell in 1932 to 407,000 quintals. These are 'luxuries' for the workers. But in the barest necessities of life, the fall was correspondingly great. Consumption of maize dropped from 27,213,000 quintals to 26,739,000 quintals in 1932. Consumption of wheat fell – and

4 A quintal is a unit of mass, equivalent to 100 kilogrammes.

this with an increase in population to 41,000,000 in 1932 – from 72,237,000 quintals to 69,204,000 quintals. Salt, which, together with the above is absolutely essential to the barest minimum of existence, fell from 2,646,000 to 2,606,000 quintals. These figures are taken from official Italian statistics. (The *Annuario Statistico Italiano* p. 198 (for 1922-25), and p. 119 (for 1933).) The *Tribuna* of 1 May 1935, revealed a terrible fall in the consumption of meat. The annual consumption of meat, which in 1928 was 22 kilograms (48.4 pounds) per each member of the population (annually) had by 1932 declined to 18 kilograms (39.6 pounds). The consumption of sugar which rose to 7.5 kilograms in 1922 dropped to 6.9 in 1932. In England the annual consumption was 40 kilograms, in France 25, Germany 23 and even in backward Spain, 13 kilograms.

The official unemployment figures in Italy in February of 1933 were 1,229,000. On 2 July 1934, an official communiqué of the Italian Government informed us that "in the winter of that year 'national solidarity' in Italy gave help 'almost every day to 1,750,000 families'." In February 1922 there were only 602,000 unemployed, and the fascists centred a great deal of their demagogy on the horrors of unemployment.

Thus, the myth that fascism can avoid the crises of capitalism is shown to be a fraud.

Once in power, fascism retains its grip for a long period because of the shattering of the working-class organisations. With all the best fighters, the most advanced proletarians in jail or murdered, the working class undergoes a period of demoralisation and apathy. Under the regime of repression and terror, the workers suffer under the greatest disadvantage for a unified struggle against the employers. The inglorious end of Mussolini was a demonstration to the world of the real hatred of the Italian people for the Duce, and an exposure of the lie that the Italian masses supported the Blackshirts.

## *Italian workers and fascism today*

It is striking to note the difference between events in Italy after the Second World War and the first.

Mussolini's fall was the signal for a deep-seated upsurge of the workers and peasants. Once again a tremendous wave of strikes and demonstrations followed the coup of Badoglio.[5] And after the defeat of the Nazis, the workers and peasants, armed in their partisan detachments, repeated the process of taking over the factories and the control of the country. One thing stood in the path of the workers taking power: the leaders of their own organisations.

This failure has meant for the Italian workers a deterioration of their conditions to a level even lower than existed under Mussolini. The workers have been able to defend themselves to a certain extent, because of the powerful unions they have constructed, far more powerful than in the past. But the middle class, ground down to standards even below that of the workers, has provided a favourable basis for the revival of fascist demagogy. They contrasted the promises of the capitalist democrats with their lot. The neo-fascists began to emerge. Armed with the experience of Mussolini's rise to power, the industrialists and land-owners proceeded on familiar lines. A May Day meeting in 1947 in Sicily was fired on, despite the fact that women and children were participating. In Naples some months before, bands of Monarchists and fascists demonstrated against the Communist Party and other workers' organisations. In the last few months of 1947 workers' meetings were fired on and bombs thrown at premises of workers' organisations. The terror of the fascists was greater in the countryside of the backward South, where the landowners organised the murder of trade union organisers and attempted to terrorise the agricultural workers and peasants against joining the unions.

Within a few months, nineteen trade union organisers were assassinated in the agricultural districts of the South.

In the North, even in such working-class strongholds as Milan, bombs have been placed in the headquarters of the Communist Party. The workers swiftly replied by a general strike in Milan,

5 Pietro Badoglio was an Italian general and war criminal. In 1943, after a coup inside the regime, the king appointed Badoglio as Prime Minister. In spite of support from Britain and the US, his government fell a few months later.

*and immediately took reprisal action against the headquarters of the neo-fascist organisations, l'Uomo Qualunque and Movimento Sociale Italiene, which were set on fire and sacked.*

Having had experience of fascism, the Italian workers have not been content to remain on the defensive. In nearly all cities, big and small, they have gone on the offensive against the fascists. Demonstrations of over a hundred thousand in Milan, tens of thousands in other cities – Turin, Genoa, Florence, Verona, Bari, Cremona, Rome, Bologna, even in Naples and Palermo (former strongholds of reaction) the workers have made militant attacks on the headquarters of the fascist organisations. The backward South has followed the lead of the North.

Naturally, the police, always conveniently absent or inactive when the fascists have attacked the workers, have been called out to protect the fascists. Troops have been called out in many towns to assist the police. Tear gas and firearms have been used against the workers.

In this situation, the de Gasperi government,[6] like its liberal predecessor of 1920-22, has surreptitiously given assistance and encouragement to the fascists. History repeats itself, but not exactly in the same way. The offensive of the workers led to the defeat of the fascists, who for the time being have been forced to lie low. The workers of Britain can learn a valuable lesson from the recent offensive movement of the Italian workers.

But this lesson has been a purely negative one. If having learned the negative lessons of preventing the fascists from rearing their heads, the workers fail to apply a *positive solution*, the menace of fascism even in Italy will not have been exorcised.

The chronic decay of capitalism in Italy continues. Already there is the mass unemployment of one and a half million workers. The first winds of the new world crisis will send unemployment soaring to record levels. Wracked by crises, the Italian capitalists will turn again to brutal suppression as the only means of stabilising

---

6 Alcide de Gasperi was a right-wing politician and founding member of the Christian Democracy party. He served eight consecutive terms as Prime Minister, beginning in 1945 and ending in 1953.

their regime. The lesson of Italy must be learned above all by the vanguard of the working-class movement. If they fail to show the alternative of the complete overthrow of the capitalist system and the establishment of workers' power and communism, the great offensive spirit of the masses will wane, and demoralisation and indifference will set in. Capitalism breeds fascism; the workers can guarantee the end of fascism only by overthrowing the capitalist system of society.

## *Germany – how the Nazis came to power*

The defeat of the German working class, on the coming to power of Hitler, set the world workers' movement back for many years. In tracing the background to the events in Germany, we can see clearly the class forces at work, the role of the German social democrats and Stalinists which led to the terrible defeat of one of the most powerfully organised labour movements in the world.

In the wake of the Russian Revolution, the German working class overthrew the Kaiser and attempted a revolutionary overthrow of capitalism in 1918.

But it was the German social democrats who came to power, though they had actually opposed the insurrection and the revolution.

They had no intention of consummating the revolution. Their programme was based on 'the inevitability of gradualism'. Having raised themselves above the level of the workers, they had abandoned the Marxist programme on which their party had been based for decades. Noske, Ebert, Scheidemann, the leaders of the Social Democracy, conspired with the German General Staff to destroy the revolution and restore 'law and order'. The Berlin workers were shot down in January 1919, and the revolutionary leaders, Luxemburg and Liebknecht, were murdered by reactionary officers on the direct instigation of the Social-Democratic leaders. The Soviets established in the revolution were eliminated, and Germany became a democratic capitalist state – the most democratic in the world, according to the boast of the Social Democrats.

At this stage the capitalists were compelled to lean on the Labour and trade-union leaders in order to save their system from complete collapse. Grinding their teeth, they were forced to make tremendous concessions to the working class. The workers won the eight-hour day, trade union recognition, unemployment insurance, the right to elect shop committees and universal suffrage for men and women. The agricultural labourers who lived under semi-feudal conditions in East Prussia under the Junkers, won the right to organise and similar rights to those of the industrial workers.

Recovering from the first shock, the big industrialists and landowners began to prepare for the offensive against the working class. Their attitude was exemplified by that of Krupp, the armament magnate who arrogantly informed his workers:

> We want only loyal workers who are grateful from the bottom of their hearts for the bread which we let then earn.

By February 1919, Stinnes, another of the iron and steel magnates of the Ruhr was declaiming openly:

> Big business and all those who rule over industry will some day recover their influence and power. They will be called back by a disillusioned people, half dead with hunger, who will need bread and not phrases.

The former Minister, Dernberg, representative of big industry, declared openly: "Every eight-hour day is a nail in Germany's coffin."

Already in these early years, the capitalists began to finance anti-labour leagues composed of ex-army officers, criminals, adventurers and other social riff-raff. The Nazis were at this time, one small anti-labour grouping among others.

They commenced a campaign of terror, which included assassinations of left-wing, and even capitalist democratic politicians. They commenced a campaign of breaking up working class meetings. "The National Socialist movement will in the future prevent, if need be, by force, all meetings or lectures that are likely to exercise a depressing influence", declared Hitler on

4 January 1921. As in Italy, so in Germany, the courts, the army authorities, the civil service, the heads of the police, gave every support to these reactionary groups. The State acted in complicity and in collusion with them. When the Munich Chief of Police, Pohner, was warned of the existence of "veritable organisations of political assassination", he replied: "Yes, yes, but too few!"

But at this stage, these fascist groups had no mass base. They comprised an insignificant social force, composed only of the dregs of society. The middle class looked to the workers' organisations to show a way out. The capitalists used the fascist organisations only as anti-labour auxiliaries, and a reserve for the future. Dealing with the development of the Nazi movement, Hitler admitted:

> Only one thing could have broken our movement – if the adversary had understood its principles and from the first day had smashed, with the most extreme brutality, the nucleus of our new movement.

Goebbels remarked:

> If the enemy had known how weak we were, it would probably have reduced us to jelly. It would have crushed in blood the very beginning of our work.

In the revolutionary crisis of 1923, caused by the inflation and the occupation of the Ruhr by France, the middle class looked towards the Communist Party which had succeeded in gaining the support of the majority of the workers. But the revolutionary situation was bungled by the then leaders of the German Communist Party, Brandler and Thalheimer, and by the wrong advice given by Stalin in Moscow to the leadership of the Communist Party.

Brandler admitted subsequently at a meeting of the Executive Committee of the Communist International:

> There were signs of a rising revolutionary movement. We had temporarily the majority of the workers behind us, and in the situation believed that under favourable circumstances we could proceed immediately to the attack.

After the possibility of seizing power had been lost, the leadership of the International tried to put all the responsibility on the shoulders of the German Party. But the German leaders had looked for advice to the leadership of the Communist International in Moscow. Stalin's advice was catastrophic. He wrote to Zinoviev and Bukharin at that time:

> Should the communists strive to seize power without the social-democrats, are they mature enough for that? That, in my opinion is the question. Of course, the fascists are not asleep, but it is to our interest that they attack first: that will rally the whole working class around the communists (Germany is not Bulgaria). Besides, according to all information the fascists are weak in Germany. In my opinion the Germans must be curbed and not spurred on.[7]

This, when they had the majority of the workers behind them! Thus tragically the German revolution was ruined and the basis laid for a subsequent increase in fascist influence.

## *Big business and the Nazis*

Scared by the perspective of 'Bolshevism' in Germany, the American, British and French capitalists poured in loans to prop up German capitalism. These loans resulted in a capitalist boom on a world scale, which particularly affected Germany. The boom in Germany lasted from 1925 until 1929. The capitalists of Germany coining enormous profits out of the rationalisation of German industry did not need the fascists, and the support for the Nazis declined. They received only sufficient funds to keep them in existence as a reserve weapon and to prevent their disappearance from the scene altogether.

Then came the world slump of 1929-33. The workers' standards of living dropped. Unemployment rose to seven million and more. The middle class were ruined in the economic crisis, and they found their standards dropping lower than the levels of the working class. The industrial workers had the protection of their union contracts

7 Trotsky, *The Third International After Lenin*, Pioneer, 1957, p. 312.

and unemployment allowances within limits, and could thus resist the worst impositions of the combines and monopolies. But the middle class was helpless.

The industrialists were alarmed at the prospect of proletarian revolution. They now began to pour fabulous sums into the coffers of the Nazi Party. Krupp, Thyssen, Kirdorff, Borsig, the heads of the coal, steel, chemical and other industrial empires in Germany, supplied Hitler lavishly with the means of propaganda. The final decision to hand power over to Hitler was taken at the home of the Cologne banker, Schroder (who, according to the Nazi racial laws was a Jew!) Enormous subsidies such as no other political party in Germany had ever received were rained upon the Nazis by the capitalists. They considered the time had come to destroy the organisations and rights of the working class.

Explaining what the subsidies meant, Hitler pointed out that:

> Without automobiles, airplanes and loud speakers, we could not have conquered Germany. These three technical means enabled National Socialism to carry on an amazing campaign.

In a confidential document published by the British Government in 1943, for the use of officials and civil servants who were to be sent to Germany, the following irrefutable facts are given:

> Fritz Thyssen and Kirdorff in the Ruhr, and Ernst von Borsig in Berlin, chairman of the German Employers' Federation (Vereinigung Deutscher Arbeitgeberverbande) were the extreme supporters of Hitler. Among other financial supporters of earlier Hitler days were the famous piano manufacturers, Karl Bechstein (Berlin), the printer Bruckmann (Munich), the well-known art dealer and publisher, Hanfstaengl (Munich) and the Reetsma Cigarette combine in Hamburg which, after Hitler came to power was granted an exclusive monopoly.
>
> But it was not only during the big crisis preceding the Nazi government that financial support by great industrial corporations began on a larger scale. Most of these did not give their contributions to the Nazi party direct, but to Alfred Hugenberg, the former director of Krupps

and leader of the 'Deutschnationale Volkspartei' (German National People's Party). Hugenberg placed one-fifth of the amount given at the disposal of the NSDAP.

Fritz Thyssen, since his break with Hitler, has stated that his personal contribution amounted to 1 million Rm., and he estimated the amount the NSDAP received from heavy industry via Hugenberg at about 2 million RM[8] annually.

At the meeting of the Dusseldorf Club of industrialists on 27 January 1932, after Hitler had enlightened them about his programme, the pact between the heavy industry and the Nazi party was sealed. Here Hitler convinced his audience that they had nothing to fear from his 'socialism', and then he commended himself with his semi-military organisation as the bulwark against any kind of 'Bolshevism'.

The economic policy carried on by the 'National-Socialists' nevertheless completely justified the confidence which the big industrialists had placed in Hitler. Hitler has in every other respect carried out *their* policy. He has destroyed the workers' organisations. He has introduced the 'leadership principle' in the factories. He has brought about an expansion of heavy industry in Western Germany by means of an immense rearmament programme and has brought the firms enormous profits. The profits which the manufacturers of the Ruhr and Rhineland were able to make are dearly shown in the so-called 'decree' regarding the surrender of 'dividends' of 1941. (*Dividend en abgabeverordnung.*) This decree, which like so many Nazi decrees, means the opposite of what its name indicates, enabled the joint stock companies to realise profits which they had accumulated during 1933-38 and which had not been paid out in dividends by way of so-called 'rectification'. About 5,000,000,000 RM of accumulated profits, which had been made in the pre-war years, were distributed to the shareholders in the form of bonus shares.

## *Trotsky calls for the united front*

In the General Election of May 1924, the Nazis received 1,920,000 votes with thirty-two deputies. But in December of the same

8 The Reichsmark (RM) was the currency of Germany from 1925-45.

year, after the Dawes Plan had restored some stability to German economy, they received 840,000 and the decline of the Nazis went even further. In the elections for the German President in 1925, General Ludendorff, the candidate of the Nazis obtained 210,000! In the General Election of May 1928, the Nazis received only 720,000 votes, losing 120,000 votes and two seats.

Then came the world slump and the frightful crisis of German capitalism. Within two years at the General Election of 14 September 1930, the Nazi vote rose to 6,000,000. The fascists had drawn to their banner large sections of the despairing middle class. The failure of the socialists in 1918 and of the communists in 1923 had driven a formidable proportion of the middle class from neutrality or even support of the workers, to the side of the counter-revolution with its denunciation of 'Marxism', i.e. socialism.

Immediately the elections results were known, Trotsky and the Left Opposition – who considered themselves a part of the Communist International although they had been expelled – issued an appeal to the German Communist Party to immediately organise a united front with the Social Democrats to prevent the coming to power of Hitler. Only thus could they hope to protect the rights of the working class from the threat of the Nazis. The Trotskyists warned of the tragic consequences which the coming to power of the Nazis could mean, not only to the German, but to the whole international working-class movement. They warned that it would make war against the Soviet Union inevitable.

But the Stalinists took no heed. Their policy in Germany was that fascism or 'social fascism' was already in power; that the *main danger* to the working class was *Social Democracy*, who were also fascists – '*social-fascists*'.

The British Trotskyists were expelled from the Communist Party in 1932 for advocating the united front between social-democrats and communists in Germany as well as in Britain.

> It is significant [wrote the British Stalinists in the *Daily Worker* of 26 May 1932] that Trotsky has come out in defence of a united front between

> the Communist and Social Democratic Parties against fascism. No more disruptive and counter-revolutionary class lead could possibly have been given at a time like the present.

Ernst Thälmann, in his closing speech at the thirteenth plenum of the Communist International in September 1932 (see *Communist International*, No. 17/18, p. 1,329) said:

> In his pamphlet on the question, 'How Will National Socialism be Defeated?', Trotsky gives always but one reply: "The German CP must make a bloc with the Social Democracy." In framing this bloc, Trotsky sees the only way for completely saving the German working class against fascism. "Either the CP will make a bloc with the social democracy or the German working class is lost for ten to twenty years."
>
> This is the theory of a completely ruined fascist and counter-revolutionary. This theory is the worst theory, the most dangerous theory and the most criminal that Trotsky hay constructed in the last years of his counter-revolutionary propaganda.

The fountainhead of this policy of the German CP, Stalin, gave the line to the German Party.

> These two organisations [Social Democracy and National Socialism] are not mutually exclusive, but on the contrary are mutually complementary. They are not antipodes but twins. Fascism is a shapeless bloc of these two organisations. Without this bloc the bourgeoisie could not remain at the helm. (*Communist International*, No. 6, 1925.)

The Stalinists even went to the extent of inciting communist workers to beat up socialist workers, break up their meetings, etc. Thälmann openly put forward the slogan: "Chase the social fascists from their jobs in the plants and the trade unions." Following on the line, the organ of the Young Communists, *The Young Guard*, propounded the slogan: "Chase the social fascists from the plants, the employment exchanges and the apprentice schools." Even the organ of the Young Pioneers, catering for the children of communists, *The Drum*, called upon communists' children to "strike the little Zörgiebels[9] in the schools and the playgrounds."[10]

They did not stop there. The leaders of the Communist International went to the extent of advocating that the German CP unite with the fascists against the social-democrats. The Social Democratic Party was in power in Prussia which consisted of two-thirds, and the most important part, of Germany. There was a traditional saying in Germany: "He who has Prussia has the Reich." The Nazis organised a plebiscite on 9 August 1931, in an endeavour to throw the Social-Democratic government out of office. Had they succeeded in this, they would have come to power in 1931 instead of 1933. The German CP leadership decided to oppose the referendum and support the Social Democrats. But the leadership of the Comintern, under the direct influence of Stalin, demanded that the CP participate in this referendum and called it a 'Red Referendum'. At the ECCI, Piatnitzky even boasted:

> You know, for example, that the leadership of the party opposed taking part in the referendum on the dissolution of the Prussian Landtag. A number of party newspapers published leading articles opposing participation in that referendum. But when the Central Committee of the party jointly with the Comintern arrived at the conclusion that it was necessary to take an active part in the referendum the German comrades in the course of a few days roused the whole party. Not a single party, except the CPSU could do that. (*Guide to the XII Plenum*, ECCI, p. 42.)

It was mad adventures of this character which disoriented the workers and facilitated the success of the Nazis. The refusal of the leaders of

---

9 Karl Zörgiebel was the Social Democratic Chief of Police.

10 This line was not confined to Germany. The tiny Communist Party of Britain advocated the break-up of Labour Party meetings. Pollitt wrote in the *Daily Worker*, on 29 January 1930:

> There should not be a Labour meeting held anywhere, but what the revolutionary workers in that district attend such meetings and fight against the speakers, whoever they are, so-called 'left', 'right' or 'centre'. They should never be allowed to address meetings. This will bring us into conflict with the authorities but this must be done. The fight can no longer be conducted in a passive manner. – *EG*

the mass workers' organisations to carry out a revolutionary policy against the fascists, resulted in this mighty working class movement, with a Marxist tradition of seventy-five years, being smashed and rendered impotent before the Nazi thugs.

It is important to bear in mind that the Nazis won only a small percentage of the German workers; the overwhelming majority were opposed to them. In 1931, the Nazis obtained only 5 per cent of the votes in the elections for the shop committees in the factories. This was after a terrific campaign to penetrate the working class. And in March 1933, after the fascists were placed in power, despite the fact that the terror had already begun, they got only 3 per cent of the votes in the elections for the shop committees! Despite the false policies of the leaderships, which led to a certain demoralisation within the ranks of the workers and helped the fascists' attempts to penetrate their ranks, the overwhelming majority of the workers remained faithful to the ideas of socialism and communism.

## *How socialists and communists faced Hitler's threat*

The workers were anxious and willing to fight the Nazis to prevent them coming to power. Millions were armed and trained in the socialist and communist defence organisations. This was a legacy of the German revolution. The organised working class constituted the mightiest power in Germany had they only had the necessary policy to fight for the defence of their organisations and pass to the counter-offensive to take power. But the leaders betrayed the workers in Germany as they did in Italy.

As the danger of a Hitler coup grew closer, these misleaders declared that the Nazis were on the decline. The socialist leaders declared, as if plagiarising their Italian counterparts: "*Courage under unpopularity.*" They urged the necessity to support the decree laws of the Brüning Government, and to support Hindenburg as against the danger from Hitler. They scoffed at the idea that a highly civilised country like Germany could fall under the domination of fascist barbarism. Fascism could come to power in a backward country like Italy, but not Germany with its highly-industrialised economy! At first, they scoffed at the crudities and insane ideas put forward by the Nazis. They urged the workers to laugh at them and disregard their provocations. It only gives them publicity, they said. It can't happen here. We know the familiar arguments of middle-class intellectuals such as Rebecca West, in Britain and elsewhere.

Constantly they underestimated the danger from the fascists and appealed to the very state machine which was protecting and shielding the fascists.

But as the fascist menace loomed nearer, sections of the socialist workers and the trade unions began to form defence groups in the factories and among the unemployed. But the German TUC, the Labour Federation, refused to support this:

> ... the situation [was] not sufficiently grave to justify the workers preparing for a struggle to defend their rights.

It was opposed to "centralising and generalising these preventive measures", on the grounds that they were "superfluous". On 6 November 1932, *Vorwärts*, the central organ of the Social Democracy wrote of the fall in the poll for the Nazis from 13,700,000 to 11,705,257 and the refusal of Hindenburg to hand power to Hitler: "Ten years ago we predicted the bankruptcy of National Socialism; it is written in black and white in our paper!"

On the eve of the Nazis' accession to power, Schiffrin, one of the leaders of the Social Democrats wrote:

> We no longer perceive anything but the odour of a rotting corpse. Fascism is definitely dead: it will never arise again.

The line of the leaders of the CP was, if anything, even worse. They declared that fascism was already in power in Germany and that the coming to power of Hitler would not make any difference. In the Reichstag, Remmele, one of their leaders, declared, on 14 October 1931:

> Herr Brüning has put it very plainly once they [the fascists] are in power, then the united front of the proletariat will be established and

> it will make a clean sweep of everything. (Violent applause from the communists.) We are not afraid of the fascist gentlemen. They will shoot their bolt quicker than any other government. ("Right you are!" from the communists.)

In 1932 Thälmann, in a speech to the Central Committee, condemned "the opportunistic over-estimation of Hitler fascism." As early as the first victory of the Hitler movement at the polls in the 14 September 1930, elections the central organ of the German CP, *Rote Fahne*, declared:

> 14 September was the culminating point of the National Socialist movement in Germany. It will be followed only by weakening and decline.

Within three years, the Nazis had succeeded in winning the bulk of the middle class and obtaining over 13 million votes.

Just at the time when the Nazis received their first check at the polls and lost two million votes, and the signs of the disintegration of the Nazi movement appeared, President Hindenburg, the army leaders, the bureaucracy and the great industrialists and landowners handed power over to Hitler.

Even at the thirteenth hour, the socialist and Stalinist leaders gave no fighting lead. On 7 February 1933, Kunstler, head of the Berlin Federation of the Social Democratic Party, gave this instruction to the labour workers:

> Above all do not let yourselves be provoked. The life and health of the Berlin workers are too dear to be jeopardised lightly; they must be preserved for the day of struggle.

This when Hitler had already come to power, in January 1933. The Communist Party leaders cried:

> Let the workers beware of giving the Government any pretext for new measures against the Communist Party! (Wilhelm Pieck, 26 February 1933.)

The leaders of these parties did nothing even after Hitler came to power. And the German workers wanted to fight. On 5 March, the night of the elections, the heads of the Reichsbanner, the military organisation of the Social Democracy, asked for the signal for insurrection. They received the reply from the leaders of the Social Democratic Party: "Be calm! Above all no bloodshed." The mighty German labour movement was surrendered to Hitler without a shot being fired.

The struggle for a united front by the Communist Party; the formation of such a united front of struggle in 1930, would have transformed the whole future course of events. The middle class would have followed the lead of the workers' organisations. Had the fascists been confronted with the organised might of the workers, they would have been smashed. Cravenly capitulating to the 'authorities', the leadership allowed Hitler to score a very cheap victory.

The reformists and Stalinists are the same in all countries. In later years the responsibility for the debacle was shouldered onto the German workers. But at the Brighton Congress of the TUC, the Chairman, Citrine, defended the trade union leaders in Germany and their failure to call a general strike in 1933. He said:

> Shortly after the elections the campaign of terror developed. The socialist movement and the trade union movement were virtually suppressed on 2 May. There had been a great deal of concern about the apparent absence of resistance to the advent of the Nazi dictatorship. German trade union leaders and German socialist leaders were openly attacked and criticised on platforms because of the absence of effective resistance. All he could say was that he knew from first-hand knowledge that very adequate means of resistance were prepared.
>
> All he could say was that a general strike was definitely planned and projected, but the German leaders had to give consideration to the fact that a general strike, after the atmosphere created by the Reichstag fire, and with six and a quarter million people unemployed at the least, was an act fraught with the gravest consequences, consequences which might be described as nothing less than civil war. He hoped they would never be put into a similar position in this country. He hoped they would never have to face that position. (*The Menace of Dictatorship*, p. 8.)

## *What happened to the middle class*

The Nazis demagogically attacked the Jews, the trusts and the combines. They even proposed the break-up of big industry and its division among small businessmen and the break-up of the big department stores and their division among the shopkeepers. Of course they had no intention of carrying out these demagogic proposals, which in any case it would have been impossible to do. Thus, they gathered support among the middle-class masses. This was the social base of the fascists.

Yet it was ironic that the middle-class dupes of the Nazis were the strata of the population who suffered the worst once the Nazis had come to power. The Nazis had bewailed the dying out of the middle class, the most important strata of the nation, the backbone of the race. The statistics tell their own story of the crushing of small capital by the giant monopolies and combines. The tendency for the concentration of capital, far from being slowed down, was speeded up because there was no means of resistance by the small man. And this process was consciously aided by the Nazis. In his book *The Coming Crisis*, Sternberg points out that in 1925 the number of proprietors in Germany, together with their dependants amounted to 12,027,000 *persons*, or 20.9 *per cent of the total population.* Owing to the havoc of the crisis by the time the Nazis came to power in 1933, the total dropped to 11,247,000 or 19.8 per cent *of the total population.* In the first six years of Nazi rule, in the period of *Wehrwirtschaft* (war economy) *the number had declined still further* to 9,612,000, or 16.2 *per cent of the total population.*

The German economic publication *Wirtschaft und Statistik* of 1940 (p. 336) brutally comments as follows on this phenomenon:

> The decline in the number of proprietors together with their dependants – their total was reduced by 1.7 million or approximately 15 per cent from 1933 – is in accordance with a long and steady trend of development. From 1895 onwards, their numbers have decreased from census to census, though the decline since 1933 is, of course, a record one.

Further evidence of this process is given in *Germany: A Basic Handbook*, which points out:

> The concentration of capital in fewer and fewer hands has proceeded rapidly. Many small and medium-sized firms have been absorbed by the big concerns. From 1937 to the end of 1942, the capital invested in joint stock companies increased by over 10 per cent. At the same time, the total number of these companies decreased. Thus, at the end of 1942, one percent of the companies owned 60 per cent of the capital invested in joint stock companies. As the *Deutsche Allegemeine Zeitung*, 6 January 1944, points out: "Of the total number of German joint stock companies with a capital of 30 billion Rms., approximately three-quarters to four-fifths are owned by large shareholders or combines."

Representatives of Big Business were given all the key positions in the economy. At the same time there was:

> … mutual interpenetration; on the one hand the leading industrialists, bankers, as leaders of the war economy, leaders of Gau (regions) Economic Chambers of Trade Groups of Reich Associations, etc., became servants of the state, and were appointed to high administrative positions; on the other hand, high ranking officials, the Nazified bureaucracy of the state departments endeavoured to obtain highly-paid positions in the sphere of private enterprise. In the end, there were a number of semi-state, semi-private, companies which may be described as public utilities in the industrial sphere. The best known of this kind is the *Hermann Göring-Concern*.
>
> … It is quite obvious that this development gave ample opportunity to the *Nazi elite* to become the new Nazi industrialists and profiteers, and thus we see these new names, together with the old and well-known names of the various branches of German and Austrian industry, in the leading positions of the management and boards of the various branches of the Göring-Combine.
>
> In this connection, a few words may be added about a typical party enterprise, *Gustloff Foundation*, which was founded on 'aryanised'

> property, the Suhl gun factory in Thuringia, in honour of Wilhelm Gustloff, a Nazi agent in Switzerland, who was shot in 1934, and which soon turned into a not unimportant machine-tool and armament combine, consisting of six companies, among them the famous Austrian Hirtenberg munitions factory. This combine is run solely by the party, that is, by the Thuringen *gauleiter Sauckel*... Nothing is known of the finances of the Foundation since, like the Hermann Göring Werke, it does not publish balance sheets or profit and loss accounts.
>
> The development of this party sector of big business does not constitute nationalisation, nor is it a negation of capitalism or plutocracy. On the contrary, it is the retention of all that enables party members to build up for themselves industrial empires and to tap new sources of income.
>
> Thus, the ranks of the old rulers of industry and commerce lent themselves to a compromise so long as the benefits accruing from the alliance with the party elite and bureaucracy, e.g. the joint spoliation of small enterprise and all strata of the 'little man' – outweigh all sacrifices by the group.

In the 30 June 1934 purge,[11] Hitler struck against those elements in the ranks of the fascists who were demagogically playing on the aspirations of the middle class, as well as against those who had genuinely been deluded by the propaganda lies of the Nazis. Having accomplished this, Hitler transformed his dictatorship into a military-police state, representing the interests of the industrialists and landlords. Instead of the Junker estates being broken up and given to the peasants as promised, the power of the former was strengthened. Instead of breaking up the big department stores and dividing them among the small shopkeepers, instead of the abolition of the combines and monopolies, the small shops were closed down in thousands, and, a further concentration of the economy into the hands of the trusts took place.

---

11 The Night of the Long Knives, where Hitler had a number of leading Nazis assassinated, including Gregor Strasser and the leader of the Sturmabteilung, Ernst Röhm.

From this we see that the only promise which was kept was the persecution of the unfortunate Jews. The middle class was despoiled, the workers' organisations crushed, and only the high Nazi functionaries and big business benefited from Hitler rule. All the worst excesses of the capitalist system found expression because no opposition or the check of public opinion was allowed.

## *Reign of terror*

Once in power, the Nazis went ahead speedily, and accomplished in months what had taken the Italian fascists years. The political parties were illegalised; the trade unions were destroyed; the funds of the workers' organisations were confiscated for the benefit of the Nazis. The concentration camps were opened, and a reign of terror commenced against the working-class socialists and communists, and Jews, such as had never been seen in modern history.

The fascists made great play of the fact that there was no unemployment under Hitler's Germany. It is true that as a result of Hitler's immense rearmament plans, the forced labour on German arms and fortifications, there was no unemployment. Of course, had the war not intervened there would have been in Germany a disastrous economic slump as in other capitalist countries. Hitler spent fabulous sums in preparing for war which he saw as the only road for German imperialism and his own regime. He staked everything on armaments production on a scale never before reached in any state in peace time.

The German workers had to work long hours for low wages in order to prepare instruments of destruction which would be no benefit to them or to workers of other lands. They were employed… to produce for the terrible catastrophe that overtook Germany in the war. Hitler regarded them as pigs to be fattened for the slaughter.

In 1935, an employers' report enthusiastically hailed the new labour laws "at the present time, precisely, which requires increased intensification of production…" (that is, speed up). Göring openly declared in a speech: "We must work doubly hard today to lead the Reich out of decadence, impotence, shame and poverty. Eight hours a day is not enough. We must Work!" On 22 May 1933, Hitler said in the Reichstag: "In Germany, private property is sacred."

Of all the twenty-five points of the Nazi 'programme' only the persecution of the Jews, a scapegoat for the crimes of capitalism, was carried out. The disillusionment was given an outlet in Jew-baiting. Even after they had been rendered helpless, deprived of all rights, thrown into concentration camps, the myth of the Jews being responsible for all the ills of society was fostered. As Hitler pointed out: *if he had not had the Jews, he would have had to invent them.* No wonder Goebbels regretted publicly that the Nazis had ever published a programme.

After the war and the defeat of German imperialism, the Allies have not brought about the destruction of fascism. The middle class, the potential mass base for fascism, is today supporting the Christian Democrats of Germany. The Stalinist policy of reparations and revenge could not rally the support of the German masses. As a result of the policy of the Allies, the German masses are nearing literal starvation. When the slump hits Germany, the collapse of the 'democratic' capitalist parties is inevitable. There is no middle road. The alternatives will be posed in Germany again: either the victory of the working class or a new fascist dictatorship.

## *Mosley before the war and the anti-fascist struggles of the workers*

The laws of the decline of the capitalist system are the same in Britain as in other capitalist countries. The legend, assiduously cultivated, in particular by the leaders of the labour movement, that Britain is 'different' has no basis in fact. This has been demonstrated on many occasions in the history of capitalist Britain. Fascism, as an expression of the decline of capitalist society can become under certain conditions as real a menace in Britain as it became in capitalist Germany and Italy.

The world slump of 1929-33 saw the emergence of the Mosley-fascist movement as a serious force for the first time in this country. The capitalist class of Britain recognised in the Mosley movement a militant and extra parliamentary weapon which they could utilise against the working class in a period of social upheaval, in times of crisis and slump. Only the fact that the British capitalists succeeded in emerging from those critical years without the need for direct action against the workers determined their limited use of fascists at that time. Nevertheless, they kept the fascist movement in being as an 'insurance' against the future.

The myth, propagated by the capitalist class, that all issues can and will be settled through parliament is exploded by the very preparations undertaken by the capitalists themselves when it seemed possible that the working class would take to the road of struggle. With the threat of an economic slump looming before the war, the British capitalists were preparing extra-parliamentary steps against the working class.

In the few years before the war of 1939-45, army manoeuvres in Britain were conducted on the basis of civil war tactics. Strategic government buildings were prepared for defence. The civil guard was created as a special strike-breaking force, composed of recruits from the ranks of the ruling and upper middle class and trained in the use of machine-guns, rifles and tanks. They were taught to drive locomotives, heavy transport lorries and to do ground staff work at aerodromes. The civil guard was to constitute the backbone of any strike-breaking force in the event of serious troubles with the workers.

A significant portent was the fact that the big insurance companies which, together with the big banks, are the decisive rulers of Britain, refused to insure against the risk of civil disturbances and civil war. The capitalists understood that Britain, no more than Italy, France, Germany or Spain, could escape the social upheavals of the sick and decaying capitalist system. If the Second World War had not intervened, the impending economic slump would have struck the country with far greater effect than even in 1929.

At this time the fascists were receiving support from numerous influential British industrialists. Towards the end of 1936 Mosley boasted in an interview with the Italian fascist paper *Giornale d'Italia*, that he was:

> … receiving support from British industrialists. [And that] a number of industrialists in the north who hitherto had given his movement secret support, fearing commercial boycott, are now stating openly that they are on the fascist side. (*News Chronicle*, 19 October 1936.)

Mosley received the backing of the powerful newspapers, the *Daily Mail*, *Evening News* and the *Sunday Dispatch*.

Then as now, the Blackshirt movement carried out its anti-working-class and antisemitic provocations under the protection of the state. The British fascists were soon to prove that in brutality and method there was little to choose between them and Hitler's storm-troopers or Mussolini's squadri. At a mass rally of British fascists at Olympia on 7 June 1934, the British working class were given an idea of what to expect if fascism triumphed. The savage and calculated brutalities inflicted by the specially trained fascist thugs upon any of the audience who dared to voice even the mildest opposition to Mosley's speech by interjections, outraged all sections of the population. Organised bands of fascists set upon hecklers, men and women alike, beating them unconscious, kicking them while on the ground.

Nurtured and aided by the authorities and the police, the fascists insolently organised provocative marches in working-class and Jewish districts, imitating the tactics of the Nazis at the dawn of their movement in Germany. The British working class gave the Blackshirts their answer. Every demonstration called by the fascists was answered by a great counter-demonstration of workers and anti-fascists. At Trafalgar Square, Hyde Park, in Liverpool, Merthyr, Newcastle – all over the country – the workers rallied against the fascists. In red Glasgow, the fascists were unable to hold meetings. In the working-class district of Bermondsey, London, barricades put up and manned by tens of thousands of workers successfully prevented the Mosley-fascists from marching through Long Lane.

Outstanding in these struggles of the workers against the fascists was the defeat of Mosley's projected march through the East End of London in 1936. Despite appeals from all sections of the working-class movement, including even the labour leaders, the then Home Secretary, Sir John Simon, refused to ban the march. On the contrary, he sought to facilitate it in every way. Ten thousand foot and mounted police drawn from all over London and the provinces were mobilised to protect Mosley and his 2,500 fascists to ensure their march through the East End. This police protection was thoroughly organised even to the extent of wireless equipment and an autogiro hovering overhead. The weight of the state was brought to bear to protect the Blackshirts in the teeth of the opposition of the London working class. The police authorities planned for Mosley's protection as though it were a military project.

Despite these measures of the state, the fascist march was defeated. Half a million workers turned out on the streets. Rallying around the slogan "They shall not pass", the workers formed a wall of bodies on the route through which Mosley was to march. From early morning, baton charges were made by the mounted police against the workers to clear a path for the fascists. But the determined opposition of the workers made it impossible. The police tried to create a diversion by clearing Cable Street. But here again, the workers of London threw up fresh barricades of furniture, timber, railings, doors torn from houses nearby, and anything that would help to bar the path of the hated fascists. This magnificent mass action, including and representing all shades of working-class opinion and organisations, Labour, Communist Party, ILP, Trotskyist, League of Youth and Youth Communist League (YCL) – forced the then Commissioner of Police, Sir Philip Game, to order Mosley and his thugs to abandon the route. United action of the workers had defeated Mosley!

The defeat at Cable Street in 1936 dealt a severe blow to Mosley. Afraid of the organised might of the working class so militantly demonstrated, the East End fascist movement declined. The spectacle of the workers in action gave the fascists reason to pause. It induced widespread despondency and demoralisation in their ranks; their victory over the fascists imbued the working class with confidence. This united action of the workers at Cable Street demonstrated anew the lesson: only vigorous counter-action hinders the growth of the menace of fascism.

At that time the Communist Party was mainly responsible for calling militant workers to counter-demonstrations against the fascists. The YCL played a magnificent role. But after 1936 this militant policy of the Communist Party changed and they now avoided any counter-action against the fascists on the wide and militant scale witnessed before. With the coming of Hitler to power the Communist Parties throughout the world had degenerated into nothing but instruments of Russian foreign policy, and their activities reflected this. When Stalin found it impossible to arrive at an agreement with Hitler at that time there was a right about-turn on the part of the then Communist International.

From a refusal to offer a united front with the social-democratic workers against fascism, the Communist International embarked on a policy of popular-frontism. In line with Stalin's efforts to make agreements and gain alliances with the 'democratic' capitalist classes, they advocated class-collaboration between the workers and the 'good' capitalists. This foreign policy of the Stalinists was reflected in the British Communist Party which even went to the extent of advocating a 'national government' of Churchill, Attlee and Sinclair.[12] Having branded the united front of workers' parties against fascism as 'counter-revolutionary', the Stalinists now rejected the Marxist class analysis of capitalist society and advocated a united front with Tories and Liberals.

In their efforts to placate those Tories and Liberals who favoured an alliance with Stalin, the Communist Party made every endeavour to paint itself as just another party of respectable and law-abiding citizens. To that end the hammer and sickle emblem of working-class unity was withdrawn from the masthead of the *Daily Worker*; the language of Marxism was replaced by that of middle-class suburbia.

12 Leaders of the Conservative, Labour and Liberal parties respectively.

More importantly, the policy of militant class struggle went by the board and this was reflected in the new 'ostrich' attitude towards the fascist movement. To take militant action against the fascists would offend the new-found Tory and Liberal 'friends' of the Stalinist party. The activities and provocations of the fascists now went unheeded; counter-demonstrations and actions of the workers against fascism were no longer organised. The former policy of militant action was replaced by appeals and pleadings to the state to take measures against the fascists. From a reliance upon the working class to deal with fascism, the Stalinists turned towards a policy of relying on the very state apparatus which had in the so-recent past demonstrated its partiality towards the Blackshirts!

How this new policy of the Stalinist leaders worked in practice was indicated by one instance of many similar examples that could be given. Just prior to the war, a monster rally of Blackshirts, imported from all over the country into London for the purpose, gathered at Earl's Court to hear Mosley. On that day the Young Communist League of London organised a ramble in the countryside!

Demonstrating against the Blackshirt rally outside Earl's Court were only the Trotskyists and a small number of anti-fascist militants. Of the Communist Party there was no sign. This new policy of the Stalinist party served to foster apathy in the ranks of the working class in the struggle against the fascists and emboldened and encouraged the Blackshirts. It seemed that the fascist movement would gain new strength in face of the lack of organised and militant action on the part of the workers' organisations. But the war cut across these developments and gave them a new direction.

## *Mosley's 'programme'*

Today, in Britain, the signs of a fascist revival are unmistakable. Having tested the reaction of public opinion to the emergence of the various fascist groups, aided and encouraged by police protection, Mosley has launched his new party, the 'Union Movement'. The new party is no different from the former BUF, the same Jew-baiting, the same promises of the destruction of the trade unions and labour organisations, the same demagogy to attract the disillusioned and despairing middle classes and backward elements.

All Mosley's publications uphold the principle of private enterprise. In one of the recent Mosley 'News Letters', he demagogically champions the 'small' man, not against the capitalist monopolies, but against the nationalisation measures of the Labour government. Mosley boasts that his "opinions remain unchanged". In his 'Greater Britain' (published before the war) he wrote that: "the making of profit will not only be permitted but encouraged". In 'An Open Letter to Business Men' published in the *Fascist Week*, in 1934, Mosley reassured the industrialists that: "In the corporate state you will be left in possession of your businesses." To the coupon-clipping parasites who live on their dividends, Mosley promised:

> Hitherto, the holder of ordinary shares, who is the true risk-bearer in industrial enterprise, has been treated for taxation purposes as the holder of 'unearned income'. The whole procedure is illogical, and calculated to discourage the enterprise upon which our industrial future depends.

Whereas before, Mosley emphasised the idea that Britain and the Empire must isolate itself for economic 'autarky', today he advocates the 'union of Western Europe'. Recognising the weakness of British capitalism and the danger of economic collapse on the continent of Europe, Mosley proposes the idea of a union of capitalist Europe based upon the enslavement and exploitation of the African peoples. In the Mosley 'plan':

> ... there will be no nonsense about 'trusteeship for the natives', [and] negroes are to have no parity with their white superiors.

One of Mosley's main planks is for war on Russia. If he were in power he would "send Russia an ultimatum that she must accept the American offer to scrap atomic weapons and submit to inspection", which, if unaccepted, would be followed by a "preventive" war.

In the press interview which Mosley gave on 28 November 1947, to announce the imminent launching of his new party, he further elaborated on his 'programme'. The present parliament would be replaced by the corporate state modelled on Mussolini's two chambers. Instead of elections there would be plebiscites where the voters would have the privilege of recording 'yes' or 'no' to whatever Mosley's government did. His government would 'resign' if defeated, but this, of course, "was most unlikely". Mosley promises to suppress communism.

By this Mosley means that his government would suppress all working-class parties and organisations. The trade unions would be 'obsolete' if they did not 'cooperate' with the fascists.

The new party of Mosley is thus openly modelled on the fascist totalitarian regimes of Hitler and Mussolini.

Mosley has clearly revealed his calculations. He anticipates being called to power at a time of crisis in the same way as Mussolini was called to power by the Italian monarchy and the Italian capitalists. In his 'Greater Britain', Mosley wrote:

> If the situation develops rapidly, then the public mind develops slowly, something like collapse may come before any new movement has captured parliamentary power. In that case, other and sterner measures must be adopted for the saving of the state in a situation approaching anarchy. Such a situation will be none of our seeking. In no case shall we resort to violence against the Crown; but only against the forces of anarchy if, and when, the machinery of state has been allowed to drift into powerlessness…
>
> Anyone who argues that in such a situation the normal instruments of government, such as police and army, can be used effectively, has studied neither the European history of his own time nor the realities of the present situation. In the highly technical struggle for the modern state in crisis, only the technical organisations of fascism and communism have ever prevailed, or in the nature of the case, can prevail. Governments and parties which have relied on the normal instruments of government (which are not constituted for such purposes) have fallen easy and ignoble victims to the force of anarchy. If, therefore, such a situation arises in Britain, we shall prepare to meet the anarchy of communism with the organised force of fascism; but we do not seek that struggle,

> and for the sake of the nation, we desire to avert it. Only when we see the feeble surrender to menacing problems, the fatuous optimism which again and again has been disproved, the spineless drift towards disaster, do we feel it necessary to organise for such a contingency.

Thus, the fascists viewed the coming struggle with the forces of 'anarchy', i.e. the working class, as an extra-parliamentary one. In the second edition of Greater Britain, Mosley deleted the chapters dealing with this problem, for they were too outspoken. Nevertheless, this remains the basis of Mosley's ideas today. Not accidentally did he declare at the meeting launching the new party on 7 February 1948 that he and his followers were "prepared to meet force with force".

The antisemitic and anti-working class activities of the fascists are on the increase and although small at present they constitute a challenge to the working class. Fascism must be defeated in its beginnings. The death camps of the Nazis, in which hundreds of thousands of German workers were tortured and murdered, should act as a permanent reminder to the working class never to allow themselves to be lulled into a false sense of security. The British fascist movement will not differ from the German or Italian fascists either in social composition, objectives or methods.

## *The Labour government and the fascist revival*

The re-emergence of Mosley and his new 'Union Movement' in Britain today is regarded with complacency on the part of the labour leaders. The bitter lessons of Germany and Italy have passed these labour leaders by. They translate into English the same false words and ideas of the German and Italian Social-Democratic leaders: "It can't happen here." The British, they claim, are "different", a "tolerant" people with a democratic tradition. Fascism is "alien" to the British and so on. Famous last words! The crime of the labour leaders is not that they lull themselves with the pretence that "it can't happen here" but they disarm the working class by sowing illusions and objectively aid the growth of the reviving fascist movement by affording them police protection.

The working class who voted Labour into power may well stand bewildered and indignant as they witness Mosley and the fascists holding provocative meetings under the protection of large numbers of police specially detailed for the job, when they witness the Labour-controlled London County Council affording facilities for Mosley and his movement to meet in schools and halls under their control. This at a time when the fascists have the utmost difficulty in booking public halls because of the pressure of public opinion. Arising out of protests Home Secretary Chuter Ede replied that he is "considering" the banning of loudspeaker equipment at public meetings. But this would apply to "all" parties who use loudspeakers at meetings. This, instead of striking a blow at the fascist movement, in practice would be a blow against working-class organisations who use such equipment for propaganda. This is the result of the 'impartiality' of the reformists. Their 'impartiality' consists in hamstringing the anti-fascists and allowing the fascists to carry on.

Despite the past six years of terrible war, allegedly to destroy fascism, at the present time, as if nothing had taken place the fascists have taken up from where they left off at the outbreak of the war. The familiar picture of police and courts taking strong action against anti-fascists while the fascists are treated lightly and even protected is once again presented.

All this, in the name of the liberal idea of 'democracy', of 'impartiality' and 'freedom for all'. In reality, this is the opposite of freedom as taught by the great socialist teachers. Under this guise of 'freedom' and 'impartiality' of the state the labour leaders used the police to baton pickets striking for their elementary democratic rights of trade-union organisation. No socialist worker who is not a traitor to his class will put on the same plane the freedom of a scab to break a strike and the freedom of the strikers to prevent him doing so. Yet this force of most despicable scabs, the fascist movement, is given every facility to flourish and prepare to destroy the very right to strike and every other freedom dearly won by the working class. This is neither freedom nor democracy. It is a violation of workers' democracy and the very negation of freedom.

As a crowning piece of folly the labour leaders have given facilities to Mosley to publish his propaganda.

Instead of welcoming the instinctive protests on the part of the workers against any attempted revival of fascist activity, the Labour government organises the police force to protect the fascists against the workers. Labour leaders worthy of the name would welcome workers' action against the reaction and would back it by legislative enactments. This would be a warning to the capitalists that any attempt to establish a fascist dictatorship would be ruthlessly acted on by the labour movement as a whole. In the name of 'free speech' the fascists are given every facility to put forward their propaganda, this to the very people who stand for the destruction of free speech and every vestige of democracy won by the working class. In time of war – and the class struggle is a war between the classes – the enemy is not given points of vantage by means of which he can better attack and massacre your own ranks at a later stage.

The election of the majority Labour government after the second world war expressed the aspirations of the British workers to establish a new social system. The masses swung left and in this swing drew behind them large sections of the middle class, whose position had been undermined during the war. The war had placed heavy burdens upon the backs of sections of the middle class, the rise in the cost of living having affected those with fixed incomes most severely. Large numbers of small shopkeepers have been driven out of business by the competition of the big capitalist combines and the measures of concentration encouraged by the state in the interests of 'more efficient' big business. Of a total number of 10,000 firms in certain trades in London alone during the war, including furriers, dry cleaners, repairers etc., there was a cut of about 40 per cent. As a consequence, the middle class looked to the Labour Party for a solution.

A Gallup Poll revealed that, in the first months of the rule of the Labour government, their popularity increased enormously as a result of the social reforms they introduced. Had the labour leaders introduced wide measures aimed at destroying the privileges and vested interests of the capitalist class, had they taken over all large scale industrial and financial enterprises without compensation and operated the economic life of Britain on the basis of an overall economic plan under the democratic control of the working class, there could have been little effective resistance from the capitalist class. This would have been the socialist solution to the ills which capitalism inflicts not only upon the working class but the middle class as well.

But what is the reality today? Under the Labour government, capitalism remains intact. Lavish compensation is given to the previous owners of nationalised industries, which continue to be run on purely 'business lines' and largely by the same capitalist managers who were in control before. The overwhelming sector of the economy remains under the control of private enterprise and the nationalised sectors are geared to and serve the interests of private ownership.

Even in the nationalised industries there is not a trace of genuine democratic control by the workers. While the labour leaders talk a great deal about the sacredness of democracy, there is no democratic control extended to the miners or the workers in the industries which are supposedly owned by 'the people'.

In Britain elements of workers' democracy exist in the form of the trade unions, the workers' parties, factory organisations and the rights which they have won. But the effective control is in the hands of the capitalist class. They control the economic life of the country through their ownership of the means of production; they have the decisive means of influencing public opinion through the control of the press, radio, cinema, schools and church and all other instruments necessary for the purpose. This is the reality of capitalist democracy. Bourgeois democracy, said Trotsky, means that everyone has the right to say what he likes as long as finance capital decides what is done. But once the workers reach out to take real democratic control, then the capitalists decide that the time has come to abolish democracy altogether.

If the labour leaders' chief concern was democracy, they would have introduced real workers' control and democracy. The elements of democracy which are already there would have been brought to full fruition.

Real democracy for the majority and not for the capitalist few, that is, workers' democracy, would mean not only the complete destruction of the economic stranglehold of big business, but the ending of their control of the means of influencing public opinion through their economic control. The Labour government should have immediately taken the press, cinema and radio out of the hands of monopoly capital and placed them at the disposal of the people. Every workers' tendency would be given the fullest free access to the means of propaganda to advocate their point of view. All political parties, including even the Tories and Liberals, who are willing to accept the democratic will of the majority, would have freedom of speech and press. But the fascists would be suppressed outright.

Having organised soviets or workers' committees in the plants and districts and established for the first time a democratic participation of all strata of the population in governing and running the country, the superiority of such a workers' state would be so obvious that any counter-revolution on the part of the capitalist class would be rendered impotent.

Instead of a revolutionary socialist solution, Labour leaders are tinkering with capitalism. The half-and-half measures of the Labour government have resulted in a swing away from Labour, particularly among the middle class and more backward sections of the workers. In the municipal elections of 1947 and in the parliamentary elections of the same year, there was a marked increase in the Tory vote.

And as a symptom of the rightward trend, the fascists re-entered the political arena.

This has taken place in a period of *full employment* and capitalist boom. British capitalism has lost the advantages she possessed in the past. Despite the efforts of the working class which have resulted in a 20 per cent increase in production over pre-war, there has not been a proportionate increase in the standard of living. Britain is far more dependent on the world market than in the past. With increasing competition the standards of life will not be raised but, on the contrary, the capitalist class will be forced to cut wages.

Already, the Labour government is waging an offensive to persuade the workers to accept a freezing of wages as the exhaustion of the sellers' market looms in sight. With the vociferous applause of the capitalist class and its press, the Labour leaders are exhorting the workers to make more sacrifices in the frenzied drive to increase production and accept a wage freeze and speed-up in the interests of reducing costs in the competitive struggle for world trade.

Cripps explains to the workers that if they do not *voluntarily* accept the yoke of capital, the British workers will he faced with the iron yoke of totalitarian dictatorship. In his own words:

> It is, therefore, essential that we should get a general agreement amongst our people to act upon sound economic lines: the alternative is likely to prove to be some form of totalitarian government.

The proposals on "sound economic" lines advocated by the labour leaders are, of course, sound capitalist lines.

Here are the symptoms of decline, of impending economic slump, of over-production. Even if the labour leaders should succeed in their objective of increasing production to further record heights, this cannot solve the problem. On the contrary, it can only prepare catastrophe for the Labour government and the British working class.

Under the impact of the radicalisation in 1945, the capitalists were compelled to retreat. But they have not been overthrown by the Labour government. Today they are biding their time. But they are systematically whipping up the discontent of the middle class and backward sections of the workers in preparation for an offensive in the future.

Under the capitalist system, with the crisis of over-production, slump will follow boom as night follows day. And if already the middle class are discontented, how will they react when the slump comes? The workers will be impelled in a revolutionary direction but unless they show the Marxist road, the middle class will be drawn into the orbit of the fascist movement. The capitalists will declare the 'Marxists' and the labour movement responsible for the crisis of their system and gain the support of the middle class for action against the workers.

In the grip of economic crisis, the capitalist class will be forced to launch savage attacks on the standards of the workers. They will find the pressure of the workers' organisations irksome, especially the trade unions. Mosley's programme of annihilation of the trade unions and workers' organisations, his defence of private property, are designed to appeal to big business precisely in such a crisis. To eliminate the unions and terrorise the workers into submission, the capitalists will need fascist bands and will look towards a totalitarian state as the means of their salvation. Then they will really commence to subsidise Mosley or some other fascist less discredited among the population.

There could be no greater danger today than to sit back and content ourselves with the idea that the fascists have little political weight in Britain. While capitalist society exists, the weapon of fascism also exists as a potential menace to the working class. Events may prove that Mosley's 'Union Movement' will not be the leading fascist movement in this country. Mosley and his followers were greatly discredited during the war. Nevertheless, some new form of fascist organisation can well arise, an organisation not overtly fascist but of a character similar to de Gaulle's 'Rally of the French People' movement which, while it disavows fascism, is, in fundamental policy and aims, designed to serve the same purpose.

As a germ of the disease already present even today in Britain, WJ Brown, Independent MP for Rugby, formerly a leader of Mosley's 'New Party' in 1931, has tentatively advocated a 'Rally of the British People'. Even more indicative is the fact that the *Statist*, in an article 'Can Our System be Modified?', on 29 November 1947, writes approvingly on General de Gaulle and says:

> General de Gaulle, naturally alarmed by the chaotic state of politics and economics as exemplified in France at present, has asked the people to

> give him power to form what he calls a national rally. At the same time he warns us that our system is so unstable that it may lead us at a date not indefinitely remote to serious trouble. It should not be wise to ignore such a warning.

Unless the working class can offer some alternative in the form of a bold programme and above all, daring action, the misguided middle-class youth who today support Toryism will be drawn into a fascist movement, whether it be a 'Union Movement' or some sort of 'Rally of the British People', or 'British Royalist Empire Saviours Society'.

## *The policy of the Communist Party*

The revival of fascist activity caused militant workers to look to the Communist Party for a lead. They have been bitterly disappointed. With the exception of a few opposition meetings at Ridley Road in the early days, the Communist Party leadership has undertaken nothing more militant than the organising of town meetings under the auspices of the National Council for Civil Liberties, and the passing of resolutions at trades councils and union branches calling upon the government to take action against the fascists. These joint towns' meetings include the representatives of the local Labour organisations, plus vociferous representatives of local businessmen, Tories and Liberals. Only the Revolutionary Communist Party has been excluded from the platforms. This 'popular front' with Tories and Liberals is a deception of militant workers who seek a fighting policy to defeat the menace of fascism.

To have a united front with Tories and Liberals against fascism is to miseducate the working class. Instead of teaching them the class nature of fascism, that the capitalist parties represent the very class which will lean on the fascists against the workers, and that only the organised strength of the working class can defeat fascism, they sow illusions and discourage militant action.

The Communist Party recently published an anti-fascist pamphlet entitled 'Fascist Threat to Britain'. We advise all workers to read this pamphlet and compare the analysis and the policy with that of the Revolutionary Communist Party. The keynote of the policy of the CP is provided by their description of the war aims of the imperialists. This is what they write:

> Many people took part in this fight. It's no use pretending that the war aims of all the national leaders were exactly the same, or that everyone in the British Army for instance, agreed perfectly. But on one thing every nation and every individual was in complete unity. And that was that the war was being fought to end this thing, fascism, for all time, to crush it without a trace.

History has shown how the 'democratic' capitalist class, how the Tory and Liberal spokesmen supported the reaction and fascism abroad. Recent history has shown in the Second World War that far from being interested in ending this thing 'fascism', the ruling class merely used the anti-fascist sentiments of the workers for their own imperialist ends. Their attempted deals with Darlan[13] and Badoglio bear witness to the fact that in the very midst of the war, their main concern was to establish regimes capable of dealing with the working class. And in Britain, throughout the so-called war against fascism, the Government refused to publish the 'Red Book'[14] of Captain Ramsay, which contained the list of names of fascist supporters in this country.

Yet the Communist Party persists in miseducating the workers that all nations, all classes were in complete unity during the war in seeking to destroy fascism. Thus the appeal to all sides of political opinion:

> You who are reading this may be a Labour, Liberal, Conservative, or Communist supporter. You may be a trade unionist or co-operator. Whatever your political beliefs we ask you in your own interest, to stand together on this. For if we do not act very soon, democratic discussion and decent living may become impossible.

---

13 François Darlan was the Commander-in-Chief of the collaborationist Vichy Armed Forces during the Second World War.

14 Captain Archibald Maule Ramsay was an Army officer and Scottish MP. An extreme reactionary and antisemite, he set up The Right Club, a secret society of Nazi sympathisers, high-ranking officers and socialites. He kept its membership logs in a small red-coloured book, which was seized by the police.

*If we do not act!* What action does the Communist Party propose?

> If the fascists come into your locality, get all the inhabitants to sign a petition of protest to the Home Secretary.

But signatures will not frighten fascists.

Following in the footsteps of the ill-fated reformists, the CP confines itself to appeals to the capitalist state machine:

> Demand that existing laws regarding 'incitement to violence' and behaviour 'calculated to cause a breach of the peace' should be strictly enforced: that police should be sent to fascist meetings to make arrests and not to afford protection.

While the CP calls for 'vigilance', they urge their members and supporters to stay away from fascist meetings.

Of course, it is necessary to conduct a campaign through the unions and Labour organisations by means of resolutions, and in order to bring pressure on the Labour Government which claims to speak in the name of the British working class. But what is more essential is that the pressure on the Labour leaders is supplemented by counter-action, by the *participation of the workers in combating the fascists*. Can anyone deny that the lack of organised counter-action on the part of the workers' organisations has emboldened and encouraged the fascists? Can anyone doubt that had the Communist Party and the YCL in London rallied its powerful organisation and apparatus to counter-demonstrate against the fascists and against Mosley when he first emerged, that they would have thought again before launching their new movement?

The Revolutionary Communist Party has been active in demonstrating and attempting to combat the fascists wherever they have appeared. We wrote to Harry Pollitt appealing for a united front against the fascists. The London District Committee of the RCP sent a similar appeal to the London CP and YCL leaderships. The essence of our position can be summed up in the following extract from the letter sent by the London District Committee to the London District Committee of the Communist Party:

> Despite the very deep and fundamental differences that separate the Trotskyist and the Stalinist Parties at the present time, the London District Committee of the RCP is of the strong conviction that not only is it possible for joint anti-fascist activity between the London members of our respective parties, along practical and specific lines, but that such a united front would meet with enthusiastic support from the rank-and-file members of our respective organisations. Recent experiences in London have demonstrated that where our comrades have been engaged in anti-fascist activity, a spontaneous united front has been established between members of our organisations with evident success against the fascists.

Our appeals went unheeded at a time when the battles of Ridley Road were at their height and it was imperative that the workers have a united front against the fascists, who were boasting that they had driven the Communist Party from Ridley Road. Instead of rallying to Ridley Road, as the Trotskyists did, the leaders of the Communist Party discouraged their members from gathering there and thus fell into the camp of the petty bourgeois moralists and reformists who said: "Ignore them." Despite the cowardly policy of the leadership, many rank-and-file members of the CP and YCL continued to rally at Ridley Road together with members of the Revolutionary Communist Party and other organisations in a united front of protest. The official line of the CP was far from welcomed by many rank and file militants, whose class instincts correctly led them to participation in the struggle against the fascists.

A revolutionary working-class policy must of necessity draw the masses into real participation in the struggle. No amount of appeals for 'vigilance' or petitions, resolutions, or appeals to the capitalist state can substitute for the real mass activity of the working class in combating its most dangerous enemies.

## *How to fight fascism – the policy of the RCP*

With the re-emergence of the fascists, the main task of the labour movement is to educate and explain to the workers the *class* nature of fascism and its function as a combat force against the working-class organisations. But to explain the class roots and function of fascism is not enough. The working class must participate in actively combatting the fascists wherever they raise their heads. For this it is necessary that the organisations of the working class rally the militants around a militant programme of struggle against the antisemitic, anti-labour propaganda meetings, against the press and other menacing activities of the fascists.

Trade unionists must refuse to print, handle or transport fascist propaganda of any description and demand that their executives make this a rule. All who violate such a rule must be blacklisted.

The first step in mobilising the workers is to unite all sections of the movement – Labour, trade union, Communist Party, Trotskyist, Cooperatives – in a common working-class united front. This is the key to a successful struggle against the menace of fascism. Fundamental differences separate these organisations from each other, but on this question of fascism it is, it must be, possible to have common agreement in forms of struggle. Retaining the right to criticise each other, it is a necessary task to organise joint counter-demonstrations, joint meetings, and joint anti-fascist propaganda campaigns. Fascism is no respecter of working-class opinions and democracy. It seeks to destroy all opposition workers' parties whether they be Labour, Communist, or Revolutionary Communist. To defend and protect working-class meetings and premises, Jewish and other minorities against fascist provocations and attacks, a Workers' Defence Corps must be established based on the trade-union, cultural and political organisations of the working class.

Mosley once boasted that he had a detachment which is joined by "nearly every man who is physically strong. They are highly disciplined in a semi-militaristic manner." Organised detachments of Blackshirts can only be combated by organised detachments of militant proletarians.

In campaigning for the Labour government to 'ban the fascists' the workers must bear in mind that history has taught that the enforcement of laws by a capitalist state inevitably acts to the disadvantage of the working class. The state rests upon the army, the police and the courts. And these are riddled from top to bottom with elements sympathetic to the aims of fascism, *especially at the top*. Even if the pressure of the workers succeeded in enforcing the passage of anti-fascist legislation, clearly it could only be put into effect by the enforcement of the workers. This means that the demand on the Labour government can only be effective when backed by the activities of the organised workers.

This does not mean that we do not strive to bring pressure on the Labour government to take action against the fascists. But it does mean that our demands can only be effective if backed by determined and organised activity on the part of the workers.

We must demand of the Labour government that it immediately:

- Publish the names of all the known pro-fascists contained in the Red Book of Captain Ramsay.
- Publish all evidence and information in the hands of the British Intelligence which reveals the connections between the Nazis and the British fascists and representatives of the British ruling class.
- Introduces legislation illegalising the propagation of antisemitism and race hatred of any form.
- Introduces legislation to make fascist propaganda and organisation illegal and at the same time to protect any section of the population which enforces this law, or is engaged in any activity against the fascists.

Today it is true that the fascist movement is only a small factor in British political life. But from a scratch comes the danger of gangrene! We must not repeat the same mistakes as the German working class.

Historical experience has shown that it is not possible to legislate fascism out of existence. The very nature of the capitalist state precludes that, for fascism in the nature of things is the naked weapon of capitalist class rule. Only the mass of the organised working class, understanding the nature of fascism and with a militant policy of struggle against it, will be capable of dealing effectively with the menace of fascism. In the final analysis the destruction of the capitalist system, which needs and breeds fascism with all its attendant horrors and repressions against the working class and racial and religious minorities, is the only means of ensuring the decisive defeat of fascism.

## *Appendix: Jews in British society – some facts*

In its attempt to find a scapegoat for the ills of a disintegrating system, fascism adopts a technique of 'Jew-baiting' familiar in the period of feudal decay. All the crimes of monopoly capitalism are blamed on Jewish finance capital. All the discontent of the small shopkeepers and professional men is turned into antisemitic channels. Mosley considered this too useful a weapon in the arsenal of his 'programme' to let go by.

The fascists attempt to arouse the basest prejudices of the small businessmen and shopkeepers and of backward workers against the Jews. They utilise a deep-rooted superstition dating back to the middle ages that the Jews own, control and manipulate the finances of the country, indeed of the world! Around this banner they do gain support among ignorant people – shopkeepers who meet the competition of Jewish shopkeepers in the same street, or workers who happen to live with Jewish landlords.

Even if it were true that most of the country was owned by Jewish capitalists, this would make little difference to the tasks confronting the working class. *It makes little difference to the system whether the capitalists are Jews or Gentiles.* Both are subject to the laws of capitalist economy and act accordingly. In a country like Spain where there were *no Jewish capitalists* (the Jews had been expelled in 1492), poverty, hunger and exploitation of the workers was among the worst in Europe because of the economic circumstances of that country. As is known, the class struggle in Spain culminated in civil war between the workers and the fascists. The Spanish fascists had to find other demagogic slogans. It is interesting to note that De Gaulle is not resorting to antisemitism at present.

However, many people, even in the workers' movement give credence to the myth that the Jews control the country. It is necessary for every class-conscious worker to know the facts regarding the real position of the Jews in British society, in order to combat the disease of antisemitism.

There are in Great Britain and Northern Ireland only 370,000 Jews out of a total population of 48,000,000. That is, there are seven Jews to every 1,000 non-Jews, or less than one per cent of the population.

The big banks, together with the insurance companies control the country's economy. Yet there is not a single Jew on the Bank of England, either among the Directors or its Executive officials. The Big Five[15] have in all 150 Directors, of these only four are Jews.

In international finance, the greatest banking company in the world is JP Morgan & Co. In this company too, there are no Jewish partners and not a single Jew in a leading position.

The Stock Exchange, which dominates the dealings in stocks and shares, and is regarded as a mysterious influence by many small businessmen, is according to the fascists, dominated by Jews. But in fact, on the Stock Exchange Committee there is only one Jew.

Before the nationalisation of the Railways, the number of Directors on the LMS was eighteen; on the LNER, twenty-two; GWR, twenty; Southern, sixteen; and the LPTB, seven. Of these only one was a Jew and one was of Jewish extraction, though his family had been of the Christian faith for several generations.

There are in all 116 daily newspapers and seventeen Sunday papers in Britain. Despite the myth that the Jews control the press, there was only one Jew who was director of a newspaper combine; he was Chairman of the *Daily Herald* but is now dead.

Gaumont British and Odeon Companies were at one time controlled by Jews. They have now passed into the hands of JA Rank, the most powerful figure in the film world, who is in control of some 600 cinemas and practically of all the important studios. The third large corporation, the ABC, was never owned by Jews.

15 The Big Five banks in the UK in this time period referred to Barclays, Midland, Lloyds, National Provincial and Westminster Banks.

Another fascist lie which has gained an ear among some backward sections of the population is that the Jews control the Government and Parliament. In fact there is not a single Jew in the Cabinet. There are only twenty-eight Jewish MPs out of 640. The four Jewish members of the Government are Shinwell, Silkin, George Strauss and Lord Nathan. None is at present in the Cabinet. (AJ Cummings, *News Chronicle*, 11 November 1947.)

It is popularly believed that the Jews dominate all black-market activities. The facts are that the overwhelming majority of prosecutions both of big and small businessmen for black market offences are not against Jews or people connected with Jewish enterprise. The capitalist press focuses attention on those cases involving Jewish offenders precisely to give the impression that they dominate the black market. Profiteers, whether they be Jews, Gentiles, Irish or Scotch, do not overlook the possibility of extra profit, whether their transactions are legal or not. The whole history of capitalism proves this. The plunder of India, of China and Africa was not carried out by Jews. The slave trade was carried out by religious gentlemen, one of the most notorious of whom named his ship *The Jesus*!

Of course, Jews do play a role in business. But in Britain in the decisive industries there is hardly any Jewish capital at all. In iron and steel, engineering, chemicals, automobiles, shipping and rubber, and before nationalisation, coal and railways, Jewish capital is negligible. In the great armaments concerns such as Vickers there is no Jewish capital. However, in certain secondary industries, where the Jews have been traditionally concentrated in different countries, Jewish capital plays an important role. Even here, it is not dominant.

Some facts: In the tailoring trade one-quarter of the total trade is in the hands of Jews, in the furniture trade one-seventh, in jewellery one-fifth, in the boot and shoe trade one-eighth, two-thirds of the Fur trade, but only eleven per cent of the electrical and radio trade, less than seven per cent in cosmetics. In food shops one-sixth of the trade in London is owned by Jews, but only one-sixteenth in the provinces.

In tailoring, Montague Burton's is a Jewish firm. The Fifty Shilling Tailors are gentile. In the bazaar trade, Woolworths, which owns

762 branches with a capital of 12,000,000 is non-Jewish. Marks and Spencer is a Jewish firm owning 236 branches with a capital of 3,950,000.

Insofar as chain stores are concerned, the co-operatives, part of the working-class movement, is owned by the workers. This is the largest chain store in the country. There are ninety-two chain store groups with a capital of 150,000 000. The Drapery and allied trade constitute about a third of the capital invested. Half is controlled by non-Jewish firms (Harrods, Selfridges, John Lewis and Barkers). The Unilever Combine, which dominates the groceries and provisions trade is not, as commonly thought, composed entirely of Jewish capital. The only Jewish capital in this concern is that owned by the Dutch Jews, the Van den Berghs.

On the retail side in the grocery and provision trade, Home and Colonial Stores, Maypole Dairies and even Liptons are not controlled by Jews. The biggest meat combine in the country is the Union Cold Storage which controls 5,000 branches. This is a purely non-Jewish firm. The Jews are totally absent from the dairy combines: Southern Dairies, United Dairies and Express Dairies are gentile firms. In the drug trade, the monopoly stores – Boots Taylors, Timothy White's, Savory & Moore's and Hodders, are all owned by non-Jews.

The decisive section of all industry is controlled by gentile capital. The number of small Jewish shopkeepers, retailers and middlemen, gives a false impression of the role of the Jews in business. In the decisive section of finance the role of Jewish capital is small. Thus, the elimination of the Jews would eliminate none of the injustices of the capitalist system.

The great majority of Jews in Britain, contrary to popular belief, are workers, employed mainly in tailoring, furniture trade and a fairly high proportion of shop assistants. About 15 per cent of the Jews gainfully occupied are in trades and industry on their own account. Of the total population, 7.5 per cent are occupied in trade.

The struggle for the emancipation of the working class is not between races or religions. It is one of class against class. Every trace of antisemitism, or any form of race hatred cannot assist the oppressed, it can on the contrary only aid the exploiters. Workers of all nationality, religion or creed must stand together against the common enemy: capitalism.

(The facts about the Jews have been collated from *The Jews in Work and Trade* by N Baron and published by the Trades Advisory Council, and *Questions and Answers – Facts and Figures of Jewish Economic Life and History*. Publishers as above.)

# *Timeline*

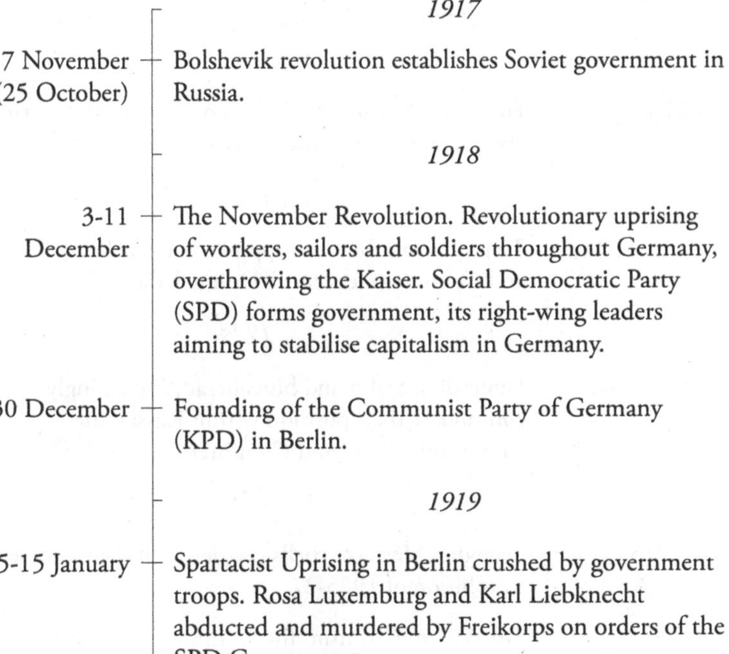

| | |
|---|---|
| | *1917* |
| 7 November (25 October) | Bolshevik revolution establishes Soviet government in Russia. |
| | *1918* |
| 3-11 December | The November Revolution. Revolutionary uprising of workers, sailors and soldiers throughout Germany, overthrowing the Kaiser. Social Democratic Party (SPD) forms government, its right-wing leaders aiming to stabilise capitalism in Germany. |
| 30 December | Founding of the Communist Party of Germany (KPD) in Berlin. |
| | *1919* |
| 5-15 January | Spartacist Uprising in Berlin crushed by government troops. Rosa Luxemburg and Karl Liebknecht abducted and murdered by Freikorps on orders of the SPD Government. |

2-6 March — Founding Congress of the Communist International in Moscow.

28 June — Treaty of Versailles concluded which results in major losses of German territory and crippling financial reparations.

*1920*

24 February — Nazi Party founded.

August-September — Revolutionary movement of factory occupations in Italy, reformist leadership fails to take power.

*1921*

17 March — Ultra-left 'March Action' called by KPD in Germany.

26 July — Hitler becomes leader of the Nazi Party.

9 November — Mussolini forms Fascist Party in Italy funded by Italian big business.

*1922*

28-31 October — Following Mussolini's 'March on Rome', Italian ruling class hand power to the fascists.

*1923*

October — Trotsky forms the Left Opposition to challenge Russian and Comintern leaders including Stalin and Zinoviev.

*1924*

21 January — Lenin dies. Stalin and bureaucracy increasingly consolidate their position within Russia, the Communist Party and Comintern.

*1927*

15 April — Shanghai Massacre spells the defeat of the Chinese Revolution of 1925-27.

November — Trotsky expelled from the Communist Party of the Soviet Union.

*1928*

9-25 February — Ninth Plenum of the ECCI. Comintern Executive declares the 'third period' or the 'final' crisis of capitalism.

20 May — Fourth Reichstag elections – Nazis only get 12 seats out of 474. Workers' parties SPD and KPD get 42% of vote.

*1929*

February — Trotsky exiled from the Soviet Union, arrives in Turkey.

1-3 May — 'Blutmai' – Berlin SPD police chief Karl Zörgiebel orders violent repression of marching workers.

28-29 October — Wall Street financial crash.

*1930*

April — Trotsky forms the International Left Opposition to draw his supporters together in the struggle against Stalinism.

14 September — Fifth Reichstag elections – Nazis get 107 seats; SPD: 143; KPD: 77.

*1931*

July — Global financial crisis leads to per capita income in Germany crashing to 24 per cent below 1914 levels. Unemployment reaches 31 per cent.

*1932*

31 July — Sixth Reichstag elections – Nazis get 230 seats, SPD: 133, KPD: 89.

6 November — Seventh Reichstag elections – Nazis get 196 seats (33 per cent of the vote); SPD: 20 per cent and KPD 17 per cent. The two parties get 221 seats between them.

| | |
|---|---|
| 17 November | Franz von Papen resigns as Chancellor, replaced by Kurt von Schleicher. |
| | *1933* |
| 30 January | Hitler appointed Chancellor. |
| 27 February | Reichstag Fire, followed by mass arrests of KPD members. |
| 6 March | KPD banned. |
| 23 March | Enabling act passed through Reichstag giving Hitler dictatorial powers. |
| Late July | Trotsky moves to France. |
| | *1934* |
| 6 February | Several thousand armed fascists and royalists attack buildings in Paris. The Radical president Daladier hands power to a reactionary government under Doumergue. |
| 9 February | General strike in France in protest of the coup. |
| 30 June – 2 July | The Night of the Long Knives – Hitler's SS wipes out the leadership of the SA (Brownshirts). |
| | *1935* |
| May | Trotsky, forced to leave France, is granted asylum in Norway. |
| 3 August | Trotsky launches call for a new, Fourth International, declaring that the failure of events in Germany to generate any debate in the Third International demonstrated that the Communist Parties and Comintern had degenerated beyond reform. |
| | *1936* |
| May | Popular Front government elected in France headed by Léon Blum's socialists. |

| | |
|---|---|
| 26 May | Strike wave begins in the port city of Le Havre. Leads to factory occupations and spreads throughout France, rapidly reaching general strike proportions. Workers leaders, including the Communist Party, negotiate concessions and the movement subsides. |
| 17 July | Fascist uprising begins in Spain against the Popular Front government. In response, workers seize power in major cities, including Barcelona. |
| 19-24 August | The first of the three major Moscow Purge Trials. Old Bolsheviks including Trotsky (in absentia), Zinoviev and Kamenev are convicted, and many are executed. |
| December | The Norwegian 'Socialist' government forces Trotsky to leave. Mexico grants him asylum. |
| | *1938* |
| September | Founding Congress of Fourth International held in France, with world war looming. |
| | *1939* |
| 23 August | Molotov-Ribbentrop pact between Nazi Germany and the Soviet Union signed. Became known as the Hitler-Stalin Pact. |
| 1 September | Outbreak of Second World War. |
| | *1940* |
| 21 August | Trotsky murdered by a Stalinist agent in Mexico City |
| | *1943* |
| 15 May | The Third (Communist) International is dissolved on Stalin's orders. |
| 25 July | Mussolini ousted from power by Fascist Grand Council. |
| 8 September | Following the fall of Mussolini, open civil war breaks out in Italy between workers and partisans and the fascists. |

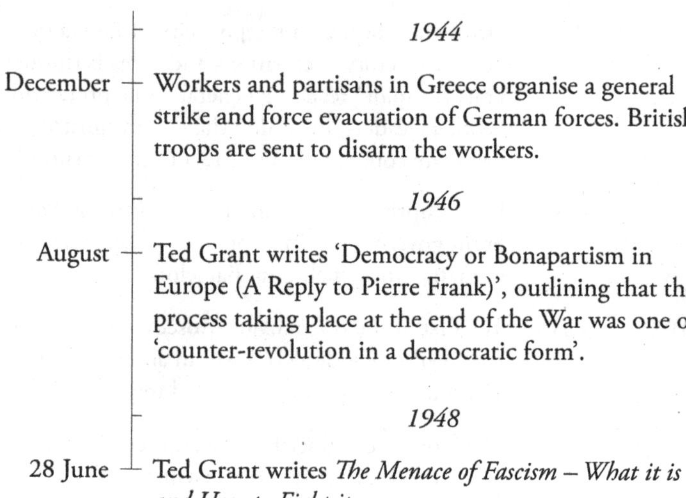

*1944*

December — Workers and partisans in Greece organise a general strike and force evacuation of German forces. British troops are sent to disarm the workers.

*1946*

August — Ted Grant writes 'Democracy or Bonapartism in Europe (A Reply to Pierre Frank)', outlining that the process taking place at the end of the War was one of 'counter-revolution in a democratic form'.

*1948*

28 June — Ted Grant writes *The Menace of Fascism – What it is and How to Fight it.*

# Index


## A

Adler, Friedrich 82
Alexander I (of Yugoslavia) 146
Alfonso XIII 123

## B

Badoglio, Pietro 287, 294, 329
Barbusse, Henri 72–3, 82, 86, 119
Bernstein, Eduard 94
Blum, André Léon 190, 197–8, 202, 204, 206, 208, 212, 215–19, 223–5, 250, 261, 266, 342
Bonaparte. See Napoleon Bonaparte (Napoleon I)
Brandler, Heinrich 11, 18, 27, 38, 136, 298
Braun, Otto 61, 96
Breitscheid, Rudolf 84–5
Brüning, Heinrich xi, xiii, xv, 40–3, 54, 91, 94, 135–6, 146–8, 151, 160, 171, 212, 234, 257, 305–6
Bukharin, Nikolai x, xxvi, 11, 15, 299

## C

Caballero, Francisco Largo 214
Cachin, Marcel 171–2, 190, 196, 206, 217–18
Caillaux, Joseph 200
Chautemps, Camille 164
Chiang Kai-Shek 24
Citrine, Walter 214, 308
Cook, Arthur 24

## D

Daladier, Édouard 147, 162, 164, 170–2, 198–9, 201, 208, 211, 218, 342
Déat, Marcel 166, 203
de Man, Henri 192
Dollfuss, Engelbert 146, 171, 183, 187
Doumergue, Gaston xx, xxii, 147–9, 151, 155–60, 162, 170, 172–3, 201–2, 261, 342

## E

Eastman, Max 242

Ebert, Friedrich 53, 106, 185, 296
Engels, Friedrich viii, 45, 67, 138–9, 198, 207, 241, 261–2, 269

F

Faure, Paul 206
Fischer, Ruth 10
Flandin, Pierre-Étienne xxii, 202, 211, 261
Foster, William Z 73
Franco, Francisco vii, xxviii, 155, 158, 215, 247, 256, 259, 264–6, 281
Frank, Pierre xxvi, xxvii, 245–7, 249–50, 252, 261–70, 272–4, 344
Frossard, Ludovic-Oscar 165, 168–72, 183–4

G

Gasperi, Alcide de 295
Giolitti, Giovanni 151–2
Gobineau, Arthur de 129
Gottwald, Klement 83–4
Gouin, Félix 247, 266
Grant, Ted xxvi–xxix, 244, 276, 344
Grzesinsky, Albert xii, 57–8, 80–1, 96

H

Herriot, Édouard 159, 162–4, 170, 172, 198–9, 204, 207–8, 211
Hess, Rudolf 129
Hilferding, Rudolf 94, 96–7, 138
Hindenburg, Paul von xi, xiii, xvii, 35, 39, 41–3, 57, 60–1, 74, 96, 109, 112, 136–8, 141, 234, 305–7
Hirsch, Werner Z 88
Hitler, Adolf vii, xi, xiii, xv, xvii–xx, xxv, xxviii–xxix, 27, 35, 37, 39, 41–4, 46, 54–5, 61, 63, 87–8, 100, 107, 109–11, 119, 123, 125–9, 132–3, 135–6, 141, 151–2, 160, 198, 201, 203, 210–11, 213, 243, 247, 250, 254, 259, 264–7, 276, 278, 280–2, 296–8, 300–2, 305–8, 311–13, 315, 317, 320, 340, 342–3

J

Jouhaux, Léon 189, 202, 215–18
Just, Claude 57, 70, 107, 127, 140, 147, 151, 198, 240, 281, 307, 318

K

Kautsky, Karl 94, 196
Kerensky, Alexander 79–80, 239–40, 267–73
Kornilov, Lavr 69, 79, 268
Kuusinen, Otto 22, 147

L

Laval, Pierre xxii, 186, 202, 211, 261
Leipart, Theodore 65
Lenin, Vladimir Ilyich Ulyanov viii, 4, 11, 25, 49, 68–9, 86, 174, 209–10, 234–5, 241, 245, 249, 251, 259, 267–70, 284, 299, 340
Liebknecht, Karl 7, 70, 80, 112, 296, 339
Louis XVI 217
Lozovsky, Solomon 69, 118
Luxemburg, Rosa 7, 48–9, 80, 296, 339

M

MacDonald, James Ramsay 146, 185
Machiavelli, Niccolò 126
Manuilsky, Dmitry 69, 101, 147
Marin, Louis 163

Marx, Karl iv, viii, 49, 62, 126, 135, 138–40, 174, 176, 182, 207, 240–1, 256
Masaryk, Tomáš 146
Maslow, Arkadi 10, 38, 105
Matteotti, Giacomo 63, 291
Maurras, Charles 198
Metternich, Klemens von 126
Molotov, Vyacheslav xxv, 22, 29, 343
Mosley, Oswald 32, 275–8, 282, 313–16, 318–23, 327, 330, 332, 334
Müller, Herman xi, 185
Münzenberg, Wilhelm 72, 80
Mussolini, Benito vii, xx, xxviii, 32, 49, 63, 126–7, 129, 131, 146, 151–2, 201, 213, 247, 252, 254, 259, 264–5, 278–80, 282, 284–6, 288–94, 315, 320, 340, 343

N

Napoleon Bonaparte (Napoleon I) 137, 139–40, 158, 203, 256, 260
Napoleon III (Charles-Louis Napoleon Bonaparte) 137, 139, 158, 203, 249, 256, 260
Noske, Gustav 80, 96, 185, 296

P

Papen, Franz von xiii–xv, xvii, 37, 39–46, 54–5, 57, 60–1, 63, 65, 74, 87, 89–91, 99–100, 106–7, 135–41, 147, 160, 212, 257–8, 260–1, 342
Paul Vaillant-Couturier 204
Perón, Juan 248
Pétain, Philippe vii, xxv, xxviii, 234, 242–3, 260–1, 264–6
Piłsudski, Józef 48–50, 146, 151–2
Pivert, Marceau 147, 187, 212
Primo de Rivera, Miguel 31–2, 146, 271
Purcell, Albert 24

Q

Quisling, Vidkun 254

R

Racamond, Julien 204, 216
Ramsay, Archibald Maule 329, 333
Remmele, Hermann 42–3, 75, 306
Renaudel, Pierre 163, 165–6, 168, 181, 184, 203
Rocque, Colonel François de La 198–9, 201, 207, 211
Roosevelt, Franklin D 247, 250
Rosenberg, Alfred 129, 287

S

Salazar, António de Oliveira 248
Sarraut, Albert xxii, 202–3, 205–6
Scheidemann, Philipp 185, 296
Schleicher, Kurt von xi, xiii, xvii, 39, 41, 44, 46, 54–5, 61, 70, 74, 87, 91, 97, 100, 107, 135–6, 138, 141, 147–8, 151–2, 160, 212, 234, 257, 260–1, 273
Schoenaich, Paul von 119
Severing, Carl 43, 96, 146
Seydewitz, Max 64, 83, 103
Sforza, Carlo 200

T

Tardieu, André 158–9, 163, 170
Tarnow, Fritz 96–7
Thälmann, Ernst xv, 10, 38, 40, 42–3, 59–71, 73, 75–6, 79, 83, 85, 88, 101, 105, 111–12, 210, 303, 307
Thorez, Maurice 206, 218
Trotsky, Leon iii–iv, viii–ix, xi–xii, xiv–xxix, 5, 7, 15, 19, 23–4,

33, 35, 76–7, 86, 155, 195, 204, 215, 233, 238–40, 245–6, 249, 251–3, 257, 259, 264, 267–72, 281, 284, 299, 301–3, 324, 340–3
Tsereteli, Irakli 68
Turati, Filippo 289–91

U

Urbahns, Hugo 105

V

Valera, Éamon de 248
Vallat, Xavier 204
Vandervelde, Emile 214

W

Wang Jingwei 24
Warski, Adolf 49
Wels, Otto 41, 55, 65, 87, 96–7, 99, 106, 135, 138, 171, 210
Wilhelm II 138, 250, 296, 339

Z

Zörgiebel, Karl xii, 304
Zyromsky, Jean 147, 171

# *Titles by Wellred Books*

Wellred Books is a publishing house specialising in works of Marxist theory. Among the titles we publish are:

***Anti-Dühring***, Friedrich Engels
***Bolshevism: The Road to Revolution***, Alan Woods
***Chartist Revolution***, Rob Sewell
***China: From Permanent Revolution to Counter-Revolution***, John Peter Roberts
***The Civil War in France***, Karl Marx
***Class Struggle in the Roman Republic***, Alan Woods
***The Class Struggles in France, 1848-1850***, Karl Marx
***The Classics of Marxism: Volumes One & Two***, Various authors
***Democracy, Bonapartism and Fascism***, Leon Trotsky & Ted Grant
***Dialectics of Nature***, Friedrich Engels
***The Eighteenth Brumaire of Louis Bonaparte***, Karl Marx
***The First Five Years of the Communist International***, Leon Trotsky
***The First World War: A Marxist Analysis of the Great Slaughter***, Alan Woods
***Germany: From Revolution to Counter-Revolution***, Rob Sewell
***Germany 1918-1933: Socialism or Barbarism***, Rob Sewell

***History of British Trotskyism***, Ted Grant
***The History of Philosophy: A Marxist Perspective***, Alan Woods
***The History of the Russian Revolution: All Volumes***, Leon Trotsky
***The History of the Russian Revolution to Brest-Litovsk***, Leon Trotsky
***The Ideas of Karl Marx***, Alan Woods
***Imperialism: The Highest Stage of Capitalism***, VI Lenin
***In Defence of Lenin***, Rob Sewell & Alan Woods
***In Defence of Marxism***, Leon Trotsky
***In the Cause of Labour***, Rob Sewell
***Ireland: Republicanism and Revolution,*** Alan Woods
***'Left-Wing' Communism: An Infantile Disorder***, VI Lenin
***Lenin and Trotsky: What They Really Stood For***, Alan Woods & Ted Grant
***Lenin Selected Writings***, VI Lenin
***On Imperialist War***
***The Revolutions of 1917***
***On the National Question***
***Lenin, Trotsky & the Theory of the Permanent Revolution***, John Roberts
***Marxism and Anarchism***, Various authors
***Marxism and the USA***, Alan Woods
***Materialism and Empirio-criticism***, VI Lenin
***My Life***, Leon Trotsky
***Not Guilty***, Dewey Commission Report
***The Origin of the Family, Private Property & the State***, Friedrich Engels
***The Permanent Revolution and Results & Prospects***, Leon Trotsky
***Permanent Revolution in Latin America***, John Roberts & Jorge Martin
***Reason in Revolt***, Alan Woods & Ted Grant
***Reformism or Revolution***, Alan Woods
***Revolution and Counter-Revolution in Spain***, Felix Morrow
***The Revolution Betrayed***, Leon Trotsky
***The Revolutionary Legacy of Rosa Luxemburg***, Marie Frederiksen
***The Revolutionary Philosophy of Marxism***, John Peterson (Ed.)
***Russia: From Revolution to Counter-Revolution***, Ted Grant

***Spain's Revolution Against Franco***, Alan Woods
***Stalin***, Leon Trotsky
***The State and Revolution***, VI Lenin
***Ted Grant: The Permanent Revolutionary***, Alan Woods
***Ted Grant Writings: Volumes One and Two***, Ted Grant
***Thawra hatta'l nasr! - Revolution until Victory!***, Alan Woods & others
***What Is Marxism?***, Rob Sewell & Alan Woods
***What Is to Be Done?***, VI Lenin
***Women, Family and the Russian Revolution***,
John Roberts & Fred Weston
***Writings on Britain***, Leon Trotsky

To make an order or for more information, visit wellred-books.com or email books@wellred-books.com.

www.ingramcontent.com/pod-product-compliance
Ingram Content Group UK Ltd.
Pitfield, Milton Keynes, MK11 3LW, UK
UKHW012253290726
14090UKWH00016B/626

9 781916 936157